The
WOOLLY WEST

ELMA DILL RUSSELL SPENCER SERIES
IN THE WEST AND SOUTHWEST

The WOOLLY WEST
Colorado's Hidden History of Sheepscapes

Andrew Gulliford

TEXAS A&M UNIVERSITY PRESS
COLLEGE STATION

Copyright © 2018 by Andrew Gulliford
All rights reserved
First edition

This paper meets the requirements of ANSI/NISO Z39.48–1992
(Permanence of Paper).
Binding materials have been chosen for durability.
Manufactured in the United States of America

Library of Congress Cataloging-in-Publication Data

Names: Gulliford, Andrew, author.
Title: The woolly West : Colorado's hidden history of sheepscapes / Andrew Gulliford.
Other titles: Elma Dill Russell Spencer series in the West and Southwest ;
    no. 44.
Description: First edition. | College Station : Texas A&M University Press,
    [2018] | Series: Elma Dill Russell Spencer series in the West and
    Southwest ; number forty-four | Introduction: Why study sheep, shepherds
    and carved aspen trees?—1st sheepscape: Searching for sheepscapes and
    finding stock driveways, White River National Forest—Sheep across the
    Southwest—2nd sheepscape: Buckles Lake, counting corrals and V-Rock,
    San Juan National Forest—The beginning of Colorado's cattle and sheep
    wars, 1880–1905—3rd sheepscape: Elkhorn Stock Driveway, Routt and
    Medicine Bow National Forests—The US Forest Service in Colorado, a
    sheep army, and the fight over government grass, 1905–1920—4th
    sheepscape: Going to the mountain, Glade Park & Pinon Mesa—Basque &
    Greek sheepmen, the Taylor Grazing Act, and end of the range wars,
    1920–1934—5th sheepscape: Dead mule on a cabin porch, Lone Mesa State
    Park and a sacred Penitente Calvario—Hispano herders, drought, and the
    Great Depression, 1934–1941—6th sheepscape: Lone Cone and Beaver Park,
    Uncompahgre National Forest—Sheepherding after WWII: from canyonlands
    to wilderness, 1945–1970—7th sheepscape: Sheepshed art in South Park—
    Recreation and restoration: Hikers, guardian dogs & bighorns, 1970 to the
    present—8th sheepscape: Cairns in the Stinking Desert & on the
    Horsethief Trail—The future of Colorado's high country: Ailing aspens,
    Peruvian herders, and ethnic lamb—9th sheepscape: Understanding
    herders' lives—Old West, new West, next West: sheep, ski areas, wolves,
    and endangered species. | Includes bibliographical references and index.
Identifiers: LCCN 2017045910| ISBN 9781623496524 (book/cloth : alk. paper) |
    ISBN 9781623496531 (e-book)
Subjects: LCSH: Sheep industry—Colorado—History. | Sheep Wars,
    1873–1921—Colorado. | Sheepherding—Colorado—History. |
    Shepherds—Colorado—History.
Classification: LCC HD9436.U53 G85 2018 | DDC 338.1/763009788—dc23 LC record
available at https://lccn.loc.gov/2017045910

A list of titles in this series is available at the end of the book.

to the lonely herders who follow the sheep

to my wife
who challenged me to write a deeper story

and to Aldo Leopold
who has much to teach us about living with nature

Publication of this book is generously supported by

Ted and Sharon Lusher,
on behalf of the Texas A&M University Press
Advancement Board,

for Lela Lusher,
who had a great love for the ranches and the livestock
of the American West;

Elizabeth Ballantine, Virginia;
Christine Harmon, Colorado;
Elizabeth "Ginger" Harmon, California;
Marcey Olajos, Arizona and Colorado;

and the Charles Redd Center for Western Studies
at Brigham Young University.

Contents

Acknowledgments	ix
Introduction: Why Study Sheep, Sheepherders, and Carved Aspen Trees?	1
First Sheepscape: Searching for Sheepscapes and Finding Stock Driveways—White River National Forest	11
Chapter 1. Sheep across the Southwest	23
Second Sheepscape: Buckles Lake, Counting Corrals, and V Rock—San Juan National Forest	33
Chapter 2. The Beginning of Colorado's Cattle and Sheep Wars, 1880–1905	43
Third Sheepscape: Elkhorn Stock Driveway—Routt and Medicine Bow National Forests	67
Chapter 3. The US Forest Service in Colorado, a Sheep Army, and the Fight over Government Grass, 1905–1920	77
Fourth Sheepscape: Going to the Mountain—Glade Park and Piñon Mesa	115
Chapter 4. Basque and Greek Sheepmen, the Taylor Grazing Act, and End of the Range Wars, 1920–1934	121
Fifth Sheepscape: Dead Mule on a Cabin Porch—Lone Mesa State Park and a Sacred Penitente Calvario	151
Chapter 5. Hispano Herders, Drought, and the Great Depression, 1934–1941	161

*Sixth Sheepscape: Lone Cone and Beaver Park
—Uncompahgre National Forest* — 185

    Chapter 6. Sheepherding after World War II from
    Canyonlands to Wilderness, 1945–1970 — 203

Seventh Sheepscape: Sheepshed Art—South Park — 225

    Chapter 7. Outdoor Recreation and Landscape Restoration:
    Hikers, Guardian Dogs, and Bighorns, 1970 to the Present — 233

Eighth Sheepscape: Cairns—Stinking Desert and Horsethief Trail — 259

    Chapter 8. The Future of Colorado's High Country:
    Ailing Aspens, Peruvian Herders, and Ethnic Lamb — 267

Ninth Sheepscape: Sheepscapes and Understanding Herders' Lives — 281

    Chapter 9. Old West, New West, Next West: Sheep,
    Ski Areas, Wolves, and Endangered Species — 297

Historical Hispanic Herding Terms — 325
Notes — 329
Glossary — 363
Selected Bibliography — 367
Index — 391

Acknowledgments

Over three decades ago while researching my first book, *America's Country Schools*, I visited the Frenchy Montero family north of Elko, Nevada, to see the small one-room school on their ranch. That was my first encounter with Basque sheep ranchers and their way of life. That trip to the edge of the Great Basin planted the seeds for this book.

Later, my understanding of sheepmen and how they operated came from researching a lawsuit in Delta County, Colorado, where I served as an expert witness on a gated historical public road. I came to realize that sheepmen had all homesteaded in the area, including the Duke family from Hotchkiss, and that they sought isolation from area cattlemen. Reviewing homestead documents before the trial helped me understand more about sheep families, their histories, and how they utilized public range.

For time to research and write this book, I want to thank the Fort Lewis College (FLC) Board of Trustees for a sabbatical in fall 2015, which allowed me to think deeply about this topic and to travel across Colorado to meet with sheepmen and their families and to visit sheepherder sites. I also appreciated funding from the FLC Foundation and FLC Faculty Development Grants. The Charles Redd Center at Brigham Young University provided valuable research and travel funds to assist with this project. I am indebted to them and their staff.

Dawn Widen and Drew Rupard provided important transcriptions from oral interviews. Bonnie Brown, executive director of the Colorado Wool Growers Association, helped me understand the perspectives of wool producers and encouraged me to attend the 89th Annual Colorado Wool Growers Convention in Montrose, Colorado, in July 2016, which I thoroughly enjoyed. The lamb served was excellent. I've never eaten better. At the convention I enjoyed conversations with Gary Visintainer, Steve Raftopoulos, Angelo Theos, J. Paul Brown, Bob Broscheid, Joe Sperry, Tom

Kourlis, and David Moreno. Thank you for answering my interminable questions.

I've appreciated formal interviews with Connie Jouflas, Bonnie Brown, Ernie Etchart, Davin Montoya, Lou Wyman, Leon Crowther, Antonio Manzanares, Carolyn Young, Raymond "Mex" Snyder, Joe Mattern, and the fun-loving Aldasoro sisters—Pam Aldasoro Bennett and Cristine Aldasoro Mitchell, among others. Thanks for taking the time and sharing your family stories.

Marie Tipping helped with sources at the Museum of Western Colorado in Grand Junction and spent a day driving me around the Glade to show me numerous historical aspen arborglyphs.

Bill and Beth Sagstetter introduced me to the Elkhorn Stock Driveway and aspen carvings in both Colorado and Wyoming. Peggy Bergon shared her knowledge of Hispanic carvers near Buckles Lake on an old sheep driveway almost in New Mexico. Bob Silbernagel generously shared his research on "The Sheep Army," which rallied between Delta and Grand Junction. Nik Kendziorski, archives director at the Center of Southwest Studies at Fort Lewis College, kept a sharp eye out for historical photographs of sheep and sheep camps. My friend and fellow researcher Chris Maschino found valuable historical newspaper accounts.

In South Park, Colorado, and Park County I photographed rare Great Depression–era sheepherder folk art paintings found in a sheepshed. Thanks to Linda Balough, Jerry Davis, Andy Spencer, Julie Koomler, Jane Goetz, Ruth Martin, and Brian Woodyard for helping with research and a historical site visit. A special thanks to Frank Wolthuis of Badger Basin Ranch for permission to visit his property.

Archaeologist and Heritage Program manager Sue Struthers assisted with my federal Archaeological Resources Protection Act (ARPA) permit, number CAN614HR, to work and photograph aspen art in Colorado forests. She wrote, "I am sure all of the Colorado Forests are looking forward to your contexts. It's an area that few have been able to take much of a look at, and of course arborglyphs have a set lifetime and many are approaching the end. Great timing!"

Archaeologists who helped with this project include Ruth Lambert at the San Juan Mountains Association, who asked me to write a conclusion to her book *The Wooden Canvas*, about the Pine-Piedra Stock Driveway and arborglyphs in Beaver Meadows and Moonlick Park on the San Juan National Forest. Working with Ruth got me committed to a larger statewide historical study. Michael Selle, BLM archaeologist at the Meeker office, helped me understand historical sheep movements in northwestern Colorado. Leigh Ann Hunt shared valuable files from the Grand Mesa, Uncompahgre, and Gunnison (GMUG) National Forests. We also had a fabulous time looking for historical arborglyphs recorded by Polly Hammer and her team in Beaver Park. Justin Lawrence on the Gunnison National Forest shares my enthusiasm for historical sheepherder landscapes—sheepscapes. Bridget Roth on the Medicine Bow–Routt National Forest is an archaeologist with a new way of looking at old glyphs and the importance of their cultural meaning. Angie Krall on the Rio Grande National Forest is also interested in sheepherder traditions.

Other US Forest Service personnel who answered my questions and shared their experience of sheep grazing and wildlife include Scott Armentrout on the GMUG; Chris Furr, Wayne Yonemoto, and Emily Braker on the Tres Piedras District of the Carson National Forest; Anthony Garcia and Kevin Khung on the Pagosa District of the San Juan National Forest; Judy Schutza on the Norwood District of the GMUG; Matt Janowiak on the Columbine District of the San Juan National Forest; and Kelley Garcia and Luciano Sandoval on the Rio Grande National Forest.

Robert G. Bailey, emeritus scientist at the US Forest Service Rocky Mountain Research Station in Fort Collins, Colorado, wrote an article titled "In Harmony with Nature: A Pioneer Conservationist's Bungalow Home" for *American Bungalow* magazine. Aldo Leopold built the house in 1912 on the Tres Piedras Ranger District of the Carson National Forest in New Mexico. A grant provided funding to restore the house in 2006. Dr. Bailey sent me a copy of his article. I applied and was accepted for the 5th Annual Aldo and Estella Leopold Residency at the bungalow, which Aldo built for his new bride. Leopold married into one of the most prominent sheep-owning families in the Southwest, which had grazed thousands of sheep for generations in New Mexico. I sought to understand the relationship between Leopold's development as one of the twentieth century's most important ecologists and his time in New Mexico.

Special thanks go to the Aldo Leopold Foundation, the Public Land Library, the Taos Land Trust, and the Carson National Forest for my four-week stay. The quiet and time away without cell phone service and internet allowed me to think clearly, gave me afternoons to listen to thunder rumbling across the San Juan Mountains toward the Sangre de Cristos, and allowed me the time to finish this book manuscript. Curt Meine, senior fellow at the Aldo Leopold Foundation, urged me to talk to sheep ranchers. He challenged me to seek the balance in my writing that Leopold himself struck between the need for conservation and the need to make a living off the land. I have tried to do that. Senior Leopold fellow and science adviser Stanley A. Temple arrived for an overnight stay at Leopold's bungalow, and we had a lively discussion that evening and into the next day.

Because sheep from Wyoming came south into Colorado and New Mexican herders came north, I very much appreciate the Wyoming State Historical Society Lola Homsher Grant I received to conduct research in the Cowboy State. At the Wyoming State Archives in Cheyenne I enjoyed excellent help and assistance from Suzi Taylor and Carl Hallberg. In Laramie at the University of Wyoming, Tamsen Hert showed me the extensive Wool Collection at the Emmett D. Chisum Special Collections. Ginny Kilander and her staff provided an important introduction to the vast collections at the American Heritage Center in Laramie, where I found vertical files, oral histories, photographs, professional papers, and original artwork.

Thank you to the anonymous Peruvian sheepherders I met and spoke to in Colorado's mountain meadows. My Spanish skills are only *poquito*, but we shared cookies, nuts, and oranges. One young herder proudly showed me his recently carved horsehead on a large, smooth aspen. Because of him I bought the same Spanish-English dictionary published by the University of Chicago that he kept handy in his sheep wagon.

Some sections of this book were originally published in a different form in the *Durango (CO) Herald*, the *Grand Junction (CO) Daily Sentinel*, the Writers on the Range column in *High Country News*, *Colorado Heritage*, *Waving Hands Review*, *Inside/Outside Southwest*, and *Natural Resources Journal*. Those sources and publication dates are cited in the endnotes and bibliography. The section on Colorado wolves in chapter 3 is abridged from *The Last Stand of the Pack: A Critical Edition*, published by the University Press of Colorado.

Special thanks go to the staff at Texas A&M University Press, especially to Jay Dew, editor in chief. Like the best of editors, he believes in his writers, and that makes all the difference. It has been a pleasure to work with such a professional staff. I am grateful for the freedom to publish so many rare and unknown photographs.

As always, my wife, Stephanie Moran, and our 40 years of marriage have helped inspire and support this research. Her encouragement, her belief in my projects, and her editing are essential and deeply appreciated.

I guess I should also thank "Happy," the bummer lamb I bottle-fed as a young boy. I hope I haven't done a baaaaaad job with this book. Any errors and mistakes are my own. Please let me know at andy@agulliford.com.

The
WOOLLY WEST

Introduction

Why Study Sheep, Sheepherders, and Carved Aspen Trees?

> In our family there is always one thing, and that is the sheep. The summer passes and the winter comes and soon it is Easter and the time for spring; but all the time, no matter when, there is the sheep.... Everything comes and goes. Except one thing. The sheep. For that is the work of our family, to raise sheep.
>
> —JOSEPH KRUMGOLD
> *...And Now Miguel*

> There are two things that interest me: the relation of people to each other and the relation of people to the land.
>
> —ALDO LEOPOLD
> *A Sand County Almanac*

Of the hundreds of books about cowboys and cowboying in the American West, there are few volumes on sheep and sheepmen. Cowboys sing to their cows and ride the long circle each night around their herd, but then they return to their bedroll and a sidekick takes over. Not so with sheepmen.

A lone shepherd might be in charge of a band of 900–1,000 sheep, and though he may have a horse, it's really his dogs that keep the sheep in line, bed them down, and guard them through the night against coyotes and bears. In the herding tradition, the morning star is the shepherd's star—*La Estrella del Pastor*, because herders rise in the dark. Before sunrise, the flock nibbles away, bunched up, moving always toward water and grass—the two elements essential to sheep grazing as described in pioneer diaries and journals.

Cowboys get the fancy hats and hand-tooled leather boots. Sheepherders wear whatever they can find and carry a staff or crook to catch errant sheep by a rear hoof. It's an ancient practice, far older than nineteenth-century cowboying and trailing cattle north to railroad terminus points as America moved west. Sheepherding stories abound in the Bible and in diverse cultures worldwide, but I wanted to learn about sheep in Colorado—where they came from, how they arrived, who owned them, who herded them, and what impact they have had on the environment for almost two centuries.

Cowboys ride the range together, or at least in pairs. Sheepherders are always alone, visited weekly by a camp tender who brings food and other necessities, perhaps tobacco, a skin of wine, more bullets, fresh peaches, news from home. "It is his ingenuity and resourcefulness, born of isolation and sharpened by experience that distinguishes the herder from the cowboy. The hired hand takes his morning orders from the boss, mounts his bronc and rides off," state Charles Towne and Edward Wentworth. "The herder, given a bunch of sheep, is sent away to remain for months in remote mountain areas, hard to reach. Here it is up to him to work out his own and the flock's salvation."[1]

This book began in an aspen grove as I studied carvings left by dozens of herders over decades. Some of the herders carved their initials each year they returned to the same grove—"the tender, fluttered, sisterhood of quaking asp," wrote Mary Austin.[2] As I contemplated the carvings and thought of the baaing, blatting sheep moving through the smooth-barked aspen, I wondered, why were sheep hated? What was behind that deep-seated animosity against white, woolly creatures by cattlemen?

Why did cowboys prosper in poetry, folk songs, and myth as rugged individuals, while shepherds, who truly worked alone, are all but forgotten in the annals of the American West? Or when they are remembered, they are despised. Yet after the cattle and sheep wars finally came to an end by the 1920s, some sheepmen came to run cattle and some cattlemen chose to try sheep.

In my life I've been blessed with time to explore three major national forests—the White River, the Gila, and the San Juan. The common thread in my writing has been describing and documenting people and communities in remote, rural places in the West. Now, as a professor of history and environmental studies, I am drawn to studying public land grazing and sheep in Colorado national forests to learn about where they came from, who herded them, and how free public rangeland became restricted and regulated under the Timber Reserve Act (1891), the US Forest Service (1905), the Taylor Grazing Act (1934), the Bureau of Land Management (1946), and federal laws like the Wilderness Act (1964) and the Endangered Species Act (1973).

I want to write about high-altitude grazing over time—its culture, attitudes, and impact on the landscape and wildlife—and, beginning in 1914, the killing of thousands of predators by trappers of the US Biological Survey, whose goal included making rangelands safe for sheep. As a historian, I know that the deeper you probe into primary sources and original documents, the broader the story goes. In Colorado history there are a few villains, and even fewer heroes. We used and abused the land in certain ways, and now we know better.

"One of the penalties of an ecological education is to live alone in a world of wounds. Much of the damage inflicted on land is quite invisible to laymen," wrote the hunter, forester, and ecologist Aldo Leopold.[3] Yet in terms of overgrazing, denuded slopes, and impacts from hundreds of bands of sheep, Leopold's wife's family may have been one of the largest sheep owners in the Southwest and responsible for much damaged land in New Mexico. He married into the Luna-Otero-Bergere family. "Mother's family had a lot to do with overgrazing of the West," admitted Leopold's daughter Nina Leopold Bradley.[4]

As a young supervisor on the Carson National Forest north of Santa Fe, "Leopold was in a precarious position. He had to reinforce new regulations in communities that had had unrestricted grazing," notes his biographer Curt Meine.[5] That job wasn't easy. Centuries of land use by *ricos*, or rich sheep owners, hiring *pastores*, or poor herders, would have to change. In the 1850s some northern New Mexican herders came north with their flocks into Colorado. A few pioneer families stayed, especially in the San Luis Valley. For decades in the nineteenth and twentieth centuries, other herders would come north from the small villages of Coyote, Gallinas, Tres Piedras, Dixon, Velarde, Española, Chama, and Tierra Amarilla, leaving signs and symbols on the "wooden canvas" of aspen trees.[6]

Prior to the establishment of forest reserves and national forests, Hispanic herders in northern New Mexico and southern Colorado simply followed the age-old practice of grazing the *ejidos*, or common lands, without rules or regulations. "Hundreds of ordinary people . . . put their sheep on the Sangre de Cristo Grant thinking they could forever use common pastures," write Colorado historians.[7] But all that would change.

Like thread hand spun from raw wool, the skein of people, place, and purpose across Colorado's high country is what I try to unravel. How did free range become government grass at the turn of the twentieth century, and now in the twenty-first century as we face global warming, climate change, and probable long-term drought, how do we evaluate grazing permits in high alpine meadows? Should past practices be continued?

And within the deeply woven story of cattle and sheep ranchers who own private land in Colorado's mountain valleys, what are those family connections to soil and sheep and ranching traditions? How do modern ranch families persevere in a complicated world of competitive uses for high country they have always grazed? Colorado remains the third largest wool-producing state.

As I seek answers and try to understand the language and culture of a few Basque, Greek, and Hispanic families who still raise sheep and graze them on public land, I am captivated by the carvings, the legacy of lone herders high in Colorado aspen groves, on foot or on horseback, etching

Peter Jouflas, a Greek who became a naturalized citizen after arriving in America in 1908, poses with his wife, Dorothy, and sons, Chris and George. According to his grandson Steve Jouflas, "The immigrant sheep ranchers were basically escaping poverty in Greece.... Like all immigrants, their only resource was their willingness to work harder than the next person." Photo courtesy of the Jouflas family.

names, dates, symbols, portraits of beautiful women, and also the occasional curse.

A hundred-year history of sheep grazing on Colorado public lands should produce some interesting stories, some deep-seated quarrels, and a new awareness of pioneer families who succeeded because of pluck, perseverance, and a willingness to risk rain, snow, coyotes, and cold nights alone, all in an attempt to raise lambs, put weight on the wethers, and make an income twice yearly—from wool and from meat.

Sheep stories abound. In Walsenburg during the Great Depression, a sheepman had his bank loan called in by the local banker, but the rancher had no funds—only sheep. The banker refused to extend the loan, so the rancher did the only thing he could think of. He brought in his woolly assets on four hooves, surrounded the bank, and closed off streets in town with baaing, bleating sheep. The banker relented and extended the rancher's loan.

In the same decade in Rifle, Colorado, a Works Progress Administration (WPA) artist thought he'd paint sheep on a mural he was preparing for the Rifle Post Office, but "before the sheep could safely graze, cattlemen raised such hell that the postmaster swore that he preferred undesecrated walls."[8] Instead, the Depression-era mural, still visible today, features a big mountain, a few horses, and a dog. Historian Stephen J. Leonard explains that the Denver Post Office did get sheep—monumental sculptures of mountain sheep.[9]

Indeed, Colorado has 15 streams named Sheep Creek and 19 peaks christened Sheep Mountain. In some cases the nomenclature refers to wild mountain sheep, probably Rocky Mountain bighorns, but often the reference is to domestic woollies.[10] The two have often shared the same high-altitude ranges, and what that has meant for both populations will be discussed later in this book.

Modern issues get tangled up when traditional pastures are bisected by hiking trails like the Colorado Trail, the Continental Divide Trail, or any of the dozens of routes that bring backpackers into Colorado's high country. What was once rural and remote is no longer. Friction exists between old-style ranchers just trying to make a living and urban vacationers out to experience nature, especially in wilderness areas like the Weminuche, Mount Zirkel, Flat Tops, Lizard Head, Big Blue, West Elk, and Maroon Bells. First impressions of sheep are lasting. "When they come through they eat everything right down to the dust," explains mountain climber Jane Koerner.[11]

In northwestern Colorado near Maybell, Steve Simos succeeded as a sheep rancher. He went back to Greece in 1934 to visit his brother and sister and to find a young wife. When Steve died in 1948 with two children, his wife, Georgia, ran the ranch successfully by herself for a year and a half. She knew she could not run the sheep ranch alone so in 1951 she returned to Greece to find a husband. Photo courtesy of the Jouflas family.

"Hoofed locusts" was the term John Muir used to describe sheep in the High Sierra of California when he worked as a herder in 1869 at the headwaters of the Merced and Tuolumne Rivers in what would become Yosemite National Park.[12] "Will all this garden be made into beef and mutton pastures? Another universal outpouring of lava, or the coming of a glacial period, could scarce wipe out the flowers and shrubs more effectually than do the sheep," complained Muir.[13]

Yet mutton provided essential meat for prospectors, miners, and others heading west. Huge flocks moved from New Mexico to California after the 1849 Gold Rush, and by the 1880s those herds had multiplied. Then sheep moved north and northeast into Idaho, Montana, and Wyoming and south to Colorado. Mormons sought sheep to build flocks to help create their small, sustainable religious communities. The nineteenth-century history of the American West is a history of sheep and settlement.

Our values have changed. Now Coloradans buy meat in packages at the grocery store, not by the herd or on the hoof. Can domestic sheep coexist in federally designated wilderness areas with bighorn sheep? Do domestic sheep pass on deadly diseases that impact bighorns? What balance exists in Colorado today among traditional grazing rights, ranching families, and long-distance hikers?

The working landscape of high-country sheep grazing in the summer and winter range in the deserts of northern New Mexico, southern Wyoming, and eastern Utah has all been modified. Sheep pastures are now leisure landscapes for tourists and wealthy second-home owners who purchase expensive private lots near Vail, Telluride, or Copper Mountain. The working West has been replaced by recreation and an adventure-driven, tourist-based economy.

Where Colorado sheep once wintered in the broken canyon country between the Green and Colorado Rivers, parts of that area are now Canyonlands National Park. Dynamite-blasted sheep trails are popular hiking and mountain biking venues used by visitors who have no idea that lonely sheepherders once clutched cold coffee cups where they luxuriate in distant views.

Thousands of alpine acres where sheep once grazed in large numbers are now federally protected wilderness areas with even more restrictions than national forests. Hikers who have walked for miles into wilderness retreats seeking silence and solitude do not favor the sound of bleating sheep from the few bands that still summer above tree line.

Herders left their names on aspen trees, yet aspens live only 60 to 100 years or so from one vast root cluster. Many of those trees are dying from old age, but also from sudden aspen decline, or SAD, which is poorly understood even by our best biologists. The trees also collapse from wind and snow and age, taking their messages with them down to the ground. Bark peels. Wood rots. Artistic images are lost. When I camp at Shepherds Rim Campground on the White River National Forest near Trappers Lake, I'm always looking for carved aspens. Finding few.

This book begins with the history of sheep grazing in the Southwest and moves forward in time through the cattle and sheep wars, the establishment of national forests, and the arrival of homesteader families who became sheep ranchers. The Great Depression and Hispanic herders are discussed, as well as the transhumance or movement of running sheep in high country in summer and in Utah deserts and canyons in winter. Basque, Greek, and

Hispano sheepmen in Colorado are described, as well as changes brought about by the Taylor Grazing Act (1934), which was originally directed by Farrington Carpenter from Hayden, Colorado.

The historical narrative goes forward from World War II up to the present, with chapters on ecological change and damage, and modern issues with wild Rocky Mountain bighorn sheep, so-called wild horses, and sage grouse. Peruvian herders are discussed as well as the expanding market for lamb, whose buyers are primarily Muslims living in cities and urban areas. They prefer fresh, unblemished American lamb to frozen imports from Australia or New Zealand.

Conflicts between hikers and aggressive guardian dogs are described as well as sheep-owning families who prospered when multimillion-dollar ski areas came to remote valleys exactly where Basque and Greek families had privately owned sheep pastures. The book ends with a look at Old West, New West, and Next West issues and the potential for wolves to be reintroduced in the Southern Rockies. Sheep stories are family stories about relationships with each other and with the land. Basque, Greek, Hispano, and Navajo herders are fondly remembered or reviled. I've tried to tell as many stories as I could.

Interspersed with the research chapters, carefully endnoted and compiled from historical sources, interviews, publications, and archives, are first-person accounts of visiting sheepherder landscapes, sheepscapes if you will, of carved aspen arborglyphs, stone cairns, and other signs of sheepherder history on the landscape. From mountain meadows to canyon cliffs, generations of herders have left their marks, yet very few hikers, backpackers, and contemporary climbers understand those signs and archaeological traces on the landscape. I hope this study will help readers learn about not only the history of sheep in Colorado and the West, and the stories of ongoing sheep-ranching families, but also how to read and understand sheepherder landscapes, or sheepscapes.

To understand winter range for sheep, I've camped at the bottom of Rattlesnake Canyon, arriving by canoe on the Gunnison River. I've hiked into Escalante and Dominguez Canyons, where sheep and cattle conflicts erupted into a shooting war. High on the Flat Tops I've backpacked in to camp among the lakes and meadows herders love, and driven by Jeep on old stock driveways from Colorado into Wyoming. In the San Luis Valley while trying to hike up into the Sangre de Cristo Mountains, I've been stopped by late spring–flooded creeks that washed out a trail that would

Harry Jacquez was a Navajo herder from Huerfano, New Mexico, who worked for the Montoya family of Hesperus, Colorado, in the La Plata Mountains in the 1950s and 1960s. Here he carved a dramatic scene of a bull rider. Author photo.

have taken me to a stone monument for a herder who died of a heart attack close to his sheep.

La Garita Stock Driveway, an ancient route out of the valley and up into the San Juan Mountains, begins in the foothills where the mountains rise. Below are the church and plaza and one of the oldest cemeteries in Colorado, where most gravestones are handmade and etched in Spanish. I've hiked the trail but really needed horses to go farther. As always, there is much to learn from landscapes in the West.

I cross-country ski up La Plata Canyon in the San Juan Mountains. Silence with deep snow. Aspens shorn of leaves. Low clouds drifting overhead. I find again the aspen tree I was looking for. Robert Martinez had carved his name on it and the date, 1953, the year I was born. That simple inscription across time and space brings me up short, as it always does. For every day of my life, this aspen tree has been waiting for me, and a herder left his name and a July date when he was there with a summer flock. I see it now in the late afternoon winter light. I was born four months later.

Often in Colorado's high country I find carvings on aspen trees. Who were those herders? What lives did they lead? What are their individual stories within the wider context of wars over grazing rights and access to grass that cattle could not reach?

As twilight deepens, my dog and I turn around. Last light reflects off dim canyon walls. White trees and white snow blend into one. I have miles to go and stories to tell. A book to begin.

FIRST SHEEPSCAPE

Searching for Sheepscapes and Finding Stock Driveways—White River National Forest

I wasn't looking for aspen art or carved aspen trees. I wasn't thinking of sheep or sheepherders or their movements through the forest. I was part of an archaeological survey team looking for something else, an ancient Ute Indian trail that wound across the Flat Tops on the White River National Forest, the second oldest federal forest in the nation, set aside in 1891. We knew where the historical Ute Trail began near the confluence of the Colorado and Eagle Rivers at Dotsero, Colorado, but we didn't know where it ended.

During the course of that summer more than 25 years ago we hiked, rode horseback, and took a small silver Cessna airplane high above the canyon system that creates the Flat Tops Wilderness, the second largest in the state. Always we were looking for signs on the ground of an ancient Indian trail and trying to understand how Ute families moved across the landscape, hunting, picking berries, searching for eagle feathers, setting up their bison-hide tepee camps. But while we found the 57-mile-long Ute Trail, which traverses the Flat Tops in a northwestern direction ascending from the Colorado River Valley to the White River Valley near Meeker, we also found another trail system that overlapped the Ute Trail.

Toward the center of the White River Plateau we found something different, equally forgotten, but in more recent use.

We found a historical sheep or stock driveway used by Hispano herders to move their flocks through the forest without arousing the ire of local cattlemen. After 1881, when the Utes had been pushed out of most of western Colorado and forced onto reservations in the far southwestern corner of the state at Ignacio and onto a reservation in northeastern Utah at Fort Duchesne, stockmen quickly moved in. They brought vast herds of scrawny Texas longhorn cattle and sheep from New Mexico, Utah, and Wyoming. The sheepmen and cattlemen sparred for decades over grazing rights. One of the solutions that forest rangers devised was to establish stock driveways so sheep could move from low elevations in the winter to higher elevations in the summer without lingering too long on cattle ranges.

We found a historical sheep driveway directly overlying the historical Ute Indian trail. Separated from my research companions, I began to walk

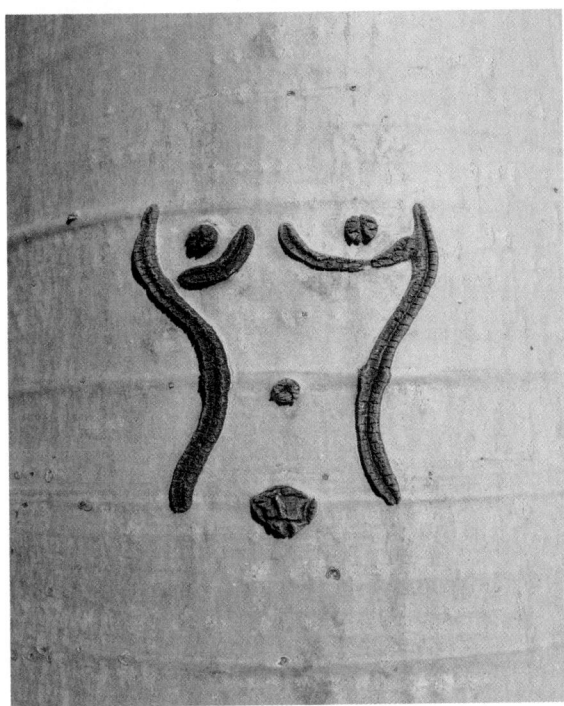

Lonely sheepherders frequently carved versions of naked women. This female torso graces an aspen high on the White River Plateau in the White River National Forest. Author photo.

from the Buford–New Castle Road, the one gravel road that cuts south to north across the high plateau, and I instantly knew this was a different landscape. From the pines and firs that spread across the forest, I entered an aspen grove and began to see carvings with dates, names, and initials from generations of herders. I was stunned by graphic depictions of sex—aspen porn—repeatedly carved into the white bark of aspens by lonely herders.

Sheep had grazed the high-altitude grasses near Meadow Lake, always under the watchful eye of herders and their dogs, but here in this one grove of trees the sun-filled meadows gave way to an aspen canopy and herders had left their messages, their signs. Little grass remained because flocks had moved through the trees nibbling it, and on a steep ascent to the west dozens of sheep had left a bare dirt trail as they had flowed up the steep slope.

In the dappled light from the quaking aspens, I realized I was in a unique cultural landscape, a male enclave of private messages left by herders for other herders, including the carved dates of all the years they had led flocks through this part of the forest. I saw the names of uncles, fathers, and sons. Some trees were dead and the original carvings dark and obscure as the bark had aged and peeled. Other carvings were hidden under spruce boughs so I had to proceed slowly, looking at the larger trees, going around to different angles, always reveling in the smell of an aspen forest, the patches of light and shadow, the wind lightly turning leaves.

I realized that like aspen leaves becoming golden and cascading down in an October breeze, these tree carvings represented ephemeral art. The trees would fall and be forgotten, yet herders wanted to leave their marks. Watching the sheep, the shepherds could never take the time to carve through the bark of spruce or fir, and there's nothing to carve in low-elevation sagebrush country, so here was their message board at this exact spot on the stock driveway.

Patterns began to emerge. Most of the carved aspens were at least 8–12 inches in diameter, and many were much larger. Herders wanted others to know they hailed from El Rito, Taos, and Farmington, New Mexico; from Chile, Mexico, Spain, and Peru. They left exact summer dates when they carved on the trees—7/9/52 for Joe J. Gonzales and 9/9/63 for Jean Bellet, a Basque from Spain.

They laughed and made fun of each other. On one tree Manuel Valdez had carved his name, and the next year a herder had carved *El Loco* (crazy) below it. In addition to the sex scenes there were also carved crosses left by Catholic believers. Julio Cordova had passed this way in 1946 and Alberto Vigil in 1958. They left messages for other male herders about their homes, about women, always signifying their presence: I am here. This is me. I have returned.

I saw the names of prominent sheep families from near Meeker, Colorado, in Rio Blanco County—Gus R. Halandras carved on 7/12/75, as did John Halandras. I began to wonder about Greek herding traditions as well as those of Hispano herders. The height of the inscriptions indicated that some must have carved on horseback, but how did they get their horses to stand so still?

There were nicknames—Nino Trujillo and Rosy Aguirre as well as Jesus Baca, Jim Atencio, Ricardo Manzanar, Charley Shields, and Hector Bruno, who fancied himself as "El Tigre," from Peru. I learned which trees to look for by following the sheep, looking where the grass had been bent down and finding carved trees in the middle of those grazed areas. Hiking longer and higher than I had anticipated, I took out a knife and made a walking stick by smoothing off the boles on a sturdy piece of weathered pine. Stick in hand, I kept walking west through the forest, trying to understand the lonely sheepherders' lives and their insistence on not being anonymous, on

Many family members all participated in the sheep business. Here Gus Halandras carved his name along a stock driveway on the White River National Forest. Author photo.

leaving their names, dates, and hometowns. I began to think about becoming a voice for the voiceless, of writing about sheep herds, sheepmen, and the herders themselves.

I had to learn from a distance what were natural black markings on an aspen tree and what could be human-etched designs. It took a while to start to see the designs, to have the awareness that this was a carved tree and not a random accident of nature.

I realized I'd found a secret in the forest, a passageway into a world of work, a type of occupational folklore. I wondered how many groves could be found similar to the one I was in.

As a deer and elk hunter I had often found carvings, but it would be years before I would try to research and write this hidden history of sheep in Colorado, to try to understand the woolly West with its unique ethnic flavor distinct from the lore of cowboys and cattle.

Herders also rode horseback, but they kept their dogs close, lived in tents or sheep wagons, not log bunkhouses, and only infrequently saw another friend, or compañero. I would come to realize that although cowboys occasionally carved on trees, herders always did.

From the Routt National Forest near Steamboat Springs to the White River National Forest east of Meeker, Colorado, a Hispano herder from Taos, New Mexico, carved dozens of arborglyphs, including his signature house. This image is found on Ripple Creek Pass along the Flat Tops Scenic Byway. As a native Spanish speaker he carved "MN" for "NM" because in Spanish the adjective goes after the noun. He also carved *Repito*, which means "I am doing it again" referring to his stylized houses. Author photo.

Cowboys often carved their ranch's brand, but herders carved their names, their hometowns or villages, the date they passed through the forest, and much more. It was part of their tradition, and it is ongoing today with new generations of Peruvian herders that I would meet and befriend in the White River National Forest.

But 25 years ago, I simply stared in awe at the carved trees and decided that someday I would want to learn more about herding traditions, about aspens themselves, and about lives spent moving through forests. Now that time has come, and I try to find the oldest, largest carved aspens in Colorado and to learn about herding patterns and family histories across the state.

I have come to realize that what I am doing is searching for sheepscapes, or traces of sheepherders on a landscape, whether a high-altitude meadow, valley, or canyon bottom. Over generations, sheepherders left their historical impact on public lands. As a practicing public historian, interested not only in the past but also in finding traces of the past in the present, I've enjoyed my search for sheepscapes.

I call a sheepherder landscape a sheepscape, and I'm discovering components or archaeological features of that sheepscape at different elevations. Combining history and historical archaeology, a sheepscape may include the following:

> 1. Stock driveways designated on national forests so that sheep could travel from lower elevations up to mountain meadows. The older driveways often have faded yellow US Forest Service metal signs that state "Center Stock Driveway," so that a herder who did not speak English would know where he needed to keep his flock. These are linear historical corridors that allowed sheep to travel for miles into and across the high country. A few segments of these have now become ATV trails, without adequate attention being paid to their historical and cultural value. Each forest had several stock driveways, and they need to be mapped and identified.
>
> 2. Blazes on trees for sheepherders in the high country, with a distinctive circle on top and a vertical rectangle below.
>
> 3. Wooden corrals wired together, usually made of locally available wood. In canyon country, canyon cliffs and walls made up the back or sides of a corral. Unlike corrals for cattle, sheep corrals had no chutes. Some corrals were simply to hold sheep, while others were for shearing and may contain fragments of metal shafts where

sheep-shearing clippers hung down. Much larger and stouter were the counting corrals, where an entire band of 1,000 or more sheep would be held and counted before being allowed to trail farther up into a national forest.

4. Lambing pens or lambing sheds, sometimes of wood or even stone, as protection out of wind and weather. These are at lower elevations where lambing occurred in the spring prior to the summer movement of sheep into the high country. In canyon country these can be low stone walls near large protective boulders. Sheep barns or sheepsheds may also include sheepherder art painted on boards with the same paint used to mark sheep.

5. V-shaped wooden bear traps in the high country where an animal carcass, often of a ewe, could be used as bait. These look like tiny, oddly shaped corrals.

6. Arborglyphs or carvings on aspen trees above 6,500 feet elevation, where herders left messages for each other. Also called dendroglyphs, these glyphs are ephemeral art because trees will die and fall. Always walk around the tree, as there may be extensions of the same image or even different images on the other side.

7. Cairns, or stacked stones, sometimes just a few in a haphazard fashion and sometimes stone monuments. These were well built, tight, and up to eight feet tall and three feet in circumference. Basque herders called such cairns *harri mutilak*, or "stone boys." Some of the best-constructed cairns on a sheepherder landscape are probably Basque built. Erecting cairns helped break the monotony in a shepherd's day, defined a shepherd's range, and became valuable as ridge finders and place markers in inclement weather.

8. Blinds or shelters of stone, erected both as hunting blinds for herders to supplement their meager meals of canned food and also as lifesaving windbreaks in case of storms. At high elevations these features can be confused with both prehistoric and historical Native American stone alignments that had similar functions.

9. Sheepherder memorials, including wooden crosses of either dimensional lumber or cut tree branches lashed into crosses, or *descansos*, which could be memorials at locations where herders may have died from a lightning strike or other cause. Sheepherder memorials that are not on any trail include rock cairns, monuments, or simple piles of

stones. Sheepmen and shepherds also built cairns to honor their deceased compañeros. Shepherds erected a stone monument to a herder killed south of Grand Junction, Colorado, during the cattle and sheep wars. In the 1880s, when Victorio and his Apaches killed nine herders and ran off thousands of sheep, owner Solomon Los Luna had nine stone monuments constructed near the home ranch at Lunas, New Mexico, "one for each sheepherder killed." No bodies were ever found.

10. Campsites where a herder's tent may have been. These are flattened, smoothed-over areas with an adjacent can scatter, the older cans with a small circle of metal that expanded as the cooked food was put in the can—hole-in-top cans. Some had vertical lead seams. There are also condensed milk cans with deep knife slits in the top, and pieces of broken blue or purple glass containing manganese that date from before World War I. Campsites may include the remains of wooden frames as a floor for platform tents eight by eight feet or larger. The diet of herders was often one dimensional, with a lot of canned food, so there may be extensive historical can scatters in the high country far from any mining activity. Perhaps even a lost sheep's bell.

11. Trenches on the landscape, including wooden troughs of cedar or pine that created basins to place salt and minerals that sheep needed during the summer. Sheepmen also had laborers dig long, deep troughs in hard adobe soil to make sheep-dip areas that were filled with water, lye, and tobacco to rid sheep of parasites.

12. Stone enclosures constructed in high desert areas devoid of available wood. These can include long walls of dry laid stone coursed approximately four feet tall, similar to European stone walls and sometimes built near a spring or water source. Large, long stone enclosures for sheep, which now enclose cholla cactus, exist at Balada Springs in the Bear Mountains on the Cibola National Forest.

13. Navajo sweat lodges, small one-person wooden structures like an upturned basket, found at the heads of canyons near water sources. Sheep often grazed below or in front of the lodges, in which Navajo herders would make small fires to heat rocks to create a cleansing steam bath, placing blankets over the wooden frame.

14. Lunate hearths, low to the ground and shaped like a crescent moon. These were very different from circular stone fire rings and offered windbreaks around small fires that herders, especially on sagebrush plateaus, used to cook and keep warm.

15. Ponderosa pine peels or scars no higher than three feet, which are narrow and short. Sheepherders used these tree peels to obtain cambium for food and medicine. They also used the inner pine *ocote*, or sappy material, as a fire starter. These are not to be confused with the much larger and longer peeled ponderosa pines used by Utes, Apaches, and Navajos.

16. Sheep bridges in the high county, built decades ago by the US Forest Service over remote creeks and rivers to enable flocks to trail into alpine meadows. Many of these bridges built in wilderness areas are not being replaced, and all that remains are stone or concrete abutments and a few logs to show where thousands of sheep once crossed streambeds.

17. Religious symbols, especially Catholic symbols, found on carved aspens as part of a sheepscape. Devout herders who were Penitentes, or religious members of La Fraternidad Piadosa de Nuestro Padre Jesus Nazareno (the Pious Fraternity of our Father Jesus the Nazarene) from northern New Mexico, carved crosses within a larger shadow-box cross shape on aspens. They also erected handmade wooden crosses on high-altitude scree fields so they could pray and offer devotions even though they were miles from a church or Penitente *morada*, a small chapel. These religious crosses and their remote locations are known as *calvarios*. A young boy would watch the sheep while the older herders attended to their prayers. One such wooden cross is still visible in the mountains of southwestern Colorado. The Spanish on the Penitente cross can be translated as "Our savior of the souls."

There may be other types of features on a sheepscape too.

Archaeologist Angie Krall from the Rio Grande National Forest has also worked on the Routt National Forest. She describes the huge density of carved aspens in Slater Park and California Park north of Steamboat Springs: "I also heard that sheepherders [probably Basque] stocked the fish in there so that's a sheepscape. That's humans changing the landscape, you know. They'd drop brookies in California Park." She found "lambing pens they built out of fire sharpened, polished trees, hardened wood, which is why it was still there to be seen and documented. It was really impressive. Otherwise if it had been dry or green [wood] it probably would have been gone, being as old as it was. So that was genius. We recognized lambing pens and camps as part of that sheepscape."[1]

Krall saw "the same names over and over again. And year after year. So you certainly recognize continuity with those folks." She found a giant mosquito carved on a tree. "Beautifully done. I mean it could have been in an entomologist's book. It was perfect." On Buffalo Pass she located carvings of "women dancing on tables [wearing] fishnet stockings that were just exquisite." The carver "was quite the artist," she smiles.[2] Throughout this book we will learn more about diverse sheepscapes, from high-altitude mountain meadows to canyon bottoms.

Colorado has more aspens than any other state in the Rocky Mountains. This September view of the White River Plateau is on the White River National Forest (1891), the second oldest national forest in the nation. Author photo.

Chapter 1

Sheep across the Southwest

> Trapper, soldier, miner and cowboy may claim title to the romance of the West, but its economic success was made certain by the great sheep trails.
>
> —CHARLES TOWNE AND EDWARD WENTWORTH
> *Shepherd's Empire*

With a knife brandished above him, the Ute Indian chief dared not move. On the sunset side of Cochetopa Pass, a Ute band had fired rifle shots to disperse westward-moving sheep, but the woollies only bunched tighter to their herders. Hired guards knew little about fighting Native Americans. Flockmaster "Uncle Dick" Wootton had to take command himself.

Luckily, the sheep moved closer, as the Utes required a toll for traversing their land. Instead of paying, Wootton grabbed Chief Uncotash, flung him off his horse, and threatened to slit his throat. Instead of giving them ewes and lambs, Wootton paid the Indians off in supplies. They rode east and he trailed his flock west. The year was 1852.[1]

The first flocks of sheep had begun to cross what would become the state of Colorado. To understand domestic sheep in Colorado and to know where they came from, it is important to begin with sheep in New Mexico and their arrival with the Spanish conquistadors. In 1540, as Don Juan Francisco de Coronado came north from Mexico amid the dust of horses' hooves and foot soldiers into what would become New Mexico, he brought 5,000 sheep. Always there were sheep. Blatting and baaing and needing to be herded lest they become lost. Sheep provided fresh meat on the hoof for soldiers, part of their daily diet. Sheep would also become one of the greatest legacies from the Spanish to Native Americans of the Southwest, especially to Navajo weavers.

Cortés in Mexico, Coronado in the northern provinces, and later Don Juan de Oñate all brought sheep. As the Spanish conquistadors traversed the landscape, resplendent in their glittering armor, herders watched the flocks, which provided movable mutton meals. The foundation stock was Spanish-Mexican merino-churro sheep. After a few concussions from falling off his horse, and after not finding gold or the Seven Cities of Cíbola, Coronado returned to Mexico in disgrace.

Rich silver-mine owner Oñate next came north in 1598 with 2,600 sheep for wool and 400 sheep for mutton.[2] As Spanish settlements began along the Rio Grande, Native Americans quickly saw the value in sheep. The Pueblo Revolt of 1680 pushed the Spanish out of New Mexico for 12 years. Navajos swooped in to steal sheep and horses. When the Spanish returned, Hispanic culture stayed, and so did sheepherding for native peoples as well as Spanish settlers.

The readily adaptable Navajos, who had moved into the Four Corners area around 1400, saw the wisdom of sheep for their lifeway, which was so different from that of the village-bound Pueblo Indian farmers. The Navajos lived dispersed across northern New Mexico, especially near Gobernador, Blanco, and Largo Canyons. By developing sheep herds, the Diné, or the People, as they called themselves, could flourish with sheep for sustenance and wool to weave into blankets and rugs. Pueblo weavers using cotton had been male, but as the Pueblos fled their villages when the Spanish returned and intermarried into Navajo clans, Navajo women became both sheep owners and skilled weavers. A woman's wealth was in her flocks, and the Spanish readily agreed that Navajo blankets, woven watertight, were superior to the textiles created by Hispanic guilds.[3]

By 1779 there were an estimated 15,376 sheep at Zuni Pueblo and 300 at Hopi Pueblo.[4] The Navajos had the most sheep. A military inspector in 1850 reported that in the prior 18 months, Navajos had stolen 47,300 sheep from Pueblo Indians alone, and probably many more from struggling Hispano families daring to live on land grants north of Santa Fe.[5]

In New Mexico, families planted corn and melons, beans and wheat. Chiles harvested in the fall became colorful red *ristras* as they dried projecting from the *vigas*, or wooden beams of flat-roofed adobe houses. But farming was subsistence only. Sheep represented pesos on the hoof.

"From the earliest days, New Mexico—which until 1863 included all of Arizona—has been a land of sheep and wool," write Charles Towne and

Edward Wentworth.⁶ For the first half of the nineteenth century, the largest export from New Mexico was sheep and woolen textiles.

Thus began a 300-year-old sheepherding tradition that would stratify Hispanic culture between shepherds and sheep owners, between poor and rich, with only the slightest chance of advancement, if one herded sheep on shares, to build up one's own flocks. In the *partido* system, *ricos*, or rich men, paid shepherds a percentage of the increase in flocks. Much grazing land was already claimed, so in search of fresh grass, enterprising *pastores*, or herders, moved farther away from the safety of plazas and villages and into areas vulnerable to predators, both four legged and human. If a herder lost lambs to coyotes, wolves, bears, late spring snows, or raiding Indians, then instead of gaining independence the herder became trapped in a cycle of debt and could never rise above *peón* labor. He and his dogs walked miles for the rich *dons* who possessed hundreds of thousands of sheep.

"It was easy to get a few hundred poor shepherds into one's debt; and once in, the *amo* [wealthy sheepman], with the aid of complaisant laws, took good care that they should never get out," writes Charles Lummis. He adds, "He was thenceforth entitled to the labor of their bodies—even to the labor of their children. They were his peons—slaves without the expense of purchase."⁷

Governor Baca of Spanish New Mexico had 2,700 herders who tended his two million sheep. When Mexico revolted against Spain in 1821, El Guero (the Blond) Chavez ran a million woollies in New Mexico. Hundreds of thousands of sheep owned by Armijos, Lunas, Luceros, Mirabals, and Oteros covered the high desert landscape, closely cropping the nutritious grama grass, which had the highest protein content of any grass in the West, and eating it down to the roots.⁸

Sheep, unlike cattle, possess a prognathous mouth with teeth that come out at an angle, so sheep can pull out grass and bite it below the buds. Conquistador accounts describe grass belly high to a horse in northern New Mexico. On Taos Mesa, overgrazing by sheep eliminated grasses. *Artemisia tridentata*, or greater sagebrush, came from seeds introduced by thousands of horses brought east from California on what became the Old Spanish Trail between Santa Fe and Los Angeles.⁹

The original Spanish sheep were rough, half-wild churros that had long, scraggly fleece but were well adapted to the deserts and mountains of the Southwest. Later, sheepmen would import blooded rams to increase both meat and wool production. "Pioneer purebred improvers, whose higher quality, larger-framed, better fleeced animals of impeccable ancestry

This historical churro skull, with its distinctive four horns, is from the collection of the Saguache County Museum in Saguache, Colorado, on the northern edge of the San Luis Valley. Author photo.

superseded the ill-bred, shaggy, undersized Churros, which for centuries had dominated the Southwestern pastoral scene," write Towne and Wentworth.[10]

Sheep went with soldiers, missionaries, and settlers. Sheep trails crisscrossed the Southwest. It is estimated there were 321,500 sheep at the California missions by 1834. During the Mexican-American War in 1846–1848, which brought Colorado, California, Utah, and Arizona into the United States, General Stephen Watts Kearny's Army of the West rode over the Santa Fe Trail and lived on mutton, boiled and baked. "Sheep have been the life of New Mexico's mountains and plateaus, the doughty survivor of Indian raids . . . the outstanding source of subsistence for explorer, Indian, colonist, and citizen," write Towne and Wentworth. "New Mexico cradled the foundation blood for Colorado [sheep]."[11]

Gold fever struck the Sierra after a carpenter found nuggets in the trace of John Sutter's sawmill. As the California Gold Rush boomed in 1849, the demand for mutton increased, and long-distance sheep drives headed west and northwest between New Mexico and California. Because the Gold

Rush swelled California's population, Antonio Jose Luna and Antonio Jose Otero shrewdly calculated a way to make a fortune. The two Hispano entrepreneurs drove 50,000 head of woollies from New Mexico, where sheep were worth 50 cents apiece, to the Sierra, where they could be sold for 15 dollars each, thus establishing family fortunes and political power that would last into the twentieth century.[12]

Heir to the San Clemente Land Grant, which encompassed 100,000 acres in the Rio Abajo or lower Rio Grande Valley, Don Jose Luna was approached in the 1880s by the Santa Fe Railroad, which needed to purchase a right-of-way through his vast landholdings. He grew concerned that the route of the train would damage his house, so the railroad paid him $13,000 for the right-of-way and enough money to build a new house, which became an impressive two-story Italianate mansion in the village of Los Lunas, though he did not live to see it completed.

In the 1850s, other New Mexican Hispanic families sought new water and grass along the edge of the Sangre de Cristo Mountains in the San Luis Valley of Colorado, but their financial gains would be far more modest than those of the Lunas and Oteros.

Jose Ilario Valdez came to San Luis in 1851, followed by Dario Gallegos, adopted son of J. C. L. Valdez, who inherited 26,000 sheep. Up the Rio Grande Valley came Luis Montoya, whose large flocks grazed the Culebra Range to the east of the valley and to the west toward Del Norte. Then came Rafael and Tomas Atencio, Francisco Lujan, Pedro Lobato, Jose Damian, Juan Jose Lopez, Luis and David Romero, and Domencio Salazar.[13] Other settlers in Costilla County included Armundo Trujillo, Julian and Francisco Sanches, Juan Pacheco, and four Vallejos—Francisco, Mariano, Miguel, and Antonio.[14]

Sheep brought Hispanics north and united the cultures of southern Colorado and northern New Mexico into a single Hispanic community.[15] Most Hispanic families eked out a subsistence living, but Anglo entrepreneurs sought California gold. Fortunes could be made by trailing sheep to the California gold fields to feed the hungry Anglos.

Mountain man and guide "Uncle Dick" Wootton tried his hand at taking 9,000 head, delivered at Taos, to California. He left June 24, 1852, with supplies and herders up the Rio Grande, across what is now the Weminuche Wilderness, then north to the Gunnison River valley and west to the Colorado River. After his encounter with Ute chief Uncotash, Wootton wintered his flock near Sacramento and sold it for the tidy sum of $50,000.

Seeing the profits to be made, other mountain men moved into the sheep business because the value of beaver plews had plummeted. A year after Wootton trailed woollies west, Kit Carson drove 6,500 churro sheep to Sacramento and earned $30,000 in the most profitable venture of his long and storied career. Soon a quarter million sheep took the southern route from Santa Fe to Los Angeles in about three months' trail time. Unlike cattle, sheep, because of their flocking instinct, could sustain their movement and eat as they walked. Sheep could move farther than cattle and had better endurance. For water they could lap dew from plants and survive.

Entire sheep caravans crossed deserts and faced dry drives and the dangers of alkali at water holes and problems with water crossings. Cracks in sheep's feet had to be covered with resin or pine sap to heal footsore stock. Poisonous vegetation needed to be avoided, and, like the Utes in Colorado, most Indians demanded a toll or a percentage of the stock if herders traversed tribal territory.[16]

Five years after Kit Carson made a small fortune trailing sheep to northern California miners, a new market opened up even closer to New Mexico. The 1858 Colorado Gold Rush near Denver, a decade after the California mining boom, encouraged thousands of prospectors to head toward Pikes Peak. As emigrants rushed to the diggings along Cherry Creek and then spread into the mountains near Black Hawk and what would become Central City, hungry miners "looked to New Mexico for their meat supply. To the mining camps trudged tens of thousands of sheep from the south, a traffic that continued for a full decade."[17]

Other bands spread across southeastern Colorado and the Arkansas River, having come north near Raton, New Mexico, and crossing La Veta and Mosca Passes. Teofilo Trujillo moved north from Taos to the San Luis Valley with his family and flocks in 1864. Despite losing sheep to Indian raids, he would prosper. "The demand for wool uniforms for soldiers in the Civil War attracted Hispanic shepherds to southern Colorado in the 1860s," historians explain. "Many of the hamlets they and others established were created by informal groups, often extended families."[18] Men of Spanish and Mexican descent ruled the sheep industry until after the Civil War in 1865, but then as other settlers and homesteaders stampeded into Colorado, competition increased for water and grass.

From Colorado, herders drove sheep into Kansas to be fattened and shipped by rail to distant markets. Over decades, California sheep multiplied and other bands left the state because of severe drought. Flocks came east to Wyoming in a profitable two-year transect because the wool clip, or wool shorn from the sheep, paid expenses. The lambs, ewes, and wethers sold at railheads represented ready cash. From Wyoming, sheep came south into Colorado across the Red Desert and into the mountain meadows and well-watered high-altitude forests. In 1870, Colorado had 120,928 sheep, but a mere decade later the state's sheep census had grown to 946,443 animals.[19]

Though cattle drives resonate in the history of the West, with colorful cowboys and crusty chuckwagon cooks, there were also great sheep drives in the last three decades of the nineteenth century and into the beginning of the twentieth century. Trailed east from California from 1865 to 1880 came bands of breeding sheep going to the Rockies and beyond. From 1880 to 1885 herders trailed both rams and ewes, and from 1885 to 1901 the sheep were wethers, or castrated males, destined for fattening and markets east of the Continental Divide.[20]

By 1880, three-fourths of New Mexico's sheep belonged to only 20 families, and four-fifths of them were New Mexico natives.[21] In that same year in Colorado, a few bands of sheep followed the South Platte River east but raised the ire of cattleman John W. Iliff, who argued that the public land was his range. Herders sought alternate routes, but waves of homesteaders came in after Congress passed the 1862 Homestead Act. As the nesters claimed their 160 acres, trailing large bands became more difficult because homesteaders erected homes, barns, sheds, and most importantly, fences, which blocked open grazing. Flocks trailed eastward from California for Colorado, which became a state in 1876. By 1884, the western counties of Wyoming teemed with California sheep.

Flockmasters moved sheep 8 to 10 miles daily by feeding before dawn and early in the morning, bedding down at noon, and moving again while it was cooler in late afternoon until almost nightfall. If water was scarce, herders pushed their sheep all through the night on long drives that covered vast ground.

New Mexican herders brought sheep north through the Rio Grande and San Luis Valleys to the upper Arkansas Valley and the hungry silver boomtown of Leadville, which boasted 5,000 residents. Sheep also trailed north by following creeks and riverbeds to Pueblo, Colorado, and along the Front Range. Increasing sheep numbers exacerbated tensions with cattlemen who also grazed free public lands. Foreign investors, specifically Scottish and English absentee owners, were grazing half a million cattle in Colorado by 1875—all on federal land. Cattlemen thought their herds immune to wind and weather, but the bitter blizzards of 1886–1887 across the open plains decimated cattle numbers and opened up landscapes to more closely herded sheep.

As farmers settled and irrigated the Platte, Arkansas, and Cache la Poudre River Valleys and planted alfalfa seed, lambs and wethers could be fed and fattened in-state. Sheep numbers reaching one million head were being fed along the South Platte and Cache la Poudre, with another 670,000 in the Arkansas River Valley, and smaller numbers in the San Luis Valley and on irrigated lands near Grand Junction. Besides alfalfa, as a sugar beet industry developed in Colorado, sheep ate sugar beet tops, and eventually Colorado fed one to two million head, or more than one-fourth of all annual sheep and lambs fed in the United States.[22]

Conflicts with cattlemen increased because of intensive sheep numbers. There were no rules about who could use public land and under what con-

In the forest reserves, sheep grazed higher than cattle. On lower-elevation mesas and plateaus, sheep nibbled grasses cattlemen needed for winter range. This historical photo from Colorado's Western Slope may be a scene on the Uncompahgre Plateau. Photo from the Walker Art Studio Collection, courtesy of the Center of Southwest Studies, Fort Lewis College, Durango, Colorado.

ditions, so by the 1880s and 1890s ranges all across the West became overstocked with both sheep and cattle. Bitter rivalries resulted and the land suffered from overgrazing, with denuded landscapes, deepening soil erosion, extensive gullies and arroyos, and mountain meadows pulverized to dirt and dust.

When herders moved combined bands of 3,000 to 7,500 sheep, they needed ground sometimes 10 to 40 miles wide, which riled homesteaders and inflamed cattlemen. Basque, French, and Portuguese herders hired their own kinsmen as they brought sheep east from California. Simultaneously, Hispano herders moved bands north from New Mexico. Perhaps as many as 15 million sheep were driven east on the sheep trails, which fell into disuse by 1900.

As railroads came to crisscross the West, mercantile stores sold plug tobacco, steel plows, knives, buckets, graniteware coffeepots, coffee beans to be ground in Arbuckle hand-cranked grinders, calico, gingham, horseshoes, Winchester rifles, Colt single-action revolvers, and striped peppermint candy. Hispano herders racked up debts at Anglo-owned mercantile general stores, and enterprising French and Irish Catholic males married into sheep-owning Hispano families and began to dominate New Mexican land grants.[23]

Lucien Maxwell married Señorita Luz, daughter of Don Carlos Beaubien, who owned 1.7 million acres near Cimarron, New Mexico. This land would come to be called the Maxwell Land Grant and be home to 50,000 sheep.[24] Perhaps the most successful sheep and mercantile enterprise was that of George and Frank Bond of Española, New Mexico, who leased and sold bands of ewes in New Mexico, Wyoming, and Colorado, carried back the debt, had thriving mercantile stores, owned 25,000 head, and handled 100,000 to 200,000 sheep as traders and middlemen.[25]

"One of his [Bond's] tactics was to obtain permanent grazing rights on forested public lands, then to rent out parcels to individual sheepherders who were unable to find pastures for their own small flocks. Their only recourse was to sign on with Bond under the partido system of old," explains William W. Dunmire in *New Mexico's Spanish Livestock Heritage*. "Contracting to rent a specified number of ewes for a three-to-five-year period, forced to outfit himself at the company store with its inflated prices and usurious rates, and then having to pay for the privilege of using Bond's grazing rights typically left the partidario in deep debt after the contract period."[26]

Many poor Hispano herders never rose out of debt. If the antiquated *partido* system continued in New Mexico into the twentieth century, so did extensive overgrazing as a result of excessive sheep numbers. Grasses and shrubs diminished. Alien weeds and nonnative plants began to thrive. Arroyos and gullies deepened, especially in the Rio Puerco watershed. Even the white-tailed ptarmigan became regionally extinct because domestic sheep ate the bird's most important food—alpine willow. Wild bighorn sheep disappeared by 1903.[27] If New Mexico's sheep barons kept Hispano herders in debt and did extensive damage to land and watersheds, back East a conservation movement had begun.

Historian Frederick Jackson Turner wrote of the closing of the frontier in 1890, the date the superintendent of the US Census declared that a frontier line had ceased to exist across the American West. "Thus had ended the first great phase in American history."[28] Out of that understanding would come the beginnings of the conservation movement and a new era of protecting American soil, water, and forests, but it also intensified competition for grazing land. Aggressive Basque, Greek, and Scottish shepherds took their wages in lambs or ewes and over time sought new pastures when they emerged as sheepmen.

In 1895 New Mexico produced 14 million pounds of wool from three million sheep. Two years later, sheep barons, or *ricos*, made fortunes when wool hit 11½ cents per pound.[29] By 1900, one-quarter to one-half of New Mexican sheep were herded under *partido* contracts. The ricos had forced small flock owners into becoming wage earners. They had lost control of their flocks and were now *partidarios*, or sheep sharecroppers. Earning 16 dollars a month and food, Hispanic men remained as sheepherders, but less and less as flock owners. As seasonal wage laborers they maintained credit for their families at mercantile stores and desperately tried to pay down their bills at season's end.[30]

North of New Mexico, as Colorado became settled and homesteaders moved in to fence their 160-acre plots of land, the days of trailing sheep and cattle ended. In the fight for grass and water, ranchers needed a private land base and access to public land. Skirmishes between sheepmen and cattlemen erupted into war.

SECOND SHEEPSCAPE

*Buckles Lake, Counting Corrals, and V Rock
—San Juan National Forest*

> Trees are poems that the earth writes upon the sky. We fell them down
> and turn them into paper that we may record our emptiness.
>
> —KAHLIL GIBRAN

Thousands of domestic sheep once grazed in the mountains of the San Juan National Forest near Pagosa Springs. Now there are none. High-country sheep-grazing allotments are vacant, and the only signs of a historical industry are stands of aspen trees carved by Hispano herders over generations. Peggy Bergon began recording and photographing those carvings or arborglyphs almost four decades ago. She knows how to "read the trees" and find patterns in the aspen art.

"Peggy's done a great job documenting arborglyphs on the Pagosa Ranger District. The value of our history should not get lost," states district ranger Kevin Khung. I have attended one of Bergon's popular aspen-art walking tours, called "Look Who's Talking: Arborglyphs," at Buckles Lake Trail no. 688 several miles east off Highway 84, which runs from Pagosa Springs, Colorado, to Chama, New Mexico.

We saw 500-year-old Spanish-style Christian crosses carved by Merejil Valdez, and Celtic knots, boxes, and stars etched by Leandro Cruz. Eturo Sanchez drew grouse, and Solomon Trujillo perfected handlebar mustaches.

When Bergon began in 1977, locals thought she was a bit daft. Who cared what messages sheepherders left on trees? She was told, "That's not important. That's just sheepherder graffiti." But now her critics realize she's sharing a historical and cultural treasure.

Her 2½-hour interpretive walks, one in the summer and one in the fall on a three-mile loop, are in their thirteenth year. The tours fill up with locals and visitors to Pagosa Springs, who delight in following Bergon as she shows off the names, designs, and portraits of her favorite carvers, including Pantelon and Pablo Casados, Solomon Trujillo, and Benigro Gallegos. "Arborglyphs captivated me from the beginning. I've always looked at these as folk art. They have become an important historical aspect of the forest and have a specific story to tell," she relates.

These Spanish Christian Maltese crosses, in a style that is 500 years old, were carved by Merejil Valdez. Religious iconography, though found on arborglyphs in aspen groves, is rare. Author photo.

Local arborglyph expert Peggy Bergon from Pagosa Springs, Colorado, has done an excellent job identifying historical arborglyphs and their carvers on the Pagosa District of the San Juan National Forest. This carving, with a distinctive handlebar mustache and long male eyelashes, is by Solomon Trujillo. Author photo.

After decades of following sheep trails and stock driveways, Bergon can recognize herders' carvings from yards away because of their distinctive writing style, caricatures, or artistic flourishes. Solomon Trujillo's smiling facial profiles always have large, glittering eyelashes, especially on men. How ironic—macho Hispanic men with truly magnificent waxed and upturned mustachios, and yet with elaborate, elongated, feminine eyelashes. "This is a hobby with a purpose," she laughs. Then she says, "The greater picture here is documenting western history, the untold story of sheepherders compared to the more famous and popular cowboys."

As early as 1893, Archuleta County, Colorado, shipped 300,000 pounds of wool annually on the Denver and Rio Grande Railroad in addition to thousands of *borregas*, or sheep. Families that ran woollies had names like Candelaria, Gallegos, Rodriquez, Martinez, Quintana, Lopez, Trujillo, Archuleta, Pacheco, Garcia, Muñoz, Lobato, Jacquez, Vigil, and Ortiz. They hired herders from Lumberton, Los Ojos, Chama, Blanco, Coyote, and Canjilon in northern New Mexico to live with the flocks from June to September.

Herders trailed sheep north into Colorado and left their names and dates carved on aspens in a beautiful curving penmanship that proved they had attended school through the eighth grade. The penmanship taught across America was Spencerian, and the herders proudly demonstrated their literacy by carving the date they passed by, their name, and where they were from.

Bergon has found thousands of separate glyphs, and her work gained a new urgency after the 2002 Missionary Ridge Fire near Durango, Colorado, destroyed aspen carvings as the fire roared over the ridge east toward the Pine River drainage. "I saw that this was a resource that was disappearing," she notes. She spent even more time searching for aspen groves, which represent only 12 percent of the 590,000 acres of the Pagosa Ranger District. "I've always looked at this as my gift to the community. It's a great history that Pagosa Springs has now embraced," she explains. She has spoken to herders and their descendants, who were "delighted that someone was showing an interest" in the carvings of their fathers and grandfathers.

She began as a camp cook in the Weminuche Wilderness, wondering about all the inscriptions and designs she found on aspens. Over the years she's learned the trails, patterns, and movements of sheep, and she finds familiar names carved in the forest with dates beginning in the 1910s up to the 1960s. Those years were the "golden age" of aspen arborglyphs and sheepherding in general, which prospered during both world wars but then declined as Americans ate less lamb and synthetic fibers replaced wool.

Popular styles of cursive penmanship taught in rural one-room schools were the Spencerian method and the Palmer method. Many Hispano sheepherders from northern New Mexico only had an eighth-grade education, and those who learned to write in cursive proudly displayed their writing skills on aspen trees, as did Mr. Madrid from Chama, New Mexico, who brought his flock north of Buckles Lake on July 24, 1934. Author photo.

Peggy Bergon searches for carved aspens on the San Juan National Forest (SJNF) in Archuleta County. Ruth Lambert, archaeologist for the San Juan Mountains Association, looks for glyphs on the Columbine Ranger District of the SJNF in La Plata County. "Aspen art is not just art images on a living canvas. The carvings are a reflection of a cultural way of life. They are artifacts of a larger story that is grounded in those traditions. They provide a window into Hispano life," Lambert explains. She leads glyph tours into Moonlick Park and Beaver Meadows along the Pine-Piedra Stock Driveway.

Esther Greenfield also hikes into the woods in search of carved aspens. In 18 years of exploring forested areas surrounding Durango, Greenfield has found and documented nearly 1,300 historical aspen carvings. She wrote *Reading the Trees: A Curious Hiker's Field Journal of Hidden Woodland Messages*, which contains about 150 of her favorite arborglyphs, along with historical research tying some of the carvings to specific people.

As Peggy Bergon returned to Pagosa Springs after her arborglyph tour, my dog and I stayed on and spent our second night in a tent close to the old herders' trail and dozens of arborglyphs. Just before afternoon thunderstorms hit on the day after the tour, we set out on our own to find more trees based on Bergon's suggestions.

Wary of lightning storms but compelled to find additional glyphs, we hiked north beyond Buckles Lake and toward a natural drainage off the steep South San Juan Wilderness, which rose above us to the east. Trails went in several directions, but I thought we'd look near a shallow natural lake surrounded by aspens. As we hiked a tall ridge, I found what I was looking for.

Numerous trees had carvings and dates from the 1930s through the 1950s, etched delicately with a penknife or even a horseshoe nail. I'd entered a private gallery with the names, dates, and hometowns of dozens of herders as well as post–World War II "Kilroy was here" symbols of a man with a large nose and two hands peering over a fence. There was a variety of carved human faces and horses, and always the names and dates of the carvers in beautiful handwriting, signifying "I am with the sheep and I am here."

Any thin scratch on the smooth white bark expanded as the tree grew. These were master carvers, and I marveled at the penmanship of a herder from Chama and his July 1941 date. Where was he when the Japanese bombed Pearl Harbor five months later? Did he keep herding? Did he return to the trees, or did he join the Armed Services, change his life, and never herd again? For many shepherds in the mountains of Colorado and New Mexico, the summer of 1941 was their last peaceful time in high-country meadows, knowing that in the winter they would return to the villages where they had been born.

Carved aspens are living monuments. Sheep ranged everywhere in Colorado. They came north from New Mexico, east from Utah, and south from Wyoming to graze on public lands. There are many stories to tell from Hispano, Greek, and Basque herders. There is much to learn because, as Bergon laments, "It's devastating to come back and see a tree that's fallen. The forest is different now because the sheep driveways are overgrown."[1] On the Pagosa Ranger District the sheep are gone. The herders are gone. Only their carvings remain.

The Buckles Lake area is rich in arborglyphs because the US Forest Service built sheep corrals there to count ewes before herders trailed the borregas higher into the San Juan National Forest. Thousands of sheep came through the area from Rio Arriba County in New Mexico and the villages of Tres Piedras, Canjilon, Los Ojos, and Tierra Amarilla. Herders "followed the sheeps," trailing them north across private ground, "but cattlemen liked for them to cross and eat the poisonous larkspur that did not harm the sheep," explains Antonio Manzanares, owner of Shepherd's Lamb.[2] His grandfather owned one of the bands of 900–1,000 sheep that were trailed in the early summer on their way to the high country, symbolized by the dramatic V Rock, a mountain with a natural V shape on a large granite face. Hispanic families had sheep "on top of V Rock." Above it was excellent browse, grass, summer pastures with water, and bears eager for a lamb lunch.

Manzanares's grandfather trapped a bear and decided to tease it for a while. Then he shot it and found that the bear had pulled and chewed and strained until only one tendon remained holding it in the trap. Had his grandfather teased the bruin just a little more, "I probably wouldn't be here," says Antonio with a laugh as we sit in the office of the New Mexico cooperative Tierra Wools, started by Pastores de Valle. "There was more sheep shipped here in the fall from Chama, New Mexico, on the railroad

V Rock is a prominent visual landmark near the South San Juan Wilderness in the San Juan Mountains on the border of Colorado and New Mexico. For decades northern New Mexican herders trailed flocks from Rio Arriba County in New Mexico north to Archuleta County in Colorado to graze them in high-altitude pastures atop V Rock. Author photo.

than from almost anywhere else. In the fall herders raced their flocks out of the forest and down to the railyards because there just weren't enough holding pens and they wanted to get their lambs on boxcars and off to market."

The sheep wintered in the desert and sagebrush country of Chaco Canyon, lambed in the spring near Los Ojos, and summered in the high San Juans. Manzanares's stories include a tale of his grandfather breaking a leg after being kicked by a mule, and once coming home covered with so many lice that he was "lousy" and not permitted into the family house.

Etched in the memory of many families, though the date is obscure, is the year of the big snow, *el Año de la Nevada*, in which thousands of sheep died, smothered under four or more feet of wet snow, probably in the winter of 1932. Dozens of sheep sharecroppers, or partidarios, lost everything and went deeper into debt with the mercantile stores that had advanced them groceries and supplies. It was those boys, men, uncles, brothers, and cousins who had carved their names and their village names on so many aspen trees near Buckles Lake.[3]

Though Manzanares's grandfather owned a flock, his father did not. So when Antonio went into the sheep business, "I learned from the sheep. They taught me what I needed to know about running sheep in the mountains, and the old experienced herders I hired like Martin Romero from Los Brazos and Elandro Chavez from Los Ojos taught me how to pack mules, how and when to move camp, where to set up camp, and what plants sheep prefer. I know now that when a herder says it is time to move camp it is time right now. The sheep have eaten the browse. Sheep are always looking for fresh food. They want to move, and the herder knows."[4]

Rain was coming. My old Labrador sensed it, and at 12 years old, he is terrified of thunder. I wanted to keep looking for glyphs, but I knew it was time to turn back. I had found a small carving of a Catholic priest on an aspen but not much else. As the mist around me became slow, quiet drops of rain, I realized I was deeper into the forest than I expected. I thought I knew the way back to camp and my tent, but I couldn't be sure because in the sunshine of the early afternoon I'd zigzagged from aspen to aspen and not paid much attention to where I was going or where I'd been.

Feeling a little nervous, I set down my pack, carefully wrapped up my camera, and retrieved my rain gear. As I walked, I wasn't quite sure of what direction to take as thunder moved closer, booming toward me from the northwest.

Hiking in groves of ponderosa pine and scattered clumps of aspen, I was not yet wet, but not sure of the route to take either. In the overcast and rain it was definitely time to turn around, so I made a slow arc, taking one last look at the aspens, their bright white bark now muted and light gray from rain. I saw a solitary carving. Nothing around it. Just a very simple horse, but exquisitely done as if carved in one or two master strokes.

What did I have to fear? I was alone on a ridge, but a solo herder had preceded me decades before. The aspen carving calmed me down, eased my anxiety, let me know subtly, succinctly, that someone else had been there. He'd left his sign, a masterpiece. Elated, I hauled out my camera for a few shots. Then my dog and I turned toward my tent, sure of our direction, moving quickly through the wet grass, thunder receding behind us.

Chapter 2

The Beginning of Colorado's Cattle and Sheep Wars, 1880–1905

Sheep eat a lot of grass. They are bound to encroach on range claimed by someone else. In the old days of swift expansion, quarrels inevitably passed from violent words to violent deeds, occasionally to open warfare that swept whole counties.

—DAVID LAVENDER
One Man's West

From the standpoint of justice, the cattlemen are right. They have done much more to build the West and do not intend to be driven out. They have the people with them.

—CRAIG (CO) COURIER
August 25, 1893

Cattlemen developed a pathological hatred of sheep people; they claimed that sheep killed the grass by cropping it too closely—a self-serving argument that was true only if their cattle had overgrazed the range in the first place. The conflict had racist overtones.

—MARSHALL SPRAGUE
Colorado

Teofilo Trujillo, born a Mexican and now an American citizen, sought justice. His herders had been threatened, his sheep clubbed and killed. Now, at last, in a courtroom in Saguache County, he sat through judicial proceedings with his entire family as insolent cowboys stood on trial.

For decades Teofilo Trujillo had grazed sheep on the slopes of the Sangre de Cristo Mountains, named for the blood of Christ. After the Mexican-American War, Trujillo became a US citizen in 1848. He prospered and his family grew. But by the 1880s cattlemen demanded his range, specifically the Dickey brothers, who settled on the Medano Ranch and forced other Hispanic ranchers to sell or give up their land. The brothers eyed Trujillo's acreage, and they had no use for his sheep.[1]

Pioneer rancher Teofilo Trujillo lost sheep to the Dickey brothers in 1884. By 1902 other cattlemen were harassing Trujillo's sheep, and in January four men attacked his flock, killing 90 head. A few days later, 14 armed men returned to kill 30 more sheep and "fired into the house in which the herders were camped. A warrant has been sworn out for one of the parties and other arrests may be made. The cattle and sheep men have had frequent collisions wherever they have attempted to range on the same territory and the sheep men usually get the worst of it," reported the *Saguache Crescent*.[2]

Teofilo Trujillo trusted American justice. He filed a legal complaint against the Dickey brothers and Bart Davis for 30 dead and 22 crippled sheep, with 90 missing. "The boys not only rode down, shot, and scattered his sheep, but also fired into a cabin where three of his herders were sleeping," reported the *Monte Vista (CO) Journal*. In court, "the evidence failed to identify either of the accused as parties to the sheep killing."[3]

Little did Trujillo know that as he awaited justice in the courtroom, other hard-riding cowboys, hired by cattlemen, had sloshed kerosene on his adobe home. Someone struck a wooden match. Flames curled up the walls and crept into the rafters.

Not trusting Anglo banks, he had hidden his money in his house. In February 1902, after decades in the San Luis Valley, the Trujillo family returned to smoldering ruins, their home demolished, its unique stained-glass windows smashed. "The ranch house of Teofilo Trujillo burned to the ground with its entire contents last Friday evening," reported the *Center Dispatch* from Saguache. "Trujillo had one of the best ranch houses in the valley and the loss was considerable."[4] Because he had lost money in the failure of the bank in Hooper, Colorado, he kept cash at home. The fire cost him his life savings of $8,000.[5] His son Pedro had warned him that cattlemen would not tolerate woollies.

Not only did Trujillo lose his house and almost all his possessions, he nearly lost his son, who had refused to become a sheepherder and "argued

This cabin was built by Pedro Trujillo, son of Teofilo Trujillo, a Hispano sheepherder whose house and life savings were burned in a fire set by cowboys. It is now a National Historic Landmark close to Great Sand Dunes National Park and Preserve. Photo courtesy of Trujillo family descendants and Patrick Myers of the National Park Service at Great Sand Dunes National Park.

with his father that the sheep would cause him trouble."[6] Pedro had homesteaded nearby and tried to appear more accommodating to cattlemen; he raised cattle and horses and built a two-story log house in contrast to his father's adobe residence, which burned. To maintain his Hispanic culture, Pedro secretly used adobe plaster on the inside to cover the logs, but in the end both father and son sold out their holdings.[7] The cattlemen had won, this round. Sheep wars in the San Luis Valley echoed those occurring across the state.

Sheep trailing and cattle drives ended in Colorado because both homesteaders and railroads had begun to change the landscape. Tensions grew between cattlemen and sheepmen, who both used public land at no charge, and violence on the range in Colorado would last from the early 1880s into the early 1920s, finally to be resolved by the 1934 Taylor Grazing Act. In the beginning, it was a wide-open West with intense competition for grass and water.

After the Meeker incident of 1879, in which Nathan Meeker and 10 other whites at the White River Indian Agency were murdered by Utes, citizens ignored the Ute Treaty of 1868. When the US Army forced bands of Utes to move to the Uintah and Ouray Reservation in northeastern Utah, Colorado's Western Slope was thrown open to homesteading and settlement in 1881.[8] Within a few months, developers platted all the major towns in western Colorado, including Durango, Delta, Montrose, Grand Junction, Rifle, and Glenwood Springs. Settlers arrived first in a trickle and then in a flood, bringing horses, cattle, and sheep to devour grass that Ute ponies had only lightly cropped.

In the fall of 1882, J. B. Hurlburt, who would settle at Parachute, Colorado, and his partner Martin Billiter brought 2,000 sheep from California. They took a northern route, arrived in Meeker, learned that the Colorado River Valley had more open winters with less snow and better grass, and then trailed the band down Government Road to Parachute Creek.[9]

The Wise brothers from Utah brought the first band of sheep into the Montrose area and the Uncompahgre Valley in 1883. Five years later, Daniel Morrison Kelly drove Utah sheep into Colorado across the border at night. Two days later, while he was cooking supper at his camp in the cedars near Kannah Creek, cowboys killed him, thus beginning almost four decades of sheep and cattle wars. "Sheep killing occurred in every section of the Western Slope. During the ten years immediately prior to 1903, about fifty sheepmen were murdered in Wyoming and Colorado and 25,000 sheep were run over cliffs or destroyed by other means," wrote Diane Abraham.[10]

The High Plains of eastern Colorado "settled up" as homesteaders claimed private land, but the formidable mountains and canyons of western Colorado and the sagebrush hills of northwestern Colorado resulted in a different ranching strategy. Ranchers settled valley bottoms and along rivers, creeks, and streams. Occasionally they would homestead a proven spring or source of water, but their private, taxable acreage remained small compared to the public-domain land they grazed.

Cattle came onto the Western Slope from all directions, and there were as many as 100,000 head on different ranges by 1890.[11] Cattle drifted north of the Colorado River into the Piceance Basin and Yellow Creek. They arrived in the Mancos River Valley and all across southern Colorado. Thousands of head of Texas cattle poured onto the public domain, cattle wild as deer. In La Plata County the Cox Cattle Company moved from the Cedar Hill country of New Mexico north up the Florida River. English investors funded the Carlisle Cattle Company, which stretched east to Trinidad and west to the Abajo or Blue Mountains, Monticello, and Bluff, Utah.

A beef bonanza was spurred on by high prices, untouched grass, and little or no competition against the speckled, rangy Texas longhorn cattle. "As is the way of 'booms' the beef bonanza mushroomed by geometric progression," wrote John Rolfe Burroughs in *Where the Old West Stayed Young*. "During the early 1880s, nature indeed was kind to the speculators; the cattle harvested the grass on schedule, the mature animals went to market, where they commanded the best prices the industry had ever seen, and investors received generous dividends."[12]

It all collapsed with the devastating winter of 1886–1887, which destroyed cattlemen from Montana to Texas, including the North Dakota cattle herd of young Theodore Roosevelt. Ranchers lost more than 70–80 percent of their herds. Estimates in the West were 900,000 cattle in 1886 but only 300,000 a decade later, compared to 875,000 sheep the same year and 3.5 million woollies by 1900.[13] As the cattle industry failed with "The Big Die-Up," sheep moved in, especially into southwestern Wyoming and then south to northwestern Colorado.

Sheep grazed in distinct patterns and time frames based on weather, topography, and available forage, but no thought was given to sustainable rangelands. "Every spring the herds of sheep followed the melting snows into the high mountain meadows just as soon as the ground was uncovered," wrote Will C. Barnes in *The Story of the Range*. "Not a thought was given to the tiny leaves of the forage plants just poking their tender points out of the soft, wet soil. The hungry sheep fed it off just as fast as it grew, and their sharp hoofs trampled and cut up the sod until bare wastes took the place of grassy meadows and bunchgrass hillsides."[14]

Sheep ranchers flanked both sides of the Union Pacific Railroad in southern Wyoming but sought grass in Colorado. Conveniently, ranch headquarters were in towns served by the railroad, and three-quarters of the flocks were churro ewes crossed with merino rams.

There was money to be made in sheep, and at least one cattleman, Ora Haley of the Two Bar Ranch in Moffat and Routt Counties, became a silent partner in sheep outfits to conceal his investment and avoid social stigma.

The Cosgriff brothers moved from Vermont to Colorado and bought checkerboarded lands, or alternate sections of 640 acres, which had been awarded to the Union Pacific under terms of the Pacific Railway Act of 1862. By buying alternate sections, the Cosgriffs could control the remaining public-domain lands. They grazed 125,000 sheep on those lands in the winter, and summer range in Routt and Moffat Counties was under the care of a trusted Mexican foreman named Adriano Apadaca. They loaned funds to other sheepmen through the 27 banks they owned, including banks in Denver and Monte Vista.[15]

On the Western Slope, ranchers sought both summer and winter pastures. In warm weather they grazed at higher elevations, but when early snows in the fall forced their stock below 7,000 feet, cowboys and herders looked for more accessible grass in canyon bottoms and valley floors. Sheep could graze much higher than cattle. With proper herding, sheep could forage in high mountain meadows and on the steep, grassy slopes of peaks 12,000 to 13,000 feet high. Problems arose when sheep and cattle grazed the same landscape at the same time, or when sheep trailed south from the Red Desert of Wyoming or east from Utah's canyon country and ate low-elevation grasses that cattlemen needed for their winter range.

Cattlemen hated the smell of sheep and believed, incorrectly, that cows would not eat where sheep had grazed because of the scent left by a gland between the sheep's toes. Because of how their jaws work, cows or steers can lower their head and chew grass, but sheep jaws open much wider, allowing them to pull up plants by the roots. Sheep thrive on steep hillsides and eat weeds and flowers cattle will ignore. If not moved daily, a flock can graze a meadow almost down to dirt, preventing plant regrowth. "Everything in front of sheep is eaten and everything behind is killed," claimed cowmen.[16] Cowboys scorned sheep as "the most helpless of animals," which were "always looking for a place to die."[17] Edward Norris Wentworth explains in *America's Sheep Trails*:

> When flocks reached fresh ranges they left very little for cattle or horses following them; while if they trailed, nothing remained to be garnered by another grazier during the same season. . . . The American public land policy placed a premium on the man who got there first—because he got the most. Hence this combination of an ability to graze deeply into the grass roots, and a national land policy that rewarded despoliation, gave rise to the long endured crime of the open range—the cattle-sheep wars.[18]

This classic photograph depicts the attitude of sheepmen and their herders in the woolly West, particularly Basque and Greek herders, in defending their flocks' grazing rights on the open range of the West. Photo courtesy of the Sheep Photo File, American Heritage Center, University of Wyoming.

While cattlemen and sheepmen fought over grazing rights, both groups ignored the damage their animals did by overgrazing, which left deep scars and gullies. Without vegetative cover on the soft soils of the West, snowmelt and hard summer rains created gullies and arroyos up to 40 yards deep where once had been grassy meadows.[19] Some landscapes and ecological habitats in Colorado will never recover. Across the West, "the land was seriously overstocked, eaten bare, trampled hard, and permanently injured. No seeds were saved to bring up the next year's crop."[20]

Compounding the problem were "tramp" or itinerant sheepmen from states other than Colorado who owned no local property, paid no local taxes, and ran their flocks on Colorado grass until they shipped fat ewes and lambs out by rail. Early in the range wars, two-thirds of the sheepmen were not from Colorado, but their flocks devoured local plants. "It is well to recall that of all the men who grow rich by hides and fleeces, not one in ten does so on his own land," wrote Mary Austin.[21]

Most of the overgrazing and conflicts occurred between 1880 and 1920, and "in reality, the problem was racial and economic. The cattleman was

Anglo and sheepherders tended to be Mexican or Basque."[22] Range wars ravaged the Book Cliffs, the Uncompahgre Plateau, Gunnison County, Archuleta County, Routt County, Plateau County, the Disappointment Valley, and the San Luis Valley.[23] Cattlemen started a variety of protective and stock grower associations, but no association ever claimed responsibility for the dozens of herders threatened, injured, and even killed; the wagons burned, sometimes with herd dogs tied to them; and the thousands of sheep shot, poisoned, clubbed, or "rim-rocked," which meant being stampeded off high cliffs.[24] Rancher and writer David Lavender claims that Colorado does not have a single record of a man being convicted for molesting sheep, yet sheepmen lost thousands of dollars and valuable breeding stock.

Cowboys wore a Colt .45 on their hip atop their leather chaps and Levi's, but shepherds were often better armed with Winchester .30–30 carbines loaded for coyotes, wolves, and bears. While cowboys on horseback always had their sidearm, shepherds usually stored rifles in their tent or sheep wagon because their troubles came from nighttime predators. The *pastores*

Originally published in *Harper's Weekly* on October 13, 1877, this drawing by Paul Frenzeny graphically illustrates the cattle and sheep wars, with cowboys on a raid at dawn to kill sheep, burn sheep camps, and bludgeon sheepherders. Drawing courtesy of the New Mexico History Museum/Palace of the Governors, Santa Fe.

rarely carried rifles during the day while they paced their sheep on foot, which left shepherds vulnerable to swift and silent attacks by armed cowboy riders with Stetsons pulled low and bandannas over their faces.[25]

Sheep made money twice a year, from wool and from the sale of castrated males, or wether lambs, for meat, whereas a cattle crop took three or four years to produce. Sheepmen became bankers and bought strategic homestead allotments as delinquent tax certificates when homesteaders failed on their mortgages. Because they moved quietly and carefully, "it was the sheepmen rather than the cattlemen who had the money with which to purchase holdings," explains John Rolfe Burroughs.[26]

Sheep were reviled throughout Colorado. Near Durango, Missionary Ridge served as an unwritten "sheepline," where cattle grazed to the east and sheep to the west. Occasionally that local custom was misunderstood. The patriarch of the Cox ranch family recalls:

> Although these old cowmen fought among themselves, they were of one mind when it became a question of sheep. This is illustrated in the end of Shepard and Clark, the original sheepmen near Parrot City, who crowded east onto cow range somewhere around O'Neal Park, and briefly wound up their career at a Pagosa Springs rooming house when they packed in for grub to take back to their sheep camp. Mexicans were blamed for this double killing, but nothing can be learned of the sheep bands ever leaving that section. Shepard and Clark were brought to Animas City and given the notoriety of being the first two men to be buried in the town's new graveyard.[27]

Throughout Colorado, cattlemen and sheepmen vied for public range. Although stories and tales abound, exact statistics are hard to determine. An Anglo's death was generally recorded, but if cowboys killed a Hispano herder, no name was remembered.

Local skirmishes in the larger war included 200 sheep shot at State Bridge. Fifteen run off a cliff at Dry Creek. Thirty-five ewes with throats slit at Whitewater. Part of the intense animosity stemmed from the different grazing habits of sheep and cattle, because sheep could survive where cattle starved. "Sheep often did better than cattle in some parts of the San Luis Valley. There they thrived on the invading forbs that replaced cowed-out grasses," writes ecologist and historian Tom Wolf.[28]

"Furthermore, sheep could move profitably onto rocky or sparsely grassed sections entirely unsuited to bovine occupation, while the cattlemen remained helpless on the stripped lower ranges. Nothing angered the cattle owner more than the dallying of sheep, across range which he normally used, while they were enroute to the foothills or mountain altitudes," notes Wentworth.[29] Sheep ate what cattle would not. As the overstocked range faltered, local cattlemen took matters into their own hands.

If sheep were bunched up, sometimes dynamite was used, but a favorite technique was putting blue vitriol or saltpeter on a bed-ground, or poisoning feed like corn. "No one was arrested in the cattle country for running off sheep, and only in rare instances were they convicted of [sheep] slaughter. When human deaths occurred efforts were greater, but the larger proportion of tragedies went unpunished. There was sympathy for the cattlemen in most communities, due to longer tenure."[30]

Racism played a role in the violence because herders were often Hispanos from New Mexico, or if the flocks moved east from Utah, then bigoted cowboys punished Mormon sheepmen. States tried to pass laws regulating grazing, but state legislatures had no authority over federal lands, and the "pirate" or "tramp" sheepmen coming onto lower-elevation public land, often winter range for cattle, knew that. An obscure federal forest law, the Forest Reserve Act, shifted what was already a precarious balance.

The frontier had officially closed in 1890. Native Americans had been forced onto reservations. The Indian Wars had ended, but the cattle-sheep wars were escalating. Well-educated easterners began to worry about the fate of America's public lands and the abuses of those lands by corporations like railroad, mining, and logging companies, which simply took from western landscapes whatever had market value. Former secretary of the interior Stewart Udall labeled the Gilded Age theft of American natural resources "The Great Barbecue."[31] In response, a conservation movement began to coalesce back East, with major repercussions on lands in the West. One law had huge consequences.

In 1891 Congress passed the Forest Reserve Act, giving the president of the United States executive powers. The law provided that

> the President of the United States may, from time to time, set apart and reserve, in any state or territory having public land bearing forests, in any part of the public lands, wholly or in part covered with timber or undergrowth, whether of commercial value or not, as public reservations; and the president shall, by public proclamation, declare the establishment of such reservation and the limits thereof.[32]

The area surrounding Yellowstone National Park (1872) became the first timber reserve, but the second was in Colorado. The White River Plateau Timber Reserve was set aside in 1891 and stretched from Breckenridge west to De Beque and north toward Meeker. It was a huge expanse, and visionary in the prospect of protecting an entire watershed. Local cattlemen howled. They had taken a beating during the rough winter of 1889–1890 and had lost 65 percent of their cattle in the White River country. This new policy seemed to be just another blow to their future.

No new regulations were promulgated. No forest rangers rode in on horseback to inspect cattle and sheep numbers. That was yet to come. All the forest reserve did was withdraw thousands of acres from potential entry by squatters or homesteaders, but for the pioneers of western Colorado, such a withdrawal was an outrage. They had rushed over the Continental Divide as soon as the Utes had been pushed out; they had "located" ranches, in pioneer parlance, and these frontier families expected to use the land any way they saw fit. Now distant bureaucrats in faraway Washington, DC, had begun to limit settlers' options.[33] It was unthinkable, but there was no one yet locally on the ground or even in the state to complain to. But as they blasphemed the new forest reserve and the implications of what it meant to

With brave herders and sheep that reproduced yearly and also provided annual paychecks for both mutton and wool, a sheep rancher could get started with only a wagon and a tent, as in this photograph. Photo courtesy of the Tread of Pioneers Museum, Steamboat Springs, Colorado.

God-fearing cattlemen, the problem with sheep continued, because there were no rules about that, either.

Joe Cain brought 5,000 head of sheep into Plateau Valley in 1890 and trailed them up on Grand Mesa for the summer season. He asked local folks whether he could drive sheep through the valley on the way to the high ranges, and he moved them rapidly and without annoyance, but two years later he was told not to return. He did not. Others did.[34]

By the winter of 1891–1892, Cunningham and Grant of Salt Lake City, as well as other sheepmen, grazed from 75,000 to 100,000 sheep on the desert in western Colorado and eastern Utah and fed breeding bucks, or male sheep, in Plateau Valley to be placed with the ewes. Later, herders would bring the ewes to Plateau Valley for grazing in the high country. "It was impossible for this to be done without stopping to lamb their sheep in the low country among the farmers and ranchmen of the valley and later taking [the flocks] to the high ranges. The ranchmen and cattlemen objected to this and immediately proposed to organize against the sheep men for their own protection," wrote forester John Lowell. He added, "The organization covered a large portion of the Western Slope and was perhaps, the strongest organization of this kind . . . in the West."[35]

In the spring of 1892, when Cunningham and Grant planned to move their breeding bucks to the desert, "the people were ready for them." The herders' camp was held up at 10:00 p.m. On the Hogback Trail, a low gap in the backbone between Grand Mesa and Plateau Valley, vigilantes killed the bucks and left carcasses strewn along the trail. The sheepmen persisted, but with no water in the desert, needed to bring their flocks to higher ground. They attempted to move 800 head of ewes over the Hogback. Seventy-five men killed the sheep. Two or three bunches were killed later, "and when fall arrived, there was not a live sheep in Plateau Valley or the high country surrounding it."[36] That same year in southwestern Colorado, a herder fought back.

In 1892 in Pagosa Springs, conflict over sheep and cattle left an Archuleta County commissioner dead in a rare altercation in which a sheepherder returned fire with deadly accuracy. On August 24, Juan Montoya, his brother, and four or five other Hispano herders from Del Norte brought 20,000 sheep westward over Elwood Pass and the West Fork of the San Juan River,

14 miles from Pagosa Springs. They had good horses and Winchester repeating rifles.

The dispute arose over how long the sheep lingered and how fast the herders kept them moving. As the Montoya brothers approached the ranch house of Commissioner William Howe, the cattleman, distraught from the recent death of his wife and baby son, rode out with two men to harass and shoot at the sheepherders. Juan Montoya quickly levered a shell into his rifle and began to fire back, fatally wounding the Anglo county commissioner. The sheriff charged the younger herder with murder.

"No other event for years so excited our people, or caused such universal regret and sympathy. There are two sides to all cases and this one is no exception," reported the *Pagosa Springs (CO) News*.[37] Because of intense feelings in Archuleta County, the murder trial took place in Durango, and because of the code of the West, the jury's main decision focused on who fired first. Archuleta County newspapers all blamed the Montoyas, and Juan Montoya refused to give a statement. Later, in Durango, he did.

> On the day the shooting occurred I was helping to drive some of the flock of sheep near Howe's ranch. Suddenly I saw three men coming toward me. When they got very close to me one went to the right, the others to the left. They were mounted and riding very fast, so fast, indeed, that I thought he who was on the right would run me down. They were all armed with Winchesters and before I was quite aware of their intentions they commenced shooting at me. I had a 40–82 Winchester and also opened fire first shooting to the right and then to the left. Not a word was said that I heard and I said nothing myself. I was much excited and suddenly received a shot in my breast, which made me stagger, the blood came from my mouth and I felt that I was choking. I felt dizzy and blind. I was so close that my face was filled with powder and some of it got into my eyes.[38]

Though shot at and injured, Montoya fired back, wounding William Howe, who turned toward his ranch and then fell off his horse into a pool of his own blood, dying later that day. Charged with murder and placed in jail, Montoya was soon out on bail. By June 23, 1893, the Pagosa Springs newspaper reported, "Juan Montoya, in attending court this week, was accompanied by twenty or more Mexicans, each armed with a Winchester and a sixshooter. Such precaution was not necessary, as no one had the least intention of harming the miserable wretch."[39]

In this drawing, Luis Montoya broods about all the trouble caused over grazing sheep in Colorado's San Juan Mountains. He spent much of the family fortune defending his son, who was acquitted of murder in one of the few cases in the American West in which a Hispano sheep-raising family received justice. Original pencil drawing courtesy of the Rio Grande County Museum, Del Norte, Colorado.

On January 12, 1894, Montoya was a free man, exonerated by a Durango jury. Closing arguments in court ended at 11:00 p.m. on a Saturday night. The jury took only 15 minutes to acquit him. Pagosa Springs papers railed against the verdict and the $1,200 trial expense to Archuleta County. But, as the newspaper concluded, "William Howe is dead. Juan Montoya killed him. Twelve men have said that the killing was done in self-defense and that William Howe made a murderous assault."[40] The death of a county commissioner and subsequent murder trial were unique. Only rarely in Colorado history did sheepmen or sheepherders have a successful day in court.

Violence escalated in part because of government policy. First came forest reserves in 1891, and then with the Panic of 1893, a severe economic depression, prices for range cattle plummeted. From high prices in 1888, prices for range cattle dropped from nine dollars to eight dollars to seven dollars a head with no buyers.[41] "Some ranches cut their herds, improved their breeding, and sought out permanent hay lands on which they could raise winter feed. Others stunned their neighbors by turning to sheep," wrote Duane Vandenbusche and Duane Smith.[42] Then the next year the ax truly fell.

In 1894 Department of Interior administrators prohibited grazing on federal land. Stockmen were stunned. Bureaucrats could not enforce this new policy, but the very idea of grazing on public land and being in trespass outraged western ranchers. Hatred increased between cattlemen and sheepmen. Cattlemen strengthened their protective associations and not only armed their range riders but employed hired guns.

On the Book Cliffs and the Roan Plateau, north of the Colorado River and west of Rifle, Mark Hurlburt told the story of John Hurlburt, who had grazed sheep on the plateau since 1882. By 1894 grass had become scarce, and good grazing meant traveling higher to more distant ranges. Hurlburt had gone to Palisade for Peach Days, as had most of his neighbors from Parachute because the Denver and Rio Grande Railroad was offering a special 75-cent round-trip fare. "Everyone who could 'rake-up' the 'six-bits' had gone to the fair," noted Erlene Murray.[43] Hurlburt was not near his sheep. The sheep slaughter, which may have included up to 3,800 head,[44] became known as the Peach Day Massacre:

> Cattlemen hired forty men [at $100 apiece] to kill the Hurlburt sheep; they furnished them with horses and guns, masks to wear and knives. They met at DeBeque one afternoon and there were a lot of cowmen that went with them to see that the job was done properly. They wore masks of red flannel cloth, a red sash around their waist and over their shoulders, and a red hat band. They killed two bands of sheep, about four thousand, the lambs were all with them.[45]

Hurlburt went on to relate that the cowboys tied up a herder, blindfolded him, tied his hands behind his back, and put him on a horse to go with them to hear the injured and dying sheep. The hired killers "went to a grove of quakers and cut clubs, about six foot long and four inches thick and would hit the sheep over the head and just kept piling them up. They also used Bowie knives."[46] "Father sold that band of sheep and never owned another sheep so I guess they accomplished their purpose," Mark Hurlburt explained years later.[47]

On the afternoon of September 10, 1894, on Roan Creek near Parachute Creek, 50 masked men visited Carl Brown's sheep camp. They fired shots. "The riders later claimed they had only intended to frighten him, but they went on to slaughter all his sheep. First attempting to drive the entire flock over the edge of a nearby cliff but finding no success at that, they proceeded to cut every animal's throat."[48] Having killed 1,800 sheep, the gang then rode seven miles to Brown's corrals and killed 2,000 more. The book *Rifle Shots* adds more details: "Carl Brown had been shot in the buttocks and had to stand up in the stirrups all the way down the West Fork Trail. Sheriff Weir said there were two bullet holes in the tent and one had just missed Carl's head."[49]

Garfield County offered a $500 reward for the arrest and conviction of anyone who had killed sheep in that incident. Private citizens offered an equal amount, and Governor Davis H. Waite also offered a $500 reward "for the arrest and conviction of any or all of the perpetrators of the aforesaid outrage, within one year." But no one came forward.[50] Perhaps the Peach Day Massacre remained unsolved because of the Plateau Valley Sheep War, which went to court in Grand Junction.

Brown's and Hurlburt's sheep had been killed in September, but J. F. Reed lost 828 sheep on May 3, 1894. "Mutton is said to be cheaper than was ever known before on the Western slope," reported the *Grand Junction (CO) Daily Sentinel*. "'Pneumonia struck them' is the verdict of the ranchmen when asked concerning the slaughter. Others claim, laughingly, that the sheep were eaten up by mountain lions."[51]

In court in Grand Junction in January 1895, sensational headlines revealed that sheep killer William Covert had confessed to being a member of a cattlemen's association and "giving a history of the members, the officers, passwords, [hand] grips, etc. . . . whose object was to exterminate all the sheep in the Plateau country" south of De Beque about 12 miles beyond the Colorado River. Guns, knives, clubs, and stones were used to kill sheep, and the killing lasted three hours. Reed's brother had been herding the flock, and cowboys encouraged him at gunpoint to "take the back trail" for the East. When the young man said he had no money, he was told, "Walking is good." He walked.[52]

"Reed has no sympathy from the small ranchman on the slope as they feel that a crisis has arrived and the ranches must be abandoned if the vast herds of sheep are allowed to pass through the country. It is claimed that last week's work was done by owners of small ranches and not by large cattlemen as was first supposed," explained the *Grand Junction (CO) Daily Sentinel* on May 7, 1894.[53]

Fears were real. Out on the flats west of town between Thompson Springs, Utah, and the Colorado state line, 20,000 sheep were lambing in the sagebrush. They would need summer pasture. Utah sheep numbered 230,000 in 1880, and that number had exploded to 3.8 million by 1900.[54]

"Nat Harrison told us he got wind of a plan to bring in thousands of sheep from Utah. There were a few local bands of sheep, which no one objected to, but more were not to be tolerated," wrote Helen Hawxhurst Young. "Everyone was sworn to secrecy and they agreed there would be no turning back, whether outside the law or not." So vigilantes killed Frank Reed's sheep. Then they killed a band on Sheep Creek. "There were several little bands of local sheep killed. McCarty's right in the town. Hebe Young's bucks in the night."⁵⁵ Cattlemen could accommodate sheep owned by local ranchers, but not large flocks moving east from Utah. Then the vigilantism got out of hand, with "the biggest killing" on Parachute Creek and sheep dynamited on Buzzard Creek.

Sylvester McCarty "was shot and killed while working on the road, supposedly because he had 300 sheep. No one knew who did it. It has been said that every man wore a gun to the funeral," cautioned Alex Hawxhurst.⁵⁶ The truth may never be known. McCarty often supported cattle ranching. "The Cowmen blamed it on the Sheepmen, but many thought it was done by the Cowmen because dead men carry no tales," wrote Bart Johnston.⁵⁷ According to newspaper accounts, the homemade coffin had rope handles and rested on two chairs during the funeral, which was held outside because the coffin could not be brought through a cabin door.

McCarty had been shot in a hurry and buried too quickly. The Mesa County coroner demanded an inquest.

On May 24, 1894, the *Grand Junction (CO) Daily Sentinel* claimed that McCarty had been "shot from ambush." Two days later, the *Grand Junction (CO) News* said that McCarty had "accidentally shot himself." Yet on June 2, the paper published the coroner's jury inquest requiring that the body be dug up from the Collbran Cemetery. The jury concluded "death from a gunshot wound at the hands of some person or persons unknown."⁵⁸

A year later, a huge sheep scare alarmed cattlemen across northwestern Colorado as they heard rumors that Wyoming sheepmen were combining flocks into a 60,000-sheep phalanx that would move through Routt County to the railhead at Wolcott, eating everything in their path. The *Cheyenne (WY) Leader*, on June 8, 1895, reported "wild excitement" near Hayden in the Yampa River Valley, where hundreds of cattlemen and cowboys were arriving from as far east as Eagle County and the Grand River (now the

Colorado River) Valley. With loaded chuckwagons, the cowboys headed northeast of Craig to intercept the invading sheep. But it proved to be a fiasco on Fortification Creek, with no large contingents of woollies. A single line rider patrolling the area had nothing to report.[59]

However, to use John Burroughs's quaint phrase, "this major stew over mutton really came to a boil" the next year.[60] On June 10, 1896, 35 or 40 heavily armed cowboys confronted Welshman Jack Edwards on Four-Mile Creek and demanded that he take his sheep back into Wyoming. The Browns Park Cattlemen's Association had forced small flock owners Frank Goodman and Charley Sparks out of the country, but Edwards insisted on his rights to the public domain. Cowboys slipped a noose around his neck, but he refused to recant. So, blindfolded and with wrists and feet tied, he suffered as three cowboys jerked the rope. As he still refused to move his woollies, the cowboys hoisted him up a second time in a small grove of alders. "The noose tightened. Once again the Welshman was swung aloft to thrash about amid the new greenery. This time he was left dangling until he lost consciousness. When, finally, they lowered him, he was purple in the face, the froth on his lips was flecked with blood, and his tongue hung limp from the corner of his mouth," wrote Burroughs.[61]

Edwards agreed to move his sheep back north into Wyoming and to sacrifice the 25–35 pounds each of his lambs could gain in the summer on Colorado grasses. But then, stubborn Welshman that he was, he changed his mind. Like other sheepmen, he had made money on woollies, bought and leased Union Pacific Railroad land in Wyoming, and understood the profits that could be made during a season in the high country. "Inevitably possession of the railroad sections (640 acres each) gave the lessees control of the intervening sections of public domain," notes Burroughs. "By means of this single coup, the sheepmen gained an invaluable—and invulnerable—operating base, whereas the cattlemen remained wholly dependent upon the public domain."[62]

Three years after his necktie party, Jack Edwards sold out at a profit. Various sheepherder and cowboy encounters continued, including one disaster in which a terrified sheepherder, having seen heavily armed men, ordered his dogs to run his frightened sheep back toward Wyoming. In dark timber the bleating ewes broke legs, became lost, and eventually crowded into other sheep bands, creating a huge woolly mess that took days to unravel at the Savery Creek sorting pens. But the sheepmen had always been more strategic than the cattlemen, and they carefully came to control the only two routes, the Muddy Trail and the Savery Creek Trail, which cattlemen needed to get their steers north from Colorado to the Union Pacific Railroad in Wyoming. Conflict would continue after establishment of the Routt National Forest. The *Craig (CO) Courier* had argued that "the Legislature should pass a law for the regulation and division of the public range," but the contested landscape was federal rather than state property, and state legislators had no jurisdiction.⁶³

After ostensibly prohibiting public land grazing in 1894, by 1897 Secretary of Interior Ethan Hitchcock had recanted and agreed to allow cattle grazing provided that the land would not be damaged. Sheep remained excluded, but with no enforcement, chaos continued on the open range. Parachute pioneer George Kerlee "was fond of saying that every time he ran cattle he went broke; every time he ran sheep he made money."⁶⁴

Mormons in Utah impacted Colorado high-country grasses. An example is the small community of Bluff in southeastern Utah, which failed at agriculture and turned to grazing. Though members of the Church of Jesus Christ of Latter-Day Saints (LDS) pooled their cattle, they also purchased sheep, which "exacted a lower initial expense, brought quicker profits, and could yield both wool and meat, giving more security because it was rare for both markets to plummet at once. Although cattle were more mobile, now that the railroad ran through Durango that was less of a concern," wrote David S. Carpenter.⁶⁵

Bluff herders began with Mexican and Navajo sheep and improved bloodlines with French merino rams. Eventually the Mormons drove wagonloads of wool to Colorado. As wool prices increased under President William McKinley's 1890 tariff, "the sheep generated most of the profits" for the tiny LDS community.⁶⁶

Sheep from Bluff, Utah, owned by Mormon L. H. Redd, grazed high mountain meadows between Rico and Telluride by the late 1890s, but not without trouble on lower winter range in the Disappointment Valley, where ranchers held land without legal deeds to it. Threatened once by cowboys, Redd's Hispano herders became genuinely scared when two cowboys tied lariats together and rode through the sheep camp pulling everything down. Herders would light large fires at night around flocks to ward off coyotes and predators, but they had no solution to keep cowboys at bay.⁶⁷

Violence crossed the Colorado border into Wyoming. Having committed murder in Browns Park under hire by cattlemen, by 1900 Tom Horn now stalked sheepmen and even the young sons of homesteaders in southern Wyoming. On July 18, 1901, Horn killed 14-year-old Willie Nickell because his father, Kels Nickell, had introduced sheep into the area near Bosler in Laramie County, just north of the Colorado line. Grieving mother and widow Mary Nickell believed that "everything that happened was because of their sheep," after her husband received a threatening anonymous letter "to get out of the country with the sheep or suffer the consequences."[68]

Horn had the gall to check on his victim to ascertain the accuracy of his rifle shots and then placed a flat stone under the dead boy's head as a macabre pillow. "The killing is the result of a sheepmen's and cattlemen's war [for control of the] range and therefore predicated on dollars and cents," stated US marshal Joe LeFors. "Kels P. Nickell has the only sheep between the Iron Mountain Country and the U.P.R.R. east-west tracks, a distance of some 30 or 40 miles. This is all open government range."[69]

Indian scout, sometime rancher, and stock detective Tom Horn had killed from ambush before. But by murdering a young boy, the son of a homesteader, Horn forced a thorough investigation and indictment. He was hanged for the killing, but other murders continued. Perhaps as many as 500 people a year lost their lives to range squabbles in the American West.[70]

Horn killed Willie Nickell in 1901. In January 1902 the *Saguache (CO) Crescent* reported, "The war which has raged at different times between the cattle and sheepmen of the state has broken out in this vicinity." The paper went on to editorialize, "The cattle and sheep men have had frequent collisions whenever they have attempted to range on the same territory and the sheep men usually get the worst of it. Sheep are, of course, entitled to the same privilege as cattle on the public range, but their presence is so detrimental to other stock that cattlemen have generally refused to tolerate them."[71]

By mid-February 1902, sheepherder Patricio Antone Gallegos of Capulin, Colorado, was shot near Cat Creek over sheep he owned being herded on the public domain. The murderers also killed his horse and pack burro. County commissioners refused to put up a large reward, and by May 10, "his widow [became] insane by reason of the tragedy."[72]

At the turn of the twentieth century, ranchers competed across Colorado, sometimes with guns, for grazing on public land. But everything was about to change. Tom Horn killed a sheepman's boy in July 1901. Two months later, because of another assassin's bullet, Theodore Roosevelt became president of the United States. Roosevelt had ranched in North Dakota, hunted elk and grizzlies across Wyoming, and as vice president had taken a train to Glenwood Springs and then a stagecoach to Meeker, where he had delighted in using a pack of hounds to kill mountain lions in the low, rolling hills west of town. His skulls from that hunt, stored at the Smithsonian Institution, are still some of the largest of the species ever taken in North America.

Roosevelt knew the West. He knew hunters, ranchers, and cowboys. He had been in the saddle with them, eaten beef, biscuits, and beans. He had drunk coffee black as a thief's heart and stout enough to float a horseshoe. He had a firm handshake and knew how to stay on horseback for hours regardless of weather, but he could also see overgrazing. He knew the damage from too many cows and too many sheep because he had seen it firsthand. He believed that federal land should come under more regulation and control.

In 1903 Roosevelt established a Public Land Commission and required it to "report upon the condition, operation, and effect of the present land laws and to recommend such changes as are needed to effect the largest practical disposition of the public lands to actual settlers who will build permanent homes upon them and to secure in permanence the fullest and most effective use of the resources of the public lands."[73]

If part of Roosevelt's vision was making land available to homesteaders, he also saw the need to withdraw public lands from settlement and to create national forests. A "wilderness warrior" during his presidency from 1901 to 1909, he set aside 8,000 acres a day, or over 230 million acres of public land. He particularly liked national forests. A report written the same year as Roosevelt's Public Land Commission justified creating one of the largest forest reserves in Colorado.

"The industries of the San Juan country are farming, sheep and cattle raising . . . although at present sheep raising brings more money into the country than any of the others, unless regulated it will soon destroy the summer range and have to be given up," wrote Coert DuBois in his 1903 *Report on the Proposed San Juan Forest Reserve, Colorado*.[74] With attention to detail, he explained, "On account of the large profits realized on sheep (some sheepmen say 100 percent annually) more people are going into this business every year." DuBois explained that sheep used the San Juans in the summer, and by July 20 they were on the mountain summits because they preferred "the tender grasses that grow above timber line."[75] Herders took the sheep down between September 15 and October 1. In the winter the sheep lived in sagebrush flats in northern New Mexico or in the San Luis Valley, where "the only water supply [is] the scanty snowfall."[76]

"These sheep are moved on regularly defined trails or routes agreed upon between the cattle and sheep owners. There is no division of mountain range; the first man up gets pick of the range and tries to protect it by placing a band of his sheep across the trail leading into it so that no other herder can get in without mixing bunches," noted DuBois. He emphasized, "If it were not for the sheep industry, such towns as Pagosa Springs, Conejos, La Jara and Antonito would practically die, for the majority of business done in them is with sheep owners, herders, and wool or stock buyers."[77]

Huge sheep numbers did extensive damage to public lands. Woollies ate spruce and fir seedlings, destroyed humus and ground cover, and damaged soils. "Cut up by the sharp hoofs of the sheep, the humus and upper soil are exposed to the drying effects of the sun, wind and air, and are washed down into the creek bottoms with the first heavy rains," DuBois described. "Until there is nothing but a layer of dust left, and each bunch of sheep coming down the trail can be located by the cloud of dust hanging over the timber above it."[78]

Herders also used fire to burn range and create new grasses and deliberately left campfires unattended. Surveying sheep damage on the eastern slope of the California Sierra, Mary Austin wrote, "Do not suppose I shall enter a proof or a denial of all the sheep have done to the watersheds, what slopes denuded, what thousand years of pines blackened out with willful fires." She added, "Also I could say something of the hills ... that once were billowy and smooth as the backs of the ocean swell, and after so many years of close-herded sheep trampling in to the annual shearing are beaten to an impervious surface that sheds the rain to run in hollows and seam them with great raw gullies."[79]

In Colorado, DuBois estimated 187,000 New Mexican sheep and 182,000 Colorado sheep for a total of 369,000 in the San Juans, chewing their way up and down mountain paths and invading mountain meadows. Something had to be done—about overgrazing, about violence between stockmen, about damage to western watersheds.

"This reckless competition could have but one end. The mountains were turned to dust heaps; the old forage plants were gnawed to the roots and so weakened that they failed to grow. Worthless weeds and annuals took their place. The willows along the streams and meadows were eaten down to walking sticks," wrote Will Barnes. "The meadows stripped of their green covering, dried out. The forage cover gone, the freshets tore through the meadows leaving great gashes in the sod and soil, which cut down deeper and deeper, draining the land."[80]

In the election of 1900, Colorado had supported President William McKinley and Vice President Theodore Roosevelt. Now, with McKinley dead and "that damned cowboy in the White House," the West was about to change.[81] TR would take moribund forest reserves in the US Department of Interior and reshuffle them to the US Department of Agriculture. The new US Forest Service he would create in 1905, with Gifford Pinchot as its chief forester, would insist on grazing fees to run stock on public land. A new breed of westerner, the US forest ranger, with his distinctive hat, badge, green serge pants, and US Department of Agriculture rule book, would come to change the Mountain West.

Ranchers felt betrayed by Roosevelt because for the first time their stock numbers would be counted. The West would never be the same again.

Decades later, high alpine mountain meadows in national forests would begin to heal, but conflict continued for 30 years over lower-elevation sagebrush lands valued as winter range for both cattle and sheep. As the twentieth century began, Colorado's cattle and sheep wars were far from over.

THIRD SHEEPSCAPE

Elkhorn Stock Driveway—Routt and Medicine Bow National Forests

Storm clouds were building to the west and north, but there was no telling when the wind and rain would hit. It was mid-September and the aspen leaves had begun to turn their vibrant yellow, with a few traces of red. Bill and Beth Sagstetter and I had met in Steamboat Springs and driven north in their two-door Jeep Rubicon, passing a band of sheep and seeing herders on horseback near their sheep wagons. Ranch roads that were more dirt than gravel twisted and turned, and sliding off a narrow road with the Jeep and dropping into the willows below seemed a real possibility.

At the Hahn's Peak store, we'd met Joe Mattern and his son Matt in their Ford F-250 pickup with a dirt bike strapped into the bed. The Sagstetters had met the Matterns years before while photographing aspen arborglyphs. Now, over 30 years later, our goal was to find the same trees again, if they were still standing, and to locate the work of a singular, distinctive Hispano artist, Ben Vigil, whose masterful tree carvings included careful portraits.

We would scout on foot while either Joe or Matt took to the trees on the dirt bike to cover ground faster. We would search from the Matterns' Medicine Bow Ranch just over the border into Wyoming where the Routt National Forest became the Medicine Bow National Forest along the famous Elkhorn Stock Driveway, which had been the scene of skirmishes between cattlemen and sheepmen at the turn of the twentieth century.

Hard to get to even in fall, the ranch was accessible in winter only by snowmobile. The ranch had been owned by a sheepman named Art Rasmussen, whose strategy had been to buy private property in Wyoming as summer headquarters close to Colorado's rich high-altitude grasses. For decades, Routt County cattlemen fought to keep Wyoming sheepmen out of the national forests, but the first chief of the US Forest Service had agreed that sheep had a right to government grass.

This remote Wyoming-Colorado border was a long way from federal bureaucrats in Washington, and here local ranchers settled their own issues. Historically, they all wore six-shooters, and on horseback most carried lever-action repeating Winchester or Savage rifles. Sheep wintered in Wyoming's Red Desert and then in spring came south toward Whiskey

On the Mattern Ranch, Bill and Beth Sagstetter photographed a variety of arborglyphs north of Steamboat Springs, Colorado. The sheepherder artist who impressed them the most was Ben Vigil, who carved this handsome couple. Photo circa 1980, courtesy of Beth Sagstetter.

Park and Hahn's Peak. The conflicts were decades old, but the stories still lingered and I wanted to hear them. Joe would be especially helpful because between the ages of 11 and 16 he had enjoyed the solitude of his grandfather's ranch. For days at a time he'd be off walking or riding a dirt bike on remote trails. He learned a little Spanish, *poquito*, and visited every sheepherder he saw. He would tell them about lost lambs or sheep he had seen. They took him in, taught him, joked with him, fed him lunch, and helped him grow up. He shared their loneliness and they shared their lives.

With the weather changing, we turned near Three Forks Ranch and kept driving north, knowing rain was coming and aware of Wyoming's legendary "suck mud" that could stop even a Jeep in its tracks. In heavy rain, equally feared was a hill on FS Road 851 that turned slick as grease, earning it the name Grease Hill. Even in four-wheel low with the brakes on, vehicles tended to slide. We hoped to have enough daylight to find the carved aspens and return to graveled roads before the storm hit. We raced the rain. It would be a close call.

We drove past a ghost town—Victoria Station, Wyoming. Nothing remained but a few sill logs hidden in long grass. At one time all this borderland had been homesteaded, but because of deep snows and distance, homesteads in little parks or grassy openings had been consolidated into larger ranches or had reverted back to public land. Most homesteaders failed. Their small ranches went into foreclosure. This area had once been a vast grazing commons and had become one again. The history would literally be written on the trees by herders who guarded their sheep and who drank clear, cold water from springs and pine-shaded streams that trickled down to become the west branch of the Little Snake River.

Joe's family had bought their ranch decades ago when no one much cared about remote high-country ranches. He grew up with herders both Basque and Hispano, and he remembered how Basque herders would set nets in the shallow streams to catch fingerling brook trout to vary their diet of mutton and canned goods. Now those streams have another purpose, and a wooden plaque in the Mattern ranch house states, "For dedicated service to the conservation and restoration of Wyoming's Native Cutthroat Trout."

As we drove toward the ranch, Bill Sagstetter sighed. Many of the aspens were dead. Was it drought? Climate change? Or just a part of the aspens' birth and death cycle not yet understood, like sudden aspen decline (SAD), which had impacted thousands of acres in the Gunnison country and south? "I should have known that it wouldn't last forever. Those colors were golden," he said, recalling a previous photography trip. "Now the forest seems drier and the colors more muted. It's like losing an old friend."

At the ranch we spread out looking for the familiar Vigil carvings. Feeling a few drops of rain, we put on jackets. Try as we might, we could find no carvings by the master. Yes, there were the occasional doodles on trees, a few names and dates, but no masterworks. Driving in we had seen many etchings by the latest generation of herders, who are Peruvians, but we couldn't find the older carvings from the 1950s and 1960s.

As the weather cleared for an hour or so, we left the ranch and drove the Elkhorn Stock Driveway. We saw carvings everywhere on both sides of the route but also hundreds of downed trees. The oldest date was 1919 and the most recent was only a few years old, with a carved outline of Peru. Decades of herders had left their signs, their symbols, but no special portraits on aspen bark.

As the sun broke through dark clouds we came to a large grove with a dramatic view of Hahn's Peak miles away to the southeast. With plenty of grass nearby, it seemed a logical place to bed down sheep. Carvings everywhere verified that, but nothing from Ben Vigil could be seen. An old metal Center Stock Driveway sign remained nailed to a fallen aspen. We took a few more photos and then reluctantly turned back the way we had come, toward Colorado and the store at the base of Hahn's Peak. The sky went gray, then

Deep in national forests across the American West, official US Forest Service signs told sheepherders, who may not have been able to read English, where to trail their sheep. Hikers and backpackers may still find these remote metal signs nailed to trees. Author's collection, Center of Southwest Studies, Fort Lewis College.

blue black. Rain splattered on the Jeep's soft top just as we descended the steepest section of road. The full fury of the storm hit as we enjoyed hot coffee, tea, and hamburgers at the store. The next day over breakfast in Steamboat Springs, Joe Mattern told his story about growing up with herders and listening to the soft tinkling of sheep's bells as flocks bedded down near the ranch.

"They loved the life they had up there," he related. "I gave them [the Basque herders] small gifts to befriend them and they would reciprocate with food or little wood carvings like sheep or other animal figures. I'd give them a sharp pocket knife as a gift and they would come to the ranch with beautiful fresh tortillas covered in a white cloth and they'd be wearing a fresh white shirt."

Mattern recalls the herders as "very kind and generous people. They didn't have much but whatever they had they were more than willing to share with you. It was a lot of fun to have herders near the ranch. They taught me about integrity and how to be good around people."

One specific memory is of catching and eating small fish. "I had lunch with one of them," Joe says, smiling. "I liked to come by during lunchtime. This herder had a net that he would use to catch brook trout when they're small and sardine-sized. He'd get them out of a pool of water and while they were still alive and wriggling he'd throw them into a bowl of flour and spices. Then he'd toss the wriggling fish covered in flour into boiling oil or lard. Soon they were ready and we'd eat the whole fish. Crunch, crunch, crunch. They were delicious." Mattern remembers, "I ate as much as the herder ate. We'd catch a big bowl of fish together. We ate dozens of fish."[1]

"They were multigenerational sheepherders from the same families. They talked about their uncles and dads before them. The camp tender would come every two weeks so the herders learned to live off the land. If they had a lamb die they would butcher it themselves but they had to be careful. If they lost a lamb it was their fault. It came out of their wages. They had no refrigeration so they hung a haunch or the entire animal in shade, salted it, and put cheesecloth on it. It would become covered in flies but when they needed meat they would just cut a chunk off."

As a young boy, Joe was impressed by the herders' dogs and the herders' understanding of animals. "They had the best dogs I'd ever seen work—Great Pyrenees. These guys were dog experts, and on our ranch if we had a sick horse I would go get a herder and they generally knew what to do or what we needed to get. They knew how to take care of animals because they had to. Animals are their life. The sheepherders learned to train their dogs to have a soft mouth. To nip the sheep but not to hurt them."

Mattern learned from the older men. He learned about where sheep liked to graze, how much chili or garlic to put in stews, how to doctor an infected horse, and, most importantly for a teenager, how to be quiet, how to listen, how to slow down and take in the sights and sounds of an aspen forest. "They had a peace about themselves. We could sit for an hour and not have to say anything," he fondly remembers.[2]

There are fewer herders now. Fewer bands of sheep graze the Elkhorn Stock Driveway. As often as he can, Joe returns to the ranch with other family members, especially his son Matt. But the sheepherders' presence, once so important in Joe's adolescent life, is almost gone.

Fences fall. Farm and ranch equipment rust. Grasses grow thick. The aspen trees delicately and skillfully etched by Art Rasmussen's herder Ben Vigil, we never found. Age and spring winds and persistent drought took them down.

Joe has a segment of a Vigil carving, signed and dated, cut from an aspen and brushed with linseed oil to help preserve it. But we could not locate the arborglyphs we sought on living trees. They've gone back to grass, and now there are fewer sheep to trim the meadows.

"From the beginning we felt the tree carvings were not graffiti or vandalism. The arborglyphs were carefully executed, and well-thought-out. The carvings exhibited a certain pride of craftsmanship and skill. Sometimes the carver had incorporated parts of the tree, like a branch or knot, into the picture. They exhibited knowledge of how the black scars form on the crisp white tree trunks, and with a light, deft hand were able to execute fine details like eye lashes and fingernails on their human portraits. And most importantly, they often signed and dated the carvings as though they were intended as art," write Bill and Beth Sagstetter. "But what did they mean? What were the carvings meant to display? We found that there were many different subject matters, but most could fit into several categories. Some were meant to be helpful, like the arborglyph that simply read 'Elkhorn' with an arrow under it pointing the way to the Elkhorn Stock Driveway that straddles the border between Wyoming and Colorado."

The Sagstetters studied arborglyphs north of Steamboat Springs along the Elkhorn Stock Driveway and in the San Juan Mountains. They came to realize that "there were arborglyphs that seemed to chronicle an event or something that the sheepherder had witnessed. One pictured two bears fighting. Another depicted two cranes, one standing at rest and the other flying. A couple of years later in the same vicinity, we were following the creek and scared a large bird that swooped up at our intrusion. We noticed it was a crane. In our bird identification books we found that cranes often migrate through this area and sometimes nest. Did this sheepherder 'scare up' a crane as we had and then record the incident? Was he recording objects and events of the landscape around him?"

The Sagstetters saw "carvings of butterflies and flowers, common sights in this area at this time of year. Horses were a favorite subject matter, and most sheepherders had a horse at their camp. But we never saw a carving of a sheep dog, and they all had more than one sheep dog at camp. And we don't recall ever seeing a carving of a sheep, even though sheep were everywhere. A herd of 1,500 at a time was common."

Of course herders carved women, and the best carver along the Elkhorn Stock Driveway was Ben Vigil. The Sagstetters note, "Ben Vigil's movie poster-like portrait of a woman and a cowboy-hatted man facing each other displayed the talents of a master carver. The woman's hair is depicted as 'marcelled' in a wavy style popular in the 1920s and 30s. She is wearing dangling earrings. Even her eyelashes were distinct in 1980 when we photographed it, though this portrait was dated 1954."

They photographed one carver's little houses, and I've found those glyphs, too. Under each one was carved "Taos Repito," but what did that mean? The Sagstetters wonder, "Was this a lonely man yearning for his home in Taos, in northern New Mexico? We were left with the impression that some of the arborglyphs reflected the thoughts and wishes—the inner landscape—of the carver. There were also complaints. One read '$30 a month and no becon [sic].'"

In their research they even found poems. "One read: '30 miles to water, 30 miles to wood, I wouldn't leave this outfit, even if I could.' This tree had already fallen nearly four decades ago. As it fell it scraped off part of the poem. Rancher Mary Mattern helped us to reconstruct the missing parts of the poem from her memory of it. So from the very beginning we were keenly aware of the fragility of the aspen carvings, and of their tenuous life span. We set about photographing as many as we could before they were gone." I agree with the Sagstetters, who note, "The sheepherders could even be philosophical. Deep in a particularly gorgeous grove of golden aspen trees, one arborglyph read: 'This is God's home.'"

But the carving that they will always remember had a different message. The Sagstetters state, "But one arborglyph haunts us more as time goes on. It was in the deepest part of the Elkhorn Stock Driveway, at the point of no return, where it was just as far forward as backward to civilization. Could it be a last will and testament? Or a suicide note? Parts were overgrown, but the legible parts read:

>The _____ says this
>
>Will is final speak.
>
>F_____. Things are for _____
>
>W_____. No hope and _____
>
>Soul is lost.
>
>Al   6–27–41[3]

Chapter 3

The US Forest Service in Colorado, a Sheep Army, and the Fight over Government Grass, 1905–1920

> We thought we had the best ranger in the Forest Service. We were strengthened in this belief by the rumor that Bill had killed a sheepherder. We were a little disappointed that he had been acquitted of the charges, but nobody held it against him, for we all knew that being acquitted of killing a sheepherder . . . isn't the same as being innocent.
>
> —NORMAN MACLEAN
> *A River Runs through It*

Slowly, tentatively, the newly minted US Forest Service began to exert its authority over federal forest reserves, which would be renamed national forests. In many places across the West, cattlemen had urged forest formation to try to control sheepmen, but those cattlemen had also assumed unlimited use of the range. Chief Forester Gifford Pinchot and his cadre of forest rangers, hired because they could pass an exam, ride a horse, pack a mule, use a shovel, and shoot a pistol, now began to discuss range allotments and specific times of year when stock would be allowed on the forests. Rangers received $75 a month and had to feed their horses out of their own pockets. To cover a large forest, some rangers owned four horses, or even five.[1]

Rangers needed to be "thoroughly sound and able-bodied, capable of enduring hardships and of performing severe labor under trying conditions." Pinchot's men had to know "something of land surveying, estimating and scaling timber, logging, land laws, mining, and the live-stock business," and across the Southwest, enough Spanish to communicate with Hispano herders and sheepmen.[2]

Generally, the rangers respected a rancher's historical grazing areas. The slow process of defining and delineating high-country range rights had begun, and though ranchers grumbled about federal oversight, their small complaints were nothing compared to the outrage when President Roosevelt and Chief Forester Pinchot decided to require grazing fees. Western Colorado became the center of a national storm over grazing rights and a legal dispute that went all the way to the US Supreme Court.

In the same decade, sheep killing continued. A "sheep army" of thousands of woollies with 100 armed guards would cross the Colorado River at Grand Junction and make national headlines in a show of force and solidarity for a murdered Swedish sheepherder killed in his own sheep camp at Kannah Creek.

Sheepmen and cattlemen continued to spar over rangelands, specifically lower-elevation winter grazing grounds on unclaimed public land not administered by the US Forest Service. And a new federal agency came into being to placate stockmen and their powerful western representatives and senators.

As the nation changed and modernized with the twentieth century, western stockmen became more entrenched, though new opportunities for immigrants, specifically Greeks and Basques, would forever change Colorado ranching. They would use an obscure revision of the original 1862 Homestead Act, the 1916 Stock-Raising Homestead Act, to acquire vast stretches of rangeland in 640-acre parcels and establish successful grazing empires, which are still managed today by their families, four and five generations later.

In another turn of events presaging the future, the US Forest Service hired its first landscape architect, Arthur Carhart, to begin to design campgrounds and survey remote landscapes for tourist cabins on 99-year leases. Carhart, surveying Trappers Lake in Rio Blanco County in 1919, had another idea, however. His epiphany would ultimately change uses of remote high-altitude landscapes across the American West in exactly the places shepherds sought good grass. Recreation would become a major forest use.

Known as the Progressive Era, the years between 1900 and 1918 featured breakthroughs in American public health and sanitation, city government, land conservation, establishment of national parks, and a deep-seated belief in standardization and efficiency. Pinchot argued that "where conflicting interests must be reconciled, the question shall always be decided from the standpoint of the greatest good of the greatest number in the long run."[3]

Everything focused on utility, and President Theodore Roosevelt believed that conservation of our natural resources was the greatest work of the nation, in contrast to the wasteful mining and logging techniques of the nineteenth century and the giveaway of millions of acres of land to transcontinental railroads. Roosevelt and other politicians, from school board members to US senators, all felt the need for efficiency and modernization. For farmers, that meant the first tractors, mechanical harvesters, and paved rural roads. For stockmen it meant greater meat production, and one way to achieve that was to systematically kill predators.

A new federal agency, the Bureau of Biological Survey, offered to do that, and though sheepmen and cattlemen fought each other over range rights, they were united in setting steel traps and spreading poison across public lands. Thousands of wolves, coyotes, eagles, lynx, mountain lions, bears, bobcats, and birds would die to make the West safe for sheep and young calves.

How ironic that as a conservation movement built momentum to protect public lands as national forests, early forest and wild game managers felt justified in killing predators. No one yet understood wildlife ecology. Even Theodore Roosevelt, one of the world's experts on large mammals and big game, did not grasp the predator-prey relationship.

Colorado landscapes, already overgrazed and damaged by too many sheep and cattle, would now be altered by a new force, the Bureau of Biological Survey's "boys," who were experienced hunters and trappers. Despite Colorado game laws, farmers, settlers, and ranchers routinely poached deer and occasionally elk under the idea of a "settler's season," and to put meat on their homestead tables so they could retain their beeves and mutton for commercial sale. Wildlife numbers decreased so drastically that elk had almost become extinct in Colorado by 1910. Predators turned to livestock.

The Bureau of Biological Survey poisoned animal carcasses to lure predators that had been killing sheep and cattle, thus upsetting natural balances and changing ecosystems, an environmental concept not yet understood. The vicious cycle of overgrazing and predator control took its toll across the state. Landscapes began to change because of the invasive plant seeds carried in sheep's wool, the loss of native grasses, and the demise of top-tier predators. Forest rangers did not realize the impacts of this chain of events. They were too busy trying to establish grazing allotments, putting out forest fires, and stepping into the middle of cattle and sheep conflicts.

The nation's first forest ranger, William Kreutzer, served in Colorado for more than 40 years. His travels and travails are outlined in Len Shoemaker's biography *Saga of a Forest Ranger*.[4] All the allotment issues, and cattle or sheep grazing on national forests without permits, Kreutzer encountered. Through his winning personality, perseverance, and steadfast resolve, he solved problems. "It was men of that type," wrote Will C. Barnes, chief of grazing for the US Forest Service, "who won the West for forestry."[5]

In the spring of 1903, Del States and Francois La Fon sought to bring several bands of sheep up on Grand Mesa near Grand Junction and fight cattlemen for the range. The US Forest Service did not yet allow sheep on the reserves, and Kreutzer had to turn back eight bands, all the while facing either herders or sheepmen with repeating Winchester carbines. He had to explain grazing trespass and civil and criminal penalties. He succeeded in averting a range war, but in riding hard out of the mountains to contact the proper authorities, he was engulfed by a snowstorm. Kreutzer's feet froze in his boots.

In a Delta, Colorado, livery stable, owner Ben Lowe helped thaw Kreutzer's frozen feet using cold water and snow. A decade later, Lowe would participate in a shootout and die in remote Escalante Canyon.

Kreutzer's story illuminates the early years of the Forest Service, the need to rely on Gifford Pinchot's *Use Book*, and the "gospel of efficiency," which required all grass to be utilized, even high alpine meadows, thus compounding cattle and sheep conflicts.

Roosevelt disliked sheep. He "spoke for many cattlemen when he called sheep 'bleating idiots' that ate the grass so close that cattle could not live on the same land."[6] At one meeting of stockmen and foresters in the nation's capital, "T.R., after giving everybody a chance to speak his piece, gave his own ideas about western range conditions, during which he pounded the arm of his chair with his clenched fist and asserted, 'Gentlemen, sheep are dee-structive.'"[7] Yet his chief of the US Forest Service, Gifford Pinchot, knew that for the fledgling Forest Service to survive the scrutiny of western politicians, grazing must be allowed. Sheep could not be excluded, because they were essential to local economies.[8]

Originally sheep had been banned from forest reserves, but when Alfred Potter of the Arizona Wool Growers Association, a cattleman turned sheepman, met with Pinchot, he convinced Pinchot to argue for sheep grazing. Later Potter joined the Forest Service to address soil erosion and overgrazing. Cattlemen grumbled over sheep on the range, but the stockmen angrily denounced the imposition of grazing fees scheduled for January 1, 1906.

The *Yampa (CO) Leader* argued that "the recommendation by Forester Pinchot that a fee be exacted . . . is an injustice the cattlemen will not submit to without a fight. . . . The stockmen are willing that reserves be created . . . but contend that the hardship of paying a fee is contrary to the spirit and custom of the country."[9] Conservation principles, especially those espoused by easterners who did not understand western ranching, bothered cattlemen and sheepmen, whose associations passed numerous resolutions. One group cavalierly stated, "Resolved, that none of us know, or care to know, anything about grasses . . . outside of the fact for the present there are lots of them . . . and we are getting the most of them while they last."[10]

In December 1905 Gifford Pinchot, dubbed "Czar Pinchot" and "King of the Forest Reserve" by local newspapers, came to Glenwood Springs to meet irate ranchers at the Glenwood Hotel to discuss his "obnoxious tax." Cattlemen, miners, and even farmers protested. "Throughout the morning Pinchot sat, urbane and unruffled, and listened intently to the cattlemen. Then, in the afternoon, they listened to him. For an hour and a half he spoke. Confident, effusing good fellowship, his rhetoric simple and persuasive, he seemed to beguile his audience," notes Michael McCarthy in *Hour of Trial*. "His message to the dissidents was simple: the grazing tax would be enacted and any cattlemen who used the range would pay it."[11]

Cattlemen would pay 20 to 35 cents a head for a grazing season, and sheepmen 5 to 8 cents a head for the regular season, with high stocking rates allowed. For ranchers this was government interference at its worst by "tyrants" who did nothing but interfere with the efforts of honest men to "build up the country."[12] After dozens of meetings across the state and much heated discussion and opposition toward forest reserve policies by stockmen's associations, one Coloradan took a stand.[13]

Snowmass homesteader Fred M. Light spent two decades developing his property on the Roaring Fork River watershed specifically to access grazing. He built a cabin and carried his cookstove on his back the last mile in to the log structure. He hand dug irrigation ditches, created hay fields, and became president of the Grand Valley Stock Growers Association. When the US Forest Service announced that cattlemen needed to apply for permits on the Holy Cross Forest and pay fees, Light refused as a matter of principle.

Instead he allowed 500 cattle to drift onto, or trespass in, the forest. A ranger charged Light with trespassing. Light filed suit. His would be a critical legal challenge to the right of the federal government to set rules, regulations, and fees on federally reserved land. Coloradans supported him, and the state legislature passed a special appropriations bill to cover his legal expenses "and sent the state's attorney general to represent him before the Supreme Court."[14]

Ultimately, the federal government prevailed with the decision rendered by Justice Joseph Rucker Lamar on May 1, 1911. Two days later the Supreme Court also upheld the Forest Service against sheepman Peter Grimaud, who had grazed his flocks on California's Sierra National Forest, also in trespass. "Together, the *Grimaud* and *Light* cases upheld the constitutional right of Congress to set aside and reserve portions of the public domain as national forests, to prescribe penalties for violating regulations, to give the Secretary of Agriculture the right to make rules and regulations for the national forest, and to impose fees for grazing permits," writes James G. Lewis in *The Forest Service and the Greatest Good*.[15] That was the big picture. The small picture was about accommodation and lending a hand.

Back in Colorado, the forest supervisor, a grazing chief from Denver, and a forest ranger went to see Fred Light to explain the court's ruling. He was haying at the time.

He held no animosity toward the Forest Service but said he could not yet pay the fees. While the ranger ran the mowing machine and Light talked with the other two men, they agreed he could wait until November to pay for the permits, after he had shipped his cattle.[16] What was important about this conclusion to Light's lawsuit was the ranger on the mowing machine.

It was that ability to help out and understand the hardscrabble livelihoods of the first generation of pioneer settlers and homesteaders that gave the new Forest Service the credibility it badly needed. Forest rangers made all the difference, and Pinchot required a courteous, loyal, professional force—"the best and the brightest" he could find.

A master at public relations, Pinchot offered formal advice and job requirements in his *Use Book*, the pages of which mushroomed each year, but he also understood the need for tact and diplomacy. "A public official is there to serve the public and not to run them," he cautioned. "Find out in advance what the public will stand for; if it is right and they won't stand for it, postpone action and educate them," he admonished. He advised, "Get rid of the attitude of personal arrogance or pride of attainment or superior knowledge." Pinchot also instructed his foresters, "Don't make enemies unnecessarily and for trivial reasons; if you are any good you will make plenty of them on matters of straight honesty and public policy and will need all the support you can get."[17]

The forest rangers on horseback, armed with a pistol for their own safety and usually carrying a rifle in a leather scabbard to shoot predators, accepted grazing permits and established grazing allotments. In 1906 they instituted grazing fees. The next year, TR added even more national forest reserves to the system, specifically in Colorado, which outraged western politicians and increased the turmoil that claimed sheepherders' lives.

Roosevelt defended grazing fees and national forests because he favored small ranchers and homesteaders fighting against large cattle herds and itinerant sheep flocks. "My first care is for the homesteader and the small stockman. The opposition we have to our proposal," TR wrote to Wyoming senator Francis Warren, as reported in the *Routt County Courier* (Craig, CO), "now comes primarily from the big men who graze wandering flocks of sheep and who do not promote the real settlement of the country. These men are the men whose interests are diametrically hostile to those of the homemakers . . . who when they have thus ruined the land of the homesteader and small stockman, move elsewhere to repeat the process of devastation."[18]

Theodore Roosevelt became president because of an assassination. Once elected in his own right, he charged ahead with declaring 14 new national forests in Colorado between 1905 and 1907, including the Pike, Gunnison, Routt, Medicine Bow, San Juan, Wet Mountains, Cochetopa, Park Range, Montezuma, Uncompahgre, and Holy Cross. Though some of the forest names changed because of consolidations, the end result was 16 million acres of national forests covering one-fourth of Colorado. Roosevelt gleefully signed proclamations within hours of losing the executive power to do so on March 4, 1907. The Fulton Amendment, tied to an appropriations bill, effectively gutted the Forest Reserve Act of 1891. After 1907 forest reserves were renamed national forests, and no new forests could be established in six western states except by an act of Congress.

Legend has it that TR, knowing that he would lose the authority to set aside forests out of the public domain, ordered Chief Forester Gifford Pinchot to come to the White House armed with maps and ideas. They cleared out a room on the second floor, got down on their hands and knees to look at potential forest boundaries, and on March 4 joyfully set aside 21 new forests in six states, including Colorado, before passage of the Agriculture Appropriations Act.

These public lands are now known as the Midnight Forest Reserves because Teddy used his presidential powers before he lost them. Pinchot stated, as Roosevelt believed, "The conservation of natural resources is the key to the future. It is the key to the safety and prosperity of the American people, and all the nations of the world, for all time to come."[19] Lofty language, yet TR's prescience prevailed.

Rangers could administer the forest, but cattle and sheep conflicts continued, especially on unregulated public-domain lands not in the forest system. Cowboys killed herders, and other herders fought back. "Wherever sheep and cattle met there was conflict over range rights. Their owners were always at sword's points and never lost an opportunity to pit their forces one against the other; their battles for range supremacy were bloody and hard fought," noted ranger Kreutzer.[20]

Across Colorado, cattle ranchers erected "deadlines," both with stone cairns in specific locations and verbally. Cattlemen claimed the tops of ridges, plateaus, and rivers as boundaries, threatening that sheep that crossed a range "deadline" would be killed and herders injured or worse. Despite the land being free and open range, the "deadline" concept resulted in range strife into the 1920s.

Stockmen joined protective associations, swore themselves to secrecy against encroaching sheep, and became Night Riders. In one group, the members promised to bind themselves "under no less a penalty than that of being shot to death" should they ever "in the least violate" their voluntary obligations.[21] Into this palpable tension, forest rangers had no choice but to insert themselves and to find solutions so that sheep could graze meadows

This painting, titled *Open Range Encounter*, a 30-by-60-inch oil on canvas by Robert Lougheed (1910–1982), shows tension between a range rider moving his cattle herd and a sheepherder and his dogs escorting a flock of sheep across the same landscape. Image courtesy of Jackson Hole Art Auction, Jackson, Wyoming.

untouched by cattle. "Cattlemen and cowboys were playing against a stacked deck—falling beef prices, depletion of their winter range by homesteaders, and opposition of the federal government," explains Wilson Rockwell.[22]

As Colorado's first forest ranger, Kreutzer initially had the job of riding over the rangelands on his district. Then he needed to secure grazing permits from ranchers. Finally, he was required to show stockmen ranges that were not overgrazed and were still knee deep in bunchgrass. Back in the mountains, close to the Continental Divide, were full stands of grass and forage. The higher the summer range, the more adaptable to sheep, but how to get flocks there without angering cattlemen had yet to be resolved. Inevitably, conflict erupted, not over high mountain forage, but over lower winter range.

In March 1907 Roosevelt set aside 21 new national forests and 40 million acres in the West, almost half of that in Colorado. By the end of April, another sheepherder, one of the small stockmen TR admired, would be dead. Thirty-year-old Peter Swanson, "a man of rugged physique and . . . a sheep man of long experience," died south of Kannah Creek about eight miles from Whitewater while trying with his brother and another herder to move 2,000 sheep toward Montrose and then to summer camp on the Cimarron.

Armed with a Winchester rifle and guarding his flock near Indian Creek, Swanson was approached by 15 cattlemen who demanded he "throw down that gun." When he refused, he was shot and left "lying upon the desert with a terrible hole in the lower part of his abdomen and a portion of his intestines exposed to view."[23] His brother Al and the other herder, Grover Cornett, had been tied up and were forced to watch Swanson's murder just as it was growing dark. They could not identify the assailants.

By May 7 the Wool Growers Association had posted a $5,000 reward for the arrest and conviction of the murderer or murderers and announced "that the sheepmen expect to strengthen their forces, stand firm and together and make a stubborn fight for their grazing rights in western Colorado." The murder capped other outrages in Delta and Mesa Counties, including sheep "beaten to death at winter quarters on Roubidoux Creek west of Delta" by masked men. One of the flock's owners declared, "This is a fight for the existence of the sheep industry and wool growers must stand together. The operation of the forest reserve law in this section has been to keep the sheep from grazing on the reserves and the sheep men have been forced to run their sheep on the lower ranges. This has embittered them against the forest reserve policy of the government," stated the *Grand Junction (CO) Daily Sentinel*.[24]

Nine months later, in January 1908, "The Sheep Army," with 21,000 sheep and 100 armed guards camped in 30 tents on the spot where Swanson was killed, erected a large stone cairn or monument. It included a cloth sheet from the Western Slope Wool Growers stating that the reward for his murderers had been raised to $10,000. In a show of force, the flocks passed through Grand Junction under an armed escort and took four hours to cross the Grand River (now the Colorado).

"The Montrose sheepmen determined to take no chances, and, without making any announcement of their movements, started their great flock of sheep through what they termed the dangerous district," including a camp at Whitewater and another at Orchard Mesa. "As far as known, every member of that grim army of determined men is a stranger to this country. Many of the men wore heavy dark beards and had their slouch hats pulled low over their faces. It was certainly a most formidable looking crowd," reported the *Sentinel*. Serious shepherds had come from afar to support their own. Scores of burros carried the camp outfits, the "army" making 12 miles daily as it headed for winter pastures in Utah.[25]

Sheepmen had crossed the cattlemen's "deadline." "No such daring move has ever been made in the history of the West," stated the *Sentinel*.[26] Publicity included a story in the *New York Sun* and an editorial condemning the protest in the *Denver News*, which argued, "We do hold that there is a place where sheepmen and stockmen can settle their disputes and that they should be compelled to go to that place for settlement—THE COURTS. The time is long past when private armies of this sort were permissible."[27]

Arthur Chapman covered the story for the *San Francisco Chronicle* and it ran in the *Daily Capital Journal* in Salem, Oregon, but no one ever claimed the reward.[28] No murderer was ever convicted. Seven years later a cowboy went to trial, but the murder case was dismissed because of a lack of witnesses.[29] Sporadic range warfare continued, with more Colorado deaths as the range itself evolved and available public grass diminished.

The huge herds of cattle that once dominated western grazing lands gave way as homesteaders moved in to claim their 160 acres of farmlands in valley bottoms, along rivers and creeks, and anywhere farming was possible. This was the great experiment at the core of the rural American dream—free government land. With railroads like the Denver and Rio Grande and the Colorado Midland piercing the mountains, would-be farmers flooded in.

During the Civil War, when the Democrats had seceded and the Republicans were in power, Congress passed major legislation to benefit the American West. The Pacific Railroad Grant provided free land and a subsidy for every mile of transcontinental rail line built, but Congress also passed a law to benefit the common man, and even the common woman.

Thomas Jefferson had believed America should become a nation of stalwart, landowning small farmers, or yeomen. Though he was a slave owner and rarely tilled the soil himself, he believed that America would prosper only if landholdings were concentrated not in the hands of the rich but rather in the hands of the many. Even before the American Constitution, Jefferson and others had supported the Northwest Ordinance of 1787, which provided the grid pattern for America to be laid out in square miles of 640 acres each.

Congress realized Jefferson's dream when in 1862 it passed the Homestead Act, providing 160 acres, a quarter section, of free land for anyone willing to live on it for five years, plant crops, and build a cabin 12 by 14

Across the West, homesteaders moved in to fulfill the American dream of owning land by claiming their 160 acres, or quarter section. Many farm families could not afford cattle, but they could purchase a small flock of sheep. These two girls pose with their favorite woollies. Photo courtesy of the Sheep Photo File, American Heritage Center, University of Wyoming.

feet to "prove up" their claim. In parts of the American West, 60 percent of homesteaders are estimated to have made good on their claims for 600,000 patents on 80 million acres of what had been the public domain.[30]

The lure of free land, with only a minimal filing fee, was a powerful tonic for both American emigrants, moving across the nation in covered wagons, and European immigrants, who crossed oceans. They arrived in large cities like New York and Boston and then took newly built transcontinental railroads west to the land of promise. Always westward. In the words of Henry David Thoreau, "Eastward I go only by force, westward I go free."[31] European peasants had no hope of acquiring acreage in countries controlled by kings, but in the United States, land was free for the taking.

When settlers finally got their patent, proving the land was theirs, the document heading began "THE UNITED STATES OF AMERICA, To all to whom these Presents shall come, Greeting." For each patent, the president of the United States signed "in testimony whereof."

A remarkable feature of this uniquely American law was its openness. The law did not require that homesteaders be American citizens, or even that homesteaders be men. Any adult could take up free land in the West, and dozens of single mothers and divorced women tried their hand at homesteading. The Homestead Act was wildly popular, and over the decades different versions of the law would be passed, such as the Timber Culture Act (1873) and the Desert Land Act (1877), to enable settlers and families to take even more land from the public domain.

And the acreage increased. Under the Timber Culture Act, perfect for areas of sagebrush, families received 320 acres if they planted a quarter of it in trees. More than 65,000 claimants did so and patented a whopping 10 million acres. Ranchers received twice that acreage, or 640 acres, under the Desert Land Act if they paid an initial 25 cents an acre, irrigated part of it, and within three years paid a dollar an acre. The Timber and Stone Act (1878) permitted the purchase of 160 acres of forestland for $2.50 per acre. In 1906, even Gifford Pinchot supported the Forest Homestead Act, which opened agricultural lands for public settlement within forest reserves.[32]

Of course there was fraud. Conniving ranchers who knew they could control thousands of dry acres if only they had sources of water would send out their cowboys to homestead key springs and land along streams, creeks, and rivers. Once the homestead became patented, or passed out of the public domain and into private ownership, the ranchers quickly paid off their cowboys and quietly urged them to move on.

Tales are told of homesteaders swearing on the Bible that they had built their 12-by-14 cabin, without admitting that it was 12 by 14 inches instead of feet. Brothers sought adjoining claims and thus built their cabins so as to straddle 320 acres instead of sitting in the center of 160 acres. To prove ownership, homesteaders had to fence their lands to keep their stock in and to keep their neighbors' out. Patented in 1874, the same year the Brunot Agreement restricted Ute Indian lands and opened southwestern Colorado's valleys for settlement, barbed wire soon adorned thousands of cedar fence posts. Midwestern manufacturers were producing 40,000 tons of barbed wire a year by 1880, and three times that much by 1890.[33]

In the early days, barbed wire was not standardized, and manufacturers produced different types, including Long Plate or Lazy Plate, Arrow Plate,

Diamond Plate, Crandall Champion, Ric Rac, Kelly Thorny, Nadel Two Point, and Brink Combination. Other styles included the Deckers Spread, Spread Reverse, Brotherton, Ross 4 Point, and Buckthorn. "The wire that won the West" forever altered grazing, and as the Forest Service took charge, it had miles of illegal fence to contend with.

Between homestead laws and barbed wire, farming had a future, and European immigrants and American emigrants moved to Colorado. The Homestead Act of 1862, enacted "to secure homesteads to actual settlers on the public domain," had been a rousing success. Settlers "proved up" their claims and sought to graze small cattle herds or sheep flocks on public land. They joined the fight for government grass.

A history of the San Juan National Forest makes it clear that "as the smaller owners came into the territory there was, naturally, considerable friction between them and the large owners. However, with the gradual settling of the territory, the fencing of ranch lands, thereby cutting down ranges, and with the gradual taking up of available winter range, the large owner had to give way to the small owner."[34] The US Forest Service began to build counting pens for sheep to assess numbers of animals and to collect fees before sheep traveled into the high country to summer pastures.

Three years after its establishment as a forest reserve, Ernest W. Shaw, supervisor of the San Juan National Forest, could state in 1908 that the sheep range "is in excellent condition for the coming year and for an inspection by the Office of Grazing." He argued, "No range is crowded and there is room for a substantial increase throughout the districts." Shaw explained, "Stockmen . . . have reached the conclusion that Government control of the range tends to give a stability to the business, unknown prior to the National Forest regime."[35] A staggering 109,359 sheep and goats grazed the forest in 1908, compared to only 14,098 cattle, yet Supervisor Shaw recommended increasing those numbers to 139,500 sheep and goats for 1909.[36] Perhaps the grass in this remote section of Colorado really was untouched, but overgrazing would occur.

Thoughtfully, Shaw also recommended that some areas not be grazed and that forest acreage be considered wildlife reserves. "To provide a refuge for the few remaining bands of elk and mountain sheep in this part of the State, which was once a sportsman's paradise, four tracts, containing approximately 58,331 acres of rough broken country which is in no sense adapted to grazing of domestic animals, have been closed to all grazing and it will be of vast interest to many true sportsmen should these areas be set aside as game preserves," he wrote.[37]

"After once riding through this country, no one whose memory can conjure recollections of the sight of those big horn sheep, or perhaps recall the sound of a big bull elk smashing off through the timber, would object to the preservation of this game-home," he noted. Shaw went on, "It is a verified fact that mountain sheep and elk will not remain in the locality in which domestic sheep are grazed."[38] A century later, contemporary rangeland conflicts between bighorns and domestic sheep would be one of the major issues facing sheep permittees on Colorado's national forests.

A true pioneer, Shaw had been to Alaska for the Gold Rush. He homesteaded up Weminuche Creek northwest of Pagosa Springs, and he later took an appointment to head Montana's Absaroka National Forest, then the largest in the United States.[39] If under Shaw's leadership sheep and cattle disputes diminished on forestland in southwestern Colorado, they increased elsewhere. For one young forester in New Mexico, trying to exert federal authority almost killed him.

Aldo Leopold came to the Southwest with a master's degree in forestry from Yale University. He came west to change the land, but in New Mexico, the land changed him. After time in Arizona, he grew to know District Forester Arthur "Ring" Ringland, who sought a new position for Leopold after he gained more experience. Ring made him assistant superintendent on the Carson National Forest, 9,000 square miles or 950,000 acres of oak brush, juniper, sage, piñon, and ponderosa north of Santa Fe and up against the Colorado state line. Like all of northern New Mexico, the Carson had been heavily overgrazed. Stockmen requested permits for 220,000 sheep; the new plan for the Carson allowed for 198,000 woollies.

By 1900, the Upper Rio Grande "was the most heavily grazed watershed in the entire country." It was the heart of public land sheep grazing, with 220,000 cattle and 1.7 million sheep, "and the families that for three or four generations had run the sheep outfits there were among the wealthiest in the West."[40] Leopold would marry into one of them. He married Estella Luna Otero Bergere, and thus the young forester who would become one of the nation's top conservationists, ecologists, and early environmentalists wedded into a family that had done immense ecological damage. Deepening arroyos and "massive gullies scissored across the landscape."[41]

Ringland quickly promoted Leopold to supervisor of the Carson, which Theodore Roosevelt had established in 1908 with headquarters at Antonito,

Colorado. Leopold moved the headquarters to Tres Piedras, New Mexico, on the Denver and Rio Grande Railroad, which he claimed was "slower'n a burro and just as sorry." Early on, Leopold noted in a letter to his father, "There is practically no game in this country. Of course the sheep have run out all the deer; there are few turkeys, and I saw one place with bear sign. Two elk were seen here two years ago."[42] Sheep impacted mule deer populations because both animals eat browse and leafy shrubs.

Married in 1912, Leopold brought his young bride to a new bungalow he had built at Tres Piedras. In April 1913 Estella went south on the train to Santa Fe. Pregnant, she would stay with her family while he went north to Durango, Colorado, hired a horse, and then rode southeast into the Jicarilla Ranger District in the Jicarilla Mountains, a 10-by-30-mile rectangle on the border with Colorado. It was the worst-overgrazed section on the forest, with ewes on their way to lambing grounds and sheepmen complaining and petitioning against the placement of a stock driveway they were required to use. Leopold was not feeling well before he left, and the trip almost proved fatal for him.

In 1912, as supervisor of the Carson National Forest at Tres Piedras, New Mexico, Aldo Leopold built this bungalow, which he christened Mia Casita, for his new bride. Now the Leopold bungalow is used for the Aldo and Estella Leopold Writers-in-Residency Program, and it is also available for rental. It is approximately 35 miles north of Taos. Author photo.

Though he wore a regulation Colt pistol and carried a Winchester rifle, he knew how to be a diplomat and kept his guns on his saddle. He settled disagreements, checked with forest rangers, visited lambing sites, and five days after arriving got caught out in a cold, wet spring storm that brought rain, hail, and snow. Leopold slept out two nights, thoroughly soaked. He rode east and took shelter with an Apache man who dried him off for a night, but the damage had been done.

On April 21, he quit riding and had to slash his boots to remove them because of severe inflammation in his knees and legs. When he finally arrived in Chama, New Mexico, a physician made an incorrect diagnosis and prescribed the wrong medicine. Taking the train back to Tres Piedras, Leopold arrived so swollen and ill that his assistant supervisor demanded that he seek medical help in Santa Fe the next day. Leopold was near death with Bright's disease, a kidney malfunction that also claimed the life of Theodore Roosevelt's mother.

After almost 18 months of rest and recuperation, he finally returned to work with the Forest Service in Santa Fe, but such were the hazards and trials of early foresters trying to enforce federal grazing regulations on mesas, mountains, and meadows that had had no rules. Not only did foresters confront antagonistic stockmen, cancel all illegal permits, and chase out illegal stock, but they also had to survive in wilderness conditions. Across Colorado and the West, stockmen fought against the Forest Service and each other.

South of Colorado, in New Mexico, Aldo Leopold grappled with sheep and overgrazing. North of Colorado, in Wyoming, cowboy and sheepherder violence escalated, with sheep raids in Big Horn County that culminated in the Ten Sleep or Spring Creek Raid. Of all the sheep raids in the American West, this is one of the best documented, with letters, telegrams, newspaper accounts, and resolutions from the Wyoming Wool Growers Association all carefully curated at the Wyoming State Archives.

Three men died. It became an international incident involving the French ambassador to the United States because one of the sheepherders was a Basque from France, and he was soon to return home to fulfill his military obligations. This became the sixth sheep raid in Big Horn County, and it would result in calling out the Wyoming National Guard to secure the local jail once suspects had been arrested.

This wooden gavel, a symbol of justice, was carved from wagon spokes that survived the burning of the sheep wagon during the Ten Sleep Raid. The Wyoming Stock Growers Association in Cheyenne presented the gavel to the Wyoming State Museum on June 12, 1935. The empty carved slot once included an embedded bullet. Photo credit: Gavel, G-1973.42.172, Wyoming State Museum, Department of State Parks and Cultural Resources.

Two years earlier, a letter from Wyoming governor Bryant B. Brooks explained, "Such outrages are growing altogether too frequent, and decided steps must be taken to punish offenders, and prevent future recurrences."[43] Later that month the governor wrote to the Big Horn County sheriff. "We can certainly never hope to build up a state unless life and property are made absolutely secure," Brooks complained.[44]

At dawn on April 2, 1909, 15 masked men attacked a sheep camp near Ten Sleep, killed popular local sheepman and naturalized citizen Joe Allemand, his young Basque herder Joe Lazier, and sheepman Joe Emge, who slept nearby in a tent. One of the witnesses left correspondence implicating several prominent cattlemen, though he himself committed suicide. What revolted Wyoming citizens and caused this event to effectively end the long range war in the Cowboy State was the manner of the men's deaths. They were shot and the sheep wagon was set afire, but no one could verify whether the men were dead when the wagon burst into flames.

"Our reports indicate that the marauders poured oil [kerosene] over the sheep wagon occupied by Allemand and Laseer [*sic*], and without ascertaining whether their victims were dead or alive, set fire to the wagon," wrote George S. Walkey for the Wyoming Wool Growers. "When officers arrived, the next day, they found the wagon had been almost completely destroyed and the two bodies burned beyond recognition. The remains of Joe Emge lay where the unlucky sheepman fell when he emerged from his tent."[45]

The same day that Walkey wrote to the governor, so did Judge C. H. Parmelee, who described 13 cases of sheep raids pending on the legal docket in Crook County. "The situation is grave," wrote the judge, "not only in its present condition, but in the prospect of what may come."[46]

Two days after receiving the judge's letter, the governor heard from the Big Horn County attorney, with additional vivid details of the murders. "Emge and Lazier were burned to a cinder, the only means of identification being Emge's gold teeth, cuff buttons, and his guns. Lazier was known to have been in the wagon and his watch and a little French medal of some sort was found together with some money under his ashes."[47]

Within a month, the sheriff had arrested seven men and asked for a dozen state militiamen or National Guardsmen to secure the county jail. Just as US marshal Joe LeFors had been involved in the conviction of paid killer Tom Horn, LeFors actively aided local law enforcement in this case. The brutal Ten Sleep Murders, with the resultant publicity, trial, and convictions, helped end sheep raids in Wyoming, but violence continued to the south in Colorado.

In the broken canyon country northwest of Grand Junction, in the heart of the Book Cliffs on sagebrush range in Garfield County, cowboys attacked a sheep camp at dawn near the tiny community of Atchee. S. A. Taylor lost between 1,500 and 1,800 ewes and lambs in May 1909. Cowboys had scouted two sheep camps from high cliffs, rode into one the day before, claiming to be looking for a lost horse, and then attacked the next day. At 5:00 a.m. they tied up, gagged, and blindfolded the herders, taking a rifle away from Abe Aragon, the foreman, and forcing the men to lie down in the dirt. "The raiders took an axe from my camp and perhaps some of the raiders already had axes, others evidently took clubs of any kind they could get and then they went into [the] corral and began their bloody work," explained flock owner S. A. Taylor.

"They clubbed, chopped, and occasionally shot the ewes and lambs but those that were killed by shooting were mighty few in number. The slaughter was awful. Legs were cut off of lambs and ewes, backs were broken, throats cut, scores disemboweled, heads were crushed and all manner of injuries inflicted," Taylor told the *Grand Junction (CO) Daily Sentinel*.[48] The raiders worked for eight hours while they left Taylor's employees lying in the hot sun.

Oddly, this was sheep range and had never been cattle country. Without live water cattle cannot survive, but sheep make do on light snow, spring runoff, and dew on green, moist grass. "We have moved our camp some distance from the scene of the slaughter and are building a new corral. We had to do this as the stench of the dead sheep is so terrible that you cannot get within a mile of the scene with any degree of comfort," explained Taylor. He added, "No one who has not been there can have any idea of the brutal nature of the slaughter.... We found little lambs buried under piles of other sheep, but still alive with their little bodies crushed awfully. We had to kill scores of fatally wounded ewes and lambs that had suffered terrible for 24 to 48 hours."[49]

The state humane society offered a $500 reward for apprehension of the sheep killers. Editorials railed against the violence. The *Denver Republican* pointed out that unlike the state's water law, which established "first in time, first in right" for water users, range rights to public land did not give stockmen priority. The newspaper argued, "It has become a custom to permit the free ranging of herds on lands for which there has been no individual demand. Because the cattleman has been allowing his stock to run on the land he has acquired no priority of right whatever and has no just basis for complaint when another chooses to exercise the same privilege."[50]

The *Pueblo (CO) Chieftain* stated, "The time has been when range wars were taken as a part of western life, but that time has long since passed.... The stockmen cannot afford to let such a deed go unpunished."[51] This was not contested range. "The sheep were in the sheep territory, right where the cattlemen wanted them to be: where they had a perfect right to be and where it has long been agreed should be sheep territory," noted the *Fruita (CO) Telegram*.[52] What no one wanted to admit was that sheep had a secret —they made money for their owners.

Woollies were easy to manage, cheap to purchase, and produced two cash crops a year—wool and lambs in a time when a range-raised steer took three years to get to market. Some of the earliest homesteaders in the Rangely area north of the Book Cliffs owned sheep. Bart Owens settled at Brush Creek. Cook and Harris lived between Carr and Cathedral Creeks. Loran Holmwood raised ewes at the head of Soldier Creek, as did Ed and Frank Colton at the head of Carr and Roan Creeks. Joe Nash, Warren Beebe, Nick Harmston, Albert Kirby, Harvey Mercer, and John Rasmussen were on Lake Creek. Ed Milner, Ed Hall, Roe Carroll, and the Bowmans had sheep on East Douglas and Douglas Creeks.[53] They were all small operators. S. A. Taylor from Grand Junction was not.

In May 1909 cowboys slaughtered Taylor's sheep. He rebuilt his corrals. There was so much money in woollies that by September 1914 Taylor and partners bought cattle, sheep, and 10,000 acres for $100,000.[54] In November 1914 they incorporated the Taylor Land and Livestock Company in Thompson, Utah, for $250,000 in stock and shares.[55] Three years later, in the "largest deal in [the] history of Grand County," the *Grand Valley Times* in Moab reported that the Taylor Livestock Company sold for $310,000.[56] Yes, there was money in sheep.

Why were his flocks killed on the sagebrush flats of Garfield County below Baxter Pass?

The *Grand Valley Times* speculated, "The enmity of the cattle men for Mr. Taylor is due probably to the fact that he is general foreman for the Utah Hide & Livestock Company, a big sheep concern."[57] Struggling homesteaders often had a few sheep in small farm flocks, but on a large scale, Colorado sheepmen hired Hispano herders and trusted foremen to run thousands of sheep. The animals produced wealth, but also intense conflict.

In northwestern Colorado, tensions ran high as entrenched cattlemen near Steamboat Springs became concerned about the potential for sheep on the sagebrush plateaus west of Craig. The threat loomed large because the owners of thousands of sheep in southern Wyoming desired the high, green grasses and meadows of newly created forest reserves in northern Colorado. For decades the Colorado-Wyoming boundary had been established as the division between sheep and cattle, with a few sheep allowed in the far northwestern corner close to Browns Park. But on the frontier, the entrepreneurial spirit thrived. Ranchers knew profits could be made from woollies.

Under the headline "Want to Put In Sheep," the *Routt County Courier* (Craig, CO) explained, "It is rumored about that a few of the ranchmen in the vicinity of Craig are banding together and will this spring make an attempt to introduce sheep into the country." The impetus was dollars but also the opportunity to strategically use sheep as a foil against large cattle herds. "By some it is claimed that the western end of the county could be profitably given over to the sheep men . . . this would drive out the big cattle outfits and by so doing would protect the summer range east of Craig." The newspaper's editor called for comments and asked ranchers to set forth their views because "the matter is one of vital importance to the country and should receive careful consideration."[58] Responses flooded in.

Established ranchers wrote against sheep, but because homesteaders were arriving with David Moffat's new railroad, newcomers had other ideas. They desired equitable public land grazing and the freedom to choose their stock. "Personally, I favor President Roosevelt's plan, namely; government control of the public range, the homesteader having first right to the lease or grazing permits," a reader wrote, describing "the class of ranchmen who are just beginning to 'get on their feet' having come to the country with practically nothing."[59]

The real issue was not small homesteaders and farm flocks of sheep but transient sheepmen and "tramp" sheep flocks, which, just like "tramp" cattlemen, brought in thousands of animals that devoured the landscape. These operators owned no real estate, paid little in taxes, and had no interest in developing or "settling up" the country. But the verdict continued—no sheep.

As for using sheep as a foil against cattle, one writer wryly replied, "We feel sorry for any deluded rancher that would get sheep around his ranch in order to keep cattle from intruding on him. In our judgment he had better send to Hayden [the railroad depot] and get some crickets, or to Kansas and import grasshoppers. They are far more desirable than sheep and are pests much easier controlled." The comment was signed "An Old Observer of Things."[60]

Other writers agreed, stating, "All the streams would be so polluted your horse wouldn't drink. The whole country would stink of sheep and would be ruined. And what for? A dozen rich men and [a] hundred or so crazy sheepherders. . . . Better bullets than sheep."[61] The Forest Service, however, looking across the entire American West, felt that sheep had a place, and rangers prepared to issue grazing permits for woollies. The *Routt County Courier* (Craig, CO) blasted, "After fighting the sheep bug for thirty years the cattlemen of Routt county have been forced through the efforts of our friends in the forestry service to admit the wooled flocks upon the sacred precincts of the heretofore exclusive grazing areas ... and the commotion is something distressing to the untutored mind."[62]

Numbers tell the story. By 1910 Colorado was grazing 1,611,000 sheep, and most of those woollies were closely cropping government grass.[63] Tempers flared and cattlemen bought extra ammunition.

By April 1911 ranchers had gathered to pass resolutions and share petitions, and "not a word was spoken in favor of the 'baa-baas.'" The assembled stockmen protested sheep and also the US Forest Service for granting sheep access to the high country. With eloquence, the resolution stated:

> Why should our forest reserves be thrown open to sheep? ... The sheep question is not a subject for argument as there can be said nothing in its favor and everything against it. Compared with cattle, sheep are an abomination and a curse to the country. ... The cattle work no harm to the range, while sheep spread a trail of devastation and ruin. ... Who is the United States government but the people? Who are the people but ourselves? Then why can not we exercise one of the inalienable rights and privileges accorded an American and govern our own section of the country?[64]

A careful reading of the resolution under the headline "Northwest Colorado Ranchmen Take Firm Stand against Sheep on Public Range" also hinted at economics. Local ranches raised hay, and sheepmen did not need it. Flockmasters wanted the high-country summer range, but in winter they fed ewes corn and did not buy local products. Reluctantly, the ranchers admitted, "Sheep are a necessary evil, it is true. Mutton is in demand in our crowded cities and sheep must have a place in the meat products of the country and we must have wool for our manufacturing industries." Yet area ranchers sought to ban sheep.

The large meeting, the "most representative gathering of ranching interests ever held in this part of the state," failed to address falling cattle markets. Ranchers met in April and apparently had consensus, yet some local families sought to diversify and bring in sheep. They paid a price.

In the end, sheep would come, but not without literally splitting the county. The high mountain meadows and deep pastures of the Yampa River valley near Steamboat Springs differed from the sagebrush flats at the western end toward Craig, which in 1911 became the 4,743-square-mile Moffat County. With the political division between Moffat and Routt Counties, tensions should have abated, but they did not.

The same year politicians created Moffat County, nine months after the ranchmen's resolutions, cowboys slaughtered sheep at the Woolley Ranch three miles east of Craig. "The news of the massacre spread like wildfire over the country until within a few hours the topic that has caused more excitement than any other since the country was settled was on every tongue," reported the *Moffat County Courier* (Craig, CO).[65]

Cowboys cut telephone wires to the ranch, and "the sheep were not only killed but they were badly mutilated, pocket knives, clubs and hammers having been used." The newspaper described similar incidents between 1897 and 1899 but made an important distinction. The earlier massacred sheep "were owned by transient sheepmen and caused nothing like the feeling that has been evidenced by the slaughter of sheep within the valley and owned by local ranchmen who were early settlers, have their own ranches and were for many years engaged in the cattle business until the doggie [sic] herds [large steer herds on the open range] made this no longer profitable."[66]

Slowly, sheepmen persevered. As Europe erupted in world war in 1914, mutton and particularly wool became highly valuable at prices ranchers simply could not ignore. The local Forest Service proposed a cooperative sheep association for area stockmen as a buffer against Wyoming flocks, and for the first time, the *Steamboat Pilot* (Steamboat Springs, CO) admitted, "Within the boundaries of the Routt national forest are thousands of acres of the best sheep pasture on earth. Feed, water and other conditions are well nigh perfect." The newspaper even grudgingly admitted, "The idea that sheep and cattle would not occupy the same range has been proven the worst sort of fallacy."[67]

A year later, American doughboys, soldiers serving overseas in "the war to end all wars," wore wool uniforms in the bitter cold winter woods of France and in the Argonne Forest. President Woodrow Wilson campaigned for meatless Sundays, wheatless Mondays, food and travel rationing, victory gardens at home, and greater food and fiber production by American farmers and ranchers. Suddenly, raising sheep became patriotic, part of the cause to spread democracy and to crush the kaiser. Coloradans enlisted in the army by the thousands. Women joined relief societies, packaged bandages and cookies, and spent hard-earned dollars buying war bonds. Yet hatred against sheep continued.

Just as America prepared to enter World War I, in a society moving toward temperance and no alcohol, President Wilson worried about American soldiers drinking in Paris, consorting with Parisian girls, and perhaps catching venereal disease. He also sought vengeance against the Mexican bandit Pancho Villa, who had raided into New Mexico and killed Americans with German Mauser rifles. On the Uncompahgre Plateau in western Colorado, ranchers worried about sheep eating their cattle's winter feed.

On March 17, 1916, the *Delta (CO) Independent* carried a story about an American military expedition under General John "Black Jack" Pershing pursuing Villa. The same front page described a sheep raid, but with limited details.[68] Cattlemen had met in darkness at the Musser Ranch before riding into the night. "For more than half a century the men who rode that night were so close-mouthed that not even their wives were told the identities of the riders," wrote Muriel Marshall in *Red Hole in Time*.[69]

She explained about Utah flocks: "Tens of thousands of nibbling mouths vacuumed up Colorado grass, leaving the range more depleted with each spring and fall sweep." Marshall added, "Western range where [sheep] have grazed for generations grows little except a certain sage that nothing eats. In the intermountain Colorado Plateau are hundreds of miles of this gnarly bush that, according to old-timers, was not here when they arrived, or could not be seen for the tall, thick grass."[70]

In a conflict known as the Escalante Sheep War, for Escalante Canyon along the Gunnison River where the slaughter took place, local ranchers determined to drive sheep from the range and to keep them off the Uncompahgre Plateau. Local sheep battles included 200 sheep shot at State Bridge, others run off a cliff at Dry Creek, and the murder of Pete Swanson, which sparked the Sheep Army. Swanson was not from Utah; he was from Montrose, Colorado. As was Howard Lathrop, whose employees sought to build a swinging-cable sheep bridge across the river. His herders crossed the sheep, and the ewes drifted 10 or 12 miles "into the middle of range where Escalante ranchers were wintering several hundred head of cattle."[71]

"We decided to take our own action, not really concerned with whether it was legal or not," remembered rancher Carl Gilbert. "We intended to kill enough sheep to eternally convince Lathrop that the south side of the Gunnison was for cows."[72] Six riders rode. They agreed not to harm herders.

At dawn, when they could see the herders' tents well enough not to fire into them, the sheep slaughter began, with empty cartridges and ammunition boxes, all sold in Delta, abandoned in the dirt. The cattlemen killed about 200 sheep. "I do know that I fired so many rounds through my rifle that the barrel got so hot I could hardly hold it," stated Gilbert.[73] Pistol-packing Ben Lowe, one of the riders, had expected Sheriff Cash Sampson to arrive, but he never came. Lathrop skinned out the dead sheep but kept the herd there. The Night Riders rode again with four more members, including the son of a Delta banker.

This time, as a Hispano herder rode for help, local men shot his horse, and then a pack mule tied in brush. Lathrop got the message and took his sheep back across the Gunnison River. "The recent high prices of wool and mutton caused many farmers to buy small bunches of sheep and it was rather expected that there would be a revival of this class of outlawry," reported the *Delta (CO) Independent*. "There is said to be little hope of running down the sheep raiders, though the period seems a little late for that class of work, be aggravation ever so tempting."[74]

Lathrop had brought his sheep into the country from Cisco, Utah, on the Denver and Rio Grande Railroad, which ran beside the Gunnison River. He intended to shear his flocks in Montrose in April and lamb in May on spring range. The train stopped in Leopard Basin on the wrong side of the river, or at least wrong for sheep. A sudden thaw shattered ice on the river, preventing him from trailing them across, so he had to make camp in cattle territory.

"He knew the cattlemen were on the prowl for any excuse to shoot up sheep. The herders tended to the pack string, made supper, unrolled their beds beside the camp stove, but Howard drank coffee and looked out from the tent to the hills. In the moonlight he noticed one lone rider slowly riding back and forth," wrote Lathrop's second wife, Marguerite, in her book *Don't Fence Me In*. "He saw a glimmer at the belt. A gun. They were coming after him with a gun, or rather after the sheep."[75]

Because nothing happened that night, Lathrop took the train into Montrose to get lumber to build a raft to move the sheep across, but cattlemen attacked. For the rest of his life he would remember "until the day he died—the crisp March air, groups of sheep that had been huddled together and fallen in a pile under the impact of bullets, their wool blending with the snow in crimson blotches, the panting sheep with the huge bleeding gapes in their wool, the horrible necessity of cutting their throats, the unharmed sheep scattered about trembling in groups bogged down in the deep snow."[76]

He would recover financially. Lathrop would own more sheep, cattle, and valuable acreage. In the end he would sell his outfit to a young Basque herder whose family, the Etcharts, continues sheepherding traditions near Montrose. But on that freezing cold March morning, Lathrop was devastated. He had to euthanize his ewes to stop their suffering, yet the killing was not over.

Within a year, one of the Night Riders, Ben Lowe, a superb horseman, sometime cattle thief, and livery stable owner, caught the former sheriff and stock inspector Cash Sampson in Escalante Canyon. Quick-draw artist Lowe never went unarmed and neither did the sheriff. After eating peaceably together at a noon meal, they found each other on the same dirt path at the bottom of a cliff shrouded in half-dead cedar trees and gray sage. Since the sheep killing, "it was as if the two men, one traveling more slowly toward it than the other, had paced their horses, their lives, to meet precisely here."[77] They fought a pistol duel and killed each other with five shots.

Over the decades rumors have swirled about motivation for the shootout, including a quarrel over horses, but the best guess is that it had to do with Lowe's fear that stock inspector and former sheriff Sampson was coming after him following a prolonged and careful investigation. Maybe there were other grudges. The truth of the antagonism will never be known. Two more human casualties in Colorado's sheep and cattle wars.[78]

An additional sheep slaughter would occur before the decade was out. Tensions would culminate in the "Oh-Be-Joyful Raid," and it would take all the skill and timing that forest ranger Bill Kreutzer could muster to prevent bloodshed, including his own. At Gifford Pinchot's orders, he had assumed charge of the Gunnison Forest Reserve and had established headquarters in Gunnison, a bastion of cattle raising. Unused by cattlemen, the good grasses that existed at high elevations were called "waste ranges" by foresters because those meadows had not yet been utilized, had not yet fallen under the gospel of efficiency fervently espoused by Pinchot and other Progressives.[79]

Sheepmen persisted, and in connection with the war in Europe and American readiness, Forest Service sheep permits had been issued in 1916 for the Anthracite–Ragged Mountain country. A storm of protest culminated in a mass meeting of Western Slope stockmen at the county fairgrounds in Hotchkiss. Hundreds of sheepmen and cattlemen arrived, but before rational discussions could occur in the fairground pavilion, sheepman Ed Duke took exception to a remark from local cattleman Clyde McMillan and punched him in the nose. "In about three minutes a dozen fights were in full swing," remembered Kreutzer. "It was the wildest free-for-all that I had ever seen, and it broke up the meeting."[80] Order could not be restored. Everyone left with sore fists and noses out of joint. A year later, the sheep permits were expanded.

Eating dinner in Tin Cup, Kreutzer received word of pending trouble on Slate River near Crested Butte, where cattlemen intended to kill sheep. Borrowing a new Ford car driven by the local newspaper publisher, Kreutzer recruited another forest ranger and the two rushed off; he believed "the cowmen would not kill the sheep with the Forest officers present, unless they also intended to kill them."[81] Later, he had a cocked six-shooter poked into his stomach and was not sure how the situation would end.

Supervisor Kreutzer found additional range for the sheep on the Sopris National Forest, and the sheep started back over the trail the way they had come. Threatened by 20 inebriated and gun-carrying stockmen, Kreutzer said, "'You fellows forgot that you were dealing with the United States Government today. You'll change your tune when I lay this case before the Department of Justice.' . . . The threat had the desired effect. It sobered the cowmen."[82]

Friction continued over the summer, with cattlemen blaming sheepmen for dead cattle and sheepmen blaming cowboys for dead sheep, when it was probably a poisonous plant, whorled milkweed, that was responsible for the losses. The Mt. Lamborn Sheep Growers' Association lost about 400 sheep on a North Fork ranch. Questions remained, although ranchers continued to bring sheep into the high mountains by the trainload. One of the grazing areas had been named Oh-Be-Joyful by prospector James

Brennan, who had camped in the area in 1879 and was dazzled by the wild basin. Soon that delightful name, Oh-Be-Joyful, would be linked "to the only sheep killing case on National Forest lands."[83]

By July 1, 1917, 16,000 sheep grazed at timberline and above at the head of the Slate, East, and Taylor Rivers. Markets favored mutton and wool. Cattlemen demanded that sheep leave the range even though the woollies had ascended to it on agreed-upon stock trails or driveways, which would be a key to defusing conflicts in the 1920s. The US Forest Service would spend considerable time and money building driveways so that sheep could peacefully, and quickly, pass through cattle ranges. But in 1917 the old animosity persisted.

On July 4, three men talked with herder Herbert Deutsch, threatened him with a gun, tied him up, and on horseback drove 250 of John Campbell's sheep over two cliffs in an exact duplication of sheep killing above Parachute Creek almost 25 years earlier. More sheep would have died, but many landed safely on the corpses of those that had already been rim-rocked. An investigation concluded that the slaughter had been perpetrated by outsiders.

Disappointed by the sheep killing, Supervisor Kreutzer laid out his ultimatum to the cattlemen: "I'm issuing an order to my rangers to be on the alert for evidence against any or all of you, and, should I find proof of guilt in this case, or any other hereafter, I'll take it to the Federal courts." In sum, Kreutzer felt, "I was determined that there should be no recurrence of the sheep and cattle war, if eternal vigilance on our part could avert it."[84] Eventually, things quieted down even in the Gunnison country. Cattleman Bert Dollard, who had poked a pistol into Kreutzer's abdomen, apologized.

Another early US Forest Service ranger got in the middle of cattle and sheep strife, but with no sheep fatalities. Beginning in 1917, at the same time that Kreutzer supervised the Gunnison National Forest, trouble arose with the Jolly brothers, who purchased a ranch on Garfield Creek west of Glenwood Springs to bring in sheep. Cattlemen protested and demanded the sheep be removed, but lambing had begun so they agreed to wait. The flock grazed forestlands, wintered in Utah, and returned to the home ranch, which angered the cattle ranchers, who felt a promise had been broken. Interventions by a local rancher and Garfield County commissioner Pierce Coulter defused the issue until the Jollys bought another ranch in 1919 near Dotsero, 60 miles away. They planned on grazing the White River National Forest.

Ranger Jim Cayton knew that Jolly had an equal right to public lands. The cattlemen requested that Cayton join them at a meeting with Jolly to avoid "undue friction." Cayton proposed a compromise, which worked. He later wrote to his supervisor in May 1919 arguing that had he not been at the meeting, the cattlemen's committee "would have been unable to reach an understanding, and that serious trouble would have resulted." The US Forest Service ranger brokered a peaceful settlement. Cayton concluded, "Mr. Jolly states that the experience has been a valuable but expensive lesson to him, and that he will not again attempt to intrude upon the range of the cattlemen."[85]

By 1920, on US Forest Service lands in Colorado, sheep killing had ceased. On other public lands, herders continued to be threatened, in part because of the success of sheep and a new law passed by Congress just as the nation entered World War I. All but forgotten, the Stock-Raising Homestead Act of 1916 forever altered the American West because now stockmen could apply for up to 640 acres and not pretend to be farmers. They had to build a cabin and try to fence their property, but millions of acres now became available on the public domain.[86] Immigrants seized the opportunity.

Greeks in northwestern Colorado and Basques in the San Juan Mountains realized they could apply for free land and move from being itinerant herders to becoming landowning stockmen with flocks of their own. The pattern had been to come to America, herd sheep, save money, and go back to the Old Country to buy a "property" in their home village. World War I devastated Europe and dashed those dreams. Instead, herders could stay here, prosper, and become American citizens. The frontier may have closed in 1890, but much of Colorado remained thinly settled. Here was an opportunity to start a family dynasty. In the shearing sheds, in the canvas tepees of sheep camps, word got around. And for at least one woman, a widow unused to hard ranch work, sheep became her salvation.

Margaret Duncan Brown and her bank manager husband left Cripple Creek in 1915 for a quieter rural life in Routt County. They placed a small down payment on a 160-acre homestead and began to brave the harsh winters with a few head of cattle. Three years later, her husband died, leaving Margaret with a mortgage and no way to earn a living. She turned to sheep.

For 47 years she lived alone on a sheep ranch learning about ewes, rams, lambs, and all the hazards sheep can get into. She kept journals and wrote flowery personal prose steeped in her own sentimental philosophy, but she also persevered in a man's world.

After World War I, when the cattle market fell, many sheepmen expanded, as did Brown. "Often I think of my step by step entry into the sheep business. In driving through the adjacent country above the ranch, I had noticed big bunches of sheep," she wrote in *Shepherdess of Elk River Valley*. "Nothing it seems to me could be more beautiful—the rolling sweeps of sage brush, the sheep broken up, little bunches of ewes and lambs shaded down under the aspens or pines, or drinking at the willow-bordered stream, the herder's wagon with horses grazing nearby."[87]

Brown bought more sheep, more acreage, and a sheep-camp cabin. "There were bare floors and log walls, but a good little sheet iron stove that got red-hot with a few sticks of wood, a cot bed, and even a set of rough shelves for food supplies. I had one single shelf for the alarm clock, lamp and a few books, also a home-made table, a bench for the wash pan and water buckets, and a few kitchen chairs." She explained, "It was completely adequate. Thoreau, or a pioneer of the very early days, would have found it luxurious." But what she really enjoyed was "a view of what looked out over all creation from the little front porch of the cabin: foothills and mountains piled on mountains."[88]

She learned about ewes lambing heavier at night and about how valuable the wool check would be. Brown came to understand not pushing sheep but drifting them, how to avoid yellow jaundice from woollies eating too much scrub oak in the fall, and the depths of loneliness. She writes of a Craig rancher who committed suicide and left a note, "which merely said: 'It was the sheep.'"[89]

Brown worked as a country schoolteacher to earn money. She added to her flocks and purchased a relinquishment, or homestead rights, to a key piece of land between her own and government range. She came to know natural sheep pasture and the diverse vegetation of wildflowers, weeds, sage, serviceberries, chokecherries, and quaking aspen. She came to own a second cabin of rough pine boards and wrote, "The grove of beautiful, quaking aspen near the cabin was the loveliest I have ever seen. With their birch-like white trunks and their heart-shaped leaves answering the slightest breeze, they have always seemed more living and human than other trees."[90] She died owning 713 acres and had made a name for herself on Elk River.

If the Shepherdess of Elk Valley reveled in nature, clear mountain streams, and sheep quietly bedded for the night, she makes no reference to the war on predators that had escalated by 1918. Any environmental history must note how many animals federal trappers pursued and killed in the early decades of the twentieth century. This is part of the story of government grass.

As the first federal forest reserves in the state became national forests in 1905, one of the duties of forest rangers was to hunt and kill predators. Daybooks or diaries kept by forest rangers on the Pagosa Springs District of the San Juan National Forest include a variety of entries. Into one of the ranger stations a rancher named Parcell "brought in [a] wolf this evening measuring 6 ft. 9 in. from tip to lip," wrote a ranger on May 6, 1920. Later that month, "Rec'd phone call from Reed asking me to join in a wolf hunt with all the men of the neighborhood. Left sta. at 8:00 and met at big mailbox and went to Robbin's where we spread out and looked for dens. Keane and Reed found two dens but old ones were absent. Traps were set at the entrance of the dens."[91]

In June the forest ranger continued to dig out dens but found them empty. In 1921 US Forest Service staff began to spread poison pellets.

Even in Yellowstone National Park, wolves were trapped, shot, and hunted to their dens so that wolf pups could be dragged out and clubbed to death, or perhaps secured to a rope or chain so their whines and howls would draw their parents back to the den to be dispatched first. Then the cubs were killed. National Park rangers killed the last wolf in Yellowstone in 1926. In Colorado it took longer because of the vast mountainous terrain and the many plateaus, buttes, prairies, and canyons that wolves roamed.

In the town of New Castle, on Colorado's Western Slope, the old fire station is now the local museum and historical society. Amid the usual pioneer bric-a-brac of black-and-white photographs, coffee grinders, knives, axes, and faded silk and cotton dresses lies one unique artifact tacked on a wall in an inner room. More than most historical artifacts, it represents the pioneer response to settling the American West in the late nineteenth and early twentieth centuries. It is a poorly done mount of a white wolf, with hair in blotches, skull open, hide torn, teeth bared. The pelt stares glassy eyed at the ceiling.[92]

The wolf has small ears. Perhaps they were clipped for a state-sanctioned wolf bounty. The hide is brittle, representing a poor job of tanning. The wolf seems fragile, as if the hide had been improperly stretched and then dried too quickly.

Among the toys, dolls, medical equipment, newspapers, and guns, two mountain lions are displayed along with a stuffed bobcat and a golden eagle. The other mounts are also part of Colorado history, but New Castle's white wolf has his own unique story. The color of his pelt means he was quite old and probably lonely when he was shot the winter of 1914–1915. In that congressional session, the US Congress decided to fund the Bureau of Biological Survey, whose goal would be to hire professional hunters to trap predators and varmints across the West to make the territory safe for sheep and cattle and to increase big game herds of deer and elk.

That winter, about five miles north of New Castle on East Elk Creek, the John Wendell family worked to improve their homestead with two feet of snow on the ground and livestock requiring grass hay. With a hired hand, Wendell would load his sled and drive his horses to his pasture a quarter mile from his house while slowly spreading the hay. His white fox terrier would come along and soon began to play with an aging timber wolf that sometimes slipped out of the forest and down to the pasture.

Each time Wendell had a rifle, the wolf failed to appear. Finally, one day the rancher had his gun, shot and stunned the wolf, and finished him off with a blow to the head from a wooden fence post. The Wendell Ranch became locally famous, and neighbors, hunters, and trappers all arrived to see the elusive gray timber wolf, so old its hair was white. Across Colorado the killing continued.

To the cattle and sheep ranchers of Parachute, the Bureau of Biological Survey sent Bill Caywood, who lived along Piceance Creek in Rio Blanco County with his wife, Laura, and six children. A farmer, rancher, and independent trapper who followed traplines in winter looking for thick fur, he joined the Bureau of Biological Survey the year Congress founded it, in 1915. A few years earlier, during 1912 and 1913, "Big Bill" claimed to have killed 140 wolves, and local stockmen surrendered the $50 per head bounty. As a government trapper, he was now on salary and could take his time to fulfill the bureau's goals of killing every last Colorado wolf.

Funded by Congress a century ago, the Bureau of Biological Survey created an ecological holocaust of strychnine-ridden carcasses and indiscriminate destruction up the food chain. We tried to kill coyotes. Instead, we brought death to eagles.

The goal was to eliminate predators to foster game populations of deer and elk and to reduce losses by stockmen who raised sheep and cattle. In 1915, "ecology" and "environment" were not household words. Interrelationships among wildlife and habitat were not understood.[93] Even a skilled naturalist and big game hunter like Theodore Roosevelt referred to wolves as "beasts of waste and desolation."[94] No one grasped the value of predator-prey relationships in maintaining healthy ecosystems.

Wolfers learned to think like wolves, to wear moccasins rather than boots, to bury #14 traps and handle gear with gloves reeking of fresh manure to hide the human scent. They learned to leave no disturbed soil and to sift dust and earth on top of trap sets. Among Hispano sheepherders, legends spoke of wolves who were not wolves at all but evil spirits of the desert, *diablos* or devils incarnate, who could not be caught, who could not be killed, and whose howls in piñon-juniper underbrush came from the dead. These were phantom wolves, spirit wolves, *lobos de las animas*, or "ghost lobos."

Government trappers dismissed such folklore, but having spent days on horseback and months on the trails of these last gray wolves, the men perhaps wondered about those stories as they silently nodded in the saddle coming back to camp in a dark, windy rain or an early wet snow.

At cow camps or sheep camps the trappers ate biscuits, steaks, lamb chops, and fried potatoes cooked on a sheet-metal stove. They devoured canned peaches and swallowed gallons of strong coffee laced with condensed milk. Wolf trappers left before dawn with a yellow slicker tied behind the saddle for rain and snow and a cold can of beans for lunch. Trappers not hired by the bureau, who chased state-based or grazing-association rewards, resented federal trappers. Both groups relentlessly pursued *Canis lupus*.

One enterprising cowboy named Edgar Williams located an old female wolf who denned up every spring under Lavender Point in the Gypsum and Dry Creek Basin. Once she had pups he would dig out the cubs and sell them for $25 apiece, but he never bothered the female. He was outraged when a trapper killed her and the cowboy lost an annual source of income.[95]

Wolfers, government trappers for the Biological Survey, became legendary on Colorado's Western Slope. "Wolf" Morgan trapped in the Disappointment Valley around 1915. Like other wolfers, he was a loner who was "not too well acquainted with a bathtub, [and] he rarely changed his clothes. Dirty, bearded, and unkempt, he lived mostly to kill wolves," wrote rancher Howard E. Greager.[96]

"Slim Hawley, government trapper ... was a superb woodsman, soft and deliberate of speech. When he hunkered down on his heels with his battered old hat pushed back on his thick shock of graying hair he looked like an embodiment of all wisdom and goodness," wrote David Lavender. "But he was an anatomical lie. His skills were with things rather than with thoughts, and beneath his admirable exterior he had the cruelest nature I have ever known. His business was killing." Hawley placed steel traps in animal carcasses and waited for predators like coyotes, wolves, and bears to return.[97]

"I believe the grass which average coyotes save by putting a check on foraging rodents and insects far outweighs the value of the stock they harm," explained Lavender, who ran his father's ranch in the Disappointment Valley.[98] Few stockmen had his insight. Instead, they poured poison onto public land. The Biological Survey managed a special poison laboratory in Denver that experimented with strychnine, arsenic, and cyanide.

In the 1918 *Report of the Chief of the Bureau of Biological Survey*, E. W. Nelson described the work of from "250 to 350 hunters under the direction of district supervisors" in which "predatory animals are destroyed by trapping, shooting, den hunting during the breeding season, and poisoning." He wrote that a "large area in southern Colorado was systematically poisoned with excellent effect."

Nelson proudly wrote that "predatory animals taken by hunters under the direction of this bureau" included "849 wolves, 20,241 coyotes, 85 mountain lions, 3,432 bobcats, 30 lynxes, and 41 bears."[99] That was only three years into the survey's work. Wholesale slaughter across the West had just begun, and states, including Colorado, contributed thousands of dollars to augment the bureau's federal funding. Colorado's remaining wolves became so famous they received nicknames.

Burt Hegewa trapped Lefty and captured Bigfoot near De Beque at the head of Roan Creek on February 13, 1922. Bill Caywood killed Rags and Whitey. Roy Spangler found the female Three Toes, and W. J. Nearing also killed wolves in Colorado. Always on the run, harassing livestock because of the depletion of game, the last wolves had names like Old Lefty from Eagle County, the Phantom Wolf near Fruita, the Greenhorn Wolf south of Pueblo, the Unaweep Wolf from Unaweep Canyon, Bigfoot at De Beque,

Old Whitey near Trinidad, and Rags the Digger at Cathedral Bluffs in Rio Blanco County.

Wolves represented raw, untamed nature, and in the early twentieth century, during the Progressive Era, we practiced the "gospel of efficiency," or the ideals of order, rationality, punctuality, and production. The randomness of nature, the way wolves could make a fresh kill every night, required retribution and torture, including slipping a muzzle of hay wire over a wolf's jaws so it would starve to death. This was "range justice."

Canis lupus harassed livestock because wild game populations had dramatically dropped. In fact, all of Colorado's elk had been shot and killed by prospectors, miners, and homesteaders. Today's elk herds evolved from Roosevelt elk transplanted from Wyoming. As the frontier came to a close in 1890 and homesteaders staked free land up every creek and drainage, they brought livestock that lured coyotes and wolves. No one questioned the value of "settling up the country," and killing a wolf became an act of heroism and notoriety for the hunter.

The location of these last wolves killed also speaks to wildness and what were once wilderness settings—Burns Hole on the Colorado River in Eagle County; Greenhorn or Cuerno Verde near Huerfano Butte, where the Rockies meet the prairie in Pueblo County; up Piceance Creek and Cathedral Bluffs, now eviscerated by oil-shale and shale-gas roads, pumps, and compressor stations. A last wolf was trapped near Thatcher, out on the plains and "down on the Picketwire," which is the local pronunciation of the Purgatoire River in Bent and Las Animas Counties. The Unaweep Wolf was killed on the Uncompahgre Plateau, and another near the Ruby Canyon cow camp for the Flying W Ranch up Big Salt Wash north of Fruita.

These final Colorado wolves represented, in their living and by their dying, the real end of the frontier, not just the symbolic end in 1890 based on settlement patterns. Up to the early 1920s these old wolves, male and female, had eluded capture. With their passing the frontier truly ended, and the industrialized West of Ford pickups, barbed wire, and repeating rifles had triumphed. Or had it?

Dominance over the landscape by stockmen, with no wolves to trim herds, meant overgrazing, grass depletion, and arroyo cutting, which has left deep scars across the state, and the replacement of native grasses with invasive species like cheatgrass that have no nutritional value. In many areas, the end of the wolves coincided with the demise of vast stretches of grama grass, bluestem, or Indian ricegrass.

The last wolves signified the end of a wild landscape that had attracted settlers to Colorado in the first place. Some of the wolfers themselves had reservations about their brutal actions. "I've just got a lot of love and respect for the gray wolf. He's a real fellow, the big gray is. Lots of brains. I feel sorry for him. It's his way of livin.' He don't know better," opined wolfer Big Bill Caywood. "And I feel sorry every time I see one of those big fellows thrashin' around in a trap bellowin' bloody murder. . . . Guess I'm too much a part of this outdoors to hold any grudge against animals," Caywood explained.[100] Most wolfers simply poisoned, shot, and trapped themselves out of business without any self-reflection.

From 1905 to 1920, Colorado and the West experienced radical changes. The US Forest Service came to regulate high-mountain ranges. Homesteaders moved into remote areas and "proved up" on thousands of acres. After 1916 and the Stock-Raising Homestead Act, even more stockmen came to own strategic portions of the range. Possibly as much as one-half to two-thirds of all northwestern Colorado private ranchland can be attributed to this law.[101]

Cattlemen and sheepmen waged war among themselves and then against all predators. Sheep and cattle continued to overgraze the West, especially on the unallocated and unclaimed public domain. That is where the last land conflicts occurred. Though state legislatures knew about the problem, they had no jurisdiction over federal property. As agricultural prices slumped after World War I and then slowly began to recover, competition for government grass remained fierce. On sheep ranges Greek and Basque herders began to run their own flocks, and in the 1920s sheepmen bought foreclosed cattle ranches from banks.

In 1930, just as the Great Depression began to affect the nation's economy, Republican president Herbert Hoover's administration tried to give what was left of the public domain to the western states. Western governors refused. Stockmen would clamor for the land a decade later.

With the election of Democratic president Franklin Delano Roosevelt, a new perspective emerged. Finally, after decades of range wars, a Colorado congressman and a Colorado rancher would create an effective plan that would forever change land-use patterns in the American West. But first the Battle of Yellow Jacket Pass, on the Rio Blanco–Moffat County line, would have to occur, complete with cowboys, sheepherders, bleating sheep, and six uniformed Colorado State Police trailing a mounted Gatling gun.

FOURTH SHEEPSCAPE

Going to the Mountain—Glade Park and Piñon Mesa

Across Colorado, researchers and historians have helped me find carved aspen trees. In Grand Junction at the Museum of Western Colorado, Marie Tipping offered to assist—first with locating important newspaper clippings on the cattle and sheep wars at the turn of the twentieth century, and then with a tour of arborglyphs in her own backyard on Piñon Mesa. Riding with her in her Ford pickup, I learned extensive family and ranching history. I began to understand the tensions between Utah and Colorado sheepmen and entrenched Colorado cattlemen who controlled the range.

From Grand Junction, far below in Grand Valley, no one would realize there are cool pine forests, aspen groves, creeks, and small canyons on Piñon Mesa above and southwest of the sprawling city. Those lands could easily have been added to the Uncompahgre National Forest but never were. Instead, Glade Park and Piñon Mesa were opened for homesteading. Marie, wearing jeans and with her hair in a bun at the back of her neck, brought a carefully color-coded map with names and dates of the early homesteaders from 1917. In an aspen grove off a private road we spread the map across her pickup hood and I began to realize how many families, over two decades, had followed their American dream south of the dramatic sandstone canyons that would become Colorado National Monument.

Both cattlemen and sheepmen coveted the tall grasses, and a variety of ethnic groups tried their hand at homesteading once the area became surveyed after 1902. Others squatted on the land before the surveyors came, and they waited to claim their turf. The Aubert family of Basque heritage acquired hundreds of acres "on the mountain" and wintered their sheep on Utah's San Rafael Swell. There were families named Beard and Burdick, and an Italian sheep-owning family named Gobbo.

Taking a firm stand against sheep was cattleman Charles Sieber, who may have had one of the largest cattle herds on the Western Slope, and like many early cattlemen, he may have illegally fenced public range. He vowed to keep sheep out, but Utah sheepmen had other ideas.

A swinging bridge for sheep crossed the Colorado River eight miles south of Cisco, Utah, in 1908. "This was the summer the first sheep were brought into Piñon Mesa and how we hated them. I was 10 and Leola was

Basque sheepherders and sheepmen have always utilized the Glade Park and Piñon Mesa area south and west of Grand Junction. This carved boot and the word *Espanola* testify to the Basque homeland.

15. Every day we got on our horses, took the dogs, and hunted up a sheep herd," remembered Catherine Moore. "Back and forth through the herd we ran our horses, hollering and siccing the dogs. We would scatter those ewes and lambs for a long ways and never once did we see a herder."[1]

From Glade Park's grass, which once had "dragged upon the stirrups," overgrazing and drought began to diminish native plants. "By now the whole country was being fenced, wells dug, ponds made here and there, sagebrush grubbed—the hard way—with a grubbing hoe. Families trying to make a living by dry-farming," Moore wrote decades later. "A few made it, but mostly they were coming and going for many years."[2]

In 1910 Big Park and Piñon Mesa ranchers met because of a rumor that herders would move thousands of sheep from Utah into the area. Cattlemen wanted a sheep exclusion zone and feared that the Sieber Ranch, then owned by Thatcher Brothers of Pueblo, would become a sheep ranch and that sheep would destroy the public range that cattlemen enjoyed. Threatening letters ensued. Rumors were rife of a range war. Reporters for the *Denver Republican* newspaper claimed that 150,000 sheep would cross the Grand River, now the Colorado, at the Utah state line. Families who had not wanted the Piñon Mesa area to become a national forest now thought they could get a forest designation with a "no-sheep" grazing clause. But not much happened. When there was actual conflict, sheep owners looked to the law.

"The long expected trouble between cattle and sheep men of Pinon mesa came near reaching a climax Wednesday when three Whitewater cattle owners leveled revolvers at the head of Frank Greening, an employee of W. T. Goslin, and forced him to move his sheep a half mile off the mesa and ordered him to keep off their range," reported the *Grand Valley Times* from Moab, Utah, on June 19, 1914. Goslin decided to "take legal steps in the matter," but the newspaper never reported on any such judicial action.[3] Instead, Walt Goslin waited out the cattlemen.

From Moab he brought in sheep and became a banker, and when stockmen lost livestock during the fierce winter of 1917–1918, which brought snow, intense cold, and the Spanish Flu, cattlemen could not pay their financial notes. The big outfits went broke. Sheepmen like Goslin acquired their property.

"Goslin called their notes and bought mortgages from other banks. The cattlemen couldn't pay them off so he purchased all their land and then resold it. He was out of the sheep business at that point, but he got the last laugh," Marie explains. She smiles. "I read the old newspapers a lot."[4]

Despite the stigma of owning sheep, there was money to be made in woollies, and some early cattlemen went to grazing sheep in part because they were easier to steal. "There was quite a few up here that got caught stealing sheep and other things," Marie told me. She added, "It was not always sheep stealing. It was also sheep killing." To get sheep from winter grounds in Utah to high-elevation summer grass, ranchers built the Serpent's Trail in 1921 through Colorado National Monument, and the Cimarron Trail, which stretched from Crescent Junction in Utah southeast to high mountain meadows above Silverton. Whatever the local families' history, Marie Tipping, whose ancestors came into the country in the 1880s, knows them all.

"He had ground everywhere. Some ranchers took the upper stuff. Others took the rocks. He'd buy property when people couldn't pay their taxes," she says of one patriarch in a ranching family. She knows who died, when, and sometimes why if there were quarrels, which frequently occurred. As we drove the mesa she would point to a rancher's "midrange" and referred to sheepmen as "land poor," meaning they had plenty of acreage but little cash.

"The big ranchers wanted more ground and so they'd hire people to homestead, pay the fees, and then pay them a few hundred dollars. The hired hands would just pretend to live on it. They were really cowboys," she explained.

We started to see carvings on the aspens. Fred Herrera, a herder from Fruita, had left his name and the date 6/21/38. We were on summer range at Snyder Flats, a mix of Bureau of Land Management and private land, much of it owned by the Aubert family. The sheepmen grazed as long as they could in the high country and then trailed their sheep west to Utah by winter. A superb local historian, Marie can see initials on a tree, know who made them, remember when they were born and died, and know who homesteaded the land we were driving through. She knows all the creeks and place names. She explained that trailing sheep through private ground always brought tension unless the herder moved fast enough to keep the sheep from eating all the grass.

We drive a country lane to Enoch's Lake, now owned by the town of Fruita. The artificial lake had been a historical resort for Grand Junction residents to get out of the summer's heat. No buildings remain, only a few traces of foundations. We drive up Jones Hill beyond the Beard place to the sheep corrals of the four Gobbo brothers. Domingo Barranca had carved a heart with a cross above it and the date July 4, 1933, and Juan Bautista Grurucla had left his inscription in 1967. Everywhere we see the name Luis Aragon.

I realize I'm looking for some of the oldest, largest aspen trees in Colorado, and I'm not sure I'll find them. Across the western landscape, stories are tied to trees and places. Marie Tipping knows those stories, but most people do not. The land remains and a few carvings still stand, but much of the grazing history is fading or lost altogether.

It's a September day, warm, overcast, with a threat of rain. Yellow aspen leaves stand muted on the trees without a trace of wind. She stops the truck and I walk a dirt road looking for carved trees. I am trying to find herders' words, which are a layer of history and meaning different from the fierce squabbles over land ownership and the shifting ranch family cycles of running cattle and then sheep and then switching back to cattle.

There are no flocks on the mountain anymore. The last sheep herds left in the 1960s, so the aspen tree signatures are frozen in time. The trees themselves are failing. "The west end of Piñon Mesa had huge groves of aspen, but now they're gone. No little tree shoots are coming up," Marie explains.

Herders left their mark. Some of the more sexually explicit carvings had been scratched over by female members of the Aubert family who found them offensive. The trees tell a story, though. Reading the trees, one learns of the Basque presence near Grand Junction, and on one tree a herder proudly wrote "French-Basque-USA" and then the nickname "BASCO" and the dates "1954, 55, 56." In a small grove of aspen with deep, dark markings where elk rubbed trees with their antlers, I find a unique carving.

Two men embrace. One wears a baseball cap, the other a Basque beret. It's a symbol of warmth and friendship.

Despite conflicts over land ownership, one of the outcomes of sheepherding in Colorado was to bring a variety of herders to the state, especially after World War II, when Europe was devastated by war. The Spanish-Basque sheepman Emmett Elizondo from Grand Junction, who ran huge flocks between Utah and the high country of the San Juan Mountains, brought many of his countrymen to the Western Slope.

The carving represents that. A new start for young men who could see little future in a war-torn Europe. They came West. Bought jeans, boots. Learned to roll smokes. They followed sheep into the high country and out to the Utah desert for winter. Now only the trees remain to tell their stories.

I turn from photographing the carving of the two men and walk to the truck. Marie and I drive in silence for a while, waiting for rain that does not come.

Chapter 4

Basque and Greek Sheepmen, the Taylor Grazing Act, and End of the Range Wars, 1920–1934

The sons of old country people everywhere must fight a little harder and do something better with their lives. Because we were born of old country people in a new land, and right or wrong, we had not felt equal to those around us, and we had to do a little more than they in everything we did.

—PAUL LAXALT, A BASQUE DESCENDANT
Sweet Promised Land

The day of the "free" or "open" range is forever gone, and in spite of occasional bunkhouse fumings over bits of local injustice, there is not a rancher who would willingly return to the former catch-as-catch-can ways of obtaining grass.

—DAVID LAVENDER
One Man's West

Grass ... invades the solitude of deserts, climbs the inaccessible slopes and pinnacles of mountains, and modifies the history, character, and destiny of nations.

—JOHN J. INGALLS, KANSAS PIONEER, US SENATOR

The 1920s produced increased tension between cattlemen and sheepmen in Colorado, particularly in the northwestern corner of the state. The US Forest Service had begun to regulate its rangelands, but disputes over the open, public domain intensified. A new element in the volatile mix, and one that would have lasting consequences, was sheepherders who were not Hispanic and were not from Mexico or New Mexico. Hispanic herders continued to tend flocks in the eastern San Juan Mountains, the Sangre de Cristos, and the San Luis Valley. In 1920 the Forest Service even issued its first publication in Spanish, *La manipulación de las ovejas en los bosques nacionales* (*The Handling of Sheep on the National Forests*).[1] But in western Colorado, from Browns Park south to Telluride, two new ethnic groups began to reshape the sheep industry in the Rockies.

Basque and Greek immigrant herders came to tend flocks. Familiar with harsh and limited grazing conditions in their own countries, they brought with them centuries of herding traditions, a pride in what they did, and a determined willingness to fight for forage. They understood isolation, were intensely loyal to their employers, and bought guns and knew how to use them. Familiar with conflicts and disputes in the Old Country, they did not hesitate to defend their employer's grazing rights in the American West. In seven years, stout Basque herders could make more money than they could earn in a lifetime in Europe, but it often meant coming into town only two weeks a year. Long seasons with the sheep. Dinner on a piece of canvas. No table. No chairs.

Both Greeks and Basques had strong family ties. Kinship bonds in the sheep industry meant that trusted relatives would be hired. Once a herder had established a business footing in Colorado, he then brought over other family members from European villages to work in sheep camps. Initially, Greek and Basque herders had come to America to earn funds and then return to their ancient villages. World War I changed that, as did the 1916 Stock-Raising Homestead Act, which allowed herders to homestead up to 640 acres. Then they applied for citizenship. Coming from poor villages on rocky Greek shores or the steep Pyrenees of Spain or France, they clearly understood that this was a life-changing opportunity. Family dynasties would be created by hardworking immigrants who believed in the promise of America.

For the Greeks, Utah coal mines, especially near Price, brought together young men and families from over 50 different Greek villages. Trapped in narrow-ceilinged, dangerous mine shafts, they longed for a different life.

For Basques who came to America to herd, two- and three-story wooden hotels, usually near railroad tracks and run by Basque wives, served as home away from home. These family hotels became common denominators for Basques, whose distinctive language no one understood. In the hotels they could relax, eat home-cooked meals from Old Country recipes, drink red wine, and discuss range conditions. One Basque herder ruefully noted that in sheep camps the shepherds all talked about women, and in hotels they all talked about sheep.

"Extreme western Colorado and eastern Utah was one of the regions of the American West most beset with itinerant sheep bands," notes Basque scholar William A. Douglass. He adds, "The largest concentration of Basques in the general area developed near the turn of the century in Grand Junction and Montrose, Colorado. Summer grazing was abundant in the high country of the western slopes of the Colorado Rockies, while the low desert lands between Grand Junction and Price, in Utah, provided adequate winter grazing."[2]

US Forest Service rangers in Colorado began to plan and build stock driveways to allow large sheep flocks to access high-altitude government grass. Most of Colorado's national forests had several stock driveways, including the Pine-Piedra and Groundhog Stock Driveways on the San Juan National Forest, La Garita Stock Driveway on the Rio Grande, and on the Montezuma National Forest (now the San Juan), the Highline Sheep Driveway and the Papoose and Wildcat Trails. Maintenance and management of the driveways became the responsibility of forest rangers at the urging of local county commissioners because "moving large herds of animals not only blocked the roads, they damaged them. Thoroughfares were not paved; the sharp hooves of sheep tore off their surfaces and dislodged rocks. In wet weather the damage was significantly greater."[3]

According to the diaries of forest ranger James G. Cayton on the Rico District, the "under-sheriff of Dolores County [is] warning sheepmen who go up the road that any damage they do, they will have to repair."[4] Rangers put up sheep boundary signs, supervised the overall surveying and construction of the route, hired workers, and arranged for tools, equipment, and camps. Cayton employed cooks and kept work crews fed, and his wife, Birdie, sewed damaged cots and tents. Cayton's diaries explain in detail the importance of managing forest access to avoid overgrazing and the careful planning of sheep movements to coincide with melting snows in June.

"He scheduled the use of driveways to allow access to grazing allotments, determining the number of animals moved. The placement of signage on the trail was the cue that a trail segment was getting close to being opened. Jim's diary entries show his ongoing involvement in creating the driveway system over the years," write David W. Cayton and Caroline E. Metzler, who explain the work involved in clearing timber and establishing routes 50 feet wide.[5]

Across Colorado the US Forest Service designed and built stock driveways to facilitate sheepmen's access to their high-elevation allotments without damaging county roads or risking wrath from local cattlemen. Many of those driveways can still be located today, and they provide historical access routes to lush mountain meadows above timberline.

By the early 1920s, another element featured in cattle and sheep grazing conflicts was successful Mormon sheepmen with property in eastern Utah deserts who desperately needed Colorado high-country grass to fatten their thousands of ewes, wethers, and lambs. A partial solution emerged—stock driveways across lower-elevation land. But these lacked the precision surveying and careful construction directed by district forest rangers. These were routes through sagebrush whereby herders could traverse considerable distances east to west or north to south without risking the ire of cattlemen. Sometimes. Without designated driveways, herders simply pushed sheep where grass was good, but that was often on cattle range.

Occasionally, Utah sheepmen advocated for large stock driveways that would cut through huge swaths of public land, ignoring cattle pastures and struggling small homesteads. Economics, ethnic solidarity, high prices for wool and lambs, and environmental damage from overgrazing all reached a crescendo on western public lands in the 1920s. Something had to be done. Soil erosion intensified from unregulated herds. Cattlemen despised sheepmen, who frequently bought them out or acquired their ranches at bank foreclosures.

Two Coloradans from the Western Slope, one a congressman and the other a lawyer and owner of purebred Hereford cattle, devised a system to defuse conflict on the range. That solution, the Taylor Grazing Act of 1934, had been a long time coming and had to be carefully worked out across the West. The more complicated issues not yet solved were the carrying capacity of the land, range improvement, and soil stabilization. In the 1920s, only one man consistently raised an ecological voice—Aldo Leopold. We should still listen to him today.

"At the start of the 1920s came the bitter battle between the cattlemen and the sheepmen," wrote Farrington Carpenter in his memoir, *Con-*

fessions of a Maverick.[6] On the night of April 5, 1920, seven armed and masked cowboys grabbed William Mann, age 22, and Dean Leonard, age 18, two young herders grazing a flock at the Keeley homestead in Rio Blanco County. The assailants tied and gagged the shepherds and then clubbed all 350 sheep in the flock to death with spokes from wheels of the camp wagon they had burned.

"The cowboys intended making an example of the two herders by lynching them," explained a Rio Blanco County pioneer. "Their youth however [and] the fact that they were not Mexicans, and the pleas of both boys that they were the sole support of several dependents saved their lives."[7] The cowboys scared one of the herders so thoroughly that as soon as he was untied he walked home to Vernal, Utah. Flockmaster Snell Johnson from Vernal sought justice, but the local district attorney claimed that "a conviction was impossible to obtain in northwestern Colorado, where juries were dominated by the cattle barons."[8]

That summer, John Darnell, a member of the Great Divide Homestead Colony, who was married and the father of one child, kept sheep for Utah sheepman William Bascom. Darnell squatted on land in Moffat County near Rough Gulch, four miles from the Utah state line. He built a cabin and reservoirs for watering sheep, and then with his father-in-law, James E. Price, herded 1,800 of Bascom's sheep. He was known to be good with a six-gun.

In the early morning hours of July 30, 1920, cowboys came calling. Price slept in the cabin and Darnell in a white canvas-covered sheep wagon. Discovering intruders at his sheep camp, Darnell fired two warning shots and then made his fatal mistake. He lit a lamp in the sheep wagon.

Cowboys fired at his silhouette, and the homesteader, in his midthirties, was murdered by a spray of bullets. He had dared to cross four miles from Utah into Colorado. Eleven cowboys killed him and then clubbed to death 686 ewes from his flock of 1,800.[9] The *Craig (CO) Courier* proclaimed on December 22, 1920, "US Arrests Six to End Sheep War. After Months of Investigation, Prominent Northwestern Colorado Cattlemen Are Indicted by a Federal Grand Jury. Accused of Attempting Fraud. Intimidating Homesteaders Charged, and Government Attorney Will Prosecute to the Limit." Yet nothing came of the federal prosecution despite the sensational headlines.[10]

As cattle prices dropped, Utah sheepmen acquired White River National Forest permits that cattlemen could not pay for. Under Republican president

Warren G. Harding, former Utah governor William Spry became commissioner of the General Land Office, and he favored Utah sheepmen. His former constituents sought a stock driveway from Utah deep into Colorado—106 miles long, 6 miles wide, with resting places for flocks every 25 miles. Spry approved it.

In shock, Colorado cattlemen complained that the sheep driveway would decimate the best of their open range and that woollies would devour grass needed for their large cow herds. "As attorney for the cattlemen, I passed along their views to the Utah sheepmen, who nevertheless decided to make a test case of the driveway," wrote Farrington Carpenter. Previously the sheepmen had shipped their flocks by rail on the Denver and Rio Grande east from Utah to Denver and then back west on the Moffat Road to Yampa before trailing their flocks into the forest. Utah sheepmen thought they could handle Colorado cowboys, but they were not prepared for the cattlemen's fast-thinking lawyer, Ferry Carpenter.

Raised in Illinois, he learned to ride on the Whitney Ranch in Colfax County, New Mexico, and ever after appeared born to the saddle. Tall, lean,

Princeton University graduate Ferry Carpenter attended Harvard Law School before settling in the Colorado frontier town of Hayden. Here he sits in his law office, where he also slept on a cot. Photograph courtesy of Dorothy Wickenden, from her book *Nothing Daunted*.

every inch of six feet in his cowboy boots, blue-eyed Carpenter could jaw with the best of the West's ranchers. He "talked cowboy" in the halls of Congress, but he was also a 1909 Princeton University graduate, and in 1907, the day he turned 21, homesteaded near Elkhead Creek north of Hayden and began his passion for raising purebred Hereford cattle. His father was not sure how long Ferry's cowboy phase would last, so he urged his son to go to law school, which Ferry did. At Harvard. Every summer he came back to Colorado and his cows.

In 1912 he graduated, and upon returning to the tiny town of Hayden, Ferry reminisced, "I soon had a nice little practice seeing as I was the first and only lawyer there."[11] He slept on a cot in his one-room law office. Because most homesteaders were bachelors like him, he schemed to get some "she-stuff" into the country. He ran for the local school board so he could keep an eye on prospective female one-room-school teachers, one of whom he later married.[12]

Labeled "America's most unusual storyteller" by the *Saturday Evening Post*, Ferry told plenty of yarns. As he tried to develop his purebred Hereford cattle, he had trouble with an adjacent rancher whose motley range bull would jump the fence and cozy up to Ferry's blooded cows. So he waited until his neighbor left on a trip, roped the range bull, drugged it, opened the scrotum, and removed the bull's balls. Later that afternoon Ferry got to thinking that the bull might look a little different, so he went to town, purchased a couple of brass doorknobs, roped the weary bull again, inserted the doorknobs into the old bull's scrotum, and then sewed him up. Next spring, the neighbor couldn't understand why his range bull seemed to have lost its customary vigor.[13]

"I'm a stubborn cuss," said Carpenter. "I like a good fight. Opposition just cheers me up. I want to accomplish what I set out to do, and I'm not in the habit of going home when I start on something. I don't like to be licked." Utah sheepmen were about to meet their match.

As attorney for the cattlemen, and as a local resident, Carpenter did not want a shooting war between cowboys and sheepherders, yet when the grazing season opened in 1921, stockmen Colthorp and Brimhall planned to take two bands of sheep up into the Flat Tops of the White River National Forest south of Yampa. N. C. Chapman was bringing a band of woollies, as were Izzy Bolten and John Kitchens.[14]

How could Carpenter stop the sheep and avoid a bloodbath? He knew the route the woollies would take. There was no time to marshal political forces to cancel the stock driveway. That would come later. The immediate problem was to turn back thousands of hungry sheep. Looking at a map and glancing at his law books, he devised a solution close to the Rio Blanco–Moffat County line. He would literally "head them off at the pass." Yellow Jacket Pass. It was only a few miles from where Northern Utes had successfully fought Major Thomas Tipton Thornburgh as he rushed to the aid of Nathan Meeker in 1879. Meeker and 11 others died, as did the major. Ferry wanted to avoid bloodshed.

"When two bands of their sheep reached the little settlement of Sunbeam [Colorado] on the Yampa River in Moffat County's rolling sage country, the sheepmen sent word to Governor Oliver Shoup of Colorado asking for the state militia to protect their sheep from the angry cattlemen," Carpenter explained.[15] The governor did not send the militia, but he did order a car full of state policemen and two motorcycle patrolmen. Six policemen trailing a mounted Gatling gun headed southeast with the sheep toward Colorado's high country. Carpenter wrote, "As long as the sheep stayed on public roads and on that part of the public domain constituting the driveway, there was no legal way to turn them back,"[16] but he realized that when the driveway crossed from Moffat into Rio Blanco County along Morapos Creek, both sides of the county road were owned by his cattleman friend J. N. "Jap" Wyman.

Under Colorado law, county commissioners can close a public road if adjacent property owners request it. Carpenter found the exact bottleneck he needed and telephoned Wyman, with whom he had enjoyed delightful days hunting bobcats. Wyman agreed to petition the county commissioners, setting the stage for the Battle of Yellow Jacket Pass, with dozens of armed cattlemen riding toward Wyman's ranch. Carpenter waited by the phone at Wyman's ranch headquarters to see how the commissioners would vote.

"At 2 p.m. Wyman's phone rang. I grabbed it, and the Rio Blanco commissioners told me that they had just signed the order abandoning the county road. The cowboys rushed forward with a roll of hogwire and built a fence across it," Carpenter remembered. "I explained to the baffled state police captain what had happened—that the road was now private property and no sheep or their owners could trespass on it without a warrant." The battle was over. Not a shot was fired. Utah sheepmen had to turn their woollies around, and it cost them dearly to take the flocks back to Craig and put them on railcars for a long trip to their summer pasture.

"All in all, testing the legality of the stock driveway had been a costly experiment to the Utah sheep owners, who subsequently admitted that it had all but ruined them financially," Carpenter noted.[17] Despite all those guns and upset stockmen, there was only one injury. A cattleman broke a bone in his foot by kicking a sheep.

Through their lawyer, Ferry Carpenter, the cattlemen appealed to Colorado senators Lawrence C. Phipps and Samuel D. Nicholson. Four of the stockmen attended a committee hearing in Washington, DC, and the secretary of the interior rescinded the 106-mile stock driveway. The Battle of Yellow Jacket Pass had been a success.

That same year, the Winder family from Utah had been threatened by telegram that if they brought their sheep into Colorado their flocks would be "rim-rocked." Seven cattlemen signed the telegram. As market conditions worsened for cattle, within five years four of those stockmen "took on sheep themselves."[18]

Economically, sheep made sense. Because sheepmen generated cash more quickly than cattlemen, they quietly homesteaded or bought land along routes where they trailed sheep from low-altitude winter range to high-altitude summer range. Sheepmen moved into banking and purchased mortgages and foreclosed properties. By the 1920s, "the open range days were over, killed by falling cattle prices, dangerous overstocking of the range which had turned once-lush pastures into dust, and by more and more homesteaders fencing in the open range," note Vandenbusche and Smith.[19]

For sheepherders willing to work hard, and for families just beginning in the wide-open spaces of Rio Blanco, Moffat, and Routt Counties, herding sheep on land no one wanted and then trailing them up into the national forests was a way to make a start. For immigrants, the goal was to come to America, earn money, and then return home. Herders often sent their wages back to the Old Country to help with family debts and preserve their farm or village landholdings.

For some Basque and Greek herders in the early twentieth century, though, America became home. They took their wages in ewes, saved every penny they could, purchased their own flocks, and homesteaded or invested in land. The 1916 Stock-Raising Homestead Act allowed an individual

With wool bags full, wagons in the San Luis Valley are ready to be driven to the railhead. Sheep-raising families still live near La Jara, Colorado, where there are wool sheds and painted murals of sheep. AUR 2100. Image courtesy of the Auraria Campus.

to "prove up" on a full section, or 640 acres. Greeks who crossed the ocean to labor in Utah coal mines gradually worked their way up and out of the mines to herd sheep on a vast sagebrush sea.

They started with nothing. Their families now own thousands of acres across western Colorado, with names like Jouflas, Halandras, Theos, Peroulis, and Raftopolous. Each family has its own American story, and each story is about hard work, perseverance, survival, and success in a foreign land.

Regas Halandras took a ship to America. His parents told him to "strike it rich" and send funds back to support the family farm in Lamia, Greece. With $25 in cash he left his homeland to go to Chicago and then on to the Utah Coal and Fuel Company at Castle Gate, where at only 13 or 14 years of age he began working in low-ceilinged mine tunnels. In 1919, at age 17, he became a herder near Price, earning $65 a month with one horse, one dog, and 2,000 sheep owned by Paul Jensen. Regas received a heartbreaking letter from home explaining that a relative had stolen all the money he had sent and that his family desperately needed $7,465. He asked Jensen for a loan and swore he would pay back every dollar. It took seven years.

Though the cattle and sheep wars had almost ended, disputes continued. In 1921, while Regas was herding at the head of Roan Creek, 14 riders threatened to kill him and another herder and gave them six days to leave the range. When the riders returned with rifles, his cousin Nick Svarnias hid behind a rock with a .30–30 lever-action Winchester while Halandras met the cowboys wearing a six-gun and riding a mule named Crazy. A cowboy lassoed a tent peg and threatened to level the sheep camp. Despite the tension, Halandras yelled in Greek to the other herder not to fire.

The next day the cattle owners themselves showed up instead of their hired guns. Halandras offered hospitality, lamb chops, biscuits, and hot black coffee in their herders' tent. "They said they sure would appreciate it if I moved the sheep, and I told them since they talked so sensible the sheep would be on the next mountain come morning. And we all shook hands. They sure did enjoy those lamb chops," he recalled years later.[20]

While the Halandras confrontation with cowboys ended in a grudging appreciation for the herders' black coffee and camp cuisine, the same year, in Utah, ranch hand Charlie Glass earned a reputation by killing a man. Born in Indian Territory with a Choctaw and Cherokee mother and an African American father, he became widely known in western Colorado and eastern Utah for his sense of humor, his card playing, and his handmade boots. The Blucher Boot Company in Olathe, Kansas, had inlaid clubs, hearts, diamonds, and spades in his boot tops.[21]

Glass also wore a high-top Stetson, liked to spur his horse to stand on its hind legs, and surprised children by giving them a silver dollar. In Fruita, Colorado, old-timers remembered Glass as a good bronc buster who would "ride the rough string—the horses no one else wanted to fool with."[22] He waited until last in the grub line, was not pushy, and ate alone unless asked to join other cowhands.

"Doing the town" in Grand Junction, he would put on a new hat, Pendleton pants, and a silk scarf and drink and gamble until he found a bordello with Hispanic girls to his liking. What cinched the cowboy's reputation, however, was killing a French Basque.

As foreman for the Lazy Y Cross, Oscar Turner's ranch in eastern Utah, on February 24, 1921, Charlie Glass shot and killed Felix Jesui, who herded sheep for Montrose sheepman William Fitzpatrick. The sheep had trespassed beyond a designated "deadline" and crossed the line of cattle range imposed by sheep inspector H. E. Herbert. A coroner's jury stated that Glass and Jesui had been close enough that Jesui died from a gunshot wound to the forehead.[23] Glass wore a Colt .38 automatic in a shoulder holster—hard to see, easy to reach.

By that February tensions had risen between cowboys and Basque herders, who fired into the air when they were approached, making it clear they had guns and would use them. At the second-degree murder trial, Herbert, the state sheep inspector, testified that herders had ignored the designated lines and, as short-tempered Basques might do, had threatened any approaching cowboys. "In a straightforward manner," Glass related his story, "and the cross-examination by Mr. Dalton, the prosecutor, failed to jar him in the least."[24]

On that fatal February morning, Glass found sheep a half mile over the line toward pasture reserved for the Turner ranch's weaner calves and weaker cattle. Glass rode to within 25 feet of the herder, got off his horse, and complained about the sheep. Jesui had a rifle and pistol and would hear none of it, acting "very defiant." Glass demurred, said his employer would take it up with the herder's boss, and walked toward his horse. The herder yelled, fired from a .25 automatic handgun, and sent a slug close to Charlie's shoulder. That was enough.

As Glass spun to draw his Colt .38, Jesui shot two more times. Charlie Glass began firing, too. Tracks in the snow were the best court evidence. They proved where Charlie's horse had stopped and he had dismounted. An investigation at the site of the killing verified that Glass had swung off his horse, walked toward the herder, and then returned to his mount. Jesui's spent cartridges glistened in the snow next to his body. His fingers clutched a cocked .30-caliber rifle that had one empty shell. Glass fired four times.

After a week of testimony, the jury took only two hours to acquit. Just as in the 1893 Montoya case near Pagosa Springs, self-defense on the open range could not be denied. The *Moab (UT) Times-Independent* reported, "The case was of more than ordinary interest for the reason that whether technically or not, it was a contest between the resident stockmen of Grand county and the transient sheepmen of Colorado, who for several years past have driven herds into Grand County for the winter months and, it is charged, have crowded out the resident stockmen with subsequent heavy losses to the latter."[25]

Did Glass pay for his own attorney, or did Oscar Turner? No one will ever know, but later Glass deeded his 160-acre homestead to his employer. The killing solidified Glass's regional reputation, and until 1934 and passage of the Taylor Grazing Act, "Charlie was given the job of keeping the sheep out of designated grazing areas for cattle. He continued that job until the grazing act became law and permits were issued designating areas," wrote Kathy Jordan. He also died under mysterious circumstances 16 years later in a pickup truck accident with two sheepherders.[26] In the Basque country in Europe, vendettas take a while.

The next year, two French Basque sheepherders were found guilty of attempting to murder Elgin, Utah, cattleman G. A. Harris, who protested when he found herders driving sheep over land he claimed. They fired on him, killed his mule, and forced him to flee into an arroyo. Raymond Tharour and Javier Burusco served jail time, but the state supreme court reversed the decision against Burusco.[27]

Also in 1922, Greek immigrant Regas Halandras brought 2,770 sheep through downtown Meeker in a tense confrontation that required six lawmen to prevent trouble. The woollies had wintered in Emery County, Utah, and would summer near De Beque. As often as he could, he "hollered at those sheep and switched at their rumps to make them move," and he got his flock through town without incident.

By 1931 Regas Halandras had become an American citizen, filed a homestead claim, owned 2,000 sheep, and begun to buy land. Halandras brought 17 Greek herders to the West. Half of them stayed. He traveled to Greece "to find a bride" in 1937, and he began a family tradition of ranching. A poor immigrant at the start, Regas Halandras persevered.

"Halandras did become rich, but it took him half a century. He did it dollar by dollar, sheep by sheep, acre by acre. Along the way he taught himself to read and write, became a proud and honored American citizen, survived natural disasters and the sheep and cattle wars, and founded a new Halandras dynasty in Colorado," wrote Olga Curtis in the *Denver Post*.[28]

The Theos family owned 9,600 acres in Rio Blanco County, leased 4,000 acres in two US Forest Service summer permits, and owned 2,000 acres and leased another 12,000 acres from the BLM in Utah for their sheep and lambs.²⁹ Steve Simos bought the George Bassett Ranch in Browns Park to graze sheep. When he passed away, his young wife, Georgia, returned to her home village in Greece and married George Raftopoulos, whom she had known since childhood. They returned to northwestern Colorado and continued to raise sheep close to Browns Park.³⁰

Like their Greek counterparts, French and Spanish Basque herders also found that hard work paid off. Young Basque men came to the United States because in their homeland a father passed down land and livestock to the son or daughter of his choice, leaving the other siblings as mere tenant farmers. In Spain, the military demanded four years of service, or for a fee, youths could depart the country.³¹ So, with few opportunities in their home pastures, they came to Nevada, Utah, California, Oregon, and Idaho. A select few found jobs, and finally fortunes, in Colorado.

But it wasn't easy. The stark western landscape of sagebrush, rocks, and scrawny junipers differed from the grasses of the Pyrenees. "There was so little feed that the sheep would wake up before daylight and never stop until it was dark, and it was all even a young man could do to keep up with them," wrote Robert Laxalt in *Sweet Promised Land*. His father remembered, "The life and the country made my heart sick, and many was the night I cried myself to sleep for ever having come to America. I would get up in the morning when it was still dark, as soon as I heard the sheep moving, and make my coffee, and I would hate for the day to come so that I would have to look at that terrible land."³² Laxalt herded in Nevada, but eastern Utah is desert country, too. Some Basques overcame their fears and loneliness and saw a future in the sweet-scented sage.

Jean Urruty, a determined young Basque, eventually had large landholdings in western Colorado and 8,550 acres near Roosevelt, Utah. Urruty came to Price, Utah, in 1925 to join his cousin Grace Aubert. He trailed 6,000 head of sheep to Piñon Mesa in spring 1926 through Grand Junction, crossing the Colorado River near the Redlands. He worked with a dozen other Basques, who would come to Grand Junction for a week's rest in the summer, but with his limited English skills, Urruty stayed in sheep camp. As winter approached, the young Basques moved their flocks back to range near Green River, Utah.

After almost five years of working as herders, Urruty and two Basque friends bought their first flock of 3,000 sheep after finding an Italian American banker willing to loan them funds. The partners transacted business and updated loans by mail. A decade later, Urruty married and with his wife bought the La Salle Hotel on Colorado Avenue in Grand Junction to serve as a way station for other Basque herders.[33]

During World War I, French Basques returned to fight the Germans, but because Spain remained neutral, Spanish Basques came to the West to herd. Antonio Retolaza arrived in Grand Junction in 1918 to run sheep with his uncle Antonio "Tony" Coscorrozza between Grand Junction and Gunnison. On September 13, 1920, they bought a boardinghouse from another herder, Jose Ocamica, on 224 Colorado Avenue in Grand Junction.

Built in 1912 as a hotel, the brick two-story building included beds, chairs, commodes, dressers, three stoves, and three pool tables. The structure had everything needed to make Basque herders comfortable while between jobs or recovering from injuries.[34] These Basque hotels stretched from Denver to northern Idaho, into Nevada, and on to eastern California and anywhere that the western sheep industry needed hired hands. Women, often relatives of the herders, ran the hotels.

For the Retolaza Boarding House and Pool Hall, women came from neighboring Spanish villages in Europe all the way to Mesa County. "Grand Junction became the hub of the largest concentration of Basques located in the region of western Colorado and eastern Utah," wrote Jeffrey Izienicki in the *Journal of the Western Slope*. "High Rocky Mountain grazing meadows and desert valleys between Grand Junction and eastern Utah produced ideal conditions for the herds of the Vizcayan Basque itinerant sheepherders."[35]

The typical Basque hotel became "a social anchor for thousands of young single teenage men far from home" and was "much more than just a room and a hot meal."[36] Here was a chance to speak the ancient Basque language without being ridiculed, to enjoy home-cooked food, to have someone write letters home, and to negotiate with other sheepmen to lease or purchase sheep through a network of lawyers and bankers recommended by the hotel owner. Often, the hotels also became Basque banks because herders did not want to leave their cash savings in their high-country summer tents. When a sheepman arrived, by custom he bought a round of drinks for the house.

These hotels regularly switched owners, but the Retolaza boardinghouse was run for 30 years by the same family. When Basques returned home, they usually took gifts and cash from other herders, as well as letters to family and sweethearts. Basque hotels served as clearinghouses for those gifts, for wages, savings, and investments, and for employers seeking dependable herders. Because Basque hotels so completely rooted young Basque men, they could remain itinerant, not own land, not pay taxes, and be cursed as "Bascos" for grabbing western grass, putting fattened wethers and lambs on train cars, and starting over each season without becoming community members. Eventually that would change, but the tramp or itinerant sheepmen became the bane of low-altitude public land, where no rules existed. They "proudly pursued the American Dream as itinerant sheepherders in what was to be the last large area of open-range sheepherding in the American West."[37]

Along with other successful Basque and Greek sheep-raising families from Grand Junction, Emmett Elizondo became the largest sheep operator on the Western Slope, owning the Colorado-Utah Livestock Company, the Emmett Elizondo Company, and the Curecanti Sheep Company, as well as being part owner and director of the Fruita Bank. He wintered his flocks near Cisco, Utah, and trailed them east of Montrose toward Cimarron and then up onto national forest land toward Lake City. He eventually owned 30,000 acres of deeded land, but he began in 1922 with 2,490 sheep on a cash lease.

He came to America from Sumbilla, Spain. "If I had the money in my pocket to repay my father for my return passage to Spain, with some cash to keep for myself, I would have gone home," Elizondo explained, "but I didn't have that much money and so I couldn't quit. I have carried that same 'can't quit' notion all my life. At first I was too young to quit or owed much money, and later I had too much at stake to stop."[38]

Like Mormon sheepmen from Utah who had run afoul of Ferry Carpenter with their 106-mile-long sheep driveway, 10 years later Emmett Elizondo, Henry Revoir, and others tried the same tactic with a proposed stock driveway along the Book Cliffs. The *Moab (UT) Times-Independent* was not amused, labeling the Basques "foreign sheepmen" and editorializing:

> If the request of the foreign sheepmen is granted, a vast area of land consisting of 65,000 acres and including the cream of the winter grazing land between the Colorado state line and the Green River, would be permanently withdrawn from entry to homesteaders, and would in fact, constitute a reserved area for foreign herds of sheep. Instead

of being a stock driveway, the withdrawn area would simply be the wintering grounds for the sheep of non-residents, and the local homesteader and stockman would be put out of business. Furthermore, all possibilities of settling the country would be at an end, since none of the area withdrawn could ever be filed on by homesteaders, and since the land applied for includes all that could possibly be of value for agricultural or stock-raising purposes.[39]

The driveway proposal failed. So instead, one of the sheepmen, Henry Revoir, purchased a ranch on the Colorado River, which is now part of the Hidden Owl Ranch northeast of Moab, Utah. Without doubt, sheep made money. Even a Jewish immigrant, a shoe cobbler from Russia, could make dollars on woollies. When Old "Izzie," or Isadore Bolten, went to borrow money to purchase livestock, he was advised to try sheep. Bolten, who lived near Hayden, Colorado, asked, "Sheep in a cattle country?"

A penniless Russian Jew who knew how to make shoes, Isadore Bolten came to northwestern Colorado to homestead and became one of the wealthiest sheep and cattlemen in the Rockies. Here he helps the sons of homesteaders learn to cobble shoes at a Routt County country school. Photograph courtesy of Dorothy Wickenden, from her book *Nothing Daunted*.

"Folks can't kill you for it—but they might try," his financial adviser warned. Later Bolten said, "Right there, if I had any friends I lost them all overnight." Izzie took his advice but almost froze to death one night as he lit sagebrush fires to keep coyotes from his ewes. He stayed alive by tramping a slow circle deeper and deeper into the falling snow. For months he lived on mutton, beans, and rice. He did not shave, bathe, or go to town. Instead he watched his sheep.

Just as Regas Halandras had had to defend against rowdy cowboys in 1921, in 1922 in Routt County, cowboys set fire to one of Bolten's sheep wagons and shot and clubbed his sheep to death with wooden wagon spokes. Eventually Isadore would come to own the ranch that had forced him to pay for food and lodging when he was a broke, itinerant homesteader. His 160-acre homestead in the steep-sloped "rim-rock country" north of the verdant Yampa River valley grew into a sprawling 400,000-acre ranch and multimillion-dollar livestock empire that stretched from Routt County, Colorado, into Carbon County, Wyoming, and included feeding lambs on Kansas wheat fields. He was the first woolgrower to graze sheep near Hayden.[40]

Other northwestern Colorado sheepmen included Dean Visintainer, Ralph Pitchforth, and Joe Livingston. Lou Wyman's father homesteaded on Milk Creek at the Milk Creek Battle Site of 1879. Wyman explains, "Sheep were more profitable and utilized rougher country better." He puns, "There was quite a lot of cowboy sentiment in Rio Blanco County. We had real dyed in the wool cowmen."[41]

In the early decades, sheepmen trailed their flocks from low-level BLM desert land up into the high country. Their strategy involved purchasing acreage every seven miles or so where sheep would need to bed down for the night. The Wyman family ran 5,000 head of sheep with a BLM permit and four permits on the White River National Forest. Their sheep trailed 50 miles to winter range, where they grazed sagebrush, and in only one year in five or ten did the animals need additional winter feed. Lou remembers hiring herders from northern New Mexican villages and some from Coyote, New Mexico. To help them take pride in having the best lambs, he would buy a new Stetson hat for the herder with the fattest lamb crop.

During conflicts between cattlemen and sheepmen, guns were often used, but so were lawyers. In 1923 a federal grand jury in Salt Lake City indicted six Book Cliffs cattlemen, including Albert Turner, Oscar Turner, and range foreman Charles Glass, for challenging the movement of sheep.

The *Moab (UT) Times-Independent* stated, "The charge against the stockmen—that of conspiring to violate the United States statute act of February 25, 1885—is the first case of alleged obstruction of the free passage over or through public lands of the United States to be brought to trial in the Utah district." The federal grand jury charged the cattlemen "to have entered into a conspiracy to prevent the sheep of Joseph L. Taylor from being ranged in the Willow Creek country."[42] And if guns and lawyers didn't work, there was always poison.

In one of the last sheep-cattle conflicts on the Western Slope, in 1926 Mormon Hans Ottoson from Utah brought sheep into Colorado onto the 2,500 acres he owned, known as Willow Springs, on Strawberry Creek in Rio Blanco County. Shearing the sheep at Watson, Utah, herders arrived with the flock at Willow Springs about May 1. His permit for the White River National Forest began July 1. He needed a month of grass and water at a lower elevation. Taking his flocks through Meeker, Ottoson was harassed by locals driving their cars through the bleating sheep. Finally he found pasture on a short-term lease.

As the sheep headed toward the high country, locals set out poisoned salt along the path near the mouth of Coal Creek where it could not be seen from the road. Ottoson, five other men, and his son realized something was wrong and tried to rush the flock down the road, but 34 sheep died immediately from the poison. Others died over the next two weeks, for a loss of 200 head. The flocks still made money, though, and a year later Ottoson bought the Nine Mile Ranch, one of the oldest cattle ranches on the White River, for back taxes.[43]

Something had to be done about the constant conflicts between sheepmen and cattlemen on the public domain. The cattle and sheep wars resulted in a devastation few westerners chose to admit. Forest Service lands were now regulated by permit, but not the unclaimed lower lands of sagebrush. Loose soil caused by overgrazing, with no vegetation to hold it during hard rains, was subject to sheet erosion, and entire hillsides slumped into gullies and became deep arroyos.

A young forester who had grown up on the Iowa prairies began to openly question custom and culture in the American West. He had seen that transition between small farms and industrial agriculture, that shift between horse-drawn plows and mechanical tractors, and he wanted wild places with sounds of bugling elk and sandhill cranes, not gasoline engines. Ultimately, he would come to define the modern concept of ecology.

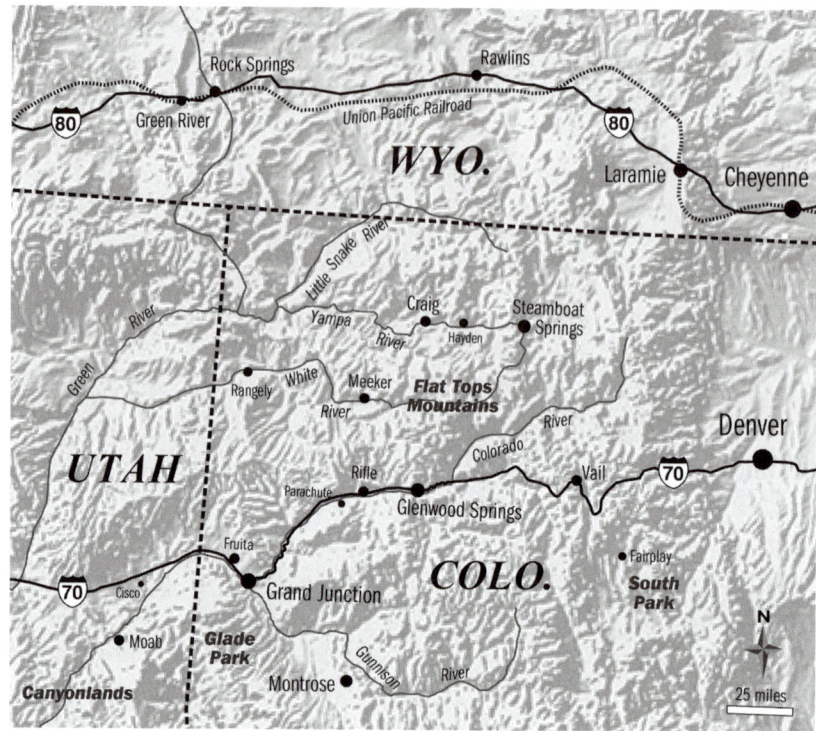

This map shows the primary area for grazing sheep on Colorado's Western Slope. Sheepherders trailed in woollies south from Wyoming and east from Utah. Sheep wintered in the Red Desert of Wyoming and the Utah canyonlands and flats near the Colorado and Green Rivers. Map by Robert Garcia.

Aldo Leopold loved to fish and hunt. He came west to Arizona before statehood as one of the recent graduates of the Yale School of Forestry, which was endowed by Gifford Pinchot's parents. Leopold had spent his early years as a sportsman in the Midwest, and he had seen some of the best natural areas for waterfowl hunting diked and drained for cornfields. He wanted unspoiled landscapes with maximum numbers of wild game and thought a career in the new US Forest Service would give him the outdoor opportunities he sought. His timing could not have been better.

Leopold arrived in the West just as the frontier was ending and the federal government, through the US Forest Service, was extending its reach and regulations. He enjoyed time on horseback, carrying a rifle in a scabbard, smoking aromatic pipe tobacco, and "cruising" timber. He looked like a "dude," and perhaps he was, but almost no one in the first decades of the twentieth century asked harder questions about the land or had a better understanding of what we now call ecological processes. "Ecology" and "environment" were not yet words in anyone's vocabulary. The Forest Service mantra was efficiency on the ground, grazing rules, and "getting out the cut" of timber for local sawmills.

Leopold questioned what he was seeing and he challenged priorities for federal spending. As momentum built across the West to do something with the wide-open public domain where cattlemen and sheepmen fought for grazing supremacy, Leopold worried about the land itself. He would join a rising chorus of fledgling federal employees concerned about the West's timber, grass, and watersheds. He focused on grass, soil, and erosion, and few stockmen wanted to hear his conclusions.

In 1922, speaking at the New Mexico Association for Science, Leopold read a professional paper that contained all the sincerity, wit, and wisdom that would mark his later writings. The breadth of his subject, his sharp analysis, and his sweep of time and place would herald a major new voice in the American conservation movement.

In his lifetime he would come to straddle that divide between conservation, the greatest good for the greatest number for the longest time, and the idea of the environment and ecology having values separate from human needs. An American spokesman for land and landscape was finding his own voice, and just as President Theodore Roosevelt and Gifford Pinchot had established millions of acres of national forests, Leopold would leave his own mark on public land. He started with gullies.

"By and large, whether or not our pioneering has been efficient, it has certainly been successful. But in certain semiarid regions like the Southwest, it seems not only to have been inefficient, but there is a doubt whether we are actually creating more useful land with the labor of our hands than we are unintentionally destroying with the trampling of our feet," wrote Leopold. He compared the waste of overgrazing and soil erosion to the federal mandate under the 1902 Reclamation Act to build dams and "reclaim" western land for farms and agriculture. "If we saw a settler perspiring profusely to put a new field under irrigation while a flood was eating away his older field for a lack of a few protective works, we should call that settler a fool. Yet that is exactly what we, as pioneers, are doing," he explained.[44]

Leopold knew that western ranchers grazed watercourses and bottomlands. With fewer plants to hold the soil, overgrazing caused floods. He vividly explained scars and gouges "eating into the very base of the hills . . . draining the natural *cienegas* and haymeadows and changing the grasses to a less-resistant forage type."[45] He bluntly wrote that overgrazing caused erosion, lowered water tables, and deepened channels so that water could not be diverted into ditches to irrigate fields.

He wrote about the problem of gully control on the open range and knew from experience that "many ranges are being so cut up by gullies as to drain and dry the soil and change or reduce the value of the grass or prevent access to the grass by stock, or access to the stock by range riders." Using Spanish terms, Leopold wrote, "Many a fine glade, park, *valle* or *cañada* has a gully gradually eating its whole length." He understood "the outstanding abuse that cries for remedy—namely the competitive overgrazing of the unreserved public domain." And he concluded, "Every year of delay further deteriorates the range, unstabilizes the stock industry, washes away the land, and dumps uncounted tons of silt into the irrigation reservoirs of the West. As always, the public pays."[46]

Just as Leopold understood the ecological disaster of overgrazing, he also came to realize the value of leaving landscapes alone. In eastern Rio Blanco County at Trappers Lake in 1919, US Forest Service landscape architect Arthur Carhart spent the summer surveying the lake for small lots to be leased for cabin sites. But after a summer of trout fishing and hiking, he suggested to his forest supervisor that the lakeshore be allowed to stay as it was, thus beginning the wilderness idea on federal lands.

Carhart presented his plan in the regional office of the US Forest Service in Denver with Leopold in attendance. The young forester instantly agreed with Carhart.

Two years after Leopold's speech on erosion, in 1924 he successfully campaigned for the Gila Wilderness to be set aside within the Gila National Forest in southwestern New Mexico. He wanted "a continuous stretch of country preserved in its natural state, open to lawful hunting and fishing, big enough to absorb a two weeks' pack trip, and kept devoid of roads, artificial trails, cottages, or other works of man."[47] A decade before passage of the Taylor Grazing Act, a new recreational value was emerging for use of American public lands.

In the years to come, the wilderness idea would have a huge impact on the sheep industry because inevitably the millions of acres of land that would be protected as wilderness were also high-altitude sheep pastures.

Two very different concepts would collide: leaving landscapes alone for hikers, hunters, and fishermen; and preserving pastures for woollies that had always grazed the high country above timberline. Those battles would occur later. In the 1920s the clamor was to do something about the lower-level public domain.

What was at stake were nearly 180 million acres and stopping "injury to public lands."[48] "Tramp sheepmen do much to keep the sheep-raising industry from taking its proper place as a stabilized industry," stated the US Tariff Commission in 1921 in a report titled *The Wool-Growing Industry*. "Numerous Americans operate in this manner, but as a rule tramp sheepmen are aliens . . . crowding in wherever they can find feed. The aliens usually begin as herders, and when they have a little money saved up get someone else, usually another alien, to act as financial partners, and together they buy a band of sheep," which they graze "by trespassing on the range of bona fide stockmen and the small settlers."[49]

A system had to be devised to rein in the itinerant herders, most of whom were Basques who owned no land, paid no taxes, and simply used and abused the public domain by allowing their ever-increasing sheep herds to eat forage down to dust. Basques traveled the West, "moving ceaselessly about the public lands" with "no possessions other than a pack animal, gear, dogs, and a sheep band," states Basque expert William A. Douglass. He adds, "Thus, in a negative sense Basques may be regarded as key architects of the land-use policies on the public domain of the American West," because the new federal law sought "exclusion of the itinerants."[50]

As Aldo Leopold argued, part of the goal for regulating the public domain would be to "stabilize the range industry," to quit the random killing among herders and cowboys, and to somehow bring peace to the stockmen. This was a tall order with social, economic, and ecological consequences.

"The history of the range country [has been] swift ruin for thirty or forty years, with a resulting wreck that it will require a century of hard work, perseverance, and self-control to save," wrote Ray Stannard Baker in "The Tragedy of the Range" for *Century Magazine*.[51] "A man might own a hundred thousand cattle and not an acre of land, though he claimed 'range rights' to fifty thousand acres, and enforced those rights with blood and iron," Baker wrote.

He explained grassland transitions. "When the rich grasses began to give out, the black, white, and crowfoot gramas, the curly mesquit[e], the sedges, and the needle-grasses, which were wonderful cattle-food, the rangers conceived the idea of introducing more sheep, knowing that sheep will thrive where cattle starve." He added, "So it happened that vast flocks appeared on the range, burning across it like so much live fire, the sheep eating out the vegetation to its very roots."[52]

Like Leopold, Baker equated overgrazing with erosion. The journalist wrote, "A wash often began with a single hillside cow-trail, down which trickled in rainy weather a tiny stream of water. With the next flood the trail became a narrow ravine; with the next it was twenty feet deep and gashing the country for miles, and spreading sand and boulders over acres of good grass country."[53]

"Each man looked upon the range forage as something he must grab before anyone else could reach it. Hence the grasses were given no chance to grow," wrote Will C. Barnes in *The Story of the Range*, published by the US Department of Agriculture in 1926. "The sheepman was much more able to cope with the elements than was the cattleman. He had his herd under his eye at all times, and could move it to better feed before the animals became too weak to travel."[54] Referring to intense conflict between cattlemen and sheepmen, Barnes concluded:

> This reckless competition could not have but one end. The mountains were turned into dust heaps; the old forage plants were gnawed to the roots and so weakened that they failed to grow. Worthless weeds and annuals took their place. The willows along the streams and meadows were eaten down to walking sticks. The meadows, stripped of their green covering, dried out. The forage cover gone, the freshets tore through the meadows leaving great gashes in the sod and soil, which cut deeper and deeper draining the land.[55]

Ignoring this ecological disaster and bowing to the demands of cattlemen and sheepmen, the Republican administration of Herbert Hoover had a single idea—give the public domain back to the western states and let them administer or sell it. A congressional committee considered the idea, and, "its labors completed, the commission proposed that the remaining vacant, unreserved, unappropriated public lands be given to the states, with any minerals present reserved to the federal government."[56] But knowing of the rangeland desolation and strapped for cash after the stock market collapsed in 1929, western governors refused Hoover's 1930 offer. As the nation spiraled toward the Great Depression, voting patterns changed. Republicans lost sway even in conservative western states. Something had to be done to fix the economy, to provide jobs for hungry Americans, to repair damaged lands.

As Franklin Delano Roosevelt assumed the presidency, drought and the Dust Bowl brought conservation issues to the forefront. A Colorado congressman would finally forward legislation to solve rangeland conflicts, heal sorely abused grasslands, and preserve the public domain by largely preventing additional homesteading. Congressman Edward T. Taylor of Glenwood Springs would have a lasting impact on the West with his legislation, but it was Ferry Carpenter, a rock-ribbed Republican, who would become the first director of the Grazing Service and who would make it work by creating grazing districts across the western states.

Carpenter would require that leasing public land meant that ranchers had to have "commensurability," or adjacent private range. That would be the end of the tramp Basque sheepmen, who would either purchase private property to maintain their sheep operations, or sell out and return to the Old Country. For his troubles, Ferry's boss, crusty Secretary of the Interior Harold Ickes, would twice try to fire him. The third time he succeeded.

The momentous federal Taylor Grazing Act had its origins at the state level with discussions in the homes of ranchers on Piceance Creek in Rio Blanco County. In 1928 Claude Harp Rees became state senator from Rifle and, with Walter Oldland, worked on drafts of a grazing bill to segregate cattle and sheep range in Colorado. Rees's son Claude Humbert Rees wrote, "My dad and Rube Oldland had experienced the anarchy that increased each year in the way stockmen used the grass on public lands. They had seen the incursion made by the flocks of nomadic sheep men without any stake in the community or regard for the welfare of the range, flocks that with their tens of thousands of hooves threatened the destruction of the already overused grasslands."[57] Despite strong opposition from sheepmen, the two ranchers got the bill through the Colorado house and senate. The Colorado Supreme Court upheld the state law on March 19, 1929, but states cannot regulate federal lands, and the Colorado law was headed to the US

Supreme Court. Key ideas in the bill included priorities based on use, grass and vegetation allocated for wildlife, and conservation of the range.[58]

Simultaneously, Dan Colton, congressman from Vernal, Utah, on the House Committee on Public Lands, tried to pass similar legislation. Concepts in both bills would be incorporated into the Taylor Grazing Act, successfully shepherded through Congress (pun intended) by Congressman Edward T. Taylor from Glenwood Springs. Taylor had vehemently opposed the Pinchot-Roosevelt conservation crusade, but he came to understand the value of US Forest Service grazing regulations. As a Colorado district judge in the 1880s, Taylor had ruled on eight murder cases in just one court term, "nearly all a result of conflict between cowmen and woolgrowers."[59] Congressman Taylor defended his bill by stating:

> There are thousands of small ranchers, local settlers, on all the little creeks, and those nomadic herds, paying little or no taxes and roaming around carrying on their grazing operations unrestrained, eating out the forage right up to the very gardens and doors of the local settlers. . . . The actual residents and taxpayers help to maintain the country . . . but as to the very large sheep men who send out a Basque or Greek or some other nonresident with a band of sheep as a shepherd, those men go out with a large band of sheep and they roam all over the country, they are not especially concerned about the principle of conservation. They are instructed by the owner of the sheep to take care of the flock for that particular season, and therefore are not interested in preserving the range.[60]

The preamble to Taylor's law proclaimed that it was time to "stop injury to the public grazing lands by preventing overgrazing and soil deterioration; to provide for their orderly use, improvement, and development; to stabilize the livestock industry dependent upon the public range; and for other purposes."[61]

It was up to Ferry Carpenter to make the new law work on 400 million acres of public land. In the beginning, no one even knew where the federal domain was or how much public rangeland existed. Ferry had his hands full, but he began with a simple premise—ranchers understood their local range, would respect their neighbors, and should have authority over federal lands they knew well. His primary concept was to establish grazing districts with local grazing boards. Now all he had to do was to get cattlemen

Two years before passage of the Taylor Grazing Act, Colorado sheepmen met in Montrose for their annual July meeting. Without a building large enough to accommodate the sheepmen and their wives, they met on a downtown street for an evening of eating, drinking, and dancing. P042. Photo from the Walker Art Studio Collection, courtesy of the Center of Southwest Studies, Fort Lewis College, Durango, Colorado.

and sheepmen across the West to sit down at the same table. That had never happened before.

Ed Taylor wanted Farrington Carpenter to administer the new Grazing Office. Ferry said, "It wasn't a very hot job, because I knew the West didn't want it."[62] But Carpenter, a Republican in FDR's administration, received the appointment and began to hold meetings with stockmen across the West. The first one was September 17, 1934, in Grand Junction, and the cattlemen openly asked him whether sheepmen had bought him off. He replied, "Maybe they have. You will have to watch and see what I do, but I think you cowboys will get a square deal."[63] Close to 900 stock growers showed up at the Lincoln Park Auditorium.

"I have a big map of the State of Colorado here," said Ferry. "I want you fellows to elect three sheepmen and three cowboys and come on up here and take this piece of chalk and mark off where these districts should be.

If there is a deep river you can't cross in your stock migrations, mark it as a boundary for your district. If there is a high mountain you can't get over, mark it as a boundary for a district." Those simple instructions worked. At the next meeting in Rifle, the sheepmen and cattlemen stayed in separate hotels. Ferry solved that problem by having a banquet at the Winchester Hotel. He "fixed up place cards and put them on the table. And I sat a woolgrower and a cowboy and a woolgrower and a cowboy, all the way around. They got in there and looked at that and kind of grinned and sat down."[64]

Across the West, the Harvard-trained attorney shuffled his feet, took off his cowboy hat, ate brisket and beans or lamb and biscuits, and got stockmen together. But Carpenter was not building the top-down federal agency that bureaucrats liked. In Arizona, Ferry got ready for a range meeting only to receive a telegram telling him to immediately return to Washington, DC. When he did so, Secretary of the Interior Ickes lit into him. "You have gone just as far in this as you can go. You are selling this out to the stockmen. They are a bunch of brigands and we are not going to have them take it over. We thought you had some honesty in you when we hired you," Ickes railed. "You are fired!"

Carpenter received a copy of the charges and later wrote a 42-page letter in response. Ickes calmed down. Ferry resumed his work and continued to make key decisions like the concept that five sheep equaled one cow for grazing purposes. Generally, each grazing district was organized under its own local customs, but what Carpenter accomplished irritated Ickes. Ferry had figured out how to manage 140 million acres with only 17 federal men borrowed from the US Geological Survey to try to find where the West was. "It must be said that Carpenter performed minor miracles of district formation. It was no easy task to determine boundaries for areas that ran to several million acres each," admitted conservationist William Voigt.[65]

Carpenter believed in advisory boards and in a spare, bare-bones administration. Given a $140,000 budget, he amazingly returned $60,000 to the federal treasury. His boss, the secretary of the interior, became livid. Ickes demanded federal, not local, control. The third time he fired Ferry, it stuck.

After a tumultuous five years, in 1939 the former director of the Grazing Service drove home to his Hereford cattle ranch near Hayden. What he had accomplished established critical legal precedent. Unlike the forestlands, lower-level sagebrush lands would have grazing districts and advisory boards. Carpenter had accomplished what needed to be done.

In *Public Grazing Lands*, William Voigt, in discussing cattlemen and sheepmen, wrote, "In the end, each would win something. The cowmen would achieve federal control and prior rights; the sheepmen could claim that district boards provided home rule on the range."[66] But even as half a century of rangeland squabbles edged toward a solution, the Great Depression and critically low farm prices ruined ranchers and displaced thousands of farmers. From small northern New Mexican villages, young men traveled north desperately seeking work. Soon they would spend their lives "following the sheeps."

FIFTH SHEEPSCAPE

*Dead Mule on a Cabin Porch
—Lone Mesa State Park and a Sacred
Penitente Calvario*

The pickup spun its tires and we couldn't get up the steep grade even in four-wheel drive. Not enough weight in the back. Then we dropped the left front tire into a ditch and were really in trouble. Finally, with me standing in the pickup bed and jumping up and down we were able to back up and drive down the hill, but we failed to reach the top of Lone Mesa to study the aspen arborglyphs. We'd have to return another day, which we did, this time with park manager Scott Elder.

Purchased from four families with Great Outdoors Colorado dollars in 1999 for about $6 million, Lone Mesa State Park is one of Colorado's most remote state parks. Though open for limited hunting, the 11,760-acre park 23 miles north of Dolores is still in the planning stages for additional visitor usage. In 1924 Clara Bow starred in a silent film set at the park with the steamy title *The Scarlet West*. From low-lying brush to subalpine vegetation 3,000 feet above, the park has several ecosystems and two endangered plants, the Lone Mesa snakeweed and the Mancos shale packera, found nowhere else in the world. Unlike 80 percent of Colorado's state parks, Lone Mesa has no lakes. Instead, it has a rich ranching history and even appears on an early 1881 Colorado map.

Grazed for decades by sheep and later by cattle, the park includes old cabins once used by the Adams, Morrison, and Redd families. A dedicated team of volunteers located carved aspen trees. I toured the park with two of those volunteers, Roger and Joyce Lawrence, who not only found carved trees at different elevations, but also used census records to research the family names and hometowns of the herders. "Anything you can learn about their lives is interesting," Joyce says. Volunteers found a large number of glyphs carved between 1930 and 1965.[1]

Joyce has a definitive list of names and dates from each stand of aspen. Some are Hispano herders, but others are from local ranch families that ran cattle and carved their names and cattle brands onto aspen trees. "Over the years we came to the conclusion that the best carvings were where the herders were camping," explains Roger. "Sometimes we found Spanish clear around the tree. We tried to read it but weren't sure what they were saying."

On our second attempt, we drove to the top of Lone Mesa and the end of the road. At a nearby pond I flushed a dusky grouse as I walked among a stand of aspen with the carved names of Manuel Aragon, Dan Lucero, Liz Toser, and former government trapper Melvin Forest, who once caught bears, beavers, and coyotes. His widow lived long enough for Colorado Parks and Wildlife to acquire the property and reintroduce three family groups of beavers. She appreciated the invitation to be in attendance when wildlife officers released the beavers.

Throughout the park are the carved names Aguilar, Chavez, Maestas, Garcia, Madrid, Gallegos, Trujillo, Suaso, Martinez, Jaramillo, Talamante, Romero, and Vallejos. One herder signed his name as "Navajo Kid from aZ." They came from Albuquerque, Bernalillo, Chama, Coyote, Cebolla, Española, Lumberton, Park View, and Gallina, New Mexico, as well as Dolores, Durango, Mancos, Cortez, and Yellow Jacket, Colorado. Every chance she could, Joyce Lawrence tried to match a herder's name, the date he signed, and census records for his home. She found family stories, obituaries, newspaper accounts, and one financial success story from the 1960s.

"A sheepherder and his family now operate the only grocery store in Cañones, a remote village in Rio Arriba County," reported the *Albuquerque Journal* on February 25, 1966, in a story headlined "Opportunity Loans Help the 'Forgotten.'" Emiliano Aragon, 59 years old and the father of three children, earned about $1,000 per year following sheep in Utah and Colorado before receiving a $2,000 loan to convert the front of his home into the only grocery store in town. He qualified for the loan in part because his daughter had an aptitude for business in high school and could help manage the store. The first year he repaid $87.64.[2]

Joyce interviewed Tony Gallegos, who explained which families ran sheep at Lone Mesa and which herders worked for them. Gallegos described moving the sheep to new feed every 10–15 days, working them across the plateau for summer range, and putting bucks in with ewes on winter range so that lambs arrived about five months later. "I was a teenager and my job was to go ahead of the herders to set up the camps. I had four mules and packed things in boxes hung from the mules' pack saddles. I took the tent, the herders' beds, groceries, and supplies to where the sheep would stay the night," he said. "I would set up camp, build a fire, and make a pot of coffee, so when the herders got there they could just get off their horses and eat. We would laze around until time to repack and move to the next camp."

He also told the story of a dead mule on the Redd cabin porch. Government trapper Melvin Forest lost a mule when winter was coming on and had to leave it. Tony found it. "When I got there next summer the mule had died on the porch of the cabin and was laying right in front of the door, all smelling. I had to drag it out of the way to get in the cabin and then wash down the porch. When the herders got there they asked me why the porch was all wet. I said because I had to clean up after a damned dead mule."[3]

Herders moved sheep from southeastern Utah into southwestern Colorado for summer range. Redd family members, especially "Jap" Jasper and Joe Redd, and Grant and Reed Bayles from Blanding, Utah, all hired New Mexican herders. Because herders worked alone, accidents could be serious. "While sheepherding, Joe Vallejos broke his leg real bad," wrote Larry Quintana for a Dolores High School English assignment. "It was on a rainy day when Joe heard the sheep crying. Something was bothering them, so Joe went to check on them. It was a steep hill where he met the problem—a fierce, mean bear. It was large and scared the horse."

"The horse reared and threw Joe, and when he fell, he hit a tree with his leg and began to roll down the hill. The bear took off running. The horse was down at the bottom of the hill, and Joe had to get on him. It was hard, for he was in a lot of pain. But he got on, and had to ride the horse for eight miles to Blackmer's camp, where he got help."[4]

Sheep are gone now from Lone Mesa State Park, which borders both BLM and US Forest land. Grasses have recovered. Flocks of wild turkeys peck for insects in the thick meadows. "Park staff have been great stewards of the land. It was heavily, heavily grazed, but now it is lush. They've even found a flower here that grows nowhere else," explains Roger, who volunteers to check in hunters at dawn and has seen 300 elk crossing the park. Hunting remains minimal, with only 25 hunters allowed per season. Recreation plans for Lone Mesa are incomplete. Some staff would prefer it to remain an undeveloped state park; others know that additional roads and visitors are in the future.

For now, park manager Scott Elder works to preserve Lone Mesa's natural and cultural resources, including counseling hunters in "leave no trace" ethics. That means not carving on aspens even though the park has hundreds of historical carvings. "Among this older generation of aspen trees, they're just dying off," Scott explains. "Those stands are not recruiting new sprouts. In many areas of Dolores and La Plata Counties there just aren't new trees among aspen stands."[5]

"We've lost a lot of trees in the ten years since we worked on the arborglyph surveys. They're down and gone," sighs Joyce Lawrence. "I'm glad we did the history when we did."

As we finished our second field trip and drove off the mesa, a red-tailed hawk wheeled silently above us. Colorado Parks and Wildlife is doing an excellent job of restoring and managing Lone Mesa, but the herder history disappears with each passing season.

Of the many Hispano herders from northern New Mexico who worked for the Redd family of Utah, a few were Penitentes, or members of La Fraternidad Piadosa de Nuestro Padre Jesus Nazareno (The Pious Fraternity of Our Father Jesus the Nazarene). *Hermanos* brought their faith with them as they trailed borregas across Utah and Colorado. Redd family descendants sold a portion of their vast landholdings to create Lone Mesa State Park. North of the park, descendants of the Penitente herder families still revere a large wooden cross where their ancestors worshipped, far from their village chapels, or *moradas*, in New Mexico.

Members of the Montaño family pose at the wooden cross erected in the San Juan Mountains by their family members, who were sheepherders and devout Penitentes who needed to worship weekly even though they were far from their local chapels. Photo includes, left to right, Sylvia Montaño Trujillo, Lilian Montaño Bayless, and Pete Montaño. Pete notes, "This was the first time two of my sisters had been up to the calvario. Many times they were overcome by emotion being there with their ancestors." Photo from 2014, courtesy of Pete Montaño.

Located on a scree field of sharp stones between two high-country pastures on national forest land, a cross on an aspen tree represents centuries of Hispano herding across the Southwest and the unique religious devotions of Penitentes, who formed brotherhoods of faith and community in remote villages without churches and priests. Penitentes were members of a lay brotherhood that would lead worship services, offer baptisms, marry couples, bless their children, and bury the dead. Of course, the Penitentes preferred that ordained priests perform these sacred rites, but in their absence the Brothers served the devoted.

"Brotherhood observances were thus not only rituals of transformation for religious individuals, they were also a reconfirmation of the original interpersonal ties which made continued existence possible and meaningful. Ideally and actually, the Brothers of Our Father Jesus were truly significant, and they have much to teach us today," wrote Marta Weigle in *Brothers of Light, Brothers of Blood*.[6]

Though much has been written about the lay brotherhood and their processions, which "wove a kind of sacred network around the community,"[7] almost no scholarship addresses the connections between Penitentes who were herders and how they carried on their devotions far from home. Penitentes may have carved saints, or *santos*, and painted scenes on *retablos*, or wooden plaques, but their true spirituality revolved around the cross as a symbol of Christ's sacrifice, death, and resurrection.

"It is this material cross, grown far beyond the symbolic, which was behind it all. Crude wooden forms of it would soon be dotting the landscape, to the wonder of uncomprehending strangers centuries later," explained Fray Angelico Chavez in *My Penitente Land*. He wrote that Christian ideals came from Spain and the Iberian Peninsula to New Mexico. "The idea of intense suffering which the cross represented would ever afterward continue simmering here in the racial blood which those first settlers were bringing into a landscape so much like the one that had nourished it for ages. It is a long story of blood in connection with landscape—a shepherd blood . . . upon upland landscapes of severe bright colors, crystal skies, and sparse rains."[8]

Though raised in the New Mexican highlands, male members of the Montaño family from Canjilon "followed the sheeps" and spent their summers in Colorado's high country of lush grasses in mountain meadows, tall fir and pine trees, and aspens round and smooth to the touch. They brought their intense faith with them and in the 1930s, in the depths of the Great Depression, erected a large wooden cross. Though the letters are almost gone now, the Spanish words remain—*Nuestro salvador de las animas*—"Our savior of the souls," or possibly "Our savior of our hope." The cross may also have had a medallion on it, but that is hard to determine.

Erected on a hill, the cross is a sacred *calvario*, representing other calvarios and crosses found across the New Mexican landscape but seen only rarely in Colorado's high country. Just as Jesus died on the hill of Calvary, so Penitentes, deep in their devotions, ascend to local calvarios at Easter and other occasions to offer their prayers and to reflect on their blessings and obligations.

In July 2017, Montaño family members came together from four different states for a family reunion in the San Juan Mountains. In a deeply moving religious pilgrimage in honor of their Penitente sheepherder ancestors, they erected a *calvario*, a cedar cross carved by Pete Montaño and blessed by a local Catholic priest. For these descendants of New Mexican sheepherders, the cross symbolizes their faith and their future. Author photo.

Near this southern Colorado calvario, a large stone monument just downslope symbolizes other, more secular herding traditions.

Pete Anthony Montaño had forgotten the family stories, but as a resident of Cortez, Colorado, who liked to visit the national forest, he returned to the sheep camps of his grandfather and uncles. As he climbed the mountains and ran his fingers over the numerous aspen carvings bearing the names of his forefathers, he remembered the stories of good times in sheep camp, the male bonding, the twilight smell of burning wood, coffee boiling, mutton sizzling in a frying pan, and the incessant bleating of sheep. Pete recalled his father, Pete Esteban Montaño, being told to watch the sheep as his grandfather Pedro Juan Montaño and others ascended the slope toward the cross. As Penitentes they walked barefoot over the sharp stones of the scree field below the calvario, heads bent in prayer.

The men repeatedly used trails through the aspens. There they left the distinctive Penitente symbol on quakies—a simple cross surrounded by an ovoid or egg-shaped circle like a shadow box. These crosses were carved

Religious iconography carved on aspens by sheepherders is rare. This image of a cross within a shadow-box design told other herders that a Penitente herder had been there. It was a sign of the Brotherhood. Photographed on state land in Park County, Colorado. Author photo.

directly and delicately with the tip of a knife, but now they are larger and raised like a scar after all these generations. Other trails and sheep driveways like the Pine-Piedra have virtually no religious symbols, but in the Uncompahgre National Forest and along the Groundhog Stock Driveway there are deliberate religious motifs and dozens of signatures by herders named Salazar, Chacon, Trujillo, Maestas, and Montaño.

Now, decades later, Pete Anthony Montaño and his sister Peggy want the entire extended family to camp in the grasses along the creek bed, to survey the aging, peeling aspen carvings, to record and document the cross, and to bring new family traditions to a historical sacred site on public land. "When we first found this place we didn't want to tell anyone, but now we know more. It's a religious site for us and we want it documented and protected," states Peggy. Pete concurs. "It's an incredibly rich family history area."[9]

"There is deep meaning here for our cultural history. It very much reflects an ongoing, living, cultural tradition," notes Pete's sister Shirley Rocha. The family had considered moving the deteriorating cross to a museum or federal repository but ultimately decided to leave it in place and add a new one, which might be six feet tall and three feet below grade, with a crosspiece four feet wide.

"There is a certain beauty to accepting the natural process rather than trying to control it somehow," Rocha adds. "Having a new cross for the generations to come holds the promise of grandchildren being as moved by this calvario as we are. I would like to see the old cross stay and a new

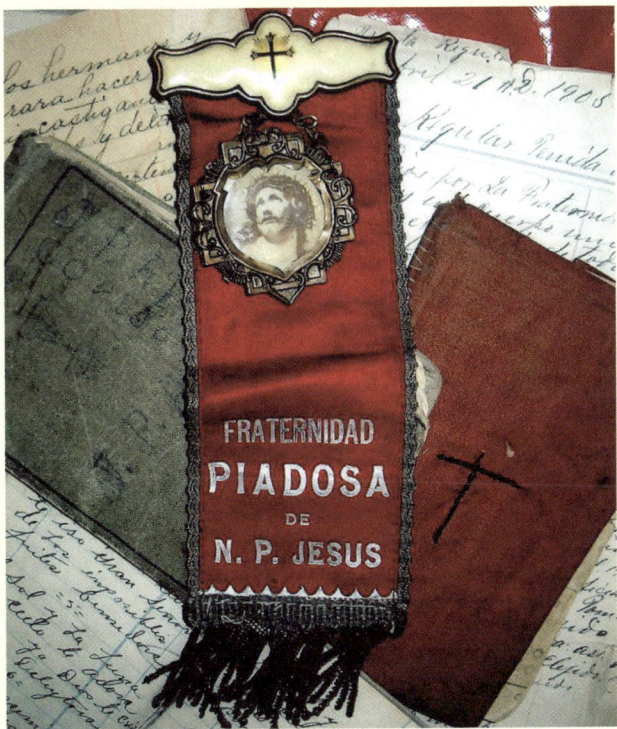

A historical ribbon for the Society for the Mutual Protection of United Workers, Sociedad Protección Mutua de Trabajadores Unidos (SPMDTU), is photographed atop journals from Penitente *moradas*, or chapels; *cuadernos*, handwritten prayer books; and *divisas*, or religious emblems from the late nineteenth century. Photo courtesy of Ruben Archuleta, from his book *Penitente Renaissance*.

cross placed nearby to continue the tradition of the calvario in the Montaño family."

Family members Sylvia and Lillian agree. "The cross should stay where it is. Let it stand as long as God wants it to. Nature will decide when that will be. If we want to erect some other symbolic cross I am okay with that as well."

The immediate goal is a thorough documentation of the Montaño Family Calvario Site by trained archaeologists and volunteers. Because all wood eventually succumbs to harsh winter weather, freezing and thawing, and the ravages of time, the family will erect a new cross. The documentation process will tie northern New Mexican Penitente families and their herding traditions to southern Colorado mountain landscapes.

Family members will come "to read the trees" and to run their fingers over carvings left decades ago by their ancestors, who in this special place will speak across time to their children and grandchildren and generations to come.

> *La vida del borreguero es muy triste.*
> The life of a sheepherder is very sad.
>
> —MELISENDRO MARTINEZ
> Canjilon, New Mexico

Chapter 5

Hispano Herders, Drought, and the Great Depression, 1934–1941

> Migration for wage work was ... an essential strategy for survival, a part of the village without which the village could not have continued to exist.
>
> —SARAH DEUTSCH
> *No Separate Refuge*

> The 1930s, which ushered in a decade of drought and depression throughout the American West, found the Hispanic villages of northern New Mexico in a state of near collapse. Long unable to sustain a self-sufficient agrarian lifestyle due to the loss of both farming and communal grazing lands, and the shift to a money economy, the native Hispanic population was inextricably tied to the national economy through its dependence on wage labor.
>
> —SUZANNE FORREST
> *The Preservation of the Village*

In a little-remembered chapter in Colorado history, in April 1936 Governor Edwin Johnson declared martial law and used the National Guard to illegally close Colorado's southern border. Of course, Anglos and those of Euro-American descent could pass through, but not "Mexicans," which was a catchall phrase for all Hispanics, whether they were from Mexico or were native New Mexicans whose families had lived in America for over 300 years. Many of those who were stopped at the border were young men seeking jobs as shepherds for Anglo sheepmen in a seasonal work pattern that had begun in the 1880s and by the 1930s had become vital to New Mexican village economies. There was simply no work at home.

In the 1920s, during the final competition for grass on the range, "cattle was king, sheep were 'woolie bitches' and lower than a sheepman was only a snake."[1] During the Roaring Twenties, agricultural prices began to slide. In 1929, with the Great Depression, they plummeted. Sheep purchased for $18 or $16 a head dropped in value to $2 a head. Lambs sold for 3½ cents a pound in 1930. Sheepmen and cattlemen barely survived. Racism escalated.

Because of the lack of employment statewide, the Colorado governor illegally declared martial law. In March 1935 he threatened to round up all Mexicans in Colorado, and two months later Governor Johnson placed local sheriffs on southern Colorado highways to prevent "Mexicans," or anyone who looked Hispanic, from entering the state. Yet Hispano herders, most from New Mexico, were desperately needed to herd flocks in Colorado's high country. Because of changing environmental conditions in New Mexican highlands, and age-old dominance by rich sheep families, or *ricos*, they had no opportunities in their homelands. Those young Hispanic men absolutely needed the work. Their wives and families depended on them to bring home cash after a summer and fall season. Few jobs existed in Abiquiu, Coyote, Tres Piedras, Las Truchas, Española, Lumberton, or Chama, New Mexico.

Arrested in Colorado, a dozen Spanish Americans, as they were then called, from the villages of Abiquiu and Peñasco, were removed from a train, forcibly placed in trucks, and dumped on the prairie on the Colorado–New Mexico state line. They traveled with passes from their sheep company employers. An Albuquerque newspaper reported that reactions to the deportation "ranged from tears to indignation." A successful regional community of Hispanic wage laborers sending funds home to northern New Mexican villages "had been cut in half." Anglo employers begged the governor to end the blockade because they needed the "Mexicans from New Mexico" during lambing season and for herding in mountain meadows and above timberline.[2]

The governor of New Mexico threatened to boycott goods from Colorado. His state comptroller, Juan Vigil, wrote to Colorado governor Johnson, arguing that "to prevent these citizens from coming into your state means they will be deprived of their only means of livelihood." Vigil's letter was prompted by urgent requests from Taos families who had always herded sheep.[3]

Not because he was concerned about racism or the legality of his actions, but because he was finally faced with the economic realities confronting ranchers, Governor Johnson relented. Hispano herders returned to the high country.

Across Colorado in aspen glades and national forests, Hispanic names and dates from the 1930s can be found. As the Depression deepened the men came north, "following the sheeps." On thousands of aspens they left their signatures and the names of their villages so that other herders would know they had been there. Greek and Basque herders, equally lonely, silently carved on the soft bark, too.

Greeks, Basques, and Hispanos herding for Anglo sheepmen had a common thread. They came from remote villages, left women at home, and "worked out" to provide desperately needed cash for small rural communities caught between an agricultural past and an industrializing future.

A prime difference, however, was the distance of those villages. Greeks and Basques herded thousands of miles from home. As World War I shattered national boundaries, leaving destruction and millions dead, there seemed less reason to return. Many herders did take ships back to the Old Country and used their American-earned savings to secure a better life. But others stayed.

They overcame the loneliness, the different desert landscapes, and began to see opportunities. Once established, Basque and Greek men sent for their wives, often young women they had known as girls growing up in their village or in an adjacent village on the other side of a mountain.

Thus, they reconstituted their home communities or at least created networks of kin in towns like Craig, Grand Junction, and Montrose. And when they began to succeed, they sent for more of their own, young men they could trust whose uncles they knew or whose brothers they had already hired. Slowly, tentatively, Basques and Greeks overcame prejudice and racism and integrated themselves into Colorado's rural communities, sought bank loans and citizenship, and even became bankers themselves.

For most Hispanics with unwavering ties to northern New Mexican villages, their goals never changed. They did not become Colorado sheepmen. They stayed as herders, migratory labor even over decades, bringing much-needed cash back to small villages and presenting their wives and mothers with dollars to purchase iron beds, sewing machines, glazed windows, oilcloth tablecloths, and most importantly, combination kitchen-range cooking and heating stoves. "The Anglo item most often listed in early accounts both by Anglos and Hispanics was the kitchen range," states Sarah Deutsch in *No Separate Refuge*. She describes a merchant in 1907 selling an

Hispano sheepherders from northern New Mexican villages worked away from home for months at a time but brought desperately needed cash home to their families. Herders frequently carved their names, dates, and villages on aspens so that other herders would know they had passed through. Map by Robert Garcia.

average of one stove a month in a Hispanic community of only 500 people. Male shepherds earned the money, but women "appear to be the spenders, or the ones for whom money is first chiefly spent."[4]

Why did some Basques and Greeks become landowners and sheepmen while the majority of Hispano herders did not? Because native New Mexicans retained their village ties. They may have spent years herding sheep in Colorado's high country, but home remained the New Mexican highlands, with one important exception—southern Colorado, where the landscape resembled that in New Mexico and young men could get a better start. The food, the terrain, the weather—all flowed seamlessly across arbitrary state lines.

"The houses of northern New Mexico blend into the land. Often they lie hidden behind or atop mesas, but even in plain sight, by their color and shape, they merge with their surroundings," wrote Deutsch. "Their plaster facades bear the same pastel earth and vegetable tones as the hills, and the dramatic rises and falls, light and shadows of New Mexico's arid north dwarf the one-story adobe structures."[5] Adobe architecture moved north into Colorado with Hispanic families.

From the broken canyon country along the Purgatoire River in southeastern Colorado to the arresting San Juan Mountains, Hispanic families, including the Archuleta, Montoya, Gomez, and Gallegos families, came north and brought sheep. For those families willing to uproot, Colorado offered lush grass and mountain meadows for expanding flocks. Some of those families would come to own thousands of sheep and alternatively graze cattle, depending on market and range conditions.

They lived in tight-knit communities and plazas along rivers, creeks, and streams, spoke Spanish, attended Catholic Mass, piled wagons high with wool, and then drove to distant railheads until trains came closer. With luck, they worked for themselves and not for others. "From at least the 1850s the villages of northern New Mexico continually if gradually expanded, sending out runners to Colorado. . . . They created a regional community bound by ties of kinship as well as economy." But by the turn of the twentieth century, boys growing up in New Mexican villages had few options.[6] Mercantile stores monopolized prices. Sheep farmers who had borrowed against their accounts at these stores found their land possessed, and they became *partidarios*, or sheep sharecroppers who owed money against their lamb and wool crops.

Hispanic sons could rarely become sheepmen; they were only herders because of a decreasing land base, the result of aggressive Anglo expansion and *ejidos*, or common grazing areas, being legally redefined as national forests with new rules and regulations. Having been overgrazed for decades, northern New Mexico had great scars upon the land, deep and dusty arroyos, and pastures pulverized to dirt by the hooves of too many sheep owned not by local families but by ricos, rich families from Santa Fe that employed hundreds of herders.

If herders stayed home, "high interest rates and low wool prices kept the sheepherder's debts in excess of his profits and the sheepherder himself, in a form of debt slavery," wrote Suzanne Forrest in *The Preservation of the Village*.[7] To stay out of debt, and to come home with cash, Hispanic men moved north. She wrote, "Villagers who did not want to become entrapped in the *partido* system of New Mexico migrated to work as sheepherders in Colorado, Utah, Wyoming, and Montana."[8]

The Bond Mercantile Store in Española, New Mexico, provided hundreds of herders with food, supplies, and sheep on shares in the *partido* system. This photo is of Bond sheep and the bare and rocky soil that came from overgrazing. Photo courtesy of New Mexico History Museum/Palace of the Governors, Santa Fe.

As the 1920s segued into the 1930s and the Great Depression, Colorado's high country offered the only hope for hundreds of young men who had limited education and spoke only *Español*. They would follow the borregas and bring home the cash that their wives and mothers so desperately needed. On their home turf in Mora, Colfax, or Rio Arriba Counties, "by the 1930s, forage in the mountains was so scarce that cattle were beginning to starve to death. The per capita income in Vallecitos [New Mexico] was just over $200. Unable to support their families, village men left to take jobs as cowboys, sheepherders, and miners in Colorado."[9] Historian Deutsch concludes, "The Depression disrupted migration patterns and strategies Hispanics had followed for ten, fifteen, and even twenty-five years. Only the skeleton of the regional migratory pattern survived," and the wives whose husbands found herding jobs in Colorado or Wyoming were considered "fairly well off."[10]

The herders who traveled brought with them centuries of working with sheep and a custom and culture familiar with high-country wilderness and weeks of being alone. They knew the exact day to turn rams in with ewes so lambs would be born under a full moon. Lambs arrived in March or April, and herders knew all about a ewe's behaviors before giving birth. She paws at bedding to make a nest. After the lamb drops, she steps forward, turns, lowers her head, sniffs it, licks the lamb's nose so it can breathe, nudges it toward her teats. The ewe moves around, adjusts herself so the lamb can suck milk. A tail starts to wag and the lamb has found its mother. Often, a second lamb drops, and the process starts over again deep in the night with herders moving through the flock, helping the lambs, ears tuned to coyotes, eyes watching their border collies for any sign of danger in this, one of the most vulnerable times on the range.

At lambing season, Hispano herders prayed to Santa Inés or Saint Agnes, patron saints for those who lived outdoors, and they prayed especially hard over lost lambs or other stray animals that they might be restored. Hispano herders knew the morning star as *La Estrella del Pastor*, "The Star of the Sheepherders," because as the star rose in the glittering cold of a mountain morning, so did the sheep.

Herders were hospitable, willing to entertain guests or strangers at sheep camp, and "a blackened coffee pot is always present on the edge of the campfire. Ground coffee and water are added as needed."[11] In a cast-iron Dutch oven atop *rescoldo*, a big bed of coals, they baked *pan de pastor*, or shepherd's bread, to serve with stout black Arbuckle coffee and canned milk. Everything had a function in sheep camp, and even the condensed milk cans were saved to be strung on hard wire like a wreath, making a rattle or tambourine to shake behind the sheep so they would move faster. Known as "tin dogs," these milk-can rattles can be found in museums across northwestern Colorado.[12]

Some stockmen kept their herders in canned food. Basques took the time to wash vegetables for stew, "but the universal and standard food was pinto beans and mutton, sour dough bread and cheese. The beans were simmered long and slowly with mutton and some onion . . . the beans were cooked until the skins burst making the juice thick and brown; the mutton to savory bits."[13] Hispano herders added roasted chilies or chili powder to taste. "With a kettle of beans simmering on the camp stove, the coffee kept warm by the stove pipe, bread baking in a pit of ashes, the men out all day with the sheep, in the evening [they] were assured of a meal such as the most efficient wife could not match," recalled one sheepman's spouse. Later, when he had leased his sheep and rented his range, the stockman complained of not being well fed at home. He teased his wife, "I'm going to sheep camp and get a good meal." To which she responded, "I'm going with you."[14]

On Christmas Eve in the low country, watching sheep in winter pastures, Hispano herders lit small fires in bags filled with sand, *luminarias*, to commemorate the shepherd campfires near Bethlehem and the birth of Christ on *Noche Buena*, or Christmas Eve. Not familiar with English and not knowing how to count to keep track of their sheep bands, herders would fill a tobacco sack full of pebbles, using a black stone to represent the black sheep, one per hundred, and white stones for how many tens of sheep they herded. If bears or coyotes came after their flock, the herders would retrieve the pelts and ears to show their *patrón*, or boss. To keep the sheep moving forward with billy goats as leaders, herders used *hondas*, or slings, to send egg-shaped rocks after stragglers. If fresh lamb was basted on the stove in sheep camp instead of rangy mutton, a herder would almost always claim it broke its leg. Who could argue?

Sometimes the herders stayed on their proper ranges or allotments, and sometimes they did not. Herders occasionally trespassed onto cattle and sheep allotments as well as onto game preserves. When confronted by forest rangers wearing a sidearm, they panicked. "A herder was grazing his sheep on a game refuge and he may or may not have known that the sheep were in trespass, but he was of the older type, understood no English, and apparently felt that he was going to be killed on the spot," a forest ranger related. "He got on his knees, prayed, crossed himself, and there is no doubt in my mind but what he thought the end had come. I helped him get his sheep onto a proper range and no further difficulty was experienced with him," wrote ranger C. B. Mack.[15]

There are stories of shepherds dying and faithful dogs continuing to move and work the sheep. And there are stories of the effect of loneliness, of "crazy" herders who could not adjust to the bustle of even a small village. "It is probably true, as has often been stated, that the *pastores*—shepherds—sometimes lost their reason after weeks and months with their flocks, accompanied only by the faithful dog who was trained to guard the sheep from wolves and bring them into the corral at night," wrote Colorado pioneer Honora DeBusk Smith. She added, "The writer has never forgotten the keen sympathy evoked by the shepherd lad who burst into tears and could not reply when accosted by a passing group of horseback riders as he stood on the solitary prairie after weeks away from any human contact."[16]

Herders cheated on each other's allotments, and occasionally quarrels became deadly. "Had to jack up Daniel Martinez for not staying on the trail. He had cut a wide circle through Tino Garcia's range," wrote a US Forest Service ranger.[17] On winter range in the Book Cliff area of Utah, a Hispano herder slayed his "countryman," another Hispano herder, with an ax after supposedly being beaten with a rifle.[18] In remote sheep camps, anger could be difficult to defuse.

Young shepherds may not have known how to combat isolation, but they knew how to assist *el ganado preñado*, a pregnant ewe, and how to help *pencos*, or orphan lambs, by tying the skin of a dead lamb atop the orphan lamb to fool another mother ewe into accepting the orphan because it smelled like her own. The herders also harvested and dried medicinal plants, *yerbas del campo*, and returned to their villages with a variety of herbs, including osha root, which grows best above 9,000 feet, and *hediondilla*, or a part of the creosote bush that serves as a remedy for kidney ailments. "Every pastor knows about *yerbas del campo*. It is well that he does, he is alone so much. Knowing them he can treat any disease that might strike him while out alone with his sheep. Only a broken leg holds any terror for a sheepherder."[19]

Herders also knew poisonous plants and had to save their sheep from larkspur, which was poisonous in the spring but not in the fall. Blue lupine was harmless in the spring but needed to be avoided in the fall when the pods formed. In the summer, sheep nipped short, tender grass, but in fall prime sheep feed was grama and curly grasses and bluestems with heavy seed heads. Sheep could also benefit cattle by eating poisonous larkspur twice a year—in spring before it reached 16 inches in height, and in fall before the plant's seeds ripened.

Stories came from the sheep camps. Stories of lost lambs, greedy coyotes, wrecks with horses, and bears—always bears—some of which became taller and taller with each telling. Leo Coca remembered:

> One time I was herding sheep and there was this mother bear. She weighed about two thousand pounds and she had three little cubs. I had a little pistol and I had a little pup and the pup seen it first. By gosh, when I seen it I didn't know what to do. I just ran right up to where she was, almost about thirty feet. Then she just stood up on her

hind feet and her cubs just start eating and then she started to come up to me and showing me her teeth. Her teeth looked like they were one and a half feet long. I started to back up and she started to stop and go down on her feet, and pretty soon after I got down the hill a little ways, why I ran just as fast as I could and I started shooting backwards, but I don't know what I was shooting at. I went back to camp and saddled my horse, and I went back but she wasn't there no more. It was a grizzly. She was white and had three little ones.[20]

When not confronting predators, in their spare time herders carved on aspens; stacked stones in cairns known as *harri mutalik*, or "stone boys" in Basque; made *teguas*, or homemade moccasins, and *reatas*, or hand-braided ropes. To heal sick sheep, herders would place animals in stone enclosures or small brush pens, called *chiceros*.

Herders knew a hundred ways to care for sheep, and every one of their strategies would be tested the winter of 1931–1932 when a severe spring blizzard decimated flocks, only to be followed by a long-lasting drought that forced reductions in numbers on the public domain after passage of the Taylor Grazing Act two years later. The drought was also felt across the Navajo Reservation under the stock reduction policies of Indian Commis-

At sheep shearing time, a variety of families all worked together. Near Cedar Hill, New Mexico, Jack Gardner and other sheepmen employed Navajo herders, who arrived with their families. Here Gardner's daughter Bernice poses for a photo with a Navajo girl her same age. Photo courtesy of Bernice Bowra.

sioner John Collier, nicknamed "Sheep Killer Collier" by Navajo women who never forgot that government men shot and killed the women's precious sheep to reduce overgrazing and erosion on the reservation.[21]

For herders across Colorado and New Mexico, the spring blizzard of 1932, just after flocks had been sheared and had no warm wool for protection, left dead sheep by the hundreds. For one young Greek herder, struggling to survive the economics of the Great Depression, the blizzard went down in family history. On April 27, 1932, a fierce spring blizzard froze young woollies that had just been sheared. Regas Halandras from Meeker lost 1,462 sheep within 40 hours. He would always remember, "I paid $18 a head for those sheep, and the carcasses were piled so high I walked on their bodies. It was the worst thing that ever happened to me." So he started over. Many sheep-owning families lost everything.

The Gomez family of Pagosa Springs and Archuleta County survived economically, but to this day grandchildren repeat stories of white, frozen sheep stuck to their bed-ground, dead in the snow, and relatives gathering wet wood to light fires, trying to warm lambs still living, while tears froze on the herders' faces amid the low, plaintive sounds of dying sheep.[22]

The Gomez family was one of the very few Hispanic families in southern Colorado to own and manage their own mercantile store next to the Denver and Rio Grande railroad. This historical building is now on the grounds of the Fred Harmon Museum in Pagosa Springs, Colorado. Author photo.

Snow melted but no rains came. For years. The drought deepened. Sharp sheep hooves cut fragile soils and hungry ewes ate plants down to the roots. Village men who had started to herd at age 10 or 12 now headed north, desperately seeking work. "Though most Hispanic migrants came from landowning families in the village, they performed only wage labor outside it," wrote Sarah Deutsch.[23]

One Mormon family that raised sheep and hired herders from Rio Arriba County in northern New Mexico was the Redd family from Bluff and La Sal, Utah. L. H. Redd took his sheep to Colorado for summer range and one spring had them near Mancos and what is now the entrance to Mesa Verde National Park. He would move his bands so he could shear close to the railroad and not have to transport heavy wool.[24] When his Hispano herders came in for supplies, Lem took them to the basement of his large stone house in Bluff to load them up with provisions for their next round of moving sheep.

Beginning in the 1890s, for Bluff ranchers New Mexican herders might tend 2,500 to 3,000 head apiece for as long as 8 to 10 months before returning home. For shearings, as many as 50 men would come north. Often they remained anonymous and were spoken of only as "Mexicans." "Lemuel Redd developed close relationships with some of his herders. But more often these workers were noted only for their tragedies, such as the poor man who fell off a heavy wagon and was crushed to death by its wheels," wrote Bluff historian David S. Carpenter.[25] The Hispano herder was buried in Bluff because no one knew his name or how to contact his family.

Lem's son Charlie Redd grew up working with herders and learning Spanish, Hopi, Paiute, and Navajo "words, phrases, customs, and ways of looking at life," according to his biographer Leonard J. Arrington.[26] That cultural education stood Charlie Redd in good stead as he expanded his father's partnership in the La Sal Livestock Company into Redd Ranches and one of the largest sheep and cattle concerns in the Rocky Mountain West, with over 25,000 sheep and thousands of deeded acres in two states, including a quarter million acres of permits and leases straddling the Utah-Colorado border.

Charlie Redd knew how to talk to people he hired. He asked about them, asked after them, and remembered their names and families. After a drop in livestock values in 1921, he inherited his father's debts of $575,000, yet he persevered. His personality helped account for his success, and Hispano herders could expect him to share their dinner of mutton and frijoles, coffee "that would take the head off a ten-penny nail," and Dutch-oven bread. Winter or summer, he would ride into camp with only one wool blanket. Charlie easily found and retained employees because "the sheep camps were comfortable, they had plenty of quilts and blankets, and the herders were better paid than cowboys."[27]

He understood his Hispano herders and they understood him. Because of that trust, he had foremen like Ignacio Martinez, Roque Garcia, and Fernando "F. R." Lopez. His employees would run up debts at the La Sal store, which Redd owned, but they did not need to pay their bills until they headed home. With a staff he could depend on, Redd expanded even in the depths of the Great Depression. "With banks that were able to survive the depression, he was able to obtain credit to buy up outfits that went broke and land that was foreclosed by failure to pay taxes or mortgages. His holdings continued to increase during the thirties," wrote Redd's biographer.[28] Redd purchased Colorado land to expand his operations even though in 1932 the value of Utah sheep fell 78 percent.

Redd ran ewes at the base of Snowmass Mountain near Aspen and up the Frying Pan River from Basalt. Those woollies arrived by train. Closer to home he leased grazing land for only $75 a section, or 640 acres, and also leased land from the diminutive but feisty land baron Marie Scott. From Marie, Redd leased ground for 30 years. He bought land for $15 an acre and with partners purchased property near Groundhog in Dolores County, Colorado, which included a permit to run 2,500 sheep. He bought the historical Pitchfork ranch from the Lavender family, the Desert Claim property of 3,500 acres, farms near Norwood, Colorado, with mountain land near Goat Creek and Gurley Reservoir, and entire canyons in southern San Juan County, Utah. Charlie Redd and partners came to own 47,000 acres near Norwood. A Utah rancher and a Mormon, he owned more land in Colorado than he did in his home state.[29] But Redd was land rich and cash poor.

By 1934, the Continental Bank in Salt Lake City began foreclosure proceedings. Bankers arrived to count Redd's assets, including 25,000 sheep. During the days they lived at the ranch, the bankers began to understand the complexity of the Redd operation, and most importantly the loyalty of the ranch hands. If the bank foreclosed, the Salt Lake business bankers would have to manage this vast agricultural enterprise and maintain threshing, herding, branding, and shearing crews. Charlie Redd's wife, Annaley, recalled:

> The bankers stayed at the ranch house and ate with the ranch hands. They ate pinto beans, home-cured ham, vegetables from the ranch garden, apples from the ranch orchard made into warm apple pie with ranch dairy cream too thick to pour. We also had chickens, so there were plenty of fresh eggs. We were almost self-sufficient at the ranch. It was the beans they seemed to enjoy the most. I am sure they observed how hard we all worked and how well the ranch was managed. The thought must have crossed their minds that if they took over the ranch, they would be responsible for all of the activity that they saw going on. They decided to finance us for another year. Charlie said it was the beans that saved the ranch.[30]

It could have been the beans, but it was probably the loyal Hispano herders from Rio Arriba County who had worked for the Redd family for almost half a century. They needed the income and Charlie needed the help. The bankers intuitively understood that Charlie Redd had a dedicated, competent work crew. Just as Regas Halandras had defused trouble on the range in Rio Blanco County with good coffee, biscuits, and fresh lamb chops, the Redd family fed visiting bankers everything from the ranch larder. Home-cooked food and warm hospitality created confidence and conviviality. By serving the right meals at the right times, Regas Halandras kept his sheep on the range and Charlie Redd kept his ranch.

Still, the old cattlemen-sheepmen feuds remained. Writing in his classic *One Man's West*, cowboy David Lavender rode miles across the Disappointment Valley before attending college at Princeton. He described Charlie's ranch:

> The map shows a town; La Sal. It is not a town. It is a sheep company; store, garage, warehouses, boardinghouses, barns, networks of corrals, and mile after mile of fodder-producing fields set like bright emeralds in a gray of sage. It is a good Mormon concern run in a good Mormon way by its horse-trading boss, Charlie Redd. Big-boned, pink-cheeked, and affable, Charlie Redd can call more men of assorted types by their first names than an electioneering congressman. But this hasn't kept his herds—they number far into the thousands—from being stam-

peded on dark nights, or strychnine from being put in his sheep salt. His barns, warehouses, and haystacks are periodic prey for arsonists. This country used to be cattle land, and the old enmities die hard."[31]

As a sheepman Charlie endured range troubles, but he made money. Lots of it. He knew Farrington Carpenter. Charlie chaired one of the recently formed advisory boards for Ferry's Office of Grazing. Though increasingly Redd traveled farther and farther from San Juan County, Utah, he could rely on Hispano herders that his family had recruited for decades from northern New Mexico.

"Hispanics were much admired by Charlie," Redd biographer Arrington explains. Charlie stated, "You could send them out with a herd of sheep and tell them what you wanted done and you knew that they would be there when you went after them. If they ran out of groceries, they wouldn't walk off; they would kill a sheep and roast it over a fire. When they lost sheep, they felt worse than I did. They worked for me; they were good fellows, and we depended heavily on them."[32]

Northern New Mexican men that Redd remembered included Roque Garcia, Mateo Garcia, Anton Chacon, Cosme Chacon, Leon Sanchez, Fernando Lopez, Benito Martinez, Tony Serrano, Melicendro "Big Mike" Lovato, and Merejildo Valdez from Española. Charlie Redd even traveled to Española for the wedding of Valdez's daughter. "These men knew sheep, were loyal, and were resourceful in getting out of any difficulty," notes Arrington.[33]

Redd realized that in order to graze national forests in Colorado or the public domain in Utah he needed adjacent land, and he "eventually developed what was surely one of the largest sheep operations in the West."[34] Sheepmen everywhere felt the sting of new rules related to the 1934 Taylor Grazing Act, which required "commensurability," or private range close to public land.[35] Often their appeals to grazing boards were rejected, so stockmen had no choice but to buy more land. During the Great Depression, if you had cash or credit, plenty of failed homesteads became available.

In the 1930s, for about $40 per month, the pattern of sheep rounds or movements on Colorado's Western Slope solidified for Basque and Hispano herders—winter in the Utah desert, summer in the San Juans. In their sheep camps complete with single bed, stove, kerosene lantern, cooking utensils, and storage, herders watched sheep all winter near Green River, Cisco, and Thompson, Utah, out on "The Big Flats." On a cold desert morning an experienced herder could roll over in his blankets, strike a safety match with his thumbnail, ignite wood chips and paper in the sheet-metal stove, and have a fire roaring before he got out of bed. Then it was coffee, check the sourdough starter, and rise in the dark as the sheep began to stir.

Eastern Utah meant big shearing events in spring, with sometimes as many as 30 bands or over 30,000 sheep with different owners. Each ewe and wether would be painted with the sheepman's brand and sometimes branded on the nose. Then herders would "graze on up" toward the high country, trailing the sheep on foot and on horseback, lambing in the brush and on the trail. They would point their flocks toward the count corrals at the Alpine Ranger Station on the Blue, up to Cerro Summit, to the Cimarron, and drive up Son-of-a-Gun Creek over the Big Blue to Baldy Peak. With a full moon, they might drive all night to get to Gladstone Basin above Silverton, Colorado, or to American Flats and pastures near Lake City.

At the height of the sheep industry in the 1930s and into the 1940s, perhaps 80,000 to 90,000 sheep would cross Utah deserts, Colorado adobe nicknamed 'dobe badlands, and head toward higher ground using the Ridge Sheep Driveway to camp near Uncompahgre Peak, to follow Pole Creek to Henson Creek, and to move on to the ghost town of Capital City. Herders sought bright, high meadows of mariposa lilies, blue columbines, red honeysuckle, yellow asters, pale phlox, bluebells, harebells, and bunchgrass that waved in the wind before a storm.[36]

Herders trailed up the North Fork to Wild Horse Peak, camped at American Flats, lunched at Mineral Point, and fished at Canadian Lake. By the ninth day they could enter Tiger Gulch and Poughkeepsie Gulch and then graze around Lake Como. For staff of the Grazing Office, created after passage of the Taylor Grazing Act, "one of the biggest headaches was the American Flats. It was an area of mountain land above timber line and not included in the Forest because there were so many patented mining claims there. Some sheepmen would lease a few mining claims and move in. It was dog eat dog, and the area was very much overgrazed," states a BLM history report. "We had no control over the mining claims and the land pattern was such that trespassing was almost impossible [to regulate]."[37] Eventually, by requiring access via a stock driveway through the forest, grazing officers could bring order out of chaos and schedule flock arrivals.

The Depression was on. Mines were closed or closing. Cabins stood abandoned and sheep chewed wildflowers. In summer, "Sheepman's Day" livened up Silverton, Colorado, with gunnysack races and barbecues. The old mining timbers are still there, the cabins now fallen in, and mine portals are closed, but the number of sheep that once grazed the mountains is one of Colorado's hidden high-country secrets.

The Redds moved sheep. Elizondo would push 12 or 13 bands of 1,000 ewes and their lambs. Chuchuru would trail 8 bands. The sheep migration could take six days. Camp gear included four pack mules per camp. The sheep wagons often stayed in the desert. In the summer high country it was canvas tents, the goatskin red wine pouch, or *chakoa*, for Basques, food for the herders. Of the four pack mules, one would carry the tent and stove, one had wooden grub boxes, and the other two brought canned goods, firewood, sheep salt, grain for horses and mules, sheepskins to sleep on, and a cot for the herder. Food for the dogs.

In the twenty-first century, a high-country sheep outfit remains essentially the same, though tents are now covered with plastic tarps to better shed rain, hail, and snow. Mutton stew and pinto beans simmer on sheet-metal stoves. When the flock and the herder are on distant slopes, bears still come around, looking to lick skillets, sniffing dog food stored in the herder's tent.

As cattle ranchers and sheepmen began to adjudicate the range because of the Taylor Grazing Act and to purchase "base property" so they could graze both in summer on the forest and in winter on the desert, another FDR program began to take hold. The Civilian Conservation Corps (CCC), one of President Roosevelt's favorite accomplishments, took young men from all over the United States and put them to work on America's public lands. They earned $30 a month but could only keep $5. The balance of their salary went home to needy family members.[38]

The CCC "boys" learned carpentry skills and masonry; learned how to swing a pick, use a shovel, move boulders, sharpen an ax; to build roads, trails, culverts, and stone bridges; and to survey and mark stock driveways. The CCC is most known for its conservation work in national forests and national parks, but "on the ground" it made a considerable difference to overgrazed Colorado landscapes. Supervisory personnel were politically appointed, and Congressman Edward Taylor wanted to be sure work was done well and efficiently. He demanded changes on the overused, deeply abused public lands, and he got them.

CCC boys went after prairie dogs and burned thousands of acres of cactus. They re-seeded denuded slopes and fenced areas so that forage plants could grow and recover. Overuse and drought had damaged or eliminated choice browse like white sage, four-winged saltbush, and native bluestem grass. On public lands, "heavy destructive soil erosion [was] in evidence everywhere. Quite drastic cuts in both number of livestock and time of use was necessary to preserve the remaining forage resource and begin some recovery."[39] Range improvement started with the establishment of grazing districts and offices across Colorado. CCC staff built fences and reservoirs, planted trees, cleared ground for stock driveways, and did a lot of "gully plugging" by putting natural brush, logs, soil, and rocks in arroyos to help heal wounds from too many cattle and sheep.

The CCC restored the land. Young men built trails, bridges, roads, and stock watering tanks and planted millions of trees. Devastation on the public domain began to be addressed. Decades of overgrazing required re-seeding and the first attempts to eliminate invasive plants like cheatgrass, Russian thistle, and foxtails—all transported across the West in the thick fleece of sheep. Young willows had to be replanted near streambeds, and eventually stock numbers were reduced.

Sheep numbers declined but remained too high for the land. In 1935 the Montezuma National Forest, now part of the San Juan National Forest, permitted 65,000 sheep between June 16 and October 15. Erosion control depended on not overgrazing, avoiding animals "getting on" the forest too early, practicing deferred and rotational grazing, and properly controlling and distributing livestock, such as changing herder patterns to keep sheep on the move and not using the same bed-ground for more than three nights. Then came drought to go with the Depression.[40]

In 1936, CCC camps continued to improve the range, especially where sheep had decimated local landscapes. The Blanco CCC camp, "made up of about 65% Spanish boys," worked hard to mitigate decades of overgrazing by fencing to exclude livestock from overgrazed areas "so that the arroyos would have an opportunity to revegetate and which will obviously be a deciding factor in retarding rapid run-off. Thousands of acres of Government and private land in Archuleta County in the vicinity of the Blanco Camp are in a deplorable condition, obviously due to erosion," stated the US Forest Service in the region's annual report. But there was hope.

Project superintendent for Camp F-29, Ralph Meager, claimed, "The work that the CCC boys did during the past four seasons for the possible

Like most sheepmen in the early twentieth century, Jack Gardner cleared his range of all predators that might harm his lambs. Here he stands with two dead bobcats. Photo courtesy of Bernice Bowra.

future utilization of these acres is really an outstanding accomplishment."[41] Yet if the ground was beginning to heal, Colorado's ecosystems remained unbalanced because the war on predators continued and even escalated.

Taking a cue from the Progressive Era and the goal of greater efficiency in public land management, the chief of the Bureau of Biological Survey, Paul G. Redington, stated in his 1930 report that "control operations directed to suppress the depredations of predatory wild animals may also be termed an essential form of regulation."[42] In essence, if they were regulating public lands for ranchers and stockmen, why not regulate animals, especially wild ones? Redington added, "The coyote is the most destructive natural enemy of livestock in the West."[43]

In 1931 Congress passed the Animal Damage Control Act, still in effect today, which created within the US Fish and Wildlife Service the Predator and Rodent Control branch, whose mission was to cleanse the range of all rodents. Congress charged the agency with the "eradication, suppression or bringing under control . . . of animals injurious to agriculture" and authorized it "to conduct campaigns for the destruction or control of such animals."

One of the agency's major targets was coyotes, which usually attack sheep on a downhill slope because frightened sheep run downhill and scatter as they descend. Stockmen routinely shot, trapped, and poisoned coyotes and then hung the carcasses on a fence post as a warning to coyote kin. The classic definition of a coyote comes from Mark Twain:

> The cayote [sic] is a long, slim, sick and sorry looking skeleton, with a gray wolf skin stretched over it, a tolerably bushy tail that forever sags down with a despairing expression of forsakenness and misery, a furtive and evil eye, and a long, sharp face, with slightly lifted lip and exposed teeth. He has a general slinking appearance all over. The cayote is a living, breathing allegory of Want. He is always poor, out of luck, and friendless. The meanest creatures despise him, and even the fleas would desert him for a velocipede. He is so spiritless and cowardly that even while his exposed teeth are pretending a threat, the rest of his face is apologizing for it. And he is *so* homely, *so* scrawny, and ribby, and coarse-haired, and pitiful.[44]

What Twain failed to add was how much coyotes love lamb. Writing for the *National Wool Grower*, Frank C. Clarke explained that the coyote is "the greatest menace known to the sheep industry of North America. His choicest food is lamb and mutton, and he will at all times make strenuous efforts to get into a flock of sheep."[45]

Hispano herders knew that and guarded their flocks accordingly. They also knew what the Bureau of Biological Survey and the employees of the Predator and Rodent Control branch did not seem to understand. If you kill off rodents, a prime food source for coyotes, then what will they turn to for dinner? *Sí, comprendo. Borregas.*

In the 1930s, just as racism caused the Colorado governor to declare martial law against "Mexicans," prejudice against Hispanos and sheepherders also existed in the mountain mining towns. One of Howard Lathrop's Hispano herders gambled on the affections of a Silverton whore. And lost. Herding sheep had no status.

A sheepherder naps with two lambs looking on. Often awake and moving sheep before dawn, herders napped in the afternoon, when sheep also bedded down prior to feeding again before dark. AUR 2175. Image courtesy of the Auraria Campus.

"We were sort of a bastard business," explained Lathrop. "We sold our lambs in Kansas City and Boston [was] our wool market. The wool that came back in long underwear for the miners in winter never was associated with the raw product. The miners were as prejudiced against the sheepmen as the cowboys. I remember the crazy peg-legged miner who thought the sheep were eating his ore, and standing on a stump, he shot into a herd turning around and around as he dropped sheep one by one."[46]

"Nothing glamorous about herders. Not like the cowboy on his horse, and the hard rock miner, the railroad men, running the little trains through the mountains, the prospector with his gold pan and his burro. Even the whores thought they were too high class for the herders," he sadly related.[47] In her book *Don't Fence Me In*, Howard's wife, Marguerite, described a young [New] Mexican with a bushy black beard. He had met a beautiful girl who said she would marry him, but she needed $25 for material for a wedding dress. The herder sought a loan from Lathrop, who found the girl in business in a crib on Silverton's notorious Blair Street, but nevertheless he dutifully paid for the dress.

When the lovestruck young man thought enough time had passed for her to have sewn her wedding garment, he asked for his wages, put on his best shirt and boots, and rode into town. The girl laughed at his dream of marriage. When he realized her profession, he agreed to take his $25 out in trade. Instead, she had him arrested. "Howard bailed him out, and rode back to sheep camp with the wiser but sadder herder," who received no justice from the sheriff.[48]

Like Charlie Redd, Howard Lathrop stayed on the move with his sheep. "No home. No headquarters . . . his office was his wallet, his bookkeeping books, his bank stubs."[49]

During cold nights in eastern Utah he would stay at the two-story wooden Desert Moon Hotel along the railroad tracks at Thompson. Like so many others during the Great Depression, Lathrop had no choice but to look to the future. The Taylor Grazing Act changed his business operation. Yes, he could still rely on the narrow-gauge railroad, the Denver and Rio Grande, to haul ewes and lambs into the high country, but not for long.

The railroad's years were numbered. So, too, would be the days of trailing sheep on gravel county roads and stock driveways. Soon they would have to be loaded onto trucks and hauled out of the deserts toward higher ground. "Paved roads and monstrous, slat-sided trucks did away with the slow foot migrations of livestock, once so characteristic a part of the country's rhythms," wrote David Lavender.[50]

As the drought began to ease, cattle prices stayed low, but sheep values stabilized. "The money's in the sheep. In the 1930s, they still made money," explained Craig rancher Doug Wellman. "There's two crops, wool and lambs, and there's money in it. My family went into sheep and paid off the note in three years."[51] Penny-pinching sheepmen covered expenses with the wool clip and set dollars ahead with the lamb crop. They used their income to buy private land closer to their public permits.

As for the herders themselves, for native New Mexicans away from home for months at a time, though wage work had been a fact of life for their uncles and fathers, the New Deal of President Franklin Delano Roosevelt provided the ultimate break, *la quebrada*, between the old, slow-changing world of their parents and a modern world with less Spanish and less tradition.

"Hispanic New Mexicans had been leaving the region for distant work for decades," notes southwestern scholar William deBuys, "but the steady current of change became an overwhelming cascade in the years of the Great Depression and World War II. Ultimately nothing remained untouched or unaltered, not agriculture, nor marriage and family, nor the use of Spanish, nor education, health, community. These are matters of record, not sentiment."[52]

There were no radios in sheep camp. No maps to find Hawaii or Pearl Harbor. Since Hitler had invaded Poland in 1939, prices had risen for agricultural products. More brothers and nephews could get jobs herding sheep. On December 7, 1941, herders mostly kept themselves warm in their sheep wagons on winter range in the New Mexican canyons of Largo and Gobernador, or on the Big Flats in Utah between the Green and Colorado Rivers. Herders waited for their flocks to bed down that night. They did not know what momentous change would occur a world away, what new products would be invented during and after the war, and what Australians would do to forever turn a generation of World War II veterans ill at the smell of boiled mutton or baked lamb.

On that December day ewes bleated. Lambs sought teats and soon, very soon, American-born sheepherders would have new opportunities and new vistas never dreamed of.

SIXTH SHEEPSCAPE

*Lone Cone and Beaver Park
—Uncompahgre National Forest*

One of the most comprehensive studies of aspen art in Colorado occurred in the 1980s near Lone Cone Ranger Station, 25 miles south of Norwood. In preparation for an aspen treatment in which older trees would be cut down to stimulate new growth of aspen shoots, archaeology field technicians under the supervision of Uncompahgre National Forest archaeologist Polly Hammer spread out to find arborglyphs. They did. They found glyphs on 4,187 trees within a few miles of the historical ranger station and filled out 164 site forms.[1]

Most prehistoric and historical sites on public lands that are 50 years old or older can be eligible for inclusion on the National Register of Historic Places, but unlike Native American pictographs or petroglyphs painted or carved on rock, aspen trees are ephemeral. They live only a century or so, and hence tree carvings are not eligible for permanent preservation. Hammer's goal was to have her crew record any and all glyphs on aspens that might be cut down.

She researched historical information about the herders, their lives, their stories, and the importance of leaving their names and hometowns in the forest. Just as golden aspen leaves fade and fall, so, too, will the trees. Aspen art is by definition fleeting, as are those lovely Indian summer days of autumn that seem to last forever under deep azure Colorado skies. When Polly retired, her successor, Leigh Ann Hunt, worked 14 years on the forest before she also retired.

Thirty years after the original survey, Leigh Ann and I wanted to return to see whether we could find some of the groves that had been recorded. She brought her friend Sharon Wangelin and a box of documents, maps, drawings, and a few black-and-white photos. Leigh Ann worried because "in 2012 in Cochetopa Park we had a site with twenty-six carved aspens recorded in the 1980s and when we went back we found only seven carved aspens and we could read only four."

Were the trees still standing? Could we locate some of the glyphs carefully drawn and described on numerous historical site forms? This would be a treasure hunt in the trees. As we walked beneath canopies of yellow leaves, could we find secrets that herders had carved?

The Civilian Conservation Corps (CCC) built Lone Cone Ranger Station, now a recreation rental in the heart of Beaver Park, a vast expanse of open grassland surrounded by aspens that flow up and around the log ranger cabin nestled at the base of Middle Peak. Lone Cone looms to the west. To study area aspen art, we rented the cabin for two nights during the height of fall colors.

I got there first. Unpacked. Had lunch outdoors on a picnic table while soaking up the silence of a glorious cool afternoon. Gray clouds scuttled across the top of Lone Cone with a promise of rain. Everywhere I looked I saw the complete color palette of aspens in the fall—shades of yellows, waxy then bright, and light red leaves a deeper color high in the canopy.

On such a day the drive south from Norwood on county and then Forest Service roads is like an approach to a mythical kingdom. The ground rises higher, sage gives way to piñon, and then aspens spread for miles, a golden carpet at 9,000 to 10,000 feet in elevation. I saw mule deer crowd Gambel oak openings. Hawks wheeled and circled above the aspens, and a fresh mantle of snow blanketed Middle and Dolores Peaks, yet the days were shirt-sleeve warm. Just to the south, the Lizard Head Wilderness beckoned.

The late 1930s ranger's cabin, with its standard 1930s floor plan, sat on a ridge above Main Beaver Creek. Skilled CCC carpenters had cut and shaped the logs. Blacksmiths had hand wrought the light fixtures, and the original kitchen table featured pine tree motifs, as did shutters on the cabin windows. A stone porch faced Lone Cone. It would be a perfect base camp for our arborglyph study.

We knew the forest held messages, carvings decades old that were left by herders who had traversed Beaver Park. A few female nudes caught my eye as well as inscriptions, dates, and the distinctive cursive script popular from the 1930s to the early 1960s. Hammer's archaeological study revealed that only 17 percent of the carvings contained drawings, while 80 percent had names, dates, and places, and 4 percent featured phrases or diary-like events.[2] I wanted to find the drawings. As I sat at a picnic table, miles of trees around me, I wondered how we would begin.

On the drive to the cabin I had found signatures of Aquilino Baca from Canjilon, New Mexico; Jose M. Salazar, Julio 23–57, Coyote, New Mexico; Filiberto Vigil, Canjilon, New Mexico, 7/23/53, and his brother Gaby in 1954 from Lumberton, New Mexico. Jose Vicente Cordova carved on 7/23/72 from Durango. From Gallina, New Mexico, I saw the name Joe Jacquez, as well as Abe Trujillo from Montrose, who always added on his tree carvings, "And my dog is Ringo." We came to recognize five different carvers named Chacon. Pacomio, or Paco, became known as a famous carver of women, clothed and unclothed, and we found vertical inscriptions by his brother Press.

A vast sheep industry had coveted the ground and grasses near Lone Cone. Early ranchers had tried to homestead the area. Some succeeded; others failed. The property where the ranger cabin looked west to the peak had been a failed homestead, lost during the Great Depression and reclaimed by the US Forest Service. This was high-country summer ground and in fall herders took their flocks west to the Disappointment Valley or even farther, into Utah.

How to find the aspen glyphs? The answer was to think like herders with their sheep. "The pictures are in places where the herders weren't that busy, where they stalled out. They sometimes had to wait for permission to cross the cattle pastures, or for the Forest Ranger to show up to count the flocks," explained Leigh Ann. "Carving was an idle sideline for a lot of them, but what's fascinating is that they carved their names. They wanted to be remembered. So carvings would most likely be found in places where there was a camp or a resting place along the drive to the high country."[3]

We knew from the paperwork that herders had left messages to each other in both Spanish and English, such as *Adios sierra pinche hoy la despedio*, "Today I'm saying good-bye you f__ing mountains." Or the simple statement "Purty damn cold." The Lone Cone area had been open range without drift fences until the 1940s, and local families shifted between cattle and sheep ownership.

Early on, antagonism existed between cattle and sheep owners. Near Lone Cone the "Goat Creek Incident" began closer to Dallas Divide when cowboys harassed a herder who had both goats and sheep. They began to shoot the goats. As the herder moved west toward Lone Cone the slaughter continued. One creek, now named Goat Creek, ran red with blood from both sheep and goats on and off between 1907 and 1909. The herd was "rim-rocked," or stampeded over a cliff. But soon sheep would be accepted because of changing livestock markets and because of a reality that cattlemen found hard to acknowledge—there was money in sheep. Lots of money if you owned them. Not much if you were just a herder.

Al Herndon grazed sheep around the peak, but not until 1916–1917. "This was due to commonly held, though exaggerated, beliefs concerning the effect of sheep on grazing pastures, and because the economic conditions were not ripe for their introduction. Incidents between cattlemen and sheepmen were few," reported Polly Hammer. She added, "The introduction of sheep was calmly received in this area because the 1915 slump in cattle prices made sheep a more profitable enterprise." So woollies were introduced by cattlemen like Clyde and Howard Davis and Arthur Dunham. After World War I, Dewey Greager and Edgar Bray switched from cattle to sheep, which covered Beaver Park by the 1920s. By 1936 the Forest Service had restricted overgrazing.

Cattlemen knew nothing about sheep. So they brought in herders who were New Mexicans, Navajos, a few Basques, Utes, and the occasional Anglo pulled from bars on Larimer Street in Denver or rounded up in Montrose. Basque herders often took their pay in ewes, saved every penny, and started their own band to run on public land. If some sheepmen employed Basques, most ranchers went to Rio Arriba County in New Mexico to pick up their herders and to hire extended families. "This pattern of many relatives working for one, or more, owners in an area seems to be common. Consequently, there are a large number of similar surnames carved on the aspens of a particular area," wrote archaeologist Hammer.[4]

Sheep grazing continued into the 1960s, when sheepmen also began to run cattle. The Forest Service required sheep to come onto the low-elevation cattle allotments on the Lone Cone Driveway in the Uncompahgre National Forest by noon, spend a night in Beaver Park, and go south toward the high-elevation sheep country in the San Juan National Forest the next day.

Hammer noted, "Cattle and sheep complement each other on the range, rather than competing for each other's forage." That's especially true if sheep graze first and trim down larkspur, which can be deadly to cattle. A critical difference in the style of grazing is that cattle can be left alone for weeks at a time, but sheep, never.

"Since sheepherders must remain with their sheep every day of the season, as opposed to cowboys who only periodically check cattle, a sheepherder has much spare time on his hands. This provides him with the time to while away his minutes carving," she wrote. As for the carvings themselves, "carving sites are most often found along the fringes of meadows or the sides of roads," Hammer explained. "And sheep camps almost always have aspen carvings nearby."

So we knew what we were looking for, and we had a good idea where to begin. I finished lunch at the picnic table. Leigh Ann and Sharon arrived. Clouds swirled over Lone Cone and we knew we'd best get moving before afternoon rains made forest roads slick and possibly impassable. We hadn't counted on hail.

We piled into my vehicle, taking along a map and site forms. A few miles from the ranger cabin we found a likely aspen grove just as rain rattled on the roof and kept us inside. Rain became pellets of frozen ice. Lightning flashed. The road disappeared. Then the weather let up, and we put on our Gore-Tex and ventured out onto the wet grass. Leigh Ann shouted first.

It was a small grove on a slight slope but had a commanding view. We found tree after tree that had been incised with names, dates, a small horse with a foal suckling at her side, a rider. "A herder friend told me the key to making these was just barely using the tip of a knife so you could almost not see the carvings. Letters expanded as the trees grew. Anglos want to see their carvings now so they gouge and damage trees. To make the delicate handwriting, you barely slice," Leigh Ann said.[5]

We found 7/15/1952 Reis Martinez from Canjilon. TXT from Thompson Park and Hesperus, Colorado. Bray 6/30/37 and a series of repetitive carvings from J.E.M., who left his initials in a shield or heart-like shape with dates like 9,9,39. The site was perfect because you could have seen all your sheep and had a view for miles. We walked up a two-track path, finding more inscriptions. The sky turned black above the golden aspens. The wind picked up. We heard thunder to the south and knew rain was returning. A low-pressure zone rumbled above us, and then I found it. On the edge of a meadow. A deer dancer or a Navajo Yeii figure so faint as to be almost transparent.

As the rain hesitated, poised to begin again, we studied the silent tree, its smooth white bark glistening with moisture, the dancer image faint and not too large, a figure in motion facing right while most images faced left. In the still moments between storms I wondered who had carved this and why. What did the symbol mean? It was so carefully executed that it would be years before the entire figure emerged with its shape outlined on aspen bark.

The wind picked up. Yellow leaves fled the trees in great bursts of falling color floating around us, landing on us, gliding in every direction. We pulled up our parka hoods and turned toward the truck. Rain resumed and drops spread across the carved dancer. I wondered whether we could make it down the soaked route without sliding sideways into a ditch or falling off the road entirely. I worried about switchbacks and tight turns.

In an aspen grove near the Lone Cone Ranger Station and the grazing meadows of Beaver Park on the Uncompahgre National Forest, the faint outlines of an Indian dancer appear as an arborglyph. This is possibly a Yeii dancer image, suggesting that a Navajo herder carved it. Author photo.

In four-wheel drive I began our slippery descent as wipers slashed at the rain, thankful that no one else was on the road when we took our half out of the middle. On that silent aspen tree the dancer continues to pirouette. Arms up. Knees in motion. Moving to an ancient rhythm with only the wind to watch.

The next morning we lolled around the cabin waiting for grass and leaves to dry. At midmorning we drove south and found a nude carved in a grove beside the forest road, as well as an odd set of letters and numbers that made no sense until we realized that elk hunters had incised the last two digits of the year they shot an elk, the size of the elk's antlers or rack, with points on each side of the head like 5X5 or 5X6, and the hunters' initials. Keeping score on aspens. Leaving messages on trees, like the girl near Main Beaver Creek who left her name and the inscription "BROKE LEG."

But we were seeking the older, hidden world of herders with their flocks far above the road, nibbling grass, passing time. With a brilliant blue sky and no hint of rain, I parked the truck and we shouldered packs and began to climb steeply out of one of the creeks and toward the snow-dusted peaks that glittered in the morning light. Walking through dark spruce, I wondered whether we could really find the historical carved trees, and then I saw my first inscription. It made no sense. Leigh Ann laughed.

A carver had written vertically on an aspen "RATERO FERMIN M." A fluent Spanish speaker, Leigh Ann smiled and explained. RATERO translates as "crook" or "thief." FERMIN M. must have been a herder who had stolen someone else's sheep, perhaps to make up for lambs taken by bears or simply lost. An indignant herder had carved the crook's name as a warning to other shepherds.

I had seen herders etch the word "loco" under another herder's name. And I knew that herders sometimes used their knives to scratch over other herders' inscriptions, but this was the first time I'd seen one herder actually call out another and name him a thief. I laughed, too. We walked into the spruce and then everywhere around us in deep shade were 40- to 50-year-old carvings. Leigh Ann explained tree cycles in the forest.

After wildland fires, aspens sprout back. Within five or six decades, fir and spruce thrive under the aspen canopy and eventually crowd out aspen trees. We had thought we were looking for isolated aspen groves, but now we realized that the oldest carvings may be on remnant aspens hidden in a mixed aspen-spruce stand. Proof lay everywhere before us.

I'd been on the other side of the mountain several years back with a friend, and we had found a series of aspen-carved faces, all pointing left, and all without necks or torsos. Simple male faces with distinctive ears and bulbous noses. My companion, Bill Quick, had smiled and immediately said, "Kilroy. Kilroy was here." I thought a minute.

American soldiers—"GIs" as they were called, as a pun on "Government Issue"—advanced across Europe and the Pacific during World War II. They left American graffiti everywhere, and a common icon emerged. On trucks, trees, buildings, or any solid surface, they'd draw a face with a large nose peering over a fence. The symbol became unmistakable. Kilroy was here. American service men and women were on the move.

Some herders fought in WWII and as veterans returned to their lives as sheepherders. A common WWII piece of graffiti was "Kilroy was here," which was a hairless male drawing that appeared wherever GIs went. This is possibly a herder's version of the Kilroy images he saw as a soldier. Author photo.

I'd seen Kilroy cartoons, and now I recognized in the woods a sheepherder's version of the same face. It was possibly done by the same herder who had carved on the other side of the mountain. If Kilroy could march across war-torn Europe, why couldn't he help move sheep? Had the herder been a World War II veteran? Now it was my turn to laugh. Kilroy was here and so were we.

We moved slowly up the hill. The three of us spread out, looking right and left at trees, behind trees, around trees. In some groves there was nothing. In other groves we found high concentrations of names, dates, drawings. Climbing a steep meadow with a high peak directly above us, we found the date 9/5/1942 and a woman's face with a cloud of curls and bangs across her forehead. This was true folk art, carved on the off side of a tree where almost no one would ever see it. The artist left no name. "This tree is like a book. It's hard to read because of the age, but it's still there," sighed Sharon Wangelin, intrigued.

With my fingers I traced the gentle curls. For all the work that Polly Hammer and her assistants Dana Isham, Rand Greubel, and Phil Born had accomplished, the trees would fall. Their official 1988 report stated, "All significant data was recovered during field work and no further work is needed. The site lacks integrity of design, materials and workmanship due to natural deterioration and possibly vandalism. It is not associated with important historic events or significant persons. It embodies no distinctive characteristics."

I disagree. Groves of carved aspen are important, and some designs are indeed significant. This should be the history and archaeology of herders, who rarely kept journals or left other signs of their passing. Many spoke only a little English. Like my Spanish—*poquito*. Their only canvas was wooden—the trees. American history has far too many stories about GWM, or Great White Men. The rich and famous. Those who succeeded often wrote their own stories and epitaphs, but what about those western workers who were just passing through? As historians and archaeologists, we need to give voice to the voiceless. This was their record, their thoughts, their inspirations. I was glad the trees had not fallen.

I turned, and Leigh Ann found an old graniteware coffeepot without a handle lying on its side in deep grass. I turned again and saw that the handle had been nailed high up on the side of an aspen trunk, and over the years, probably from the weight of repeated snowfalls, the enamel pot had separated from the handle, which was now deeply embedded in the aspen's bark. Although she had over 25 years of archaeological fieldwork, Leigh Ann had never found an actual artifact at a former sheepherder camp. We both smiled and looked beyond to the snowcapped peak high above the fluttering aspens. Why nail a coffeepot high up on a tree? We shook our heads. "Perhaps a place to leave notes?" she queried. Who knows? *Quién sabe*? We left the coffeepot where we found it.

Far above us on an aspen, Lee Jones had carved his name and the date 8/10/71. Had he stood on his saddle to write that inscription above our heads? Another mystery.

We also found a series of large carved hands, almost baseball-mitt size. Humans on every continent have carved and painted hands for thousands of years, but perhaps these carvings reflected the impact of La Mano Negra, or the Black Hand Society, regional rebels from Rio Arriba County who resented the US Forest Service takeover of what had been village ejidos, or common lands, in New Mexico. Many of the herders near Lone Cone came from Rio Arriba County. Were they sympathetic with La Mano Negra? Were they members? The mysteries and questions continued. History was all around us if we read the trees.

Late for lunch, we walked downhill. On other trees I found a woman's carved face and an ancient Celtic-style cross. Names, dates, scribbles. Headed west in bright sunlight, I found it hard to peer at the trees even with polarized sunglasses. I spied more Kilroy heads, perhaps carved by Gabby Vigil. Had he been in the US Army? The date on one tree was 8/7/53.

Then I thought I saw something in the shadows, an aspen caressed by spruce branches. I couldn't be sure if I was seeing the natural dark lines of boles on the tree's trunk or a human-made pattern.

Closer into the spruce trees I walked and then the carving lit up in a shaft of sunlight, the white aspen bark prominent against the dark spruce near it. I caught my breath. I was staring at the complete carving of a walking woman in a striped dress. The artist, Jose Emilio Salazar, had finished the drawing on 7/19/1942. Did he have brothers in the war? Was he a young man carving an image of his mother, whom he missed? Was he homesick this far north into Colorado with only a dog and borregas for companions?

For long minutes I looked at the portrait. Few people had ever seen it or ever would see it. The light changed and the woman went from sunshine into shadow and then shone again. Clearly, this four-foot-tall carving had

Though sheepherders frequently carved nude women on aspen trees, it is rare to see a fully clothed, full-length female. This is probably the carver's mother or some other important woman in his life. This glyph was found deep in the spruce and aspen trees south of Beaver Park on the Uncompahgre National Forest. Author photo.

been a labor of love. I respected the artist. Had I arrived at the wrong time in the silence and shadow of the forest I never would have seen her, but she appeared to me, and I am grateful she did.

Deeper into the spruce I walked, dark and thick in the afternoon. I found the date 7/25/45 and the faint words "Hoy de dia Santiago" by the same Jose Salazar who had carved his mother. I think he was describing a feast day for Santiago, the patron saint of shepherds and all who work the fields. Jose left his name and the town "Park View, New Mex," which had once been Los Ojos, just north of Tierra Amarilla in Rio Arriba County. A developer had given the village a more English-sounding name to lure potential immigrant farmers from Chicago, but the plan had failed and the town had resorted to its old name of Los Ojos, "The Eyes," christened because of nearby springs that run with water similar to how one's eyes tear up.

I thought of the decades since Jose had carved his woman in the striped dress, and I wondered how he had spent his herding income when he returned to his village. Deeply moved by his carvings and inscriptions, I stepped out of the spruce and into warm sunshine. We slowly descended the steep slope.

Though we climbed and looked, the rest of the day we found nothing comparable. Perhaps we misread our maps or perhaps the patron saint Santiago had nothing more to share. We returned to the cabin and sat on the historical stone porch. Later that night around the woodstove, Leigh Ann Hunt told me more about her sheepherder friend George "Junior" Valencia (1937–2015) from Blanco, New Mexico, whose family had homesteaded near Marvel, Colorado, and then moved to Montrose, where he lived. Strangers mistook George for a Native American. Like many born in New Mexico, he experienced subtle and not so subtle racism most of his life.

Speaking in both Spanish and English with Leigh Ann, he told her a variety of stories about herders and their ways. He felt that Basques succeeded in moving up from herding sheep to owning sheep because they were white. "We would get turned down for bank loans because of our brown skin. Hispanics rarely went from being herders to owning their own flocks. How could New Mexicans who dropped out of elementary school to go to work, get loans and understand the requirements of grazing allotments?" George argued. There was simply too much paperwork.

Even though members of his family herded sheep, once a young man got older and wanted to start a family he usually needed more money. So, as George had done, he went into the mines or worked for the railroad. All these occupations kept families separated for months at a time.

As a herder for nearly 30 years, Valencia paid in no Social Security. Employers did not withhold any wages. They provided food and sometimes paid doctor bills. They'd give herders new leather gloves or maybe a jacket.

How did the herders feel about the jobs themselves? Leigh Ann recounts, "They had to be totally self-reliant like the time George pulled an infected tooth by himself with a pair of pliers. Or having a horse suffer a high-altitude heart attack and roll off a cliff at night. George did not even have a flashlight to scramble back up to his camp."[6]

He told her many stories. He spoke of two herders near Ouray who argued over what was on the label of a Log Cabin syrup can. Legend has it that they killed each other back at camp.

George was afraid of ghosts in the night, coyote packs, bears snuffling around his 10-by-10-foot canvas tent, which had no floor. He slept with a .30–30 by his bed for the rest of his life.

Good herders swept the floor, kept clean tents, and were excellent cooks. Poor herders abused their dogs and lived in filth, and their food could not be trusted. On a cold night one herder heated his stove too hot and burned his tent to the ground.

Sheepmen had total power over their herders and either misunderstood what food to bring to camp or did not care. One boss continued to bring canned salmon to Valencia, which he would not eat. Finally, having left full cans around the tent for his boss to see, George gave up and buried them so he wouldn't have to move them. Every male in his family worked a few seasons in sheep. New Mexicans, having grown up around horses, had an early advantage over Basque and Greek herders, who had much to learn about riding horses and packing mules. Basques from the Pyrenees had many adjustments to make in America. Initially they did not understand horses and were as clueless as anyone else about herding. They had herded only small flocks. They didn't know what to do with 1,200 sheep, George had commented.

There was virtually no cash in northern New Mexican villages, so men who "followed the sheeps" into Colorado or Wyoming brought much-needed income back home. With his wages, Valencia bought his mother her first refrigerator, and he was still making payments on it when she died. Relatives appropriated it. The theft angered him the rest of his life.

We talked about George late into the night. Leigh Ann had helped him through his last days with cancer, and he had given her a sheepdog pup that had accompanied us here, full of fun and frolic, with a mat of gray and white hair. In the morning we parted ways, vowing to meet again to try to find more Colorado aspen drawings.

She asked me to write about George and his life because he had been so vital and had worked so hard most of his life on behalf of the owners, but as a herder he was nearly forgotten; and that's why these carved trees are so important today. Valencia had kept his sense of humor and mischief to the last. I saw tears well up in Leigh Ann's eyes like Los Ojos, like springs. I told her that yes, I wanted to tell the herders' stories. Someone should.

"Important information on range usage was obtained from aspen carvings," wrote Polly Hammer. "It was possible, in some instances, to determine changes in allotment lines, seasonal movements, weather, location of salting areas, periods of range use or non-use and to make deductive inferences concerning economic trends." Archaeological fieldworkers found enough carvings by Gabby Vigil to monitor most of his movements through the 1953 grazing season.

Grazing records and aspen carving dates dovetailed perfectly with the rise and fall of lamb and wool markets. Carvers left phrases about the environment, rain, work, sex, and sheep. Samples include the following:

This road up	Working for Hughes
Salt Ground #9	Lost 600 sheep
Put salt 7–18–52	Bray sheep range
My bed overnight	The sheep died here
We have made this corral	The sheep are very sick
This place is worth shit	Here I stayed at my camp on Sept. 1937
I was sick here today	Come for my horse from the Preacher
I am barefooted in camp	What fucking animals I am taking care of [7]

Hammer and her colleagues also noted the lighter side of herders' phrases infused with romance, philosophy, humor, and respect for nature.

Rain like hell today	Rain for 50 days straight
Hallo fellows	October will soon be here
Kiss me dear	A beautiful day
It is beautiful and raining	Abe honey lets go home
With my Maria	Love oh love
Me and you only sweetheart	Stays up all night
He who watches for thieves	Rest in peace
With closed mouth no flies will enter	Sunday, Oct. 1935 [8]

"One could detect the acculturation process of the more prolific carvers by noting the progression from Spanish, to broken English, and finally, to correct English over time," notes Hammer in the *Cultural Resource Inventory of the Lone Cone Aspen Treatment*.[9] Researchers found abundant drawings of flowers, leaves, and animals, including dogs, cows, horses, deer, bears, birds, and one butterfly, but no fish.

Resident artists included Pacomio Chacon, Moses Galvez, M. A. Montaño, who may have carved the bald-headed "Kilroy was here" faces, Hilario Maestas, Celso Martinez, and Filoberto Galvez, who perhaps carved the female profiles we saw. Dates of carvings match women's hair and dress styles for those periods in American fashion.

There is much to learn from aspens; they reflect the loneliness and isolation of sheepherders' lives, especially the large number of Hispano herders who worked in Colorado but came from villages in the highlands of northern New Mexico.

Outdoor adventure hikers seek solo experiences and live a few days on a mountainside or deep in a desert canyon. For herders, those days become months and years. They live in a world of silence, solitude, and starlight. Always listening for the sound of distressed sheep, the agitated tinkle of a bell on a wise old ewe, or the low growl of a dog smelling a bear near camp.

I took Road 611 from the Uncompahgre Forest south toward the San Juan National Forest. Along the route I found another carving about Fermin, this time on two trees with "ratero" on one tree and "Fermin M." on the adjacent aspen. I had to smile. Herders complaining about other herders.

I drove by myself, except for my Labrador on the front seat beside me. I thought about what we'd seen and where we'd walked. I scouted a few small white groves and found nothing of consequence. Hunting camps had moved in, and by the next day the first fall rifle season would bring hunters and their bright fluorescent orange clothing moving beneath yellow aspens. I was alone, driving higher into north-facing fir and spruce, the dark timber where willows cloak small streams and sunlight filters softly through pine needles.

As I drove on, aspens spread below me shedding their autumn leaves. The herders' carvings would soon stand on bare trees. Alone like the herders themselves. Silent on the steep slopes, waiting for the first snowfall.

South of Norwood, Colorado, the aspens on the Uncompahgre National Forest and in nearby mountains contain some of the densest concentrations of arborglyphs in the state near the congressionally designated Lizard Head Wilderness. Author photo.

Chapter 6

Sheepherding After WWII from Canyonlands to Wilderness, 1945–1970

> We abuse land because we regard it as a commodity belonging to us. When we see land as a community to which we belong, we may begin to use it with love and respect . . . That land is a community is the basic concept of ecology, but that land is to be loved and respected is an extension of ethics.
>
> —ALDO LEOPOLD
> *A Sand County Almanac*

> The greatest factory on this earth is the lonely sheep. Its raw materials are the grasses and weeds that grow on our mountains and prairies, and its product of essential food and raiment goes farther than any single factory in the world to meet the needs of mankind.
>
> —US SENATOR CHARLES H. WILLIAMS, MONTANA

Deep in the canyon country of southern Utah on winter sheep range, Howard Lathrop lost two saddle horses to a rugged, tortuous trail. One horse began to pitch and buck and when Howard rolled out of the saddle the horse slipped, plunged onto rocks below, broke its neck and died. On a narrow stone ledge a year later, as he led another horse by the reins, the second animal panicked and fell hundreds of feet to its death snapping an iron saddle horn off a well-worn saddle. Lathrop climbed down the cliff to retrieve the broken saddle horn and gave it to his wife Marguerite "telling her it showed how near she came to becoming a widow."[1] She used it as a paper weight.

After World War II the hard and sometimes dangerous work of sheep herding continued, but change was in the air. The 1934 Taylor Grazing Act had created the Grazing Service but it met with limited success and congressional hostility. A decade later ranchers pushed not for regulatory reform but for the land itself. "Little major decision-making in the West has entailed more pain and uncertainty than that of determining what should be the ultimate fate of the remaining public domain after homesteading had run its practical course," notes William Voigt, Jr. in *Public Grazing Lands*.[2]

Ranchers grabbed every blade of grass they could find. Soil had been scalped. Rain-caused sheet erosion gullied what had once been meadows. Severely overgrazed landscapes required conservation measures and re-seeding to slow erosion. Grappling with difficult land-use questions, former forester Aldo Leopold had moved from New Mexico to Wisconsin. In Madison at the University of Wisconsin, he began the radical work of re-seeding a Midwestern prairie and he helped create the new concept of ecological restoration. He liked the challenge so much that for back taxes he bought a run-down farm full of sand and cockleburs and on weekends he and his family planted trees and tried to restore their own prairie. Across the West, half a century of overgrazing had taken its toll. Federal land managers pushed to accomplish on the public domain what Leopold was attempting in Sand County, Wisconsin.

In 1947–48 in the Valle Seco area near Pagosa Springs, Colorado, on 300 acres, US Forest Service employees utilized a Caterpillar bulldozer and a 10-foot disc to plow and then broadcast seed for crested wheat grass, brome, and yellow sweet clover.[3] Many national forest districts followed suit.

Continuous overgrazing also had damaged private land creating ditches or arroyos where once natural runoff had moistened deep grasses. William deBuys writes of ecological damage near his home in northern New Mexico:

> The intermittent stream that once meandered these flats and nourished them with silt now cleaves the meadow in a raw gully twenty-five feet deep. Pines that are decades old grow in it, their tops barely reaching what used to be ground level. You cannot cross the arroyo, not here; you need to search a better spot, and still you would expect to fill your boots with dirt as you slide down one steep side and scramble up the other, clawing with your hands. Year after year of goats and sheep

and milk cows and horses helped to unravel this place, and probably a wagon track once ran down the center of the meadow preparing a naked strip of earth for storm flows to gnaw away.[4]

On public lands the damage was often worse. Ecological changes had occurred during the droughts of the Great Depression that would take years—if ever—to reverse. The western landscape had paid the price of sustaining ranchers. With limited resiliency on the land, after the war some of the West's sons and daughters simply did not return home but found other opportunities in bustling cities.

As World War II ended and a generation of Americans came home to attend college on the G.I. Bill, buy new houses in the suburbs, purchase fancy two-tone cars with big engines and flashy fins, other changes occurred, too. In World War I it had taken ten sheep to clothe one soldier and provide for woolen Army blankets. During World War II the US Army had needed wool uniforms for soldiers in the European theatre and the government had guaranteed markets for wool, but no more. Men's fashions changed. Dress pants no longer had cuffs. Few gentlemen wore wool vests.

Though Pendleton Woolen Mills in Oregon still sold shirts for between $9 and $12, and a Texas company marketed the $25 "Stockman's Shirt" of wool gabardine with pearl buttons and silk-lined yoke in tan, black, green and wine, natural fibers gave way to rayons and nylons. Carpets and drapes utilized less wool. A new world of plastics supplanted wool products and used Jeeps brought waves of uranium prospectors and tourists into the intermountain West.

Returning GIs started the baby boom when they came home to the girls they had left behind. For the thousands of US Marines who had been in the Pacific Theatre the war had given them an aversion to mutton and lamb.

My father, David Oliver Gulliford, had been a US Marine Corps major flying aerial reconnaissance in B-24 bombers off the Solomon Islands. He could not stand even the smell of roasted lamb. With little fresh meat available, soldiers in the Pacific had been fed strong, tough, aged Australian mutton which they came to revile. Marines swore they could smell boiled mutton a mile away from their military bases and it turned their stomachs. Once home they told their young wives to cook any kind of meat—pork, beef, chicken—anything but lamb. So a younger generation of Americans grew up without knowing the delicacy of roast leg of lamb for Sunday dinner.[5]

Still, Colorado's sheepmen prospered because of expanding world markets and the need for food and fiber in war-torn Europe, even though across the West sheep numbers gradually declined. A significant change after World War II was new residents moving into uncrowded western states. Thousands of veterans who had seen the West for the first time while stationed on western military bases or traveling across the country on troop trains, longed to live in a land of snow and sunshine away from the heat and humidity back east. As the West's urban centers boomed after the war, and with the 1956 Interstate Highway Act and new paved roads, tourism increased with fishermen and their families coming in station wagons to fish Colorado's gold standard rivers and streams. Couples crossed the West while visiting national parks, and deer and elk hunters enjoyed record harvests because for five years no one had been home to hunt. In Colorado, hunters could kill two deer with one license.

In the decades after the war as the American market for wool and mutton began to trend downward, federal agencies realigned themselves based on new principles of multiple use that included the old mainstays of lumbering, mining, and grazing, but now also included recreation and public access to lands whose primary users had been ranchers.

The most dramatic shift was the elimination of the century-old General Land Office and the recent Grazing Service and the 1946 consolidation of those lands under a new agency titled the Bureau of Land Management. These were millions of acres of primarily lower elevation lands that no one had wanted to pay taxes on. Few ranchers had homesteaded these desert and sagebrush areas, they'd just used them. Conservationists argued that ranchers had not just used those lands—they had abused them. In the late 1940s the conservation movement had not yet become the environmental movement, but change was forthcoming. [6]

A new generation of men in sheep camps rolled their own cigarettes and rolled the bottoms of their Levis up a few inches above their boots. They were the grandsons and sons of men who had pioneered in the West when there were no rules. They tilted their sweat-stained Stetsons above their foreheads and pondered new ways to kill coyotes. The landscapes they had always had to themselves would soon have additional visitors. From Colorado's lush mountain meadows long used for summer sheep grazing, to Utah's canyon bottoms perfect for winter feed, those acres held a different meaning for post-World War II tourists who saw only scenery not the working landscapes of livestock owners.

Through his journals and his writings Aldo Leopold had begun to evolve his thinking. He had always sought a balance between Americans and their landscapes, but now he came to see the value of large predators to control prey populations of deer and elk. He held the radical idea that wolf bounties should be eliminated and that wolves should be allowed to inhabit their traditional ranges. He grappled with ecological ideas, created conservation and wildlife management principles, and finally moved from applied science and ecology to philosophy with his statement on a land ethic.

Leopold was far ahead of his time. Out west predator populations plummeted because of steel leg traps, repeating saddle rifles, and more lethal poisons. Cattlemen and sheepmen had ceased to quarrel among themselves. Instead, they focused their anger on the federal government and newly minted, college-educated range cons or range conservation experts who suggested reduced numbers on grazing permits to let the land heal. Leopold would have understood, but he wasn't trying to make a living raising sheep on Western ranges. There the big livestock operators sensed change and moved to block it. Politicians did their bidding.

Wesley Calef dedicated his book *Private Grazing and Public Lands* to federal employees who were "district graziers in the Middle Rocky Mountain basins, who, during the lean and difficult years of the Grazing Service, badgered by politicians, ignored by those they were supposed to regulate, unsupported by their department, and neglected by the electorate, nevertheless carried on their work with intelligence, energy, and astonishingly, with enthusiasm." [7] Federal land managers and their lower level employees faced a public land grab. Cattlemen and sheepmen not only wanted no rules and no regulations on the Taylor Grazing area lands, they wanted the lands themselves.

In the 1940s western ranchers, many of them sheepmen, doggedly denied that the land they had always used primarily as winter range did not belong to them but instead belonged to the American public. Thus, World War II veterans from the West returned home to another war, a struggle over federal dominance of western landscapes and a 1940s fight for government grass. At the heart of the dispute, the unspoken truth was the deplorable condition of Western rangelands and the absolute necessity of reducing livestock numbers.

At higher elevations, the US Forest Service effectively managed public grazing on national forests, but in the lower level areas of sagebrush plateaus, mesas, benchlands, and canyons, a struggle for the heart and soul of the interior West had begun. "The principal argument of the western livestock interests seemed to be that they wanted the land, and therefore it was grossly unfair, illegal, unconstitutional, and immoral for the federal government to continue holding it; moreover it was 'communistic,'" explained Calef. The ranchers demanded that rangelands be sold "with an absolute preference for the current lessee." [8] How ironic that stockmen argued that they would gladly pay in property taxes what they had opposed as grazing fees.

In 1946 sheepman and Wyoming Senator E.V. Robertson introduced S. 1945, a bill designed to transfer the entire public domain to the states for private ownership as well as grazing lands in national forests and even lands suited for grazing in national parks.[9]

Proponents of giving federal land back to the states to later be sold to area ranchers included G. Norman Winder of Craig, Colorado, president of the National Woolgrowers Association and a permittee on the Routt National Forest, as well as J. Elmer Brock of Kaycee, Wyoming a permittee on the Big Horn National Forest and former head of the American National, a cattlemen's organization.

The Denver and Rio Grande, Colorado's mountain railroad, off-loads sheep that herders will trail into Colorado's high country. OP-8024. Photo courtesy of the Denver Public Library.

Brock explained in an opinion essay written for the *Denver Post* on February 2, 1947 that stockmen should be allowed to buy the grazing lands they coveted on the "basis of 10 per cent down, the balance to be paid over 30 years and to carry interest at 1 ½ percent." [10] And the price? From nine cents to $2.80 per acre. "Brock's article provided the spark needed to fire the conservation organizations," explains Voigt. [11]

Far-thinking sheepmen did not just rant against the government. They bought abandoned homesteads for back taxes or purchased farms and ranches from families moving towards western cities in the great post-war migration to urban and suburban areas. Some of those ranches were sagebrush and pinon but others were high country meadows close to national forests making it easier to acquire and keep USFS permits because of having nearby land or "commensurability." Some ranchers simply bought land near railheads so they could corral their sheep waiting for the right trains to take them to market.

US Senator Pat McCarran from Nevada, a state with hard-working, successful Basque sheepmen, had begun in 1941 to hold field hearings to listen to the frustration of stockmen. Short-tempered and vindictive, by July, 1945, McCarran had led a fight in Congress to block appropriations for the Grazing Service closing most district offices in eleven western states. Only two government employees remained in Colorado to work with the grazing advisory boards.[12]

Stockmen thought their problems would be solved with the 1934 Taylor Grazing Act but they now argued for privatizing public lands. Anticommunist McCarran listened hard. "The public land users were restless. They had believed with passage of the Taylor Act their problems would disappear," writes Voigt. He explains that the McCarran investigations "would close with the consolidation of the Grazing Service and GLO into today's Bureau of Land Management under conditions that virtually assured that the thoroughly cowed new agency would have the utmost difficulty in rising from custodial into genuine managerial status."[13]

In Wisconsin, Aldo Leopold was trying to restore prairies. Out west to avoid stock reductions, ranchers wanted to own the public lands they grazed so they could not be told what to do. The post-war years on the public domain can be defined as the era of the Great Land Grab. The environmental movement had not yet taken shape but hunters, anglers, and other sportsmen realized that private ownership of public lands would mean little to no public access.

In 1947 Lester Velie wrote, "They Kicked Us off Our Land" in *Collier's Magazine*. Arthur Carhart published, "In Defence of our Public Domain" in *The Land*, and Bernard De Voto fired salvo after salvo in *Harper's Magazine* with articles titled, "The West Against Itself," "Sacred Cows and Public Lands," and "Statesman on the Lam." [14]

That same year stockmen grazing livestock on Grand Mesa in western Colorado met with US Forest Service officials to appoint a committee on range improvement to avoid a 30% reduction in grazing numbers. The land was poor and needed a rest. Eventually policies were worked out, salt licks relocated, and depleted lands re-seeded. [15]

As ranchers fought against stock reductions, as sportsmen rallied to the defense of public lands, conservationist and hunter Aldo Leopold was asked to sum up the land grab threat at the prestigious North American Wildlife Conference held in San Antonio in 1947. He rose to the occasion and eloquently remarked:

> Let no man think the issue is a western affair of no consequence to other states. The defeat of public land conservation in the West would be felt by every state. Let no man think this is a Grazing District fight. Disrupt the public domain and the national forests will follow; disrupt the national forests and the national parks will follow. It is pure evasion to say the states or private owners could practice conservation on those lands. Neither, by and large, has demonstrated either the capacity or the wish to do so. To organize the practice of conservation on large areas takes decades of hard work.[16]

As always, Leopold spoke the truth. One of the nation's foremost conservationists and an early environmentalist, as a forester Leopold had spent time in Arizona and New Mexico. He knew the impact of public lands grazing. In 1947 he sought to stop the public land grab. A year later at age sixty-one he would be dead.[17]

Just before his death, Oxford University Press had agreed to publish his edited essays as *A Sand County Almanac*. He was to be one of America's representatives at a United Nations sponsored conference on conservation in 1949. Instead, he died fighting a wildfire on a neighbor's property near his beloved Shack. [18] The world had lost a great naturalist and conservation leader, but his thoughts have lived on in *A Sand County Almanac*.

"The idea that all species properly make up a community, and that human beings have a moral obligation to expand their idea of community to include other species . . . and even natural processes, was first clearly articulated during the 1930s and 1940s by pioneer conservationist Aldo Leopold," explains William R. Jordan III in *The Sunflower Forest*. He adds that Leopold, "has become one of the defining legends of environmentalism" based not only on Leopold's land ethic, which argued for the greatest distribution of natural species on a piece of land, but also because, "he avoided the extremes of utilitarian conservationism and hands-off preservation . . . His writings are marked by a sense of moderation and an undogmatic respect for diverse cultural traditions combined with a passionate commitment to the well-being of the land community." [19]

Leopold's writing on diverse cultural traditions includes respect for sheepherding and sheepmen and trying to understand the need for ecological balance. He wrote about riding the White Mountains of Arizona and of mountain meadows that "were scrolled, curled, and crenulated with an infinity of bays and coves, points and stringers, peninsulas and parks, each one of which differed from all the rest. No man knew them all and a day's ride offered a gambler's chance of finding a new one." [20]

He describes "the profusion of initials, dates, and cattle brands inscribed on the patient bark of aspens at every mountain camp site" and how the trees traced the rancher's evolution, his acquisition of stock, and even the birth and coming of age of his children. Leopold concludes, "The old man was dead now; in his later years his heart had thrilled only to his bank account and to the tally of his flocks and herds, but the aspen revealed that in his youth he too had felt the glory of the mountain spring." [21]

In his lifetime Aldo Leopold gave momentum to ideas and ideals that would transform the West and impact the West's sheep-owning families exactly like the Hispanic New Mexican family he had married into. While Leopold argued for landscape restoration and new conservation values, out on the highly contested public domain in the West, to bend to the demands of stockmen for more grass, Caterpillar bulldozers worked side by side dragging huge anchor chains between them to destroy native sagebrush and pinon juniper trees in a hundred-foot swath.

This episode of "chaining," to make it easier for sheep and cattle to eat limited grass, ruined native plants and ecosystems, threatened wildlife, and destroyed archaeological sites not yet recorded. The goal was to obliterate sagebrush and replant public lands with Indian rice grass and non-native crested wheatgrass. The end result was more invasive species and shrubs that have crept back. "So that's not a really good solution to the problem. Once you've destroyed the native plant community, I don't think you're ever going to bring it back," says Utah native Julian Hatch. "You might be able to bring it back in one-acre, five-acre pieces that look like little pastures or something. But generally, throughout thousands of acres, you've lost all of those native plants." 22

Yet opportunities existed both for conservation and for establishing new sheep families and empires of wool and lamb. Senator Pat McCarran who had held hearings on privatizing public land continued to rail against the threat of communism, but he also acknowledged that sheepmen across the West needed shepherds. Valuable employer-employee ties had been broken because of the war. Always attentive to his Nevada constituents, McCarran supported bringing in more herders and passed "Sheepherder Bills" for that purpose.

"The story began during the war. In the manpower shortage all farm labor became hard to get," wrote Peter Edson in the *Times-News* of Twin Falls, Idaho on March 13, 1951. "Self-respecting white men refused to have anything to do with tending silly sheep. Neither would the native Indians of the western range country."23 Sheepmen needed herders and powerful Senator McCarran introduced bills to bring in Basque herders from the Spanish Pyrenees even though they came from Franco's fascist Spain while other immigrants were denied visas. Basques come from France or Spain, but McCarran targeted Spanish Basques. Without herders, sheepmen sold their sheep. They had no choice.

"The request had come from ranchers in Nevada, Idaho, and California. Herds were shrinking; wool production was down. Ranchers believed that the able hands of 'sturdy Basque sheepherders' could help staunch the decline of herds," explains Basque descendant Vince J. Juaristi. 24

As chairman of the Judiciary Committee, silver-haired McCarran wielded enormous power. He started submitting bills bringing in 250 Basque herders a year. Other immigrants were carefully scrutinized before being allowed to come to the United States, but "Basque sheepherders were considered immigrants with special skills, giving them preference over average immigrants. That they hailed from a fascist country no longer mattered," notes Juaristi. McCarran brought in a total of 1,135 Basque shepherds. They were not political. They were not fascists. They were young men desperately seeking work outside of war-torn Europe.

"No other group of immigrants enjoyed such preferential treatment, or expedited attention," states Juaristi. "If a Basque sheepherder in the Pyrenees applied for a visa, he received an interview at the American consulate, a physical, and a plane ticket. Within a month he found himself with a dog at his side and a willow in his hand herding a band of 1,000 sheep in Nevada or another western state, sleeping by a campfire, and eating beans from a can."25 Some of those Basque herders became famous Colorado sheepmen whose sons carry on proud herding traditions.

If the 1950s saw a flood of Basque herders, other post-war changes included a successful fight to stop a dam in Dinosaur National Monument on the Colorado-Utah border. Stopping a dam might not have had much to do with sheep grazing on public lands, but out of the Dinosaur fight the environmental movement emerged from the 19th century conservation movement. Flush with victory over stopping a dam on the Green and Yampa Rivers, the Sierra Club and the Wilderness Society then advocated for a national wilderness bill. Leopold's thinking can be found in both campaigns.

Aldo Leopold fought against dam-building projects on Wisconsin's rivers. In an unpublished essay left in pencil draft he wrote, "Flood-control dams, hydroelectric dams, channelization and dyking of rivers, watershed authorities, drainages, lake outlet controls and impoundments, are running riot, all in the name of development and conservation." Leopold explained that these water projects "involve irreversible changes in the organization of the biota . . . . In all of them, control of nature by concrete and steel is held to be inherently superior to natural or biotic controls." 26

Leopold did not live long enough to fight the proposed dam in Echo Park, but stopping a dam in a unit of the National Park System became a galvanizing action that pushed the old style conservation movement into the modern environmental movement. Dozens of organizations became involved and for the first time the Sierra Club acted outside of California.27

Dams and wild rivers do not seem linked to domestic sheep, but momentum from halting the dam in Dinosaur convinced the Wilderness Society, created in 1935 with Aldo Leopold as one of its founding members, to seek passage of a federal wilderness bill. The bill would create a national Wilderness Preservation System, and the high altitude lands that were targeted for inclusion were exactly those grassy mountain meadows flush with wildflowers in July, where sheep did best.

Having failed to privatize Bureau of Land Management lands that they utilized in winter, now sheepmen faced another potential threat to their summer ranges on public land. American sentiment had shifted. Youthful baby boomer backpackers desired to camp in the same mountain meadows where herders had once had the landscape all to themselves.

In the 1840s Henry David Thoreau had argued "In wildness is the preservation of the world." By the end of the century, John Muir, in a state of ecstasy in the high Sierras above Yosemite National Park, proclaimed wild landscapes essential to the American soul and the perfect antidote to modern civilization. He had begun his experience in that granite boulder strewn country as an itinerant sheepherder who would later claim sheep to be "hoofed locusts."

Momentum had grown with formation of The Wilderness Society in 1935 and by the mid-1950s Executive Director Howard Zahniser sought a national wilderness bill to create a permanent system of wilderness areas "where man is a visitor who does not remain." The wilderness idea had evolved into a goal or an ideal that became bottled up in committee when it met Colorado Congressman Wayne Aspinall, an old-style conservationist who believed in the full utilization of natural resources for grazing, mining, and lumbering. He thought that every river needed a dam. His sheepherding constituents could not imagine a mountain meadow without a band of woolies grazing contentedly and a few Border collies dozing at the edge of the flock, one eye open.

Zahniser had his work cut out for him. Aspinall blocked passage of the Wilderness Bill 66 times in his Congressional committee. Zahniser had a new vision for public lands. He wanted them preserved for their wilderness values, for the mystery of nature, not just for forage production. "We are not fighting progress, we are making it," he proclaimed, buoyed by the fact that in 1960 Congress had passed the Multiple Use Sustained Yield Act which gave equal status to recreation, range, wildlife, and fish on US Forest Service lands.

Zahniser sought untrammeled areas where natural processes prevailed. His biographer Mark Harvey explains that the word "untrammeled" held special meaning because "this word best captured the essence of wildness, because it indicated how wilderness lands were 'not subjected to human controls and manipulations that hamper the free play of natural forces." It did not mean pristine. He defined wilderness "as a place that, though damaged from overgrazing or prospecting, might be healed." [28]

Touring potential western wilderness areas Zahniser often saw the effects of decades of overgrazing and denuded grasslands. Congressman Aspinall insisted, because of his Colorado constituents, that any wilderness bill would "grandfather in" grazing. Existing permits would be honored. As for Zahniser, "Generally he was inclined to advance the wilderness cause by making allies, and he was troubled by the prospect of alienating ranchers."[29]

In the end, both Aspinall and Zahniser won. Aspinall required grazing and a full Congressional vote to add any wilderness areas to a national wilderness system. Zahniser got his wilderness bill passed with the stirring words that "it is the policy of the Congress to secure for the American people of present and future generations the benefits of an enduring resource of wilderness." But just as Aldo Leopold did not live to see the publication of *A Sand County Almanac,* Howard Zahniser died two months before President Lyndon Johnson signed the Wilderness Act in 1964 preserving nine million acres. Wilderness lands have now grown to over 110 million acres of American soil, yet that's a mere 4% of the United States. We have an equal percentage of paved roads.

The backpacking boom continued and congressionally designated wilderness areas became backpacking destinations for thousands of able-bodied hikers who would return again and again for the silence, solitude, and darkness they found in wilderness landscapes. That's what they expected anyway. In many areas they found herders' tents, sheep smells, and silence broken by ewes bleating for their lambs. Sheepmen felt the sting of backpackers' scorn, but young lambs put on rapid weight in the high country found in national forests above timberline.

One Colorado rancher who did well with forest grazing was G. Norman Winder of Craig, Colorado who served in a variety of organizations and on boards always looking out for livestock interests. In the sheep business all his life, his family acquired the Two Bar Ranch on the Little Snake River and using six Mexican herders with six flocks Winder sheep could "stop on Two Bar land every night during the 70-mile drive from winter headquarters on the Little Snake to the forest summer grazing lands without traveling on a main highway." [30]

He increased wool production and meat production, re-seeded the worn out homestead lands he had bought and served on senate committees on public lands, with wool freight rate investigations and hearings on livestock rates for shipping meat. He also brought comely blonde models to Craig for a publicity stunt during shearing time.

They posed with steel clippers and docile ewes on the high school football field. The models with their tight-fitting blouses and high heels hovered over Winder's best shearer when he won an award for clipping the most wool. By the early 1960s stockmen like Norman Winder made Craig, Colorado one of the top wool shipment depots in the United States.

In the beginning cattlemen hated sheep and spurned sheepmen, but the money in woolies transformed Northwest Colorado. In 1949 envelopes mailed through the Craig Post Office stated "World's Largest Wool Shipping Center" on the cancellation. By 1956 more than half of Routt and Moffat Counties were owned or leased by sheepmen who shipped 3.5 million pounds of wool from Craig. Four years later in 1960 the *Rocky Mountain News* proclaimed Craig "the largest shipping point for wool in the country." Hayden, Colorado had become a national shipping point for young lambs.

In the *Rocky Mountain News*, Pasquale Marvanzino wrote "Tenders of the Sheep" about successful Greek families who wait for September when the sheep come home. "Then begins a series of feasts—all of them based on religious name days and great celebrations. Their ladies turn out the *dolmates*—the hamburger and rice wrapped in grape leaves, the lamb curry, the great mounds of green bread. And the husbands sit around and talk and dance over homemade Zinfandel wine oddly flavored with pitch."[31]

Norman Winder came from a Utah Mormon family and helped establish the family's Colorado ranches in Moffat and Routt Counties. Other families who did well had Greek ancestors. Their descendants adapted to the rolling terrain of northwest Colorado with its sparse natural cover and plenty of room for winter grazing. Local ranchers prospered from a sheep economy.

Through their politicians, stockmen continued to assert authority over public land management. Environmentalists had successfully scored with passage of the Wilderness Act protecting millions of acres, but what about wildlife? Decades of predator control by the Biological Survey had killed thousands of wolves, coyotes, bobcats, lynx, eagles, and even magpies. In 1946–47, in the middle of the Great Land Grab, paid professional hunters controlling predators in Colorado turned in a record 304 pair of scalped bears' ears. Their goal was to make the high country safe for sheep and cattle.[32]

High in the San Juan Mountains, in country traversed in the 1850s by sheep being trailed to California to feed prospectors and miners, predator control continued because bears munched mutton. Colorado has thousands of black bears, but grizzlies are gone.

In 1952 at the headwaters of the Los Pinos River, in a beautiful small park, Lloyd Anderson built a "cubby" or v-shaped bear trap, which is a log corral with large bait, often a dead sheep, and a hidden steel trap. Once the bear springs the leg-hold trap he or she would have been encumbered by a "toggle" or drag log. Anderson used a heavy freshly cut green tree, eight-foot long, one foot in diameter. "If a trapped bear tried to run for it, the long heavy toggle would get snagged on trees and brush, slowing or stopping the getaway, at least in theory," writes David Petersen in *Ghost Grizzlies*. "In this case, the trap-bound grizzly dragged its improvised ball and chain five rugged mountain miles." [33] Following on horseback with a mule in tow, Anderson fired twice as the bear reared up on its hind legs deep in the willows. He kept the claws and skull.

The last legal kill of a grizzly in Colorado occurred in a place christened by the Spanish, a magic site, in the Weminuche Wilderness appropriately named *Rincón de la Osa* or hiding place of the female bear. Supposedly the sow had recently killed 35 sheep. Now she was dead and a valuable part of the San Juan Mountains' biodiversity had died with her.[34]

Aldo Leopold could not mourn her loss, but writing for the National Park Service, one of his sons would soon propose a new goal for wildlife in national parks. A decade before passage of the Endangered Species Act in 1973, and twenty years after the last legal kill of a grizz in Colorado, another Leopold would advance a wildlife ideal.

While sheepmen continued to pursue predators on public lands, A. Starker Leopold had a different mission. Stewart Udall, Secretary of the Interior under Presidents John F. Kennedy and Lyndon Johnson, asked for recommendations on ecosystem management in national parks. Aldo Leopold's son made a name for himself in his own right. The Leopold Report stands as one of the most significant ecological documents in the history of scientific management of national parks. Plagued with too many elk at Yellowstone National Park, Leopold suggested predators could prevent habitat degradation and that parks should represent "a vignette of primitive America."

The report stated, "We would recommend that the biotic associations within each park be maintained, or where necessary recreated, as nearly as possible in the condition that prevailed when the area was first visited by the white man."[35]

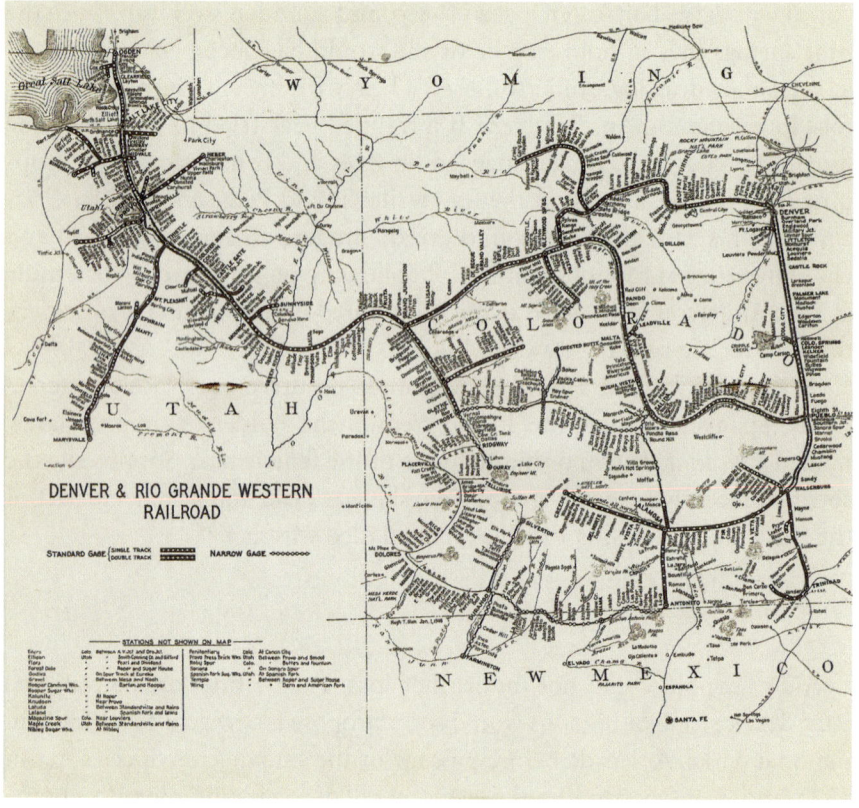

The narrow-gauge Denver and Rio Grande Railroad accessed mountain towns throughout Colorado's Western Slope. Rail routes allowed sheepmen to winter their sheep in Utah deserts and then have the sheep brought by steam locomotives to Colorado loading yards, where sheep could then be trailed to mountain meadows above 10,000 feet in elevation. This 1952 map is courtesy of the Jouflas family.

Just as his father Aldo was often decades ahead of his time, his son Starker recommended ecosystem management before the term existed and before conservation biology had become an emerging field. His report would help provide a rationale for the Endangered Species Act (1973), and it suggested the important ecological role of natural wildfire as a management tool.[36]

It would be years before Starker Leopold's goals would be achieved, but the idea of restoring wild animal populations to their previous habitats would become more accepted in the 1970s. As the environmental movement expanded, non-hunting environmentalists would become more interested in wildlife and game populations. Watchable wildlife would delight hikers.

Secretary of the Interior Stewart Udall had asked for Starker Leopold's report, which would come to impact sheepmen because predators now had a restored place in natural ecosystems. Udall also wanted more national parks. A Southwestern native, he came to focus on Canyonlands, on the jagged, barren red rocks of southeast Utah where on lands that no one had wanted, Utah and Colorado sheepmen had routinely found winter pastures. "What we save now, may be all we save," Udall believed.[37]

Howard Lathrop who lost two horses to the rough terrain, would now have to fight for his winter grazing. The red rocks that were hell on horses would become a tourist magnet and a backcountry challenge for hikers near Moab, Utah. The days of the canyon sheepmen were numbered.

On a 1960 study trip through Ernie's Country in the Maze, ranger Lloyd Pierson asked sheepman Art Ekker about giving up grazing. "He thought a moment and then said, 'It might be better if you did make it a park, then I wouldn't have to worry about getting the sheep down here,'" quotes Jen Jackson Quintano in her biography of Bates Wilson, the first superintendent of Canyonlands.[38] Like other sheepmen, Ekker believed it was his duty to utilize grass on BLM lands, even if it was hard to get to. For sheepmen the desert desolation that would become Canyonlands National Park was just one more working landscape they needed in a constant round of moving woolies to available grass.

Bates Wilson captivated strangers with his Dutch oven cooking diplomacy and his penchant for sharing bourbon. When it came time to discuss swapping BLM lands into a unit of the National Park Service, at North

Point a well-soused BLM ranger camping with Bates agreed to give all of southeast Utah to the Park Service in exchange for three shots of Jim Beam.[39] A shining example of interagency cooperation, sheepmen still needed to be phased out.

US Senator Frank Moss, a Democrat from Utah, understood the shift from a grazing to a recreational economy. He knew the economic potential that would transform the West. He stated in the early 1960s:

> Two great space races now confront us. On the one hand, there lies a great challenge of outer space. One the other there is the problem of play and living space for the American people. We dare neglect either .... there is hope that in groping for the infinite, man will find new dimensions for peaceful living down here.... But it will gain us little to win the moon, only to lose our earthly heritage. [40]

As Bates Wilson worked his job as Superintendent of Arches National Monument, he campaigned for Canyonlands and national park status. He could talk to politicians, locals, tourists, and "then sit down in a Basque sheepherder's trailer over a plate of beans to discuss—in passable Spanish —the driving of livestock across the monument." [41]

Sheepmen grazed on The Big Flats, the name for a wedge-shaped piece of desert plateau between the Green and Colorado Rivers. Referred to as the Utah Desert its red sand and dry yellow earth contained grassy knolls, curly grass, pinons and cedars for shade, and meadows of gramma and blue grass. Chinook winds melted snows in February and March so sheep thrived.[42]

Montrose County, Colorado sheepman Howard Lathrop took his sheep to Dead Horse Point and then dropped into the Big Flat. He also trailed them down the Shafer Trail, which his wife described in her book *Don't Fence Me In* as, "a series of switchbacks, zig-zagging downward and climbing up and looping down again, vanishing on ledges of sandstone too slick to hold tracks. The trail dipped in V's where the horses had to back up to make a turn." [43] What would become thrills for backcountry hikers began as a rugged trail for determined stockmen seeking rims and benches of gramma grass, saltbrush and blackbrush.

Marguerite Lathrop often camped with her husband. She writes about having seen many sunsets, "But in the canyon the land borrows the colors of the sunset to supplement its own. The pinnacles in the distant rock

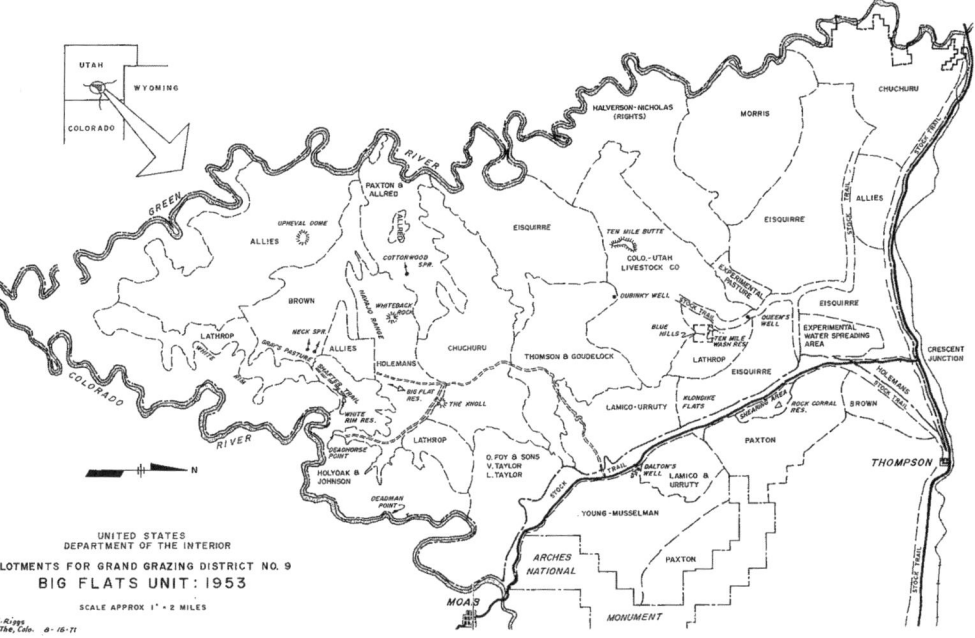

Colorado sheepmen wintered their sheep north and west of what is now Arches National Park in Utah. This map of the Big Flats Unit in 1953 shows the names of the sheepmen, many of them Basque, who had winter grazing allotments in areas now included in Canyonlands National Park, which Congress created in 1964. Map from Marguerite Lathrop, *Don't Fence Me In*. Original allotment map in the Lathrop Collection at the American Heritage Center, University of Wyoming.

took fire from the sun, the buff and browns turned orange, and slowly the canyon was filled with shadows of different intensities of darkness." [44] She wanted to write about those sensations but her husband told her not to. That she'd bring people down into the canyons. Then they'd make it into a national park, "And the first thing you know they'll kick sheep out of here. They don't seem to understand a sheep eats grass and browse nothing else can use and makes it into meat and clothing."[45]

His wife never wrote her article, but Howard Lathrop was correct. In 1964 Congress created Canyonlands as a breathtaking national park where sheep grazing permits have since been retired.

Tourists brought dollars, purchased gas and ice and beer and filled motels. Sheepmen only bought grub for their herders, medicines for the sheep, and biscuits for their dogs. Natural resources became recreational resources. A New West began to replace the Old West of bubbling beans in a camp cookpot and herders moving flocks to bed grounds. "The influence of the population-leisure-travel complex since World War II has been sharply felt in our national and state parks," argued an assistant to the secretary in the Department of the Interior. "In the beginning we labeled this a trend, but in the words of our park superintendents, 'it soon became a stampede.'" 46

If national parks put out the welcome mat for tourists, the Bureau of Land Management, having survived a bumpy beginning with reluctant ranchers, also saw a future in recreation. "By the mid-1960s, the BLM had fully embraced multiple use as a land management tool meant specifically to include recreation in addition to wildlife and grazing management," notes land use scholar Leslie Carr Childers. 47

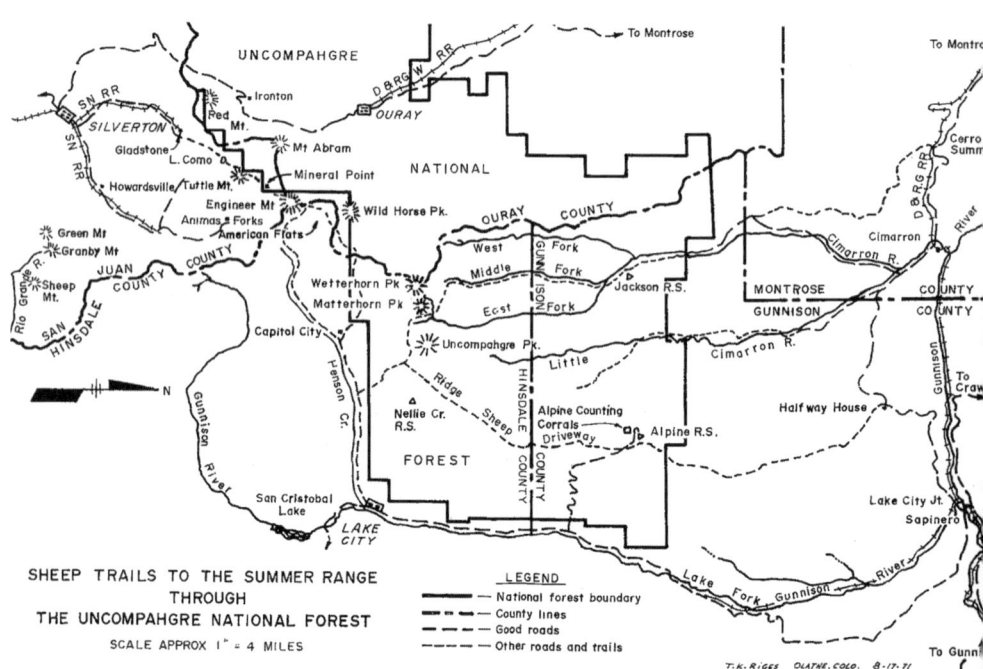

This map shows sheep routes into American Basin and the high country between Silverton and Lake City in San Juan, Hinsdale, Montrose, and Gunnison Counties. Map from Marguerite Lathrop, *Don't Fence Me In*. Original composite of USFS maps in the Lathrop Collection at the American Heritage Center, University of Wyoming.

Once, sheepmen had the high mountain parks to themselves. Then came the Wilderness Act, Vasque hiking boots, Kelty aluminum frame backpacks, Gore-Tex, and lightweight packable tents. Sheepmen's summer ranges became compromised with other users equally at home on public lands. In the desert canyons of southeast Utah ewes lambed thousands of sheep. Stockmen shipped wool on the railroad from Cisco and Thompson Springs, but redrocks and stunning geology made scenery out of working landscapes. Winter sheep camps became a national park.

Sheepmen had expected changes after World War II, but not to this extent. The future would bring additional federal laws, more hikers and backpackers, and an even bigger boom in outdoor recreation. The 1960s meant passage of the Wilderness Act, creation of Canyonlands National Park, and the last decade of northern New Mexican herders traveling into Colorado "following the sheeps."

Of course, some herders still went north into Colorado and Wyoming, but reading the trees, studying the carved aspen arborglyphs, reveals a dramatic reduction in Hispano names linked to New Mexican villages. The names and dates are there in the post-war years but by the end of the 1960s they taper off. A few New Mexican herders continued to looked after the *borregas* but a centuries-old tradition was ending. Basques came now and young men from Mexico. Sheepmen stayed proficient in Spanish and their sons learned to speak it in the sheep camps, but trail drives had given way to trucking sheep. As much time was spent in pickups as on horseback. Native New Mexicans had gone home to Canijlon, Los Ojos, Tres Piedras, El Rito, and Taos. They would not return to the Colorado high country and the mountain meadows where they had spent some of the best summers of their lives.

SEVENTH SHEEPSCAPE

Sheepshed Art—South Park

As we drove from Fairplay toward Hartsel to get a key to the ranch gate, the width and breadth of South Park opened out before us. Miners had explored this vast park ringed by mountains, known by fur trappers as Bayou Salado, in the 1850s. Mining had occurred on the fringes of this southernmost of Colorado's three high-mountain parks, but cattle and sheep grazing had also been an important part of the local economy. I'd seen photos of unique sheepherder or sheepshearer art in a long, low barn at what had been the Colton Ranch. Now I wanted to see the images themselves. So did my driver, Brian Woodyard, who had spent 10 years on the Park County Historic Preservation Advisory Commission.[1]

Unlike Colorado's Western Slope or the San Luis Valley, the 2,100 square miles of Park County were home to sheep ranchers of primarily English and Scottish background in the 1870s and 1880s. The Wadley, Galloway, Meyer, Rogers, and Chalmers families often ran both sheep and cattle.[2] They hired "Mexican" herders and sheepshearers. The bloody conflicts between cattlemen and sheepmen that had erupted in other parts of Colorado had not occurred in South Park because the same ranch families owned both types of livestock.[3] They wisely alternated between sheep and cattle, depending on market conditions and prices.

The Gilley Ranch herded sheep across South Park and took two weeks to trail its woollies up Boreas Pass and into the high country. Clyde Gilley stayed with his sheep.[4] The Trout Creek Ranch ran a few thousand sheep. Sheep ran on the Slater Ranch east of Como and on the Burns Ranch. In summer sheep grazed Buffalo Peaks and crossed Breakneck and Brown's Passes, which are minor crossings of Sheep Ridge southwest of Fairplay. "The sheep range might best be described as the alpine country along the entire Mosquito Range west of South Park, as well as the same along the Park Range and east into the alpine country south of Mt. Evans," notes local historian Jerry Davis.[5]

By 1882 Meyer and Wadley had shipped 17,000 pounds of wool. A year later, over 10,000 sheep nibbled away at South Park's grasses and flowers.[6] Between 1885 and 1910, the Galloway-Wadley Livestock Company ran cattle and sheep at Red Hill. The Harrington Ranch also sprawled across South Park.

The sheep industry got a start in the 1870s, with the 1870 census documenting the Guirauds' 900 sheep and the flocks of Myers and Maxey on or before 1876. Later, lambs, wool, and ewes between five and seven years old, with teeth worn down, would be shipped by rail. Herders arrived from Taos and Santa Fe and the industry thrived in the first decades of the twentieth century, allowing Park County to become one of the leading wool and mutton growers in the state.

New Mexican sheep from Española and Chama also came into South Park on the Denver and Rio Grande Railroad. Herders off-loaded their woollies at the Y-railroad junction near Salida and grazed them all summer, moving them toward Woodland Park. Lonnie Lantz from Poncha Springs told me that his grandmother was Finnish but knew Swedish cooking and baked Swedish rolls with lots of sugar. Hispano herders traded her bum or orphan lambs for sweet rolls, and she built up her own flock of 22 sheep.

Photographs and stories of the local sheep ranchers and their families exist, but there are almost none of the herders. That's what I wanted to see. What paintings had the herders created as informal folk art in a drafty, windblown sheepshed or barn? What messages had they left, and how did they want to be remembered? The Badger Basin Ranch, part of the old Colton/Hartsel Ranch, now runs bison, which had historically roamed South Park. We stopped to get a key to the ranch gate and I watched storm clouds build to the west over the Buffalo Peaks. I knew I had a short window of time to take photos. It was late November, and the first of many winter storms had begun to arc across the mountains.

Congress voted to create the South Park National Heritage Area in 2009, and ranch preservation was a critical part of Park County's preservation goals. But wind, rain, and snow continued to take their toll on South Park's wooden buildings, and no one knew how long sheepherder art would last. Wind scours hillsides and drifts snow for miles, and in the harsh environment at 9,000 feet and higher, Park County has the oldest living tree in Colorado—a bristlecone pine over 2,300 years old. "Where there's trees there's snow, and where there's no trees there's wind," chuckled Brian Woodyard as he spoke into his beard. Where we were headed there were no trees or bushes and very little grass. But once, there had been sheep by the thousands grazing the high mountains in summer and wintering on native grass and hay in South Park.

"The crest of our continent, as the mines work out, is becoming all one great pasture for climbing, close-cropping sheep whereof the staple summer diet is timber-line clover," wrote Will Irwin in 1922 in the *Saturday*

Evening Post near the height of Park County's sheep numbers.[7] At Hartsel he described "wide-spreading lambing and shearing sheds ... bunk houses, blacksmith shops ... garages ... corrals."[8] Irwin explained, "The sharp little hoofs of sheep cut the ground like steel knives in the days of universal open range, when men were more concerned with ripping a fortune out of the West than providing for our national future."[9] By the 1920s, the range had been regulated, though the US Forest Service in the mountains above South Park charged only 9.75 cents per ewe and lamb each summer.

The Hartsel Ranch ran 30,000 sheep and shipped 14,000 lambs in a normal year. In late fall, the ranch's 17 herders returned to Taos or Santa Fe, leaving the flock tenders to stay in sheep wagons and watch over the remaining ewes. By January, the thermometer could dip to 25 degrees below zero. Bitter winds out of the west could force flocks to the lee of low hills to seek shelter, and in desperate situations to crowd into lambing sheds for warmth.

That's where we were headed. Toward lambing and shearing sheds on a historical ranch with dramatic views of the Buffalo Peaks. What paintings and inscriptions had the herders left behind, with no aspens to carve on for miles? "The boss employs only Mexicans, as we call them, Spanish as they call themselves," wrote Irwin. "Comparatively few of them speak English, and psychologically they are still Spaniards of the sixteenth century.... And among them the tradition of sheep has been handed down, father to son, for as many as ten generations. They have an instinct for the desires and troubles of the wool-bearing species."[10]

By 1929 Park County had shipped 400,000 pounds of wool and 40,000 lambs, becoming one of the leading wool and mutton growers in the state. Those years between World War I and World War II saw sheepmen thrive because of the demand for wool blankets, socks, jackets, gloves, and military uniforms. A special corridor, now Park County Road 15, had to be built between homesteads to allow sheep to move north from Hartsel to Como. Under manager Hollis Russell Mills, the Hartsel Ranch, with 5,000 acres of bottomland along the South Platte River, led the South Park sheep industry in producing the soft white fleeces of merino sheep for wool. Merino ewes mated with black-headed and black-legged Hampshire rams for meat quality.

Hispano herders and one or two dogs led 17 bands of 1,500 to 2,000 sheep per band. They trailed up into the high country all along the east side of the Mosquito Range, using deserted mining cabins for summer camps and employing over 100 seasonal workers. Drought, overgrazing, and poisonous weeds devastated the industry, which had thrived during the wars and went into a rapid decline throughout the 1950s and 1960s. In the 2012 census, only 11 sheep or goat farms remained. As had happened almost everywhere else, ranchers had switched to cattle, though the Badger Basin Ranch chose cattle and bison. We could see their herd of buffalo as we unlocked the gate.

Dennis, the ranch hand, told us the bison were curious and would come up to us, but we didn't quite expect that. Instead we left the truck, slipped through the barbed-wire fence, and made our way to the shearing shed. There I saw paintings from 80 years ago. Standing in decades of dried manure, we peered at the weathered boards. Our eyes adjusted to the dim light and we began to see a folk art legacy left by New Mexican shepherds

Though sheepherders are known for their aspen carvings or arborglyphs, they also painted in sheepsheds using the same paint they used to mark or brand sheep on their backs. This self-portrait, probably with a wife or girlfriend, is from an old sheepshed in Park County on a ranch that now raises bison. Author photo.

or shearers who had used sheep paint to decorate the barn's interior—the same paint they would have applied to mark ewes with a daub on the back of their fleeces. Slowly I began to see a portrait of a couple, and beside it a single woman, pensive, stared back at me. The artist had painted a mocking self-portrait with a girlfriend or wife. Who the single woman was could not be determined. Maybe another girlfriend, probably the artist's mother. Her eyes stared at me across space and time.

The artist, Alfredo Romero from Arroyo Hondo, New Mexico, had painted the images on May 19, 1934. His work appeared on the north wall of the barn, which included a thoroughbred horse and jockey. On the west wall he painted a small churro sheep with four horns, and a large horse with perfect proportions and a distinct, smooth neck. I saw the inscription of Patricio Santistevan from May 30, 1929, and the name Max Gomez.[11]

This handsome race horse in a Park County sheepshed was painted by Alfredo Romero from Arroyo Hondo, New Mexico, on May 22, 1931. He also added subsequent dates through 1935. Photo by author.

Wind whistled through the boards and around the cracks. A large pack rat nest above me seemed destined to split a roof rafter. We walked from the shearing shed into the lambing barn and found more initials, dates, and colors of sheep paint. We found "A.R.T./ 4+5—1946" and "Pablo 1954–55." We found names and letters painted vertically, initials pounded in and shaped by nails, and enough colored paint drips on boards to resemble "a Jackson Pollock painting," quipped Woodyard, thinking exactly what was on my mind.

A vibrant painted chicken emerged on a back wall, perhaps reminiscent of a good meal or maybe a symbol for cockfighting, long a tradition in Hispanic villages. We came out of the lambing barn and found ourselves face to face with a young female bison behind barbed wire a few feet away, curious about our presence. As we left the barns, winter clouds rolled in over the Buffalo Peaks. The bison herd moved toward us, prompting a quick return to our truck. We drove out and locked the gate, and I thought it was ironic that bison, which had been hunted out of South Park, had returned, while domestic sheep, which had made fortunes for some ranchers and a critical paycheck for New Mexican herders during the Great Depression, were now all but gone.

Later that day I looked at carved aspen trees and a signature cross etched by herders working for the Silbano-Medina Ranches. Many of the trees were dead or dying. At Mud Spring in the 17,000-acre James Mark Jones State Wildlife Area, we found more carved trees, including an inscription by Delfino Medina from Ranches de Taos on 6/27/41. But now the herders were gone, and irrigation water, which had made South Park famous for its nutritious grasses, had nearly all been sold to Colorado municipalities. The real wealth in South Park had not been gold, silver, or grass, but water. Ditches had dried up. Grazing had become secondary to water rights, and a national heritage area preserved remnants of a lifestyle that had largely disappeared. Second homes on ridges, anywhere near trees, replaced ranch houses.

I can't get my mind off the woman's portrait. I see her now, poised, staring, looking at me across generations, probably worried about the loss of her sheepherder son, gone from Arroyo Hondo for most of the year. Sheep numbers in South Park are a fraction of what they once were. Maybe I should write a "ewelogy" about the loss of flocks, of shepherds, of tinkling sheep's bells and of black sheep as single markers to herds of 100. The sheep are gone as well as the loyal dogs, which could locate lost lambs even in thick timber and bring them back, bleating, to their worried mothers.

This haunting woman's portrait, painted on the rough boards of a Park County sheepshed, is probably also the work of sheepherder or shearer Alfredo Romero. Sheepshed art is a unique form of folk art. Photo by author.

Mountains where sheep grazed are now the Buffalo Peaks, Mount Evans, and Lost Creek Wilderness Areas. Recreation has replaced grazing. A working landscape that knit the floor of South Park with the high peaks above is now scenery for hikers, challenges for mountain climbers, and a backdrop for photographers. Not much remains to tell the story of sheepherders and sheepmen except a few carved aspen trees, dead or dying, and barn boards, luckily still intact, a palimpsest from the past, painted by hardworking men who could laugh at themselves and still share their longing for loved ones.

Chapter 7

Outdoor Recreation and Landscape Restoration

Hikers, Guardian Dogs, and Bighorns, 1970 to the Present

> There are some who can live without wild things, and some who cannot.... Like winds and sunsets, wild things were taken for granted until progress began to do away with them.
>
> —ALDO LEOPOLD
> *A Sand County Almanac*

> eat lamb ... 100,000 coyotes can't be wrong
>
> —STICKER ON A SHEEPMAN'S TRUCK

In the 1970s in the high country of the San Juans, the Flat Tops, and the Elk Mountains of Colorado, come July shepherds would move their flocks up old, established trails to cool mountain meadows where lambs would do their best. Gaining weight. Staying close to the ewes. Sleeping at noon and eating flowers and grass until almost dark. In the high country not much had changed. The herder had the same canvas tent with no floor. Wooden grub boxes passed down from generations contained essentials—salt and pepper, chili powder, canned goods, a few utensils.

The herder's cot stretched out at the back of the tent, farthest from the canvas door. Dog food came in on the left to keep it from bears. Woodstove on the right for cooking and for heating when the summer storms rolled in and rain switched to snow and sometimes hail. The border collies remained the same, with their bright eyes, black-and-white coats, and

Historic corrals in American Flats was a strategic high altitude sheep grazing location between Silverton and Lake City. The corrals are near Alpine Loop, a popular summer route for Jeeps and ATVs. Author photo.

In the La Plata Mountains of southwestern Colorado, sheep trails and trails to mines occasionally intersected. Along this old sheep trail heading west from La Plata Canyon is an arborglyph for the Lucky Moon Mine. Author photo.

dogged diligence in watching the sheep, gathering them up, and coming at a run with a voice command, hand signal, or whistle.

On the cot lay old sheep pelts as a kind of mattress. A pillow and a few blankets, wool of course. A .30–30 Winchester lever-action rifle lay in the tent's corner in case of bears or hungry coyotes. Maybe even one of those newer .30–06 Remington bolt-action rifles with a scope and greater killing power at a distance. Binoculars. A couple of jackets. Levi's, faded and worn. Shirts that needed washing.

Herders still spoke Spanish, but instead of coming up from northern New Mexico they now came from Mexico itself, from Spain, and slowly, little by little, more herders arrived from South America, especially Peru. But wherever they were from, their dreams remained the same. Work a few years in the sheep camps. Make money. Go home with cash, *dinero*, in their pockets to strut around town, show off in their local plazas with new clothes, a new Stetson hat, shined boots. Most were young and unmarried. Some had tied the knot and deeply missed their young wives, their growing children. But they all had dreams. Lolling near camp, seeking the shade of a tall pine on a lazy afternoon with the sheep contented. Scratching one of the collies behind the ear. It was a good life and an easy way to make American dollars—most of the time, but certainly not always.

Also on a sheep trail above La Plata Canyon, a sheepherder went to great lengths to carve an Aztec god in homage to the Aztec Mine, where Montoya sheep once grazed nearby in high mountain meadows. Author photo.

If only the camp tender who came by every week would bring fresh fruit, oranges, something sweet. Instead it was usually canned meat, soups, and bread that was stale before it even reached the horse's panniers for the long twisty trail up the mountain's flank. Sometimes, rarely, there were a few cans of Coors beer the herder could place in the creek to stay cool and drink just as the stars came out, when the sheep were bedded down and the watchful dogs listened, paws together, one ear cocked to a slight sound down in the valley below.

David Lavender, born and bred a western rancher, wrote about sheepherding in Colorado in his classic book *One Man's West*:

> Higher and higher you go, onto range too rough and too near the peak tops for even cattle to follow. Now you are in the wide green basins above timber line. Splintered, snow-creased peaks rear on every hand. It is the climax of your year. . . . The nights are crisp, star-hung, the days an indolent delight. Everything is open, everything clear. From yonder pinnacle you can see your whole fattening flock without stirring.[1]

As the 1970s began, things stayed the same in sheep camp except that fashionable western shirts had more snaps instead of buttons. Battery-

Sheepherder aspen art often includes drawings of nude women. Sometimes the women's hairstyles can help date the arborglyphs. Photo from the author's collection.

powered transistor radios played static during the day, but at night on top of a ridge, sounds came from powerful AM channels across the West—country music, rock and roll, and sometimes, faintly, a station playing *Español* with horns, trumpets, and acoustic guitars. Then, alone, the herder could dance a few steps in the dark, holding an imaginary woman in his arms, giving her a kiss, a tight *abrazo*, or hug. But a solitary two-step is not the same as dancing in a full cantina. Down from the ridge he would go, radio off, headed for his lonely tent, guided by the stars.

In Washington, DC, on January 1, 1970, embattled Republican president Richard Nixon, caught in an escalating Vietnam War, signed the National Environmental Policy Act (NEPA), which would create sweeping changes across the nation and require paperwork and environmental audits for grazing permittees. The law established the Environmental Protection Agency and new concepts of environmental assessments (EAs) and environmental impact statements (EISs) that Aldo Leopold would have approved of.

Herders knew nothing about this, and sheepmen not much more, but slowly the impacts of the law would trickle down into even the most remote grazing districts, and a new generation of foresters and BLM managers would be obligated to consider land health and ecosystem management. What to do with invasive plants and how to protect riparian areas, or those acres near lakes, streams, and creeks that represent only 3 percent of the West but contain 75 percent of vertebrate species?

A burgeoning environmental movement back East also took pity on so-called wild horses and burros in the West. In 1971 Congress passed the Wild Free-Roaming Horses and Burros Act, which "added wild horse herds to the panorama of public lands management" on BLM lands that had been the exclusive pastures of remote ranchers.[2] What had been marginal sheep and cattle country on the public domain would find itself under a media microscope as the BLM became caught between ranchers legitimately complaining that feral horses ate too much forage, and wild horse advocates arguing about inhumane horse "gathers" and the use of helicopters as roundup tools. Predator control also came under scrutiny.

"One of the most insidious invasions of wilderness is via predator control," lamented Leopold.[3] A year after Nixon signed the National Environmental Policy Act, rancher Van Irvine of Casper, Wyoming, pleaded no contest to illegally shooting pronghorn and lacing their carcasses with poison, which killed eagles and coyotes. He paid a $675 fine. Compound 1080 had become a popular poison. Highly toxic and slow acting, it kills predators in "two to five hours," reports the federal Wildlife Services agency, which states that death "may result from gradual cardiac failure; progressive depression of the central nervous system with either cardiac or respiratory failure as the terminal event; or respiratory arrest following severe convulsions."[4]

Van Irvine killed predators with thallium sulfate as the lethal agent, but the popularity of Compound 1080 and the bad press received from killing eagles resulted in Executive Order 11643, signed by President Nixon in 1972, which banned the use of poisons on federal lands. President Reagan would bring back Compound 1080, but only in special collars worn by sheep. Sheep ranchers found it too ineffective to use and preferred to lace animal carcasses with large amounts of poison. "I think the coyote is smart enough that they soon are going to learn to leave those sheep (with collars on) alone," said Lawrence Aubert, a sheepman from Glade Park near Grand Junction.[5]

On the heels of the EPA came an even more powerful law that would affect sheepmen, protect eagles, guard lizards and toads and salamanders, and even bring back wolves. The Endangered Species Act of 1973 codified into American law some of the values Aldo Leopold strove for with his land ethic. For the first time in history, Congress proclaimed that the will of the American people was to preserve habitat to protect endangered and threatened species whose range had been reduced. Species could be protected if remnant populations could be found and animals could be reintroduced to areas where they had once thrived. The act protects species and "the ecosystems upon which they depend."

Ecological restoration, as sheepmen feared, meant fewer woollies on government allotments. Sheep numbers would decline as ranges were restored. Reductions included the number of sheep allowed on an allotment and the length of time they could be grazed. On the Bear S&G Allotment in the Norwood District of the Uncompahgre National Forest, reductions included fewer days on the forest and sheep numbers cut in half.[6]

Sheep claimed the high country because they can eat subalpine larkspur, which is poisonous to cattle. "Effects of livestock grazing vary with season of use, intensity, length and repetition of grazing, and the characteristics of the pre-grazing community; but preferred forage species have declined relative to less palatable plants across much of the West," write Deborah D. Paulson and William L. Baker in *The Nature of Southwestern Colorado*.[7]

Near Lizard Head Pass between Rico and Telluride, sheep predominated. Reviewing US Forest Service range conditions, Paulson and Baker write, "The first memo indicating damage dated September 22, 1949 reads: 'All the high range on this allotment is in bad shape[,] also that portion on the Uncompahgre Forest—it looks like the permitted number of 1,000 for 80 days is just too many sheep.'"[8]

Those same conditions prevailed in 1957, with no change by 1967, when a forester reported, "Roads and sheep trailing [have] contributed to some of the gullies and [are] causing a great deal of damage on the already damaged area. . . . It will never recover under present management."[9] In the 1980s, a Trout Lake resident, annoyed by too many sheep, fired a rifle over a herder's head and said he was going to shoot any sheep that grazed closer to Hope Lake. The permittee removed the sheep and the US Forest Service eventually closed the allotments because of landscape damage that could be seen from the highway. Higher up, on Sheep Mountain, sheep grazing and poor range continued, but at Lizard Head recovering grasses have become home to the savanna sparrow, a Colorado Species of Special Concern. Nearby, sheep have been taken off Wilson Meadows. Paulson and Baker report:

> Today, Wilson Meadows is recovering from a century of sheep grazing, and recovery is slow . . . the damage goes beyond changes in the plant community. Gullies are deep and still eroding upstream. No scientific knowledge indicates how long recovery might take in a high-elevation setting like this, where elk still graze heavily in the summer. It could be several decades before the natural plant communities and stream channel are restored.[10]

Near Weminuche Pass and the Rio Grande Pyramid, in the heart of the Weminuche Wilderness, Lloyd Anderson trapped and killed one of the last grizzly bears in Colorado. "Certainly, this place is prime-time for sheep grazing, and I imagine them—the horror!—blighting this tranquil scene by the thousands, summer on summer, cropping plant life to the roots, fouling God's own drinking water with their filthy excrement, displacing natural prey species such as elk and deer and torturing hungry predators with their nonstop bleating," complained David Petersen in *Ghost Grizzlies*.[11]

How ironic that Anderson trapped one of the last grizzlies in a place that the Spanish had named *Rincón de la Osa* centuries before, a name that translates as "refuge or hiding place for the female bear." Because a sheepherder complained of bears attacking his flock, one of the last grizzlies was killed deep in the Weminuche Wilderness within the San Juan National Forest. Yet because that grazing allotment is so remote, sheep no longer summer in that high mountain meadow.

"Consequently, the native flora are returning: Among big bunchy grasses and the darker sedges . . . grow a gleeful abundance of monkshood and alpine bistort. The latter (*Polygonum*) support bulbous pink-white flower plumes atop long stalks, resembling Texas-size Q-tips. The thick, twisted, starchy roots of bistort are grizzly candy. Indians dug them, too. I've been known to munch a few myself," admits Petersen.[12]

Slowly, carefully, federal land managers have tried to address the decades-long problems of overgrazing and erosion. Sheep numbers fell because of both market and range conditions, but in Colorado's high country, the hidden history of sheep grazing has given way to the scrutiny

In Colorado's high country and in many federally designated wilderness areas, sheep graze high-altitude grasses and the tops of watersheds. Where sheepherders and their flocks once were the sole summer visitors, now Old West high-country grazing lands are crowded with ATVs, hikers, climbers, backpackers, and mountain bikers as part of the New West. Author photo.

of ecological conditions by thousands of day hikers and backpackers as they now regularly traverse mountain meadows. On specific routes such as the Colorado Trail, the Continental Divide Trail, or access routes up Colorado's popular Fourteeners, which are the 54 peaks higher than 14,000 feet, recreational visitors proliferate and bring thousands of tourist dollars to Colorado coffers.[13]

What was once a working landscape for sheep and shepherds is now a leisure landscape for hikers and climbers "bagging peaks." New environmental awareness does not bode well for sheepmen still shooting coyotes and using aggressive guardian dogs, now that there are restrictions on poisons and traps. In northwestern Colorado on sagebrush flats far from hikers and mountain climbers, European guardian dogs have been in use for 30 years.[14] In the central Rockies, friendly, floppy-eared border collies have recently given way to much larger Turkish Akbash, Anatolian, and

Increasingly across the West, sheepmen have augmented their border collies and other herd dogs with large and sometimes aggressive guardian dogs. A strong supporter of public lands sheep grazing and the use of guardian dogs is painter and sculptor Veryl Goodnight, who painted this canvas titled *Trek to the High Country*. Painting courtesy of Veryl Goodnight.

Great Pyrenees guardian dogs that have threatened and attacked hikers and mountain bikers. Yes, they do a better job of guarding sheep than the faithful herding dogs, but they have given woolgrowers much pause and lost sleep.

As damaged meadows recover from Old West overgrazing, New West confrontations occur among public land users. Hikers have threatened to carry pistols to shoot any guardian dog that comes close. If the US Forest Service permits sheep ranchers and those ranchers' dogs attack hikers, is the government liable? Time will tell. Sheep numbers are down but conflict is up.

Sam Robinson is one of the last sheepherders near Vail, Colorado. He had an Akbash but worried about being sued, so he switched to an Akbash–Great Pyrenees mix. On a given summer night in the dark of the moon, the only thing between him and economic devastation from sheep loss was a canine affectionately named Big Dog.[15] For Robinson to make a profit, his lambs need to put on 100 pounds, most of it in mountain pastures.

Because of the location of his allotment, at the intersection of the Colorado and Continental Divide Trails, hikers disturb, run off, and even want to pet his sheep. "Sam estimates that the summer foot traffic costs him $2,000 each year in lost weight. Every pound counts when he goes to sell his crop of lambs in the fall each year," notes Frank Clifford in *The Backbone of the World*. "His profit is the margin between his annual expenses and the price he can get for his lambs. The leaner the lambs, the thinner the margin."[16]

In 1999 the price of wool dropped to one of its lowest levels in US history. In Colorado, sheep permits on federal land plummeted by 40 percent. In John Muir's day, eight million sheep gorged in the forests of the West. Now there are only 5.3 million sheep in the entire United States.[17] On Colorado's White River National Forest, sheep numbers are down 60 percent since 1940.[18] In 1930 over 216,000 sheep grazed the San Juan National Forest. By 2004 that number had dropped to under 11,000.

With thin margins and a narrow line between loss, sustainability, and profit, sheepmen like the security their flocks receive from large, aggressive guardian dogs, but those same dogs have created a public relations nightmare.[19] In San Juan County, Colorado, the small town of Silverton, with a

Silverton, Colorado, in San Juan County, once sponsored annual Sheepmen's Days, with gunnysack races, barbecues, dances, and other events. Sheep came right through town, as seen in this photograph. Photo courtesy San Juan County Historical Society, Silverton, Colorado.

current population of fewer than 600, celebrated Sheepmen's Day in the 1930s with games, a barbecue, and gunnysack races. Now the county commissioners have banned domestic sheep.

Sheepdog incidents in San Juan County have occurred on the Colorado Trail, at the Highland Mary Trailhead, at Velocity Basin, and on the county road to Kendall Mountain.[20] Hikers and mountain bikers have been surprised that "suddenly those cute little border collie dogs have morphed into those giant, white, salivating, vicious, aggressive, nasty dogs . . . [that] definitely want to bite your face off."[21] A letter writer stated she had to put her mountain bike between her and two of the dogs and squirt water in their faces. The US Forest Service has tried to warn hikers, but she said, "The ridiculous sign the Forest Service put around is misleading and could potentially lead a person to be passive around these dogs when really you need to be aggressive, throw rocks, squirt water, and if a person has one on hand, shoot them with a gun."[22]

Many Silverton-area hikers have had frightening encounters with aggressive guardian dogs and have contacted the sheriff's department, called the BLM and the Forest Service, and written letters to newspapers and county commissioners. Describing a terrifying encounter in which snarling dogs charged him, a mountain biker stated, "Sheep shit is one thing, but an Akbash lunging for the unmentionables is where my patience ends. If I'm taking that dreaded heli-ride out of the high alpine, a dog bite better not be the culprit," wrote Will Sands in the *Durango (CO) Telegraph*.[23]

Faced with numerous complaints and first-person accounts of children and families threatened by sheep guardian dogs, Silverton's San Juan County commissioners voted unanimously that "the grazing of sheep within San Juan County is detrimental to the health, safety and welfare of the citizens and visitors of San Juan County." The commissioners also correctly argued that not a cent of federal grazing fees ever returned to their county. They determined the following:

- Sheep protection dogs pose a health risk to residents and visitors of San Juan County.

- The use of sheep protection dogs has made some residents and visitors of San Juan County fearful to use their public lands for recreational purposes.

- Sheep are detrimental to the environment of the fragile alpine tundra within San Juan County.

- San Juan County receives no economic benefit from sheep grazing within San Juan County.

- San Juan County is dependent on a tourist-based economy, and the grazing of sheep within the county is detrimental to the tourist economy.

- The grazing of sheep destroys the fields of mountain wildflowers that attract tourists, photographers, hikers, and backpackers to the public lands of the San Juan Mountains.

- Sheep grazing has no respect for private property, placing the burden on property owners to fence the sheep out.

- Therefore, the Board of County Commissioners is unanimously opposed to sheep grazing within San Juan County.[24]

In their decision, which cannot be binding on a federal grazing permittee, the members of the board of county commissioners may have been thinking about Renee Legro, who participated in a mountain bike race in Eagle County's Camp Hale and was mauled by two Great Pyrenees. She suffered injuries to her left eye, torso, ankle, and right thigh. She needed 60 stitches. The dogs were put down.

News stories included statements from Peter Orwick, executive director of the American Sheep Industry Association, who said, "We have more and more dogs in use and more and more encroachment into traditional agricultural areas, and we're running into the need for more management of our dogs and education for the public as to why the dogs are there and what they do." Rancher Tony Theos from Meeker, Colorado, added, "When you come to terms where we can't protect our livestock and can't protect our livelihood, it's just not worth it anymore."[25]

Acknowledging the shared use of public lands, Bonnie Brown, executive director of the Colorado Wool Growers Association, stated, "A hiker or biker has just as much right as we do. We are making a concerted effort to work with producers to let them more intentionally manage these dogs."[26] Eagle County jurors convicted dog owner and Rio Blanco County sheepman Samuel Robinson of owning a dangerous dog and committing a misdemeanor, and they ordered him to perform community service and pay a fine. Robinson was sued by the mauled bike rider, and his insurance company agreed to a $1 million policy limits settlement. After giving up guardian dogs to protect his sheep, he claimed that the next season, predators and domestic dogs killed 26 percent of his flock.[27] The current annual loss of sheep and lambs to predators averages about 3.5 percent.[28]

In Colorado and across the West, the guardian dog issue is far from over for area sheepmen. Any rancher who grazes on public land must realize that public access to public range has long been established in federal policies. The problem is much more acute, however, in those mountain counties where summer recreation brings hikers, mountain bikers, and climbers into direct contact with grazing sheep. The sheep industry will have to evolve.

In the 1940s stockmen tried to privatize the public domain. In the 1980s the Sagebrush Rebellion renewed those claims, but a new generation of environmentalists responded with scorn. Edward Abbey, never one to mince words, wrote in *Harper's*:

> The rancher (with a few honorable exceptions) is a man who strings barbed wire all over the range, drills wells and bulldozes stock ponds,

drives off elk and antelope and bighorn sheep, poisons coyotes and prairie dogs, shoots eagles, bears and cougars on sight; supplants the native grasses with tumbleweed, snakeweed, povertyweed, cowshit, anthills, mud, dust, and flies. And then leans back and grins at the TV cameras and talks about how much he loves the American West.[29]

Abbey's extreme position did not reflect the mainstream media's love of doing stories on the West, though almost always omitting sheepmen for more glamorous cowboys herding cattle over a hill. But attention began to focus on grazing fees and what the government received from lessees for animal unit months, or AUMs, and what it cost to administer grazing programs.

A sheepman can run five sheep, or one AUM, which in 2004 was $1.43 per month. The rules defining AUMs were established decades ago during the first years after enactment of the Taylor Grazing Act. But regarding the federal government's management of grazing programs, the General Accounting Office stated in 2005, "The grazing permits and leases the 10 federal agencies manage generated a total of about $21 million from fees charged in fiscal year 2004—or less than one-sixth of the expenditures to manage grazing."[30] Rural, remote ranch families needed access to public grazing to stay in business, but environmental groups and scholars jumped on these statistics, and a wave of books and reports began to equate overgrazed, eroded, weed-infested public lands with federal grazing policies on 300 million acres.

"Public land grazing is economically inefficient and inequitable and causes severe, sometimes irreversible, impacts to the land, it is unthinkable that we would continue to allow cattle and sheep to graze large portions of our public lands," began law professor Debra L. Donahue in her book *The Western Range Revisited*.[31] She noted that millions of people use public lands but that permit holders number about 22,000, and that "livestock are permitted to use more than two-thirds of all public lands, yet those lands contribute but a tiny fraction of national livestock production."[32] She acknowledged that "the public land ranchers of today are something of a paradox. Their numbers are few, but their political power is substantial," and "the current federal grazing policy is a largely unintended artifact of history, perpetuated by myth."[33]

Amid the wave of articles and books discussing grazing on public lands, Lynn Jacobs published *Waste of the West: Public Lands Ranching*, and George Wuerthner and Mollie Matteson edited *Welfare Ranching: The Subsidized Destruction of the American West*.[34] Both books focused more on cattle than on sheep, but economic analyses began to point out how little public lands ranching contributed to the nation's food supply and what extensive damage had been done to landscapes and ecosystems.

Effective March 1, 2016, the Bureau of Land Management and the US Forest Service raised grazing fees to $2.11 per AUM. That equals one cow and calf or five sheep. Though this was a 25 percent hike over previous fees, it was still woefully below fair market value. The Trump administration lowered the fees back to $1.81 per AUM.

The fees affect 8,000 permits on Forest Service lands and 18,000 permits on BLM leases, which together cover over 200 million acres. Both the Public Lands Council and the National Cattlemen's Beef Association supported the Obama administration's fee increase, but environmental groups called it welfare ranching and a waste of the West. Why? Because in 2014 the BLM and Forest Service spent $144 million on grazing programs and earned a piddling $19 million in lease income.

We have an Old West legacy in a New West economy. It costs more to manage grazing on federal lands than the public sees in financial returns. "Taxpayers are getting a raw deal regarding grazing," believes Travis Bruner, executive director of the Western Watersheds Project. "Americans are supporting a narrow welfare program for the benefit of Western livestock operations."[35]

Some ranchers complain about federal fees, but in 16 western states, grazing costs on public land are 80 percent cheaper than on private land. Where do those grazing fees go? Ironically, half the dollars return as cattle guards, fencing, corrals, stock ponds, and other improvements to benefit stockmen.

Then there is Wildlife Services, a branch of the US Department of Agriculture that slaughters native predators like bobcats, wolves, black bears, and a coyote every 8½ minutes, according to *High Country News*.[36] Though Compound 1080 is no longer available to ranchers, paid trappers for Wildlife Services can use the M44 set-gun, or "coyote-getter." When a predator bites the bait, the gun fires a cyanide shell directly into its mouth. On the Servilletta Allotment on the Tres Piedras District of the Carson National Forest, in one summer a rancher lost 75 lambs and 25 ewes to particularly hungry coyotes. A federal trapper used set-guns to solve the problem.[37]

For a century, taxpayers have footed the bill to make public lands safer for sheep and cattle. Western public lands ranching may be a proud tradition, but less than 5 percent of livestock consumed in the United States is produced on public land. There is better feed in Missouri and Florida, and more of it.

Old West sentimentality and western heritage bump up hard against twenty-first-century economics. "Grazing on federal land accounts for less than one percent of total income and employment in most of the region, according to the economist Thomas Power. Meanwhile, recreation and tourism have become ever more important," writes James Surowiecki in the *New Yorker*. He adds, "Demonizing the federal government and trying to resuscitate the past may have its demagogic appeal. But the Old West is gone, and it isn't coming back."38

Yet public lands ranching sustains historical custom and culture. Rural ranch lifestyles represent an important part of American and western history. Ranching is vital to small rural communities, and ranches provide open space and room not only for cattle and sheep to roam but also for wildlife that needs large blocks of land for adequate habitat.

Howard Lathrop grew tired of losing horses over steep canyon rims in Utah. He had heard about a young Basque herder from France who was so dedicated to sheep that he had stayed with 1,500 woollies six straight years and had never once come to town. Basques kept clean camps, served delicious mutton and lamb, and "wanted their camp axes so sharp they could shave. They always kept a file handy." Lathrop went to Martin Etchart's camp and, as one sheepherder to another, lifted the lid on a pot of traditional Basque cooking, seasoning all day on a sheet-metal stove. He said, "That smells good." The men began to talk about the future and about selling sheep.39

Etchart had saved his money by not going to town, and he had cash in the bank. Lathrop agreed to a down payment and said he would carry a loan against the sale of his own flocks, leases, and permits near Silverton up Cement Creek, on Uncompahgre Peak, and in Utah in what would become Canyonlands National Park. As a French Basque herder, speaking no English, Etchart had gotten off a train on May 12, 1947. His boss, another Basque named John Allies, handed him a hand-drawn map and a band of sheep, telling him to be back in eight months. Now he could acquire his own sheep from Lathrop, make even more money, and return to the French Pyrenees a comparatively wealthy man. "I learned everything the hard way," Etchart says. "The sheep, they teach you the business."[40]

In 1954 he went out on his own, packing in to summer allotments high in the San Juan Mountains and bringing his children along as soon as they could ride. His sons, Ernie and George, now have their father's allotments, which range from 10,000 to 13,000 feet in elevation. Their father's goal was to return to France, but his children preferred America. The family stayed.

The Uncompahgre Valley once raised as many as 200,000 sheep and is now home to suburban sprawl and ranchettes. "Growth is what continues to force us to change the way we operate," Ernie Etchart argues. "We have plenty of room as far as our public land leases go, but it's becoming increasingly difficult to find and maintain our private leases."[41]

Etchart specializes in high-country grazing, confronting predators like bears "that want a little meat protein to go with their greens." Now only 15,000 sheep graze the San Juan Mountains, where at least 150,000 woollies covered earlier allotments. "We could see these changes coming. When I was in high school you could sell a band of sheep with the permits by putting them up for sale at noon and have them sold that night. Now there are so many restrictions and issues with endangered species. As for grazing, we probably only take 15 percent of the available forage. If that."[42]

Ernie speaks fluent Spanish with his Peruvian herders, who take pride in what they do. Their lambs grow and put on weight, which happens easily in mountain meadows with abundant grasses. Much of the high country around Silverton belongs to the Bureau of Land Management as well as the US Forest Service. "Sheep probably trample 50 percent more than they eat. In the high country with summer rains, grasses come back. They're leaving 75 percent of the vegetation. My goal is to keep them dispersed," states Garth Nelson, a range conservationist with the BLM who monitors Etchart's herding rotations.[43] Ernie agrees. "There's a lot of country to cover in only sixty to seventy days," he says.

"As ranchers we realize that recreation is encroaching on us, but it's federal land and we can't stop it, so we try to work with everyone, but we're running out of this land to graze, and not just this land but the lower land as well. So much of the lower country gets bought up for homes," Etchart states. Near Gladstone Pass, beyond Silverton, he muses, "This is really good sheep country. This piece happens to be a little steep, but the sheep hold really well in this country. The cool temperatures, the feed and the water—that's what makes this great. The sheep don't go looking for feed or water; it's everywhere, and they don't have to shade up."[44]

The Etchart family now represents three generations in sheep and agriculture. Julie Hansmire also runs sheep in the high country of Eagle County, on 200,000 acres of US Forest Service permits in aspen, spruce, fir, and pine habitat and above timberline. The sheep move to 50,000 acres of Utah desert in winter. Just as Howard Lathrop provided a young Basque herder, Martin Etchart, with his start, Julie and her husband, Randy Campbell, bought sheep, leases, and permits from the Greek sheep-ranching family of Chris Jouflas.

Hansmire hires six Peruvian herders annually on H-2A visas. "They're very dedicated to what they do," she says. "They appreciate the work for one thing, but we try to take care of them just like family."[45] Etchart sees his herders at least every five days, packing in supplies and moving their tent camps to other mountain basins. "I'm their psychologist, their banker—whatever they need, I provide—without them I don't survive."[46]

Public lands ranching has a place in the American West. Stockmen can continue to parry environmentalists and environmental groups, though ranchers must attempt to create better range conditions and adhere to ecological plans to improve allotments. The high country includes some of the last strains of rare Colorado cutthroat trout, and to the chagrin of sheepmen, a small but striking predator has resumed its former range.

In Colorado, lynx had disappeared, but the species thrived in Canada. So, staff from Colorado's Division of Wildlife (before the name changed to Colorado Parks and Wildlife) sought to restore nature's balance and brought back the silver-haired cat. When Kip Stransky retired after working 30 years for the Colorado Division of Wildlife, his last five years on lynx reintroduction, his colleagues gave him shit, literally. Poop on a plaque. And he could not have been happier.

Kip is so proud of his unusual retirement gift that "it hangs on my living room wall and it's quite a conversation piece," he says. The plaque reads "The fruit of your labors." Covered with a light coat of shellac is genuine lynx poop, glued to a piece of mahogany and naturally embedded with rabbit hair, "probably from a bunny that I purchased somewhere," Kip says with a smile.[47]

Working with lynx can be like that. You get dedicated to the three-foot-long, 20- to 30-pound cats with their beautiful silver and gray coats, huge ear tufts, and black-tipped tails. Kip's job was bunnies. Lots of bunnies. Stransky was the rabbit man, and in the complicated world of reintroducing an endangered predator, Kip's position as wildlife technician was to find food to keep Canadian lynx alive as they adjusted to Colorado in a secure Division of Wildlife (DOW) rehabilitation center near Monte Vista. It wasn't easy.

He had to convince bunny breeders across four states to sell him between 1,500 and 2,000 four-pound rabbits a year. In Price, Utah; Shiprock, New Mexico; and Grand Junction, Colorado, he would meet rabbit raisers with a horse trailer full of cages to buy live bunnies to stockpile for the approximately 50 lynx a year that the DOW wanted to release into the San Juan and Rio Grande National Forests, which had been the southern range of lynx before they had been trapped almost to extinction.

Started with the best of intentions under DOW director and conservation biologist John Mumma, lynx reintroduction began poorly. Captured Canadian lynx, released in the spring, died—three starved, and one was badly malnourished when it was recaptured. At the University of Colorado, students held candlelight vigils to mourn the lynx loss. There had been almost no research on lynx reintroduction, and wildlife biologists had not adequately prepared the lynx. The biologists learned.

That put Stransky in the bunny business, looking for fresh food for furry friends. The failure of the "hard release" resulted in a dramatic rethinking of how to put lynx into the wild, with the goal of fattening them up to adjust to their new mountain home. But feeding captured lynx rabbits and roadkill was the least of the DOW's worries.

There were angry farm and ranch groups that were terrified of these small, elusive, gray-and-white cats with their huge back paws up to eight inches wide—perfect for traveling in snow in the same deep powder that has made Colorado an international ski destination. There were irate loggers, worried ski-industry executives, and even arsonists and ecoterrorists, who in 1998 firebombed a ski lodge near Beaver Creek, Colorado, close to Vail, where the last confirmed lynx had been illegally trapped in 1973.

Clearly, this small, stunningly beautiful cat, with its oversized paws and its large pointy ears, stirs controversy even though it is rarely seen. It is the mystery cat of the southern Rockies and a vital link in the predator-prey food chain, which conservation biologists seek desperately to maintain despite increasing habitat fragmentation. No stranger to controversy, Mumma supported his staff in bringing back lynx. It was a fateful decision, and one of the best he ever made.

The biologists knew there would be shouts of criticism as well as applause. They did it for the lynx, and out of a belief in Aldo Leopold's land ethic and the understanding that biodiversity means having as many species as possible in their original habitat, or on landscapes where they had always roamed. No one thought it would be easy. But no one imagined the piles of paperwork or the professional protocols necessary to put a small predator back onto spruce-fir slopes in wilderness settings. Now backcountry travelers could anticipate rare encounters with the legendary lynx.

Successful restoration of the species to its former habitat had to coincide with the 10-year predator-prey food cycle with snowshoe hares in Canada. Instead of Canadian trappers catching and killing lynx for their pelts, trappers were paid a higher amount to use live traps. Living lynx were then flown from Canada, where they are abundant, to the United States, where they had virtually disappeared. But it had to happen during an upswing in the lynx population, because nature rules.

By 2005, 218 animals had been released. After eating Kip Stransky's dead bunnies, lynx found their ecological niche and now munch on snowshoe hares, grouse, ptarmigan, squirrels, and other small game, including mice. In turn, lynx are eaten by coyotes. A few lynx have had difficulty adjusting to the San Juan Mountains. Lynx were never numerous in the southern Rockies. Ute Indians have lived in the San Juans for hundreds if not thousands of years, and there is no Ute word for the small felines.

A new 10-year project will be one of the first of its kind to monitor a high-country predator. Released from 1999 through 2006, lynx will now be studied to determine their territory and food supply, and whether their numbers are stable or fluctuating. Biologist Scott Wait says, "This type of long-term monitoring has never been done with lynx or forest carnivores. It may give us information that no one has ever had."[48]

No one knows whether lynx have taken lambs—perhaps they have taken a few—but if issues with guardian dogs and threatened and endangered species trouble sheepmen, perhaps an even more serious threat to their way of life is another kind of sheep—Rocky Mountain and desert bighorns, which inhabit the same range.

Wildlife is a measure of wilderness character. As a nation, we have agreed to protect wilderness, but wilderness without wildlife is just scenery.[49] Bighorn sheep represent wilderness. "There exists no animal more hardy, nor any better fitted to grapple with the extremes of heat and cold. Droughts, scanty pasturage, or deep snows make it shift its ground, but never mere variation of temperature," wrote Theodore Roosevelt about bighorn sheep, which have gamboled in the Rockies for over 200,000 years. The Endangered Species Act mandates keeping them there. TR continued, "The lofty mountains form its favorite abode, but it is almost equally at home in any large tract of very rough and broken ground."[50]

For decades sheepmen in the Rockies have shared range allotments with small numbers of bighorn sheep, *Ovis canadensis*. But as the wild sheep have died off—hunted for their succulent meat in the nineteenth century and susceptible to diseases transmitted from domestic sheep—new ecological awareness and contested scientific studies are reshaping allotment lines and eliminating some grazing allotments entirely.

Though sheepmen grumble about hikers getting too close to their flocks and guardian dogs, and about the revolving door of federal employees who

This young desert bighorn was photographed near the Gunnison River and the Dominguez-Escalante National Conservation Area, which was once highly contested winter range for sheep and cattle. Author photo.

come one year and are gone the next, new protocols for managing bighorn herds on public land have them truly worried. Families that have used allotments for years in the lower San Luis Valley are now being told they have to find grass elsewhere. At least one Colorado sheepman now grazes his flocks south into New Mexico on the Carson National Forest, where he is permitted for 500 Rambouillet. Leon Crowthers from Sanford, Colorado, is not sure he can make ends meet with such small permitted numbers and the distances he needs to travel.

Bighorns have not done well with the settlement of the American frontier. The smaller desert bighorn sheep, *Ovis canadensis nelsoni*, was a favorite food for native tribes in the Southwest, and prospectors and miners also liked the delicate flavor and the status of killing large rams with a full curl to their horns. Roosevelt wrote, "Throughout most of its range the big-horn is a partly migratory beast. In the summer it seeks the highest mountains, often passing above timber-line; and when the fall snows deepen it comes down to the lower spurs or foot-hills, or may even travel some distance southward."[51]

Their coats are different shades of brown, and their horn shapes differ, too. On males the horns curl outward from the top of the skull, and the older the ram, the fuller the curl. The massive head and horns can weigh up to 40 pounds and sometimes exceed 10 percent of the animal's total weight, which is usually determined by habitat quality. From 10 yards away, males can turn, run, and rear at each other at 20 miles per hour, butting heads while suspended in midair with a sound like boulders crashing together in a flooding canyon.

Bighorns need open country to flee their most serious predators—cougars, or mountain lions. From the plains to the tops of the Rockies, bighorns once ranged widely on landscapes now often dominated by domestic sheep grazing in the mountains in summer and in canyons in winter.

"Diseases and parasites carried by domestic sheep are easily transmitted to bighorns. Lacking the immunity domestic sheep had developed during their centuries of domestication, bighorn populations were decimated by diseases from domestic livestock," writes Jack Ballard. "To this day, disease transmission from domestic to wild sheep is one of the greatest perils to bighorn populations, and on numerous bighorn ranges wildlife managers have worked diligently to keep wild sheep separated from their domestic kin."[52] Bighorn numbers remain low; there are approximately 7,000 Rocky Mountain bighorns and 500 desert bighorns in Colorado.[53] "We're trying to recover bighorn sheep—Rockies or deserts. I'm willing to take risks for bighorns," offers Colorado Parks and Wildlife director Bob Broscheid.[54]

Disease transmitted by domestic sheep to just one wild ram in a nose-to-nose meeting can reduce an entire herd by 80 percent in an "all-age die-off." Like domestic sheep, wild sheep head higher into the mountains as snows melt and forage greens up.

Writing about wild sheep, John Muir explained, "Possessed of keen sight and scent, and strong limbs, he dwells secure amid the loftiest summits, leaping unscathed from crag to crag, up and down the fronts of giddy precipices, crossing foaming torrents and slopes of frozen snow, exposed to the wildest storms, yet maintaining a brave, warm life, and developing from generation to generation in perfect strength and beauty."[55]

With eyesight eight times better than that of humans and able to detect movement at 1,000 yards, these rock-clinging, ledge-climbing beasts, sculpted by the Ice Age of the Pleistocene, represent wild nature. Able to outrun and outmaneuver leaping, lunging mountain lions, they can be brought down by something as simple as contact with domestic sheep.

Writing about desert bighorns in *Eating Stone*, Ellen Meloy explains the imminent danger from "domestic sheep that can infect a roaming bighorn with pathogens, making him a vector of disease for his herd mates. There are feral dogs, cattle, roads, fences, poachers, impenetrable thickets of politicians." She adds, "These creatures become who they are by adapting to a particular geography and biotic condition. They are idiosyncratic and local. They are nature's specialists. If their populations are small or confined to remnant habitat, or they depend on a precarious niche or food source, the risk of extinction can intensify."[56]

Reestablishing bighorns onto their native range has met with limited success because they have a singular fidelity to place. They seem to imprint on a mountain landscape, a steep ridge, and certain rocks and soil types, and once they are removed, their adjustment is tentative, careful, and cautious, and few lambs are born. Survival rates for lambs into their first year can be as low as 20 percent. Two years after 20 bighorns were transferred into the Cave Basin allotment on the San Juan National Forest, "transplanted bighorn sheep have not been seen alive."[57]

Pneumonia is the main disease transmitted by domestic sheep, and "reducing contact between bighorns and domestic sheep is considered by biologists to be essential to the survival of the *Ovis canadensis* species."[58] The problem is that domestic and wild sheep eat mostly the same grasses, shrubs, and forbs, including wheatgrass, fescues, rabbitbrush, bitterbrush, and species of sagebrush. Biologists worry that what happened in Colorado in 1953 might occur again. In a single winter in the center of the state, a thousand bighorns dropped to only 30 animals, a 97 percent decline in population in just one season.[59]

"During the last thirty plus years we have advanced from circumstantial evidence to laboratory studies that demonstrated transfer of *Mannheimia hemolytica* (Mh) from domestic sheep to bighorn and fatal pneumonia in the bighorn," writes Dr. Nike Stevens, who has worked for the US Forest Service as a wildlife biologist in Colorado and Montana and as a seasonal researcher for the National Park Service at Rocky Mountain National Park. She adds that more recent studies show that a different pathogen, *Mycoplasma ovipneumoniae* (Movi), results in "significant declines followed by years (or decades) of poor lamb survival. Both these pathogens are carried by a large majority of domestic sheep (typically 80% or more) without showing any ill effects."[60]

Looking back historically, biologist Stevens notes, "Grazing of domestic sheep on public and private land has resulted in the decline of bighorn sheep to 1 or 2% of their original numbers. The decline of the domestic sheep industry since 1940 or so has allowed restoration of bighorn sheep through transplanting throughout the west." As for the recent era, she explains, "During the last decade or two recovery of bighorn sheep has stalled in many states due to a lack of suitable habitat free of significant risk of contact with domestic sheep."[61]

In 1908 the San Juan National Forest grazed 110,000 domestic sheep and recommended that numbers go to 139,000. By 1920 the estimated number of bighorns on the same forest stood at only 251.[62] Forest resources have never been effectively managed to account for bighorns, but across the West and in Colorado, that is changing with the acknowledgment that bighorns have special needs for "proximity to steep cliffs, slopes and other rough, rocky terrain."[63] Management for bighorns has become risk management, with politicians weighing in asking for clarity on rules, and with Colorado wild sheep populations stagnant after disease outbreaks in the 1990s and the first decade of the 2000s.[64] Respiratory diseases can eliminate 50 to 75 percent of a herd.

The wake-up call came in the sheep state of Idaho. A federal judge reduced domestic sheep numbers by 70 percent on the Payette National Forest.[65] Recommendations by the Wild Sheep Working Group in the bulletin *Recommendations for Domestic Sheep and Goat Management in Wild Sheep Habitat* "remain current and robust" and are now becoming a BMP, or best management practice.[66] According to biologists, "many native herds have declined to less than 10% of historical size."[67]

The question is, what is the safe distance between bighorns and domestics? Currently in Colorado five miles are recommended, but that distance may soon spiral upward to a mandatory buffer zone of nine or more air miles, which in mountain or canyon country can mean disqualifying a sheepman from his allotment. "Recent court rulings have mandated separation between domestic sheep or goats and bighorn sheep, including mandatory non-use of grazing allotments where effective separation could not be assured," states the Wild Sheep Working Group report.[68]

Biologists argue for the value of Rocky Mountain bighorns. They are an iconic wild species. Their contribution to biodiversity is unquestioned. But what few scientists want to admit, and what state wildlife agencies don't want to talk about, is how much a full-curl ram is worth to wealthy big game hunters—thousands and thousands of dollars.[69]

Native American tribes also seek bighorn restoration. Taos Pueblo charges thousands of dollars for a special bighorn hunt, which is why another serious threat to bighorns isn't domestic sheep—it's poachers either seeking the heads of full-curl rams or guiding unethical hunters to kill them. If a Colorado hunter draws a rare bighorn hunting license (which takes years and extra points to achieve) and successfully shoots a ram, the head must be brought into a Colorado Parks and Wildlife office. There an employee will drill a small hole into the back of the horn and insert a metal plug with a number so that the ram's head will always be accounted for and will never be confused with a poached set of horns.

Bighorns have enormous value as watchable wildlife, but they also allow hunters to demonstrate their hunting prowess. With their acute vision, they are difficult to hunt. But the high country is changing. With beetle-killed trees dying and falling, some ridgelines are opening up. Because the animals need long sight lines to survive, their habitat is increasing. Herds may be moving beyond their historical ranges.

In southern Colorado, the East Vega–Treasure S&G Allotment on the Rio Grande National Forest, like all US Forest Service allotments, has annual operating instructions for the sheep-grazing permittee. The 34-page document that sheepherders must thoroughly understand states bluntly, "This permit can only be issued if there will be mechanisms in place to achieve separation with wild sheep." A number of protocols are mandated to keep domestic sheep separated from Rocky Mountain bighorns, including strict accounting for all sheep, dead or alive; changing salting practices to keep bighorns from domestic salt sources; restricting breeding seasons to keep bighorns from being attracted to domestic ewes in estrus; and even the potential for radio collars and GPS monitoring of domestic sheep to be sure they are kept away from bighorns.[70] "The sheep industry is declining. There are only 3–4 permittees remaining," states Luciano Sandoval, a range conservationist with the Conejos Peak Ranger District. "They run wherever they can, but it's a battle of attrition."[71]

For working ranch families in southern Colorado on the Conejos Peak Ranger District in La Jara, proximity to bighorn sheep on the families' historical range can be devastating. "For the permittee it's a harsh awakening," says sympathetic range specialist Kelly Garcia. In the 1980s the district stocked 15,000 sheep, and now six families are down to only 4,000 sheep. Under tightening environmental assessments and environmental impact statements, every time an allotment becomes vacant it is analyzed for range health, riparian values, and increasingly for wild sheep habitat.

When radio-collared bighorn males cross three canyons and a historical stock driveway or domestic sheep trail like the Hot Creek Driveway, it changes the way families can get their sheep up the mountain.

"There's so much data that we're dealing with. It's like drinking out of a firehose. It's tough for me because I'm the messenger," laments Garcia. "Our families have grazed here since the 1800s and there's still bighorns so we've done nothing wrong. As a Forest Service employee I'm caught in the middle between the permittees and the biologists."[72]

Sheepmen feel caught in the middle, too, between making a living and complying with federal policies protecting wildlife, which are our intellectual inheritance from Aldo Leopold. After all, he pioneered the field of game management. Ranchers try to live on a landscape that their families have called home for generations, yet they wonder whether they themselves are an endangered species. Leopold left us with hard questions, but no easy answers. Retaining biodiversity in the Mountain West comes with personal costs.

EIGHTH SHEEPSCAPE

*Cairns—Stinking Desert and
Horsethief Trail*

All across the American West, sheepherders have piled stones. Idly watching their flocks, some herders have randomly gathered and placed flat rocks a few feet high. Others have erected true stone monuments, *harri mutilak* in Basque, or "stone boys," to mark their range while tending sheep. Each rock was intricately placed, the final courses so high that the herder could have reached them only on horseback. To be hiking almost at timberline and to see these magnificent cairns gives pause, wonder, and admiration. These monuments have stood and will stand for generations. Lonely herders on vast landscapes regularly pile stones. So do native peoples.[1]

When the Canadian government created the indigenous province of Nunavut above the Arctic Circle, the first postage stamps the new province issued were photos of inuksuit, or stone cairns. I have long been interested in cairns as more than random piles of stone. Here in the West, at high elevations and off remote trails, we also have abundant stone messengers.

In the snow-covered Arctic, the horizon remains flat and unbroken, the light flat with no sun for direction. Traveling across the great expanse, "as the distance closes, you are compelled to stop, transfixed by an ancient message left upon the landscape. Stone upon lichen-encrusted stone, it is an *inuksuk*, the signature of an Arctic hunter who passed this way on a journey that would last a lifetime. . . . You marvel at the perfect balance of stones selected and arranged with great care. The size of a young boy, the *inuksuk*, its mere presence attaching you to its unknown builder, warms you with its sense of humanity," writes Norman Hallendy in *Inuksuit: Silent Messengers of the Arctic*. He continues, "As thanks, you leave a piece of your precious food tucked between its lower stones and move on. Only you know what you said to it the moment before parting. Soon you meet another *inuksuk*, and another. You are no longer alone."[2]

In Colorado, we have all manner of cairns. We have stones that were piled for high-altitude game drives 9,000 years ago in what is now Rocky Mountain National Park, and there are stacked stones on mountain summits left by the F. V. Hayden surveyors in 1874. Modern climbers of those summits often add a stone or two in gratitude for a successful climb. The act of piling stones in remote places is ancient human behavior.

"Cairns can be seen as one of the earliest forms of communication . . . for thousands of years, and across cultures and continents, we have piled up stones to mark our way," explains David B. Williams in *Cairns: Messengers in Stone*. He adds, "Explorers across the centuries have left their mark by erecting a pile of rocks. It may be the one feature uniting world exploration."[3] The word "cairn" comes from sixteenth-century Scotland and occurs in all Celtic languages, including Old Irish and Welsh. The Scots themselves, wool-wearing sheepherders to the core, have 450 cairns scattered across the moors.

Trail markers can be as simple as one stone atop another, or the more common aggregation of two flat rocks and one round stone, especially at a point where a trail splits or diverges. But larger, more complex cairns are what intrigue me—big piles of stone far removed from trail systems. I seek out cairns that took hours to construct with hundreds of pounds of rock that had to be moved to the site and then artfully assembled for balance, form, and structure.

Across the West, when I see cairns on a ridgeline, I'll stop the truck, whistle to my dog, grab a camera, and take an impromptu hike. Why is that cairn where it is? What does it mean? Who built it and when? Often the answer is sheepherders, standing silently and watching their flocks below, determined to leave a message for other herders.

Two decades ago, a Yakama Indian elder told me to look for a row of cairns high on the Columbia Plateau before the road dropped down to the Columbia River. I found that ancient line of stone piles, some finished with a hand-sized, rounded basalt rock on top, and others incomplete. He said they were clan boundary markers delineating fishing territories and were created by generations of Yakama families who had passed that way. On top of the ridge, with grass waving in a steady breeze, the cairns had been there beyond remembering, would always be there.

In the Bitterroot Mountains of Idaho, as Lewis and Clark hurried home in the spring of 1806, their Nez Perce Indian guides insisted that the Corps of Discovery stop at stone markers indicating the Smoking Place, where tradition required offering a pipe of tobacco to the Creator and to all the directions. Though those cairns have come down and been rebuilt several times, the stones remain.

What is it about stones, special places, and human memory? At Bosque Redondo and Fort Sumner in eastern New Mexico, where Navajos were forcibly confined between 1864 and 1868, tribal members today bring stones from the reservation as a remembrance and as an offering to their ancestors who suffered.[4]

At Skeleton Canyon in southern Arizona, a rock pile from fallen cairns marks the spot where Geronimo surrendered after 25 years of Apache wars. If indigenous people have left stone markers across the western landscape, so have Basque and Hispano sheepherders in the Stinking Desert along US Highway 50 in northwestern Delta County on the way to Grand Junction. Over 50 cairns have been recorded that were built by herders who have grazed their flocks in the area since the early 1900s.

"This stretch of real estate along the base of the Grand Mesa and overlooking the lower Gunnison River of western Colorado has been labeled the Stinking Desert, as in 'it's nothing but a stinking desert.' The implication is

The public BLM land between Delta and Whitewater, Colorado, on the east side of the Gunnison River, has been labeled "a stinking desert" in Bill Harris's article in *Southwestern Lore*. "The implication is that this area has little or no worth. The area's prehistoric and historic use demonstrates otherwise," explains Harris, whose team located and mapped over 50 cairns, probably all erected by sheepherders. Author photo.

that this area has little or no worth. The area's prehistoric and historic use demonstrates otherwise," writes avocational archaeologist Bill Harris in an article in *Southwestern Lore*.[5]

I know that country. I've walked it along the top and seen it from the bottom while canoeing the Gunnison River. It's perfect winter sheep country and was once a sheep haven from antagonistic cowboys. They let the herders have the desert—the adobe, locally pronounced 'dobe—hills of grasses dried and yellow in the winter but full of nutrition. This is open country, primarily wind, shallow soils, and rock, yet the small cairns of volcanic stones make a difference, break up the vast range, offer proof of human presence.

"Most of the cairns are found along prominent ridgelines or on high points or pediments. Several cairns overlook domestic sheep bedding areas," notes Harris. "All of the cairns are made with basalt boulders. Several have a large, imbedded rock as their base."[6]

Cairns also reside high in the Flat Tops Wilderness of northwestern Colorado near Deep Lake and Bison Lake. These are ancient cairns with lichen growing between the stones. They are Ute landscape markers positioned within sight of wallows made by a smaller mountain bison, which is now extinct but was once pursued by Ute hunters with bows and arrows centuries before the Spanish brought horses to the West.

But sheepherders have been there, too, and have used the same landscape and also piled up stones. Short of expensive tests to identify the age of lichen growing between or under rocks, it's hard to tell the age of cairns. The tradition is ancient and is found wherever there have been herding peoples.

Cairns are scattered across the Weminuche Wilderness above Dollar Lake, on the peninsula between Pine River and Vallecito Creek, on the Cave Basin Trail, and on Middle Mountain. Most of these came from the hands of herders.

Two huge stone boys, also nicknamed "stone Johnnies," are on a straight line northwest of Perins Peak near Durango, Colorado, stacked with perhaps 1,500 pounds of rock. There are two matching monuments.[7] One, at latitude 37° 17.977 N on Colorado Parks and Wildlife land, is at least eight and a half feet tall and three feet around. "You can see the entire town of Durango from the cairn," notes San Juan National Forest public affairs specialist Ann Bond. "You also have a clear 360-degree view of surrounding landmarks. It is in a location that is difficult to reach. The round-trip hike took me five hours from the trailhead at Rockridge into the Perins Peak State Wildlife Area."

The matching cairn, at the same latitude due west, is on a public land bench below Lewis Peak, just south of the La Plata Mountains on a south-facing ridgeline west of Lightner Creek. As a hunter, I have hiked to both cairns and realized the only way to get those final stones on top would be on horseback. What a lot of work!

Are these sheepherder monuments? Are they boundary markers for livestock allotments or for some early government survey? Whatever they are, they're worth the hike. There are also dozens of cairns in the San Luis Valley, along the flanks of the Sangre de Cristos, to the west near Penitente Canyon, and north of Saguache on ridgelines and above deep draws.

Just as herders follow the sheep, I follow the herders, sleeping at night in a small backpacking tent beside a creek high in the San Juan Mountains. It's

Sheepherders leave cairns but also erect monuments, which may be seven or eight feet high and are often found on ridgelines having nothing to do with trails or trail intersections. This dramatic stone monument was erected on the Horsethief Trail between Ouray, Colorado, and the top of Engineer Pass. Author photo.

July, but I'm wishing I'd brought long underwear—come dawn there's ice in the creek. Hot tea but no breakfast. I break camp and head even higher, finally finding the start of Horsethief Trail, so named because stolen horses, gathered in Utah in the 1880s and 1890s and sold in Telluride, would be stolen again, taken along this trail, and sold a second time in Lake City, Colorado. The trail conveniently leaves Ouray out the back door, so to speak, but goes straight up into the high peaks.

Alone, my Springador (a springer spaniel Labrador) and I walk across the tundra. Dew on the grass and on the tops of tiny flowers. No wind but huge puffy cumulus clouds beginning to appear to the west. Rain in the afternoon by 3:00 p.m. at this elevation. Guaranteed.

I'm not seeing anything but rolling green meadows perfect for sheep, and then, far off in the distance to the north, jutting up like a finger, I see a stone monument. Get out the small birders' binoculars. Zero in. Yes, worth the hike.

Once up on that scree slope, not only do I see a Basque stone boy, but also a possible Ute Indian vision quest stone alignment—an open horseshoe-shaped pile of stones, west facing. And another low stone feature like a short wall. As I clatter across the scree in my hiking boots, careful not to slip and gouge my knees on the sharp, splintered stones, farther west on the ridge I find another large monument, but this one is hollowed out with a space big enough to sit in out of the wind, which is increasing as the belly of those previously white clouds turns blue black.

Up on Horsethief Trail I think about lightning, rain, sideways-driven sleet.[8] What would it be like to try to huddle sheep in such open country with a thunderstorm pounding out of the west? But in summer, either later that afternoon or the next morning, there's warm sun. To be up on a forest allotment too early in the spring or too late in the fall could mean serious snow in a landscape above timberline with no visual markers, no guidelines on the horizon; similar to the Arctic, it suggests the reason Inuit peoples build *inuksuit*. Not because they herd sheep. But because they know about getting lost on the tundra in plant communities similar to these in Colorado at 12,000 feet and higher.

This special stone structure would work. I could sit in it. It would put the wind at my back. I've never before seen a monument so large that I could sit in it, but here it is. The clouds darken. It'll take a while to get back to the truck. I don't have a herder's horse, so I'd better begin to hike. Like herders past and present, I have a dog, a good one, and he's ready to turn around,

Sheepherders endure wind, hail, rain, sleet, and snow at high elevations when they are alone and tending sheep. They must also be aware of dangers from lightning storms. This enclosure or shelter along the Horsethief Trail may have provided a small amount of protection for herders caught in inclement weather. Author photo.

too. I say good-bye to the cairns and wonder whether they are all Basque—or are some of these stone features Ute? The wind picks up and I descend the ridge, hiking poles clicking on the slate-like scree.

I'll keep looking for sheepherder cairns. I believe in a "leave no trace" hiking ethic, so I won't be making any large piles of stones myself, but I'm fascinated when I find them. Okay, maybe as darkness descends after hours of trekking I'll place one stone atop another. Just a few. It's such a human thing to do.

Chapter 8

The Future of Colorado's High Country
Ailing Aspens, Peruvian Herders, and Ethnic Lamb

One of the penalties of an ecological education is that one lives alone in a world of wounds. Much of the damage inflicted on land is quite invisible to laymen.

—ALDO LEOPOLD
A Sand County Almanac

Hard frost came and passed. Aspen leaves fell and lay crisp and briefly yellow in the valley, and the dark flame of the scrub oaks faded to the brown of their bitter little acorns. The sky was clean and clear. The air was crisp. The season turned to that pause when the mountains rest between summer and winter and a man knows, if there is any understanding in him, the truth of his own being.

—HAL BORLAND
When the Legends Die

Aldo Leopold linked plant and human ecology. He knew that humans influenced landscapes and were themselves changed by the mountains and meadows they inhabited. He was one of the first to raise the alarm about soil erosion, but he would be astonished at the changes in the forests of the Southwest today because of too many trees and too little rain.

The poetry of the high country is aspen trees in the fall. The light green leaves, dappled with sunlight and moving slyly in the wind, begin to yellow with cool nights, and yet days stay shirt-sleeve warm and pleasant. Bugs are gone. The skies clear of smoke from summer fires, and views get longer and longer. It's the perfect time to hike, to hunt, to train a pup, and to measure the world from a rocky outcrop on a ridgetop. Spring may bring flowers and migrating birds, but autumn in the high country is a world unto itself, of creek water cascading over smooth stones, aspen leaves turning golden day by day, and winter coming yet far away.

Herders bring sheep off the mountains, down the old trails and into valleys where the corrals and sheep wagons wait. At night large stock trucks come to load lambs and ewes at dawn. For hours it's been a cacophony of baas, bleats, and grunts beside the tinkling of bells and the quick movements of collies. Grass lies trampled. Flies whiz about, and then, after the woollies are loaded, sheep wagons pull out behind pickup trucks and another public land grazing season has ended. It's back to the home ranch for showers, better food, local chores. Winter away from the canvas tent and into the wagon, with the woodstove close to the single bed for those cold nights that are coming but not yet here. It's mid-September or early October. The aspen leaves are turning and sheep have left the mountains.

High up on those ridges between 6,500 and 11,500 feet, the golden leaves shimmer in the sun. Each leaf is distinct, but each quaking aspen tree, or *Populus tremuloides*, is a clone of the trees nearby because they have the same root system, which may live 8,000 years or more.[1] There may be hundreds of trees in an aspen grove, but they come from a single root system. To walk a mountain trail in a slight breeze as aspen leaves descend with their distinct clean scent is a sensory experience of blue Colorado skies and swirling yellow to red leaves.

Unlike other leaves, aspen leaves have the ability to photosynthesize on both sides, soaking up the sun as they shine, quake, and shimmer in September and into October in a visual delight, their colors a glorious tribute to the high country.[2] Quakies move the way they do so that sunlight can reach all leaves on the tree. Their characteristic flutter results from flat leaf stems that give them the strength to twist and turn in fall breezes. Aspen bark also photosynthesizes, and the white powder contains salicin, a chemical similar to aspirin, which is why animals eat the bark, particularly cow elk after giving birth. Native Americans used it as a fever remedy and to prevent scurvy. Scientifically, "aspen is an important habitat for a wide range of wildlife, supporting a greater richness of bird species and numbers than any other mountain habitat in North America."[3]

A wet fall means brighter colors when the leaves change, as the green of chlorophyll decreases and carotenoids, the same chemicals that produce the orange color in carrots, increase.

The chemical analysis is simple. The impact on hikers is glorious and profound.

As the leaves turn, sheep descend from the mountains, but the aspen arborglyphs will remain, at least for a few more years. Across the West, aspens are dying. From drought. From disease. The cultural commentaries of the older herders will fall with the trees and become lost, forgotten. Generations of carvings made by northern New Mexican herders, Greeks, Basques, Chileans, Englishmen, and Scots will fall as the trees decline, blown by wind, ravaged by disease, or simply felled by age. Aspen generally do not live beyond a century at most. Then it will be impossible to read the trees, to understand the sheepherders' codes. Messages the bosses, or *padrones*, never saw because they usually stayed at the ranch and rarely came to the high country. That was the camp tender's job.

Colorado has more aspen trees than any other Rocky Mountain state. Aspens are a climax or disturbance species that thrives after fires have killed spruce and pine. As the trees age and fall, stories from the herders will be lost. In campgrounds like Canjilon in northern New Mexico, dead and dying aspen have been cut down so they will not pose a risk to campers, but cutting the trees erases hundreds of messages the herders left for each other. The plight of the aspens has been literally sad, known as SAD—sudden aspen decline.

A drought at the beginning of the twenty-first century and increasing impacts from climate change are affecting sheepherders' landscapes. Half a million acres, or one-fifth of Colorado's aspens, have been affected by fungus and multiple other factors that have killed aspens for 1,700 square miles. The aspen decline was exacerbated by drought, which left the trees dying of thirst, resulting in the cutting of thousands of acres of trees to stimulate regrowth from the aged root systems.[4]

The die-off peaked about six years after the drought, and the water-loving trees have since stabilized and are recovering. What will never come back are the numerous aspen carvings, some of which were recorded by archaeologists prior to a planned forest cut. The message trees, with split bark and white trunks faded to gray, were sacrificed to stimulate new root growth. With earlier snowmelt, faster runoff, and hotter, drier summers occurring in southwestern forests, aspen growth may never be robust again.

Miners came west to find gold in rocks, crevices, and creeks. But the real gold is in the turning of aspen leaves in autumn. "In the fall, with aspen gold and scrub oak red, another month or six weeks and they would be beautiful," wrote Hal Borland about the San Juan Mountains in his classic

When the Legends Die. "Then the leaves would fall and you would be able to see forty miles in the clear autumn air. Those perfect fall days when you felt that the whole world was yours and you had been here forever. Mountains did that to you, these mountains."[5]

Yet the changing climate is leaving aspens behind.[6] Although small patches may be clear-cut, these "patch cuts" should be limited in acreage because "aspen clear-cutting is not favorable to native birds, may increase non-native weeds, and is prone to regeneration failure. No ecological need exists to clear-cut aspen forests. . . . Society's relationship with aspens is now more complex and contested than it was previously."[7]

Spruce and pine trees are also threatened by bark beetles. Milder winters have enabled beetles to thrive. Endemic in the high country, beetles are not an invasive species but have been kept in check in the past by deep snows and cold winters. Now the beetles are blown by wind currents across the tops of ridges and have appeared throughout Colorado, devastating the high country and leaving red, dead trees where evergreens once offered sheep shade and rest.

Fire has a natural place in western forests. Instead of a single mass of trees, a healthier ecosystem would be a forest mosaic with patches of pine, fir, and spruce, open grassy meadows, and stands of aspen coming back in burned-over areas. Forests should contain trees of different ages. Because we put out wildfires in the twentieth century, we now have too many trees in the forest, in what are called "dog-hair thickets," and we have dramatically altered natural landscapes. As global warming affects ecosystems, small, lightning-caused ignitions become catastrophic megafires, costing taxpayers millions of dollars and endangering the lives of firefighters and citizens. In the highest mountains, locals have thought they lived near "asbestos forests," or trees that would never burn. No more.

Bark beetles are chewing their way across the tallest forests, including the mountain pine beetle in northern Colorado and the spruce beetle in southern Colorado. Tiny bark beetles, half the size of a thumbtack, can alter miles of living green forests and create vast stands of dead red trees.

There are so many acres of dead trees that cutting them down, or "treating," the national forests is not possible. When trees blow down in big windstorms, they limit the way flocks and herders move through the high country. Colorado's famous green-clad mountains, proudly proclaimed on license plates, are turning dark brown as pine needles die.

The earlier mountain pine beetle devastation killed lodgepole pines across northern Colorado. In the south, the spruce beetle is changing Wolf Creek Pass, the Upper Rio Grande, the Sangre de Cristo Mountains, and miles of spruce forests along the Continental Divide north of Monarch Pass. In Colorado's wilderness areas so many spruce and fir might fall across trails as to make hiking impossible because crews with handsaws will not be able to keep trails open. The cycles of beetles and fire will take 200–400 years to restore natural ecosystems and replace the forest mosaic that Americans have inadvertently damaged by putting out too many wildfires.

Fire on steep slopes burns hotter. As the forest understory gives way, soils and sediments loosen, damaging watersheds for mountain towns and communities. How much grass will remain for high-country herders, and who will those herders be?

Often, ecological change and human change occur simultaneously. The latest generation of herders hails from Peru. They are familiar with hard work, high altitude, bitter cold nights, and days of aching loneliness. They know sheep, and if they are treated with respect, Peruvian herders can be loyal year in and year out. Unlike earlier generations of sheepherders who took their wages in ewes and started their own flocks, these South Americans will probably never become American citizens, but they maintain the old traditions of living out of sheep wagons and riding on horseback part of the day. Faithful dogs trained in Spanish and English watch the sheep.

"With consistency over time, the Peruvians are some of the best," explains Gary Visintainer, whose Austrian grandfather came into northwestern Colorado over a century ago. "Most of herding is a lonely life and other workers don't want to do it even at $20 an hour."

Peruvians know winter and high altitude, can take the cold on a high-desert landscape, and are used to hard manual labor. Visintainer had one herder who worked 27 years on nine three-year contracts. The herder finally retired and went home for the last time.

"We've lost sight of agriculture and where our food comes from. So much of the West is well suited to sheep," argues Visintainer.[8] Aldo Leopold agreed about food. He wrote, "There are two spiritual dangers in not owning a

On Clark Ridge in the White River National Forest, a young Peruvian herder stands next to the horse's head he has just carved in an aspen grove. Note that the tree is scratched, not deeply carved, so that as the tree ages the design will become more pronounced. Author photo.

farm. One is the danger of supposing that breakfast comes from the grocery, and the other that heat comes from the furnace."⁹ Peruvians are patient and know how to keep lambs and ewes thriving on summer grass and in the coldest of winter months, but they have also been some of the lowest-paid agricultural workers in the United States.

Sheepmen, also called livestock producers, have come under increasing scrutiny related to working conditions. Peruvians now have H-2A temporary visas or work permits designated for special types of work that Americans either cannot or will not do. Abuses have occurred, and unlike other agricultural workers, sheepherders who are on the range with their livestock 24 hours a day are not covered by minimum wage laws. The US Department of Labor administers the work program and the Immigration and Naturalization Service grants the visas, which have been given to as many as 600 herders annually in Colorado. Most herders like their bosses and have them send their wages directly back to family members in Peru.

"I don't have many problems," Serapio Velastegui told a newspaper reporter. He lived in a sheep camp in northwestern Colorado with two sheepdogs named Charla and Vagabundo, or Chatter and Nomad. The dogs always kept track of the band of 1,000 sheep. It was a lonely occupation, but he received regular mail from Peru. Like most herders, Velastegui was provided an airplane ticket to the United States and "all tools, supplies, and equipment required to perform the duties assigned," though there have been gray areas about costs and expenses.

For instance, are winter gloves and winter clothing personal attire or work-related equipment? Allegations of physical abuse of herders have surfaced, but only rarely.[10] Most herders have good bosses who want them to return, but wages have been abysmally low.

Over a 20-year period, sheepherder pay rates rose only $50 a month, though the herders were with their animals 24 hours a day and rarely got a day off, much less longer breaks to socialize and speak to someone—anyone. "The nature of these occupations—on call 24/7 in remote locations—and the scarcity of US workers in the occupations have made setting an appropriate minimum wage difficult, resulting in wage stagnation," the Labor Department reported in a *Wall Street Journal* article.[11] In October 2015, the

Sheep camp materials at high elevation have barely changed in the last century. Herders still use canvas tents, cots, sheet-metal stoves for cooking and heating, and wooden boxes for kitchen utensils and supplies. This Peruvian herder works for Ernie Etchart from Montrose and was photographed high above Silverton, Colorado, in McCarty Basin. Author photo.

wage rate increased to $7.25 an hour, double the previous rate, though Nina DiSalvo, executive director of the Denver-based legal-services group Toward Justice, argued, "The men doing this work across the American West are working in terrible conditions and working for absurdly low wages that are not enough to support them or support their families."[12]

Though some sheepmen have complained about the wage increase, Ernie Etchart from Montrose agreed that he could pay the higher wages for the five to six herders he employs. Etchart candidly admitted, "I think our industry has known that we've needed to get the wages up."[13] Colorado has ranked third in the number of sheep in the United States, most of them grazed on public rangelands, with sales of sheep and goats at $87 million in 2012. Wages for shepherds became "a human-rights issue" for Tom Acker of the Hispanic Affairs Project. In 2014, Colorado had 338 H-2A temporary herders working on 63 sheep ranches.[14] Many herders return year after year out of loyalty to the same ranchers.

New definitions and regulations for the H-2A program will be monitored by inspectors who will check on herders in their remote locations and see exactly what tasks they perform both on the range and at the home ranch. Effective communication is a safety issue, but most herders now have cell phones and solar-operated chargers. Ranchers have paid bonuses to herders for their good work and experience, but they have been penalized for it because the bonuses were not disclosed as part of the original contract. From the ranchers' perspective, it's just one more example of government overregulation and scrutiny of a rangeland industry that has not changed much in a century.

Well-intentioned ranchers will follow the new rules, pay the higher wages, and hope that lamb and wool prices go up. They hire international laborers, and their products must compete against international markets. A strong and unlikely American market for lamb is also emerging.

New studies indicate that 62 percent of Americans have never tasted lamb, yet a vibrant lamb market continues to grow from an unlikely source—urban ethnic groups like Hispanics, Latin Americans, Greeks, and Middle Eastern Muslims. Immigrants from Lebanon, Syria, Yemen, Palestine, and Saudi Arabia "prefer American lamb, blemish-free, want to see how the lamb is finished out and often purchase an entire animal," according to researcher Julie Stepanek Shiflett.[15] Americans generally eat less than one pound of lamb per capita per year, but Colorado lamb is a favorite, especially paired with beer or wine. Ethnic consumers eat three times as much. Sheep and lambs are raised on the range in western states but are eaten on both coasts, especially in Los Angeles, New York, and Boston, as well as Detroit.

Sheepmen generally come from long-established American families, and half the US lamb market consists of imports from Australia and New Zealand. Ironically, America's new minorities, particularly Muslims, account for 58 percent of total US lamb consumption. They prefer lamb from the United States. One of the largest lamb markets is in San Angelo, Texas, where as many as 25,000 head have been sold over the four-week Muslim holy days of Ramadan.[16] For Muslims these are Halal-killed lambs, butchered only by men as ritual sacrifices for family celebrations, weddings, births, funerals, and the end of the holy days of Ramadan. When the animal is sacrificed, the butcher must pause and say, "In the name of Allah." Goats are killed, too, but lambs provide more meat for large dinner tables surrounded by relatives and friends.

A Peruvian herder high on a mountaintop in summer or out on a sagebrush range in winter may think he is isolated, and he is. But the American sheep industry is linked to foreign markets, especially wool. Sheep shearers are also international workers hailing from Japan, Spain, Australia, and New Zealand. Young men, bent over most of the day, seem to dance with the sheep as they use electric clippers to remove fleeces. Shearers enjoy loud music with a heavy beat, "perhaps to drown out the interminable drone of the electric shears. Sheep after sheep after sheep, 12 shearers work in a nonstop, no-nonsense methodical manner ... constantly bent at the waist."[17]

"The lifestyle's good. It's hard sometimes to put your finger on it, but you always meet new people all over the world. It keeps us alive. No one's getting rich. We keep coming back, we've got to," says one shearer. "And it makes the beer taste better afterwards. We do play fairly well, too."[18] Hardworking shearers can clip 250 sheep a day at $1.50 per fleece, and the fleeces are pressed into a bale that contains the wool of 40 sheep and weighs between 400 and 450 pounds.

White American wool is tightly packed in huge bales and travels to China in cargo containers. Millions of pounds also go to Bulgaria for processing into finished products. Only a few small woolen mills remain in the United States, though a fibershed movement regionally tries to support local sheepmen. There is an expanding domestic market for special long-fiber wools like churro wool from the original double-coated Spanish sheep now reintroduced across the Southwest to the Navajo Nation and in herds run by Antonio Manzanares and the Tierra Wool Cooperative at Los Ojos, New Mexico. Churros may have black hair in their fleece.

If wool and lambs are finding new markets, recent research also points to holistic rangeland management. Just as sheep once devastated landscapes through overgrazing, now theories abound about how effective sheep can be at eating alien weeds, which in the high country can include yellow toadflax, oxeye daisy, diffuse knapweed, leafy spurge, and musk thistle. Woollies may also help with carbon sequestration, in other words getting plants to soak up and absorb more carbon by nibbling on them and promoting additional growth.

If aspen and pine trees are in danger from climate change, so are piñon pine and juniper across the Southwest. Because of "a high likelihood that widespread mortality" will occur in piñon-juniper forests, so many trees could die that 10 gigatons of carbon, or 36.67 gigatons of carbon dioxide, could be emitted into the atmosphere, causing additional global warming.[19] But sheep to the rescue.

Sheep eat grass and plants other animals will not eat. They stimulate plant growth, which then absorbs more carbon dioxide, or at least that's the premise of *Grass, Soil, Hope*, a book by Courtney White.[20] "Besides taking large amounts of carbon out of the air—tons of it per acre when grasslands are properly managed . . . that process at the same time adds to the land's fertility and its capacity to hold water," explains Michael Pollan in the book's preface. He adds, "Every time a calf or lamb shears a blade of grass, that plant, seeking to rebalance its 'root-shoot ratio' sheds some of its roots. These are then eaten by the worms, nematodes, and microbes—digested by the soil, in effect, and so added to its bank of carbon. This is how soil is created: from the bottom up."[21]

So sheep may help create soil and possibly stabilize and improve watersheds, providing ecosystem services through tightly managed grazing circuits. "They clean up the dry grass and litter by which the smoldering fire creeps from pine to pine; ranging moderately on the hillsides. They prune the chaparral which by smothering growth and natural decay covers great areas with heaps of rubbish though the shrub stems barely lift their leaf crowns to the light and air. Frequently in such districts after a fire, trees will spring up where no trees were because of the suffocating growth," wrote Mary Austin in *The Flock*.[22]

The French believe "a skilled herder is analogous to an 'ecological doctor' who at his finest has learned how to maintain the health of communities by providing ecological medicine in the form of ecosystem services."[23] France even has four herding schools, but also a manipulated and controlled landscape far different from the vast acreage in the American West.

Holistic management, involving short-duration grazing and rapid-rotation grazing, also has its critics, who state that what works for grasslands and previous Great Plains bison habitat does not apply to the drier Intermountain West, especially in drought conditions.[24] Sheep as saviors? Woollies as an effective edge against climate change? Perhaps, but that's a controversial claim.

Certainly as the Southwest gets drier, watershed protection, one of the original goals of the US Forest Service in 1905, will become even more important. But the woolly west has changed over decades. Many sheep ranchers have gone out of business or switched to cattle. It's easier.

Cattlemen do not need an on-site herder 24 hours a day. They put their cows out on public land pastures in summer and gather them up in the fall. They have less trouble with predators, as coyotes prefer smaller lambs to newborn calves. There are no issues with H-2A visas and foreign workers, and no disease transmission to wild bighorn sheep because cattle will not pass it on nose to nose.

America eats beef, not lamb. Sheep producers grazing the high country in the Mountain West have become a minority unto themselves. Angelo Theos of Meeker, Colorado, remembers where 30,000 to 40,000 sheep once grazed along the highway between Meeker and Rifle, Colorado. There are now only 5,000. No sheep graze on allotments in the Pagosa Springs Ranger District, where once roamed thousands. In the Norwood Ranger District, the only sheep permittee is Ernie Etchart. Aspen carvings can be found by the hundreds, but no borregas. In La Plata County, Davin Montoya's family epitomizes changes in land use.

His grandfather started with sheep and ran two bands up Cascade Creek and in La Plata Canyon, which the US Forest Service designated as sheep range in 1908. Members of the family grazed sheep on shares, in the *partido*

system, which impacted all of northern New Mexico. In the 1930s, seeing into the future, Belarmino Montoya homesteaded and bought land to go with his permits. He hired herders and worked wherever he could. "He started buying up land and people wouldn't buy land. They says, 'Why would you buy land when it's free grazing every place?' Well, he could see that this was not gonna last forever," explains Montoya, whose mother's family also ran sheep near Silverton, Colorado. The family made money on their lamb check, their wool check, and their incentive check to raise wool once Australian wool had flooded American markets after World War II.

The decades-old tradition of sheep raising did not last. The land did. In 1978 the family switched to cattle. Montoya explains:

> The reason we went out of the sheep business was because of the predators. I was what we referred to as a camp mover and I took the groceries to them and took care of the herders and whatnot. But the coyotes, the bears, just every night, was killing them. In the end sometimes several of them. Bears. And we would go up there and we'd get somebody to go up there with dogs and kill the bear, find the bear, kill it. Find wool and stuff in his gut knowing that he was the culprit, and the next night we'd have another kill. Another bear. I mean, it was just like they were standing in line. And so our losses were getting just terrible. At that time nobody was talking about using guard dogs.[25]

So a heritage of sheep raising, on both the Montoya side and on Davin's mother's side, the Jacques family, came to an end. It was difficult to hire herders, too. The family had always found local Hispano herders or Navajos. "You know, a sheepherder's got a tough job. I mean, it's a seven day a week job. You live by yourself, out in the hills, and I could understand why no one would want to do it. But we couldn't survive without having somebody to tend the sheep."[26]

Like so many other ranchers, the Montoyas switched their Forest Service allotment from a sheep permit to a cattle permit. But the sheep stories remain, along with the bear stories, and all those years of checking on herders, riding deep into the mountains. Montoya remembers:

> One night I rode into one of the camps. I got in after dark and I thought the herder was gone. It's after dark. I'm like, "I wonder where the hell this guy's at?" So I just turned my horse loose and found something to eat and I just slept outside 'cause those tents, they didn't have a lot of room. By the time you put your camp boxes in and a bed

and stove in there, there wasn't much extra room, so I just rolled my bedroll out on the ground outside. There was stars in the sky. Then about ten o'clock at night I hear him come riding in. I think he'd been over visiting another herder someplace. Well, he went to bed and then about one o'clock in the morning it is raining cats and dogs. I'm in my wet bed trying to figure out what to do. Pretty soon I hear him holler. He says, "Hey! Hey, it's raining." I says, "I know it's raining but I don't want to get up!" So he runs out there and grabbed a hold of my bedroll and drug me into the tent. That was a cold night.[27]

Cattle just aren't the same. They do not require constant attention and so the stories differ, the human relationships change. Herders now are mostly from Peru, though one Wyoming sheep family uses herders from Nepal and has learned the Nepalese language. As aspen leaves turn in autumn, there are fewer sheep in the high country.

Like their Hispanic counterparts and like generations of other herders, Peruvians gently carve on the white bark. Young herders will learn to carve

Considered a "master folk artist" in Colorado, sheepherder Pacomio Chacon carved dozens of arborglyphs, particularly female portraits. This section of a cut aspen tree from the Dick Moyer Collection is at the White River Museum of the Rio Blanco County Historical Society in Meeker, Colorado. Author photo.

with a light touch. Their writing is often too blocky. Recently arrived herders must develop cognitive maps of their territories—where to take sheep in the cool mountain mornings, where to bed down at night. The foreign herders must learn the diverse ranges and hidden pockets of water, shelter, grass. That hasn't changed, and neither has their longing for female companionship. Recent carvings attest to that—a thread of continuity among all lonely male herders who have only the stars and their dogs when the moon rises over mountaintops.

On the Pyramid Lake Trail at the eastern end of the Flat Tops in the Routt National Forest, this woman's portrait quietly stands among other uncarved trees with no artist's signature or date. Author photo.

NINTH SHEEPSCAPE

*Sheepscapes and Understanding
Herders' Lives*

> The forest resists exact understanding as much as the deepest dream. The roots of its mysteries reach into time and into the earth, as the roots of our dreams reach into the far, dark corners of our souls.... It is a place where bones, memories, and myriad other things, some with names and some without, vanish and later reappear, only to vanish again like an unremembered dream. But in the forest, as in the soul, nothing is lost.
>
> —WILLIAM DEBUYS
> *The Walk*

> The sheepherder has never been a member of the fraternity of western heroes.... His "wooly pests" were damned and dynamited ... the sheepherder has been an outcast in the American West ... it is his loneliness that comes to mind when we think of the sheepherder.
>
> —J. S. HOLLIDAY
> "The Lonely Sheepherder"

> Es triste estar solo
> It's sad to be alone
>
> —ANONYMOUS ASPEN CARVING
> California Park, Routt National Forest

Carvings on aspens inspired me to research and write this book. At first I wanted to find the largest concentrations of aspens in Colorado national forests, go there, camp in the woods, and walk the trails to read the trees and understand messages left by generations of herders. But even with aspens aging and dying, there are too many trees. History got in the way for me, as it always does. Digging deeper into the subject, I realized there was so much more to write about than just the arborglyphs. I sought to become a voice for the voiceless, for those herders who spent years of their lives, almost always alone, with their sheep and their dogs and a horse or two. But also a voice for the land—how it was used, abused, and restored, and how it is being utilized now primarily for recreation.

I started this book because the places I like to go best have always had sheep and sheepherders. From the mountain high country in the summer, above the old mining roads and wagon roads into federally protected wilderness areas of meadows, peaks, and the beginnings of rivers, to stark, steep canyons in winter with rocky trails, Indian ricegrass, and thin, green ribbons of riparian areas.

For outdoor education or outdoor recreation programs, the apex of weeks outdoors is a few days' solo experience—alone with one's thoughts, fears, strengths, joys, and weaknesses. Yet think of the months and even years sheepherders not only spent time alone, but spent time faithfully guarding their flocks, knowing each ewe and their lambs, always alert for cunning coyotes that would steal a sheep or two, or worse, a bear that could wade into a flock at night and kill a dozen ewes and lambs with the brute swipe of a paw.

Imagine that instant panic when dusky grouse explode off the ground and fly up into tall pines. One herder with grouse near his camp carved *Mucho Gallinas Aqui*, or "Many Chickens Here." Of course, the herders and camp tenders would arrive once every five or seven days to bring supplies, but there were still hours and hours alone, and sometimes ghosts in the forest. Certainly there are stories. Sheepherder lore drifts and settles like mist rising off a mountain stream at dawn. Tales reverberate of a place named Dead Mexican Gulch on the Routt National Forest, where a herder paid the price of being too successful in a poker game and was killed by avenging losers who followed him back to camp. It's marked on the forest map with the symbol of a grave.

How many sheepherder graves are out there? How many herders died from being struck by lightning or from a bad fall off a horse? One mesa has a unique rock alignment that appears to be in the shape of a horse. Perhaps a horse died and the herder buried it and covered it with stones out of love and respect.

On Snow Mesa near Creede, Colorado, lightning killed a herder. Another died up Cotton Creek near Henderson Gulch in the Sangre de Cristos. A wooden cross with a design of intricate nails marks the spot on Hermosa Mesa near Rambouillet Park on the Rio Grande National Forest where a herder died from lightning. Taken by a storm.

Near Ouray stories still remain of herders killing each other over an argument. On the Flat Tops a persistent tale has a Greek sheepman waiting until herders had worked for him for three years and then killing the men rather than paying them and sending them home.

The mountains, parks, and canyons have stories that modern hikers and backpackers never hear. Too busy. They move too fast, often wearing headsets playing modern music. They fail to listen to the land, to hear the stories told by the wind at twilight as it moves up canyon or across a ridgetop as the first stars light the heavens.

I've talked to herders, though my minimal Spanish is a barrier to effective communication. On Clark Ridge in the White River National Forest, I've been taken to a wide, healthy grove of aspen to see a fresh carving of a horse's head, the tender bark just recently cut with the sharp point of a horseshoe nail, not gouged with a large knife. The Peruvian herder and I spoke quietly and shared snacks until the dogs came and it was time to move the sheep.

On narrow mountain trails covered with willows and overgrowth I've seen aspen carvings with the standard template of a herder's name, the date, and his hometown or village. I have come across the occasional folk drawing of a house, a cabin, always with smoke drifting out of a chimney, symbolic of a herder longing for a real home with four solid walls and a door instead of his windblown canvas tent. Walking miles on the East Fork of Williams Fork as it drains the White River Plateau, I've turned to backtrack on a trail and then seen what wasn't there before. As the sun dips low late in the afternoon it can shine like a spotlight. There, high on a tree, was a hauntingly beautiful woman's face. How could I have missed it? Who was she?

Men talking to men, writing messages on trees as a unique expression of folk art. They carved tasteful, respectful portraits of women, erotic nudes, and sometimes pornography, explicit sex acts, aspen porn. Yet herders also etched religious symbols—crosses of various shapes and styles, the Penitente cross in its shadow box, the Virgin of Guadalupe, and on Maestas Ridge south of Taos even the Jewish symbol of the Star of David, carved on aspens by herders who may have been crypto-Jews from families that hid their Jewish heritage for centuries as they lived in New Mexico's Catholic communities. In the forest no one would know. You could carve the woman of your dreams or the symbol that signified your secret religion.

There are fewer and fewer sheep grazing Colorado's public lands. Maybe I am writing a eulogy, or rather, a ewelogy. I try to understand the world of sheepherders and sheepmen in an ancient lifeway that began the history of the American West and now diminishes each year. Sheepmen blame predators.

"Used to be you could have a day in the country. Now the bears are taking sheep right off the truck," laughs Joe Sperry. He then gets serious and adds, "The predator thing is about to get us. Out of a band of 2,800 I'm now losing 200 a year. I could buy a brand new truck with what the predators take. Bears scatter the sheep then the coyotes come in. And I've got three lions on my range, too."[1]

"Coyote. He sees you before you see him," relates sheepman Wayne Brown from the San Luis Valley. "That's why you need the herder to keep the predators away."[2] There will never be public lands sheep grazing without herders. In the high country, in the canyons, they often use the same trails that Native Americans used, and just like Native Americans, they leave minimal signs on the land, yet these are worth looking for. One of the most dramatic signs of sheepherders is their tall stone monuments. A cairn may be a trail marker of only three stones piled atop each other, but a monument is distinctive and can be seen from miles away.

All herders seem to have piled up stones, regardless of their ethnicity. Though herders have left us few records of their thoughts, their stone monuments remain. "As the Irish dominated the ranches, Basques and Mexicans emerged as specialists in the herding business," noted S. J. Cranshaw in the *Douglas (WY) Budget*. "Less susceptible to the temptations of the bottle than the gringo and more given to the patience and gentleness essential to proper sheep handling, they also accepted the solitary life on the trails and mountains where they whiled away the hours building pillars of rock on the hilltops." Cranshaw concluded, "These monuments remain in much of the country, silent testimony to the passing of an unprecedented era."[3] In fact, another nickname for stone monuments was "sheep herders' wives."

One of the best explanations of sheepherders' monuments is from a Works Progress Administration (WPA) interview with Tomás Antillon in Wyoming in 1939. "Before I was twenty, my father and I went to Colorado to work for a large sheep company, and my strongest impression of that country was the deep snows. Now the 'monuments' I had built began to serve a practical purpose," Antillon told an interviewer. "For several times, when blizzards struck, the piles of stones were my only means of getting back to the main camp, in a country which was all new to me. When an old, grizzled herder asked me how I ever found my way back to camp, in a blinding storm, I told him I followed the 'monuments' I had built. He answered, 'Well, I'm glad to know them danged things can be used for some purpose.'"[4]

Antillon continued, "Some of the Mexican boys in Colorado even had names for certain monuments—such as 'Dinner Table Monument' (where we ate our lunch); 'La Mesa Monument' (because we had put a flat, table-like rock on top of a big monument); and 'Frijole Monument' (because some of the rocks we used in building it looked like frijole beans). We took a great deal of pride in seeing who could make the largest and best monuments, and building them helped while away many lonely hours."[5]

Antillon added other details, including an attempted murder by a Mexican herder named Comerciano who had fired a shot at another herder. Comerciano pled innocent and insisted that Gregorio had shot at the victim. The aggrieved man did not know who fired the gun, but he knew exactly which monument the shot came from. Gregorio's friends proved that no one else built their monuments quite like Comerciano, so it had to have been him with the pistol.

Folktales include herders hiding money near monuments and their friends searching in vain for gold or silver coin supposed to be buried at a certain distance from a special pile of rocks. Herders arranged for girlfriends to meet them at special monuments, and one such secret tryst evolved into an elopement and marriage. But perhaps the most poignant story is Tomás Antillon's own account:

> I would have frozen to death had I not followed a line of monuments. The blizzard started suddenly and I was far from camp. As I tried to make my way blindly along, the wind and snow grew worse and worse. It is a terrible feeling to know that you are lost, and so cold you can hardly move. Finally, I saw a "hump" of snow that I thought might be a monument I had built. I scraped away some of the loose snow and found the "hump" to be a pile of stones I had put there, weeks before. It may sound absurd to say you can "recognize" such a monument. But actually it can be done, for you remember some certain stones, where you got them, and how you set them in place. I remembered that this monument was due north of an old, deserted shack, so I began trying to make my way there. For a while it looked as if I was beaten, but I finally did get there, and got a fire built. But some of my fingers were so badly frozen I had to have them taken off.[6]

Thus, sheepscapes have meaning. Stones tell stories. There are many such stories across the landscapes of the West, and signs can be found in nature as well as in culture. I look for history not just in archives and old newspapers, but on the land itself.

In a long-standing tradition, sheepherders offer both friends and strangers coffee and a bite to eat. Bill and Beth Sagstetter photographed Joe Maestas in his sheep camp near Engineer Pass, around 1980. Photo courtesy Beth Sagstetter.

Aldo Leopold looked each year for signs of the first plant blooms or the return of migrating birds, but at his home place, "the Shack," in Wisconsin, he and his family also paid attention to Native American artifacts that his children found. He would appreciate an understanding of sheepherder landscapes just as he would note where scars from overgrazing have healed on western landscapes and where they have not.

Archaeological features remain where sheep have been, but stories stay, too, and the silent soliloquies of being alone. Hal Borland wrote the novel *When the Legends Die* about an angry Ute Indian bull rider who returned battered and bruised to Pagosa Springs, Colorado, to heal wounds both mental and physical. He got a job herding sheep and the landscape helped heal him. "It was unbelievable. He had forgotten. Then he heard the bubbling of the creek, the whispering of the aspens just across the creek, but those sounds were part of the silence, the peace," Borland wrote.[7] The herder reconnects with his sense of place, his home in the high country, the rhythm of grazing sheep.

> He rode now to his camp, unsaddled the horse and hung the saddle from a rope over a low branch of a pine near the tent to keep it out of reach of porcupines. He built a fire, opened a can of beans and set them to heat in the frying pan, made a pot of coffee. By the time he had eaten and fed the dogs the sheep had bedded down and the first stars were out. He washed his dishes, put them away. Then went with the dogs for a slow walk around the flock. The stars glinted, the air was cool, the aspens whispered to the night. The sheep were quiet. He went back to the fire, poured another tin cup of coffee and sat sipping it, watching embers darken and die.[8]

Borland wrote a fictional account of sheepherding, but the Frenchman Pascal Wick tells of his actual experiences herding in the Absaroka-Beartooth Wilderness in Montana. In his memoir he describes seeing ravens and facing grizzly bears, but also the terror of a summer lightning storm. "The logger, the mountaineer, trapper and hunter can choose their days. The flock has to feed, sun or rain. I must go with the weather. I have no choice, no alternative," he writes. "When everyone goes home, I go out; we herders are not out in the storm by accident; it's where we have to be."[9]

Hikers and backpackers seek shelter from a storm, but herders have to embrace it. "The intervals between thunder and lightning become uncomfortably shorter; feeling the fear of a thunderbolt, deciding to be one with it, protecting yourself as best you can, but also tasting the fog rising and filling the wood, clinging to the trees and invading the clearing. For that takes over little by little, fog which brings fear, fog which all at once makes it impossible to see the whole flock, disorientating, stifling the bells, bringing isolation," Wick explains in *Beartooth: Diary of a Nomadic Herder*.[10]

What remains of a herder's experiences? Stories passed down and a few scattered artifacts. On lower-elevation BLM lands with potential for massive solar installations, required archaeological clearances of those lands are revealing sheepherder camps and sheepscapes spread over decades. The old stories of sheep and cattle wars are being remembered and documented. Traces are found on the landscape of sheep camps, condensed milk cans, scattered wood fragments from corrals, and at an archaeological site on the North Desert near Grand Junction, a rusty shearing blade, once used because sheep required "crutching," or trimming of the wool around their anus, groin, and teats in winter or early spring.[11]

The story of Navajo herders on Colorado's public lands is almost forgotten. Raised with sheep on the sprawling 17-million-acre Navajo Reservation, young Navajo men made good herders, but they were far from home, far from their families, their ceremonies, their traditional foods. They worked across Colorado and New Mexico, and still do. On some high forest trails, remnants of small Navajo sweat lodges can still be found, sticks crossed in an upside-down basket shape, with the entrance to the east. Their herding history blends in with that of Hispano herders, especially if the Navajos had Hispano surnames, which many of them did. Occasionally a herder could move up the ladder and progress to owning his own flock and public land allotment for summer grazing, but few did. Johnny Tom was the last Navajo to run sheep in the La Plata Mountains in the southern San Juans. He ran churros near Jackson Lake and Windy Gap.

Hispano herders learned English late at night while listening to transistor radios as they finally relaxed in their tents. The old herders stayed so close to the sheep that when flocks were sold they literally went with the sheep, like indentured servants, explains Antonio Manzanares, who runs a band near Tierra Amarilla, in Rio Arriba County, New Mexico, a county once dependent on proceeds from lamb, mutton, and wool.

North of Tierra Amarilla in southern Colorado, Aaron A. Abeyta remembers herding sheep with his grandfathers in what is now a federally designated wilderness area. In one blizzard the family's herd almost suffocated in deep snow. Abeyta writes:

> I reach the rocks and aspen trees where the herd was nearly buried. The natural world is intact, as it's been for centuries. The human side has faded in the proper order of things. The place is made sacred by my memories, strength and the brief kindnesses displayed there so long ago. There are names carved upon the trees, but there is no need to read them; I know all they have to say.[12]

But the rest of us who do not have such close memories need to record the trees, to document who was there and the decades they passed through.

On the Carson National Forest, at 10,000 feet at Canjilon Lakes, a favorite campground and fishing spot for Rio Arriba locals, dying and dead aspens needed to be cleared to make the campground safer. Archaeologists recorded 347 inscribed aspens. Consistent carving dates for Hispano sheepherders included almost every year from 1904 to 1966, with a wealth of male names, symbols, initials, carved faces, designs, and direct links to New Mexican villages like Canjilon, El Rito, Chamita, La Madera, Cebolla, Abiquiu, Mora, and Taos.[13]

Sheepmen and shepherds are reclaiming their rightful place in western history. After a century of being ignored and forgotten, the stories are being told of Teofilo Trujillo, who sought justice for the killing of his sheep and the abuse of his shepherd only to have his house firebombed while he sat in court with his family. There is the true tale of Juan Montoya, who raised his rifle to fire on a cattleman, an Archuleta County commissioner, but only after the young herder had been wounded in the shoulder. Montoya killed the irate cowboy and sought justice, too.

On the Utah desert in the winter of 1920–1921, cattlemen wearing black masks routinely burned sheep camps, harassed herders, and ran off horses and mules. "On some occasions, they were known to catch a lone herder out by himself, rope him, tie him up, double up their hard twist ropes and beat him almost to death. They would steal the pack animals at night," remembered Elmer Bair.[14] No help came from the law. It was every herder for himself.

In Elmer Bair's self-published autobiography, he describes being jailed in Moab in an attempt to have him convicted for horse theft. Grand County cattlemen, the sheriff, and his deputies were in collusion against Mormon sheepmen like himself. Luckily, he got out of the legal scrape, but he always kept his .30–30 Winchester rifle close by.

"One Basque outfit, not too far from us, lost two good pack strings and a camp. Their banker was in Price, Utah, and when they tried to borrow money to buy their third pack string and second camp outfit, the banker turned them down and sold their outfit to another Basque. A Greek sheepman on the other side of us was roped and beaten over the head until the blood soaked through his hat," Bair recounts.[15]

These are the stories of Basques and Greeks who came into a new country and made it their own, fighting with cattlemen for free range, yelling the *irrintzi*, or Basque war cry. These stories need to be told. The historical balance must be reset to describe who lived on the frontier and who settled the West. And those stories must include cultural concessions like the celebrated victory of Greek sheepman Regas Halandras riding with his wife in the Meeker Range Call Parade as its chief marshal, waving from the back of a convertible, finally given the status his family deserved. Cowboys and cattlemen tipped their hats and nodded with respect as he rode by. Yet his grandson, also named Regas, told me, "We're out of the business these fifteen years. It was so much work and Dad was getting older."

So I'll write the stories and seek the hidden histories of sheep and sheepherding. I'll spend time in the archives, locating historical documents, reading old newspapers, finding personal accounts, but I'll also walk the land, hike the trails, look for carved messages on aspens, on the wooden canvas. I'll read the trees.

One of my favorite places to do that is the Groundhog Stock Driveway, where sheep moved from the high country near Lizard Head Pass west toward lower country and Utah winter range.

Imagine being an artist working alone in a grove of shimmering white aspens, carving a portrait that you will never see. A full decade will pass before the design will appear, subtle, serene. Like the skilled calligrapher making a quick stroke on parchment, the Hispano carver leaves the gentlest mark for the tree to embrace. As the aspen grows, the bark expands and the art appears like magic, but the artist never sees his work. Now, half a century later, the sheepherders are gone, and soon the trees will fall, too.

Deep in the forests, beneath barren ridges but above the sides of creeks, stand elder aspen groves with thousands of carvings etched by sheepherders who passed through beside their bleating sheep. Carving symbols on trees is a cultural tradition vanishing along with the trees themselves, lost to drought, blight, and other unknown impacts that are decimating the aspen forests of the West. The issue is acute for Colorado, which grows half of the aspen trees in the Rocky Mountains.

Aspen trees tell stories. When we read the trees we glean a new understanding about the lonely lives of Basque and Hispano herders, some from the Pyrenees in Spain and others from northern New Mexican villages, or more lately from Peru. Among thousands of square miles on the Colorado Plateau, certain sections of aspen groves are covered with aspen art. In

This is possibly a carving of a sheepherder with a stomach ailment. It may be a self-portrait or it may be a portrait of another herder, whom the carver was trying to make sick using magic and a spell. Found in the San Juan National Forest along the Groundhog Stock Driveway. Author photo.

special places, herders and cowboys left messages for their compañeros and created a sense of community.

On the Pine-Piedra Stock Driveway at Beaver Meadows and Moonlick Park in the San Juan National Forest, where the trail begins to climb at the ecotone boundary between aspen and fir trees, the carvings become profuse. Names on the trees include Trujillo, Montoya, Bates, Isgar, Aragon, Archuleta, Gonzalez, Sanchez, Jacquez, and Valdez.[16] Herders bringing sheep from one grazing area to another and back again as the seasons changed moved north from Ignacio, Colorado, along Spring Creek on the edge of the HD Mountains and up Yellow Jacket Pass to Moonlick Park. They spent a few days resting sheep in the park, and as the light played upon the aspen groves they left their marks. Inscriptions include the poignant "Thanks to God" and the high-country haiku by cowboy Jim Bates: "NO LUCK, DAMN HORSES GONE! SNOW WALKING OUT DAMN!"[17]

Calligraphy decades old and inscriptions in flowing script nestle among the aspens clawed by bears and rubbed by elk antlers. Proud of their literacy and the ability to write their names, herders carved who they were, where they were from, and the date so that other herders would know of them. Some herders added a subsequent date each succeeding year they herded to explain to anyone who read the trees that they had returned. They were back. Think of that continuity over time. Year after year to come to the same grove with the daughters and granddaughters of the sheep you trailed before.

Rival herders occasionally vandalized each other's names. Carving categories included inscriptions; portraits of males with heads in profile and females from a frontal view; religious art like crucifixes and churches; poems; political slogans; and artistic expressions of mermaids, rifles, burros, sheep, maps, a flying saucer, and even a lifelike Elvis. Women were depicted artistically. "Aspen porn" became a significant subset as "a cultural form of expression" set back in groves, "almost like a private gallery," notes one archaeologist, whose favorite glyph read: "VIA INFERNAL, MAL VITAS SEAN LAS BORREGAS," or in English, "INFERNAL LIFE, CURSED BY THE FEMALE SHEEP."[18] One memorable contemporary carving is of a female forest ranger complete with badge and braids.

"The archaeology of the mundane. You have a guy who in the end is just standing at a tree and he's tagging it essentially for whatever reason that he's tagging it. He's putting the places that he's been. He's putting the places that he's from. He's putting some sexually suggestive art," laughs Bridget Roth, archaeologist with the Routt National Forest, who says "the cheap forest porn ... is always entertaining to come upon." But she adds that there is "not a consistent way to record aspen art. And aspen art is essentially one feature within a broader cultural landscape. The Elkhorn Stock Driveway is a good example of that."[19]

Unlike other archaeological sites, sheepscapes, and aspen art in particular, pose unique problems. "How do you manage these sites? It's a tree and because it's gonna die, the best thing we can do is thorough documentation." Yet, Roth asks, "How do we fit all these pieces ... and then how do we tie those individual trees to the broader cultural context they may be associated with? I think it's interesting how normal people live their lives.

We spend a lot of time in history deifying the great people. You know, we do big things about big people [but what about] the idea of an individual person's dreams? The way they lived their life is what I find interesting."[20]

Archaeologist Scott Ortman adds, "The facts of history matter for redressing past wrongs, adjudicating disputes between present day communities, revitalizing traditions, and promoting truth and reconciliation. Archaeology contributes to these positive outcomes by working to get the facts of history right."[21]

The key to locating aspen carvings is to know the route herders took through the forest. In the 1940s these traditional routes were marked with yellow signs stating "stock driveways" in order to help herders, who may have varied from year to year. Some of those signs can still be found.

On the Groundhog Stock Driveway near Dunton, Colorado, carvers competed not only to leave their name and date but to do so in exquisitely fine penmanship as they carved the smooth skin of the aspens. The best carvers used a light touch, a lover's touch, to caress the trees as they remembered caressing their women, so many months ago and miles away. Now, decades later, the herders' flourishes stand out in vivid, beautiful detail. The best carvers never gouged or cut but rather made a gentle scratch, a pinprick with the sharp point of a knife, and their ephemeral art lingers upon trees beginning to age and die.

This technique is one of the primary distinctions between historical aspen art and contemporary graffiti, which, because of brutal gouges, can damage and even destroy trees. The ethic now for all forest campers and hikers should be to "leave no trace" and leave the trees alone.

In the summer of 1955, New Mexican Joe R. Martinez was one of the best carvers. Folk art is generally anonymous and speaks to members of a select community or group, but Joe's style was unique and can be seen in marvelously simple cowboys with hats, women with hats, nudes, and other tableaux. He was good and he signed his work. On July 2, 1955, he carved one of the most amazing images in the forest.

A woman in profile wears a fancy feathered hat, and below her, at the level of her chin, another woman appears, this one a crone. Somewhere Martinez may have spied this drawing, in which the viewer is challenged to see both the well-dressed woman and the witch simultaneously. It's a

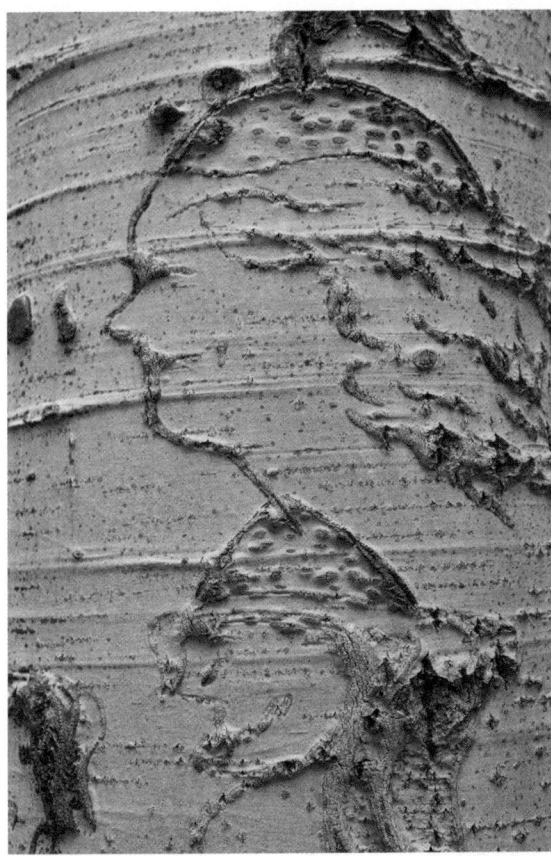

In this arresting arborglyph, the woman's portrait also contains another face, perhaps a witch, at her throat. Carving by New Mexican Joe R. Martinez, probably in 1955. Found in the San Juan National Forest along the Groundhog Stock Driveway at the edge of the Lizard Head Wilderness. Author photo.

figure/ground trick to see which image appears first, but in a sheepherder tradition, is the crone really La Llorona in an amazing double portrait? Is this a herder's version of the beautiful Hispanic seductress who lures men with her body but is really a witch?

Statistical analysis from one national forest reveals that 75 percent of the carvings were inscriptions with names or initials, hometowns, and dates; 5 percent were phrases or comments; and 20 percent were drawings in the categories of nature, buildings, portraits, guns, and symbols, including crosses and hands, and erotica such as images of the "Venus of the Forest."[22]

Who knows how many carvings are yet to be found? With a light touch and a sharp knife, how many forest folk artists etched images as yet undiscovered? How many of those trees remain? Who will pass on stories from the sheep camps and share the sensory smells of sweet *rosa de castilla* (wild rose), *paleo* (wild mint), and meadows combed by wind just before a rain?

So many sheepherders carved nude women that carvings of fully naked females are categorized as a special artistic type—Venus of the Forest. Found in the San Juan National Forest along the Groundhog Stock Driveway. Author photo.

Now fewer and fewer bands of sheep munch on forest grasses and the herding tradition is declining, as are stands of older aspens. Most of the men are gone now. They went back to their villages and small towns. On winter nights sitting in small kitchens, coffee in hand, they must have looked out their windows and thought of their trees—white in the moonlight, soft and silky to touch, silent except for the rhythmic rustling of leaves. They remembered the incessant bleating of their sheep and the way a herd moves through the forest, slowly in a meadow and faster through the trees, like a river flowing around rocks. Finally, the flock beds down for the night, circled by faithful herding dogs.

Shepherds remembered their quiet evenings smoking, carving, dreaming of home. The trees remember. Now we must read the trees to glean and understand a western tradition that's almost gone.

Chapter 9

Old West, New West, Next West
Sheep, Ski Areas, Wolves, and Endangered Species

> The world of the [Continental] Divide was animated by feuds—between cowboys and conservationists, sheepmen and coyotes, wolves and elk—and it would be a lesser place for the loss of any of the antagonists. Its appeal comes not only from mountain meadows and sculpted canyons, but from the relics of history—the bones of homesteads, the names of immigrant herders carved in aspen bark.
>
> —FRANK CLIFFORD
> *Backbone of the World*

> Our problem is John Wayne didn't film any movies chasing sheep.
>
> —JOHN FIELD
> Colorado woolgrower

The famous Two-Bar Ranch, owned and operated by cattle baron Ora Haley, had range that stretched for miles in Colorado and abutted Wyoming in Browns Park. Haley's ranch foreman ran thousands of cattle and earned the animosity of Anne Bassett of the homesteading Bassett family, southerners who had moved West. The Bassett Ranch became a safe haven for outlaws, and Butch Cassidy once served coffee at the ranch during Thanksgiving dinner.[1] When the Two-Bar had Anne's fiancé murdered for alleged cattle rustling, Anne ran an entire Two-Bar herd off a cliff above the Yampa River. In those days, westerners took things into their own hands and settled range disputes without the benefit of the law.

So it's odd that Ora Haley's cow boss never knew that Haley hired a sheep foreman who ran thousands of woollies, gobbling grass near the Wyoming state line. They took feed that the cows could have eaten. The two foremen, not knowing they worked for the same employer, often glared and yelled at each other but did not draw their revolvers in anger. As for Haley himself, he just went to the bank with his profits. He started his own banks and never let on in his social set that as a cattleman he also had sheep shit on his hand-tooled leather boots.

The Two-Bar is now a sheep ranch owned by Steve Raftopoulos, who runs as many as 14,000 sheep and has 30 Turkish Akbash dogs, 40 border collies, and a $30,000 ranch budget for dog food.

Other Greek ranching families with a sheepherding tradition include the Theos, Jouflas, and Simos families. Connie Jouflas was from the Simos family, with an enterprising Greek mother who had married a sheepman 30 years her senior. Georgia came to America from Greece at 18 and did not know how to read, write, or speak English. When Steve Simos died, she knew she couldn't run the outfit herself, which included various properties at Browns Park, Lay, Greystone, and Milner, Colorado. Greek sheepherders who decided to stay in America went back to the Old Country to find wives. So when her husband died in 1948 of pneumonia after a hard winter, she returned to Greece to find a second husband. She sold the sheep but wisely leased and did not sell the land. That second union, with George Raftopoulos, created an even larger woolly empire of sheep-owning Raftopolouses, and Steve, vocal former president of the Colorado Wool Growers, is part of it.

The historical Bassett Ranch has had numerous owners since the 1880s, but one of them was Tom Kourlis, another Greek sheepman running ewes on public land, with his operation headquartered out of Craig, Colorado. "The immigrant gene," he says with approval. "That's what made America great. That's where our families all came from. Our grandfathers and great grandfathers came here with nothing and were willing to take risks to make a change, to establish a family. They created a country that's very energetic, dynamic, and with great livestock producers willing to do what it takes."[2]

An orphan, the patriarch of the Kourlis family came from Greece in 1924. He worked as a lumberjack, Utah coal miner, restaurateur, and finally a sheepherder paid in ewes, who trailed sheep to Axial Basin and stayed to homestead 160 acres and more under other homesteading laws. Then he purchased more homesteads, grazed more sheep, and brought other Greek herders from the Old Country, another link in the chain of migration.

The Old West of hardworking immigrants—Greeks in northwestern Colorado and Basques in central Colorado—also included Scottish and English families spread evenly across the state, with names like Swisher, Duke, Hutchinson, and Hotchkiss in the North Fork Valley. The Olsons, Nottinghams, Pappases, and Burfords ran woollies in Eagle County. Others raised sheep in the great high parks—South Park, Middle Park, and North Park. They began their operations to feed the nineteenth-century tide of Colorado gold and silver miners, and they stayed, always by expanding, to pass on huge ranches acquired patiently as homesteaders left one by one.

Overgrazing blistered and broke the land, but in the high country much range has recovered. In the Uncompahgre Wilderness, a few cairns can still be found on Forest Service Trail 223, a historical stock driveway that sheepherders used to bring thousands of sheep from the bottom of Big Blue Creek to the top of Uncompahgre Peak. Sheep numbers today are 10–15 percent of their historical highs, and in the past 20 years, lower stock numbers have made for sustainable grazing and land use. Aldo Leopold would be astonished and delighted.

"Back in Aldo's day there were so many more sheep. Things have changed dramatically. We had thousands of sheep here at the dawn of the Forest Service. We've seen marked improvements in range conditions," states the supervisor of the Grand Mesa Uncompahgre Gunnison (GMUG) National Forests, Scott Armentrout. "In the unregulated era most of the high elevation lands suffered greatly. The average person wouldn't even notice that sheep are still using the Uncompahgre Wilderness. We've reached a very sustainable place. Aldo would be proud."

The San Juan Mountains now have healthy riparian zones along creeks and rivers, with good cover of willows, grasses, and forbs. The rare Uncompahgre fritillary butterfly is doing fine. "Through years and decades of good partnerships we've been able to change the impacts of overgrazing," Armentrout adds.[3]

On lower-level sagebrush and desert lands administered by the Bureau of Land Management, damage remains. Those lands were used and abused longer, and because of a lack of annual precipitation, rest and recovery will extend into the next half century—if they can recover at all.

The Old West became the New West with a post–World War II vacation and recreation boom fueled in part by Interstate 70, authorized by the Eisenhower-era Federal-Aid Highway Act of 1956. The carefully designed four-lane road split Colorado in half and opened up sheep ranches that had always been remote. "This landscape finds its highest worth in being pretty to look at or nice to play in—it is more valuable to us for aesthetics, atmospheric, or recreational values than for any resources it may yield," writes William Philpott in *Vacationland: Tourism and Environment in the Colorado High Country*.[4] "In Colorado, the vacation mystique that came to surround the high country inspired many people to reshape their lives, identities, and politics around the state's leisure amenities."[5] The high country, which no one had wanted if it had no minerals, now became sought after for a new outdoor pastime—downhill skiing.

Vail Resort began its operation 100 miles from Denver in 1962. "Whenever motels appeared in an old mining town, campground facilities in a forest, or an entire resort village in a former sheep pasture, a setting that had been unremarkable or unwelcoming to vacationers gained the ability to attract and accommodate them. Suddenly the setting became an entry in travel guides, a spot on the tourist map," explains Philpott.[6]

Vail and Vail Mountain were the permitted grazing areas for the Jouflas family. Connie Simos, whose stepfather was George Raftopoulos, married Chris Jouflas at age 16. In Greece, the villages where the Simos and Raftopoulos families came from were only 10 miles apart. Both family dynasties began with Greek grandfathers struggling in the coal mines at Castle Gate, Utah, and longing to get out of the dark, dangerous mines.

In the late 1950s, in a secluded valley on the back side of Vail Mountain, Chris Jouflas looked up to see several men coming his way, wading through his bleating sheep. He wasn't sure why they were there. As they came closer and began a conversation one man said, "We're going to build a ski area here."

"Oh really? Good luck with that," Jouflas responded to Vail Mountain founders Earl Eaton, Peter Seibert, and other investors.[7] Over the years, acres of Jouflas property would become prime Vail real estate, and the Greek drink ouzo—alcohol distilled from olive leaves—would be toasted to consummate deals. At one location, "Vail had already built the chair [lift] to go up there and discovered that we owned the land," remembers Connie Jouflas. Though Vail Associates sent a check, "we came to a price after a lot of negotiations and when they did the final sale, Chris took a bottle of ouzo

Chris Jouflas, the son of Greek immigrant Peter Jouflas, was a passionate sheep rancher who served the agricultural community on local, state, and national levels. On the far left in this photo, in a white shirt, Jouflas serves barbecued lamb for the American Sheep Producers Council on a Tall Timber Tour above Vail, Colorado. Photo courtesy of the Jouflas family.

to 'em and so they had a shot of ouzo. They named the ski run 'Ouzo.' So that was the first time we sold and then we sold some other land after that and every time we did, they brought the ouzo afterwards."[8]

A handshake closed the deal for a ski lift near Lost Boy. Additional acreage became the Game Creek Club. Two world-class golf courses at Red Sky Ranch and Golf Club once pastured Jouflas sheep. What's left of the Greek sheepherding heritage can be found in food, as in the Lil Spicy Lamb meatballs served at the Wolcott Yacht Club.

The family's Lazy J Ranch once encompassed 7,000 acres in the valleys of the Frying Pan and Eagle Rivers, with 14,000 sheep. Winter range included 4,000 acres in Utah and Colorado, and grazing rights and permits in Ruby Canyon, Rabbit Valley, Thompson, and Cisco.[9] Now the family businesses include oil, gas, real estate, and the potential development of an entire town on the only large parcel left in the Vail Valley—acreage that Chris's father bought near Wolcott as sheep pasture to graze his flock while waiting for shipment out on the Denver and Rio Grande Railroad.

Sheep stories are a vital part of family folklore, like the story of hardworking grandfather Peter Jouflas, who when he succeeded bought a new car every other year. Once, driving a deep maroon Cadillac with a white leather interior, he spotted a few of his lambs outside a fence and placed them in the back seat. At a gas station the attendant said, "That's a beautiful new car. Why do you have sheep in it?" The rancher answered succinctly, "Why shouldn't they ride in it? They paid for it."[10]

Another family that successfully transitioned from Old West sheepherders to New West entrepreneurs is the Basque Aldasoro family from Telluride. Grandfather Joaquin came to the United States on March 15, 1913, to herd sheep for the Aubert family up on the Glade west of Grand Junction. Not being the eldest, he stood to inherit nothing in his home country. He

Sometimes multiple brothers married multiple sisters. This wedding photo shows three Aldasoro brothers marrying three sisters. Almost all immigrant sheep ranches were tightly run family businesses in which everyone played a role. Photo courtesy of the Aldasoro family.

would have to make his own way, which he did. Joaquin's brothers Miguel and Jean and cousin Sarapio also arrived.

In Price, Utah, the Spanish Basques purchased the French Hotel, a local Basque boardinghouse and sometime gambling parlor and speakeasy in an era of prohibition. Handsome Jean would be shot and killed through the window while playing a card game.

Joaquin worked for the Auberts until he could purchase his own herd. Cristina Aldasoro Mitchell and Pam Aldasoro Bennett explained that the carousing trait has stayed in the family. "That's how our dad was. He did the sheep. I think he liked the sheep okay, but the day in and day out it wasn't his favorite thing to do, but oh my gosh, get that man with a bunch of other men and then some whiskey and all they'd want to do is talk."[11]

Grandfather Joaquin, who had limited English skills, started purchasing property in 1926 on Deep Creek Mesa "because it reminded him of the old country." He bought 5,000 acres, one homestead at a time, "during the time when a lot of the people up here were ready to move out of the area because the mining had crashed and they didn't know what they were gonna do up here," relates Pam. "He would buy a piece of property and then the adjoining property brothers would say, 'Hey would you buy ours?' And the story we heard is that he would go away for a season, sell his wool and lambs, and

Imagine the fears of young girls from the Old Country leaving the only home they knew to travel to America to marry a hardworking sheep rancher. Cristina Basterrechea Aguirre came from Spain to marry into the Aldasoro family from Telluride, Colorado. Photo courtesy of the Aldasoro family.

he'd buy the next piece of property. And we always heard that it was for a fair price; whatever they asked for, he would pay."[12] Joaquin ran Rambouillet sheep with Suffolk and Hampshire bucks.

The homesteads he acquired are now a high-end real estate development, Aldasoro Ranches, near the Telluride Airport. The family fortune came down as a partnership, and when family members could not agree on distributions and a lawsuit was filed, the holdings were eventually to be sold at auction on the San Miguel County courthouse steps. The Telluride branch of the family prevailed, though with serious loans to pay off because of investing in both cattle and sheep when both markets had collapsed.

Finally, the Aldasoro sisters' father's estate was settled, but with additional expenses. They paid those by selling another piece of land, 2,200 acres, originally bought to avoid trespass fines. Pam Aldasoro Bennett explains that in 1940 their grandfather was trying to move sheep from the high country out to the Utah desert. He became stalled in Mailbox Park, near Redvale:

> It was the Norwood area, and a hell of a storm came in. And it was deep enough that they were not gonna be able to move the sheep. So they said, "Well, we'll just stay here for a period of time until we can move on." And during that period they brought in some feed but Grandpa Joaquin found out who owned the property, which was Marcelino Alchu, is what we found on the deed, and said, "We'll need to stay here. We'd like to lease pasture from you because we can't move our sheep." And he said, "No, I won't lease you the pasture. I'll trespass you unless you purchase the property." 'Cause he was trying to get out of the area. Grandpa Joaquin didn't want to get into trouble so he said, "Okay then, I'll buy it." And I think that was the only time, well, I know that was the only time we ever used that property for sheep.

Selling that property tidied up their father's estate, and funds have been invested in other ventures, but the sisters still own their grandparents' homestead. They are diligently trying to put together their family history and have a trunk full of deeds, photographs, pay stubs, and newspaper clippings. They love to share family stories. Just as the Jouflas family did, the Aldasoros have returned to Europe to see the churches and pastures, ancient farmsteads, and roots of their herding heritage.

In Colorado resorts with multimillion-dollar homes, water features, security alarms, high-speed internet, and hiking and biking trails, shepherds roamed before mountain meadows became littered with exclusive, gated McMansions. Starter castles and second, third, and fourth homes and condos have replaced sheep camps, canvas tents, and herding dogs. The herders' Dutch-oven cooking on a bed of spruce coals has been replaced by stainless-steel 10-burner gas grills costing more than shepherds earn in a few years.

The aspen groves where herders once camped now sprout huge patio decks. The alpine view is the same, but without the band of bleating sheep and their softer sounds at sunset. No more baaing ewes. Just scenery. Not a working western landscape. The working West of mountain meadows and a thousand grazing sheep is now the domain of outdoor enthusiasts using forests for recreation but not for producing lamb and wool.

Ever-attentive herders, always alert, listen for their marker sheep, their guard dogs, the proximity of coyotes or bears at night. More often than not, bikers and hikers listen to no natural sounds at all. Their ears are plugged. They wear tiny headsets so they can rock and groove to popular music as they exercise across the landscape, treating the mountains as a place for cardio, for workouts, but not for work.

"The spread of recreational developments, recreational values, and recreational consumers into ever more rural areas is the 'new normal' for regions like the American West," notes scholar William Philpott.[13] These new values in rural regions have even created a twist on the term "ghost town." He adds, "The new land uses conspired with newcomers' environmental values to crowd out traditional resource-based livelihoods, while spiraling real estate values pushed residential and recreational space beyond the means of longtime locals, service workers, and even many in the middle class. In an ironic recycling of regional lingo, some invaded communities were termed 'ghost towns' where neighborhoods full of seasonal residents' 'trophy homes' sat empty much of the year."[14]

Away from the ski resorts, sheepmen still run sheep, but it's getting harder on those mountain peaks where wild bighorns live, and equally difficult in the valleys and sagebrush areas where threatened and endangered species of greater sage grouse and Gunnison sage grouse have their leks, or nesting grounds. Sheepmen seek grass. Environmentalists campaign to protect a vanishing species.

Across the West, politicians and oil and gas industry spokesmen are wringing their hands, shaking their heads, and saying "no" to Bureau of Land Management proposals to set aside large swaths of land for the greater sage grouse. Federal plans may also include listing the separate Gunnison sage grouse as an endangered species.

Colorado governor John Hickenlooper wants the BLM to "look at the public-private partnerships that have been so successful in Colorado as a model on how to get things done."[15]

Perhaps. But who speaks for the sage grouse?

What is at stake are thousands of square miles of the Intermountain West, because prime habitat for both species of grouse is also prime turf for oil and gas rigs, cattle, and sheep. In Mesa County, Commissioner Rose Pugliese said that stringent federal management of the greater sage grouse "will kill us" economically. Commissioner Chuck Grobe, in Moffat County, worries that $1.1 billion worth of minerals are at risk.

"San Miguel County wants to have the US Fish and Wildlife biologists make a determination based on science, not politics, as to whether the [Gunnison sage grouse] is threatened or endangered," said Commissioner Art Goodtimes. He added, "Losing another iconic Western species to extinction is a threat to the web of life, and the repercussions could have lasting consequences that we are not even aware of today."[16]

Sheepmen argue that back when they could use poison to control coyotes and other predators, they remember more sage grouse. They claim that coyotes do the damage, and with poor predator control, grouse numbers decline. Whatever the truth, sage grouse issues cannot be sidestepped. Conservation biologist E. O. Wilson explains, "The causes of extinction intensified throughout the 20th century. They are now the highest ever, and still rising. Almost one in four of Earth's mammal species and one in eight of the bird species are at some degree of risk."[17]

It's about habitat. But it's also about restraint. The Endangered Species Act of 1973, signed into law by President Richard Nixon, was prescient and powerful because the legislation represents humility. The law posits that we are only one species on this continent, and that it is our moral responsibility to protect and preserve the diverse life forms our forefathers knew in abundance and bequeathed to us.

Conservationist Aldo Leopold said it simply, "The first rule of intelligent tinkering is to save all the parts." Now there are believed to be fewer than 5,000 Gunnison sage grouse. We are losing the parts we need to interweave ecosystems back to land health—another Leopold concept that included air, soil, waters, and the land itself.

Like bighorns on rocky crags above timberline, the lower-elevation sage grouse controversy continues, with lawsuits filed by both ranchers and oil and gas companies and countersuits by environmental groups. A federal listing of sage grouse as an endangered species could change the way the rural West does business because grouse range encompasses a 257,000-square-mile region in 11 states.[18] Colorado has 4 percent of the range of the bird, but half of that is private land. The Gunnison sage grouse has been listed as threatened, but the greater sage grouse, found in 11 states, teeters on the edge of ecological intervention. No one knows "what is best for the bird" and whether science can effectively inform rangeland management.

Wild horses—really feral horses—are also an issue for sheepmen in northwestern Colorado. The Sand Wash Basin has 700 horses, yet the appropriate management level (AML) is 162. For 20 years ranchers have complied with "voluntary nonuse" of that grazing area to allow vegetation to recover, but it's still being hammered by too many horses.

Sure, they look great. Manes flying. Tails outstretched as herds gambol across open spaces, but in the process they endanger native plants, introduce invasive species, hog rare water holes that other mammals need, and continue to multiply. What kind of symbol is this for the American West? Unlike mule deer, elk, or mountain lions, wild horses aren't really wild. They are feral. Set loose. Perhaps a few rare specimens represent the genetics of Moorish ponies brought over from Spain five centuries ago, but most so-called wild horses were simply abandoned. Owners continue to release domestic horses onto public lands, especially when the economy turns or hay prices rise.

The Wild Free-Roaming Horses and Burros Act (1971) protects herds on public lands. But what the act never considered was equine fertility. One of the icons of the West, enshrined in myth, is now being scientifically reexamined. Four decades after the law was passed, we know a lot more about ecosystem balance and the carrying capacity of animals on public lands. Factor in drought, and ecological conditions are getting desperate.

According to a December 2010 report by the Office of the Inspector General, the number of wild horses and burros adopted out decreased from 6,644 in 2004 to only 2,960 in 2010. The herd size doubles every four years, and "each year the number of wild horses and burros the Bureau of Land Management manages increases as does the level of public interest and scrutiny."[19]

Where the animals grazed in 1971 there are now designated herd management areas, or HMAs, covering 32 million acres in 10 western states. The BLM controls 180 HMAs, which in Colorado include the Spring Creek herd in the Disappointment Valley, the Piceance Basin/East Douglas Creek herd west of Meeker, the Little Book Cliffs herd northeast of Grand Junction, and the Sand Wash herd.

Approximately 30,000 head of feral horses from BLM land are in "long-term holding facilities" where animals no longer inhabit desert and sagebrush landscapes but instead are shipped east. We simply have too many feral horses and burros threatening ecological balance. So by default we now practice equine birth control. Volunteers shoot mares with contraceptive darts that lose their potency after a few years. Then it's time to pull the trigger again.

For wild horse lovers, that strategy exceeds the bruising benefits of helicopter roundups, now called "gathers" by the BLM, which can run animals into dense oak brush or box canyons, and can certainly produce panic and fatigue as the horses are crowded into corrals. The Office of the Inspector General admits, "The risk that horses or burros will be injured or killed is an unavoidable consequence of gathering. Injuries and broken bones can and do result from the effort to herd, capture, and transport the animals."[20]

After the gathers, it's off to pleasant pastures in Kansas, Oklahoma, or South Dakota, at a total taxpayer cost for the horse and burro program of $66 million annually and climbing. It's time to stop and smell the sagebrush. We need laws that allow federal agencies to sell or auction feral horses and burros to be recycled into food products.

Republican president Theodore Roosevelt said, "We're not building this country of ours for a day or even a year. It is to last through the ages." Yet environmental rules and regulations often strike at the heart of traditional grazing practices and rural ranch livelihoods operating on thin economic margins.

For sheep ranchers, where does it end? Where is the middle ground where everyone can meet? Historically, the US government tried to give away the West, to open it up for free land via the Homestead Act of 1862 and subsequent other laws. So families came West, out beyond the prairies, across the mountains and into basins and parks to try to earn a living any way they could. "Herding hasn't changed. The sheep wagons have propane refrigerators and stoves. Solar lights. But it's still a rustic life. It's tough making ends meet. We've got all these regulations and yet as ranchers we've made habitat for wildlife and sage grouse," explains Gary Visintainer. "All I want is the land to make me a living."[21]

Like many descendants of homesteaders far from the lush, green landscapes of mountain resorts, Visintainer needs public land to earn a living, yet excessive rules and regulations continue to burden small ranchers. He has one band of sheep. Hires one herder.

Small family ranches have "consistently lost out to the needs and interests of the nation. Their dependence on public lands placed them at the mercy of the American public, symbolized by the federal government and the BLM and put them at risk when public lands shifted from unallocated, unreserved, and unwanted territory to the treasured landscape of the nation," writes public land scholar Leisl Carr Childers.[22]

On BLM land, authorizations for animal unit months (AUMs) to graze on public land have dropped from over 18 million in 1953 to near 8 million in 2014.[23] AUMs may change annually depending on range conditions, and the agreed upon number is often lower than what a rancher's permit allows. "The advent of range science—which aims to use a coherent scientific method to determine how much grazing the land can sustain—changed everything," and now federal managers, and many ranchers themselves, seek sustainable grazing levels so they are not whipsawed by the market and caught with bank loans in a down year.[24] If good rains bring better grass, AUMs are not increased because severe droughts may be next.[25]

What was once marginal grazing land used by adjacent ranchers has now become weekend playgrounds for hikers, hunters, and ATV users.[26] In Colorado, the agricultural economy tied to public land grazing softens while the state's annual $13.2 billion outdoor recreation economy booms.[27] Heritage tourism is also doing well, and soft, cuddly lambs and sheep have a unique niche. In Cortez, Colorado, for a $10 fee children between the ages of 3 and 10 can sign up for "Mutton Bustin,'" a lighter-weight version of bronc riding for tykes.

Every September, Bayfield, Colorado, has Sheep Trailing Days, when J. Paul Brown's flock comes down from the high country and parades through town. There has even been a recent set-to reminiscent of the old cattle and sheep wars but with a new twist. This took place in a subdivision among residents squabbling over homeowners' association rules.

The conflict is known as the Shenandoah Sheep War after the name of an exclusive subdivision near Durango. Terri Warner had border collies and

Though public land sheep grazing is in decline, small flocks on family farms are increasing. In the West, young children practice a form of rodeo bull riding called "mutton busting" as they try to hang on to a sheep's fleece and ride around a paddock layered in straw. In Bayfield, Colorado, sheep rancher J. Paul Brown always brings his sheep through town in a popular September event known as Sheep Days. Author photo.

wanted to properly train them, so she purchased eight sheep. An irate neighbor sued over subdivision covenants. Eight years and $600,000 in legal fees later, the Warners won in court and even received reimbursement for their legal expenses because a judge ruled it to have been a frivolous lawsuit. An award-winning member of the Colorado Wool Growers Association, Warner smiles and correctly says she's owned the most expensive sheep in the state, worth $80,000 each. After the legal hassles and disapproving stares from her neighbors, she and her husband relocated to a historical sheep ranch near Cimarron, Colorado, where they have privacy and many more sheep. Ironically, the Shenandoah subdivision had once been a sheep pasture.

If sheep wars have moved from the open range into subdivisions, sheep wagons have been transformed, also. One of the premier manufacturers of modern camp wagons is Wilson Camps of Midway, Utah. Rules under the H-2A regulations dictate a minimum of 98 square feet per herder, or about 7 by 12 feet for camp wagons. New thick-gauge aluminum-sided camps have beds, shelves, propane cooking stoves, woodstoves for heating, solar and propane lights, showers, and a small tub for washing clothes, though "in reality herders are going to wash 'em in a stream or ditch and lay 'em on rocks to sun dry," says Mark Wilson, whose camps are so popular that as of September 2015 the company was 44 camps behind in production.[28] "As soon as we get them done they leave," he says proudly. They can cost $25,000 and up.

Sheepmen place an order and then wait a few years to be able to purchase their new camp. The camps hold their value and are so well insulated that Wilson claims, "A propane gas light will keep them warm at thirty below. In a sheep camp you can have any color you want as long as it's white. Owners can almost always sell them for one or two thousand dollars more than they paid." That's because at 3,300 pounds, the camps are built only one at a time, with a lifetime guarantee on hinges. The camps have a distinctive thin red stripe and a serial number on a steel builder's plate.

Just as sheepmen now have competition for the use of public land, hunters, fishermen, loggers, and rockhounds have all bought Wilson Camps, which are found in every state west of the Mississippi River. "We have 'em in Alaska for hunting, but not yet in Hawaii," Wilson laughs.[29]

Public land grazing of sheep has declined since World War II. American families eat less lamb and wear less wool, so old sheep wagons are often abandoned or sold at auction. These wagons were on display at the Wyman Living History Ranch and Museum, Craig, Colorado. Author photo.

Painted sheep wagons have become trendy vacation rentals, as in this re-created traditional wagon available for rent at Avalanche Ranch Hot Springs between Carbondale and Marble, Colorado. What was once functional is now fashionable. Author photo.

There is even sheep camp tourism, in which older rustic wagons, well used and retired, have become recreational lodging next to historical cabins. Given some bright coats of paint and a few modifications like electricity and Dutch doors, and permanently lifted off their worn-out axles, these vintage wagons provide a unique place to sleep, especially if rain drums down across the rounded metal roof.

As the West shifts and changes from resource extraction to recreation, and as fewer jobs exist in agriculture, the historical Bair family of Mormon sheepmen from Carbondale and Glenwood Springs, Colorado, have placed part of their Golden Bair Ranch under a conservation easement of 4,300 acres with the Eagle Valley Land Trust. This provides open space along Interstate 70 for the 15,000 travelers a day who see the ranch east of Glenwood Canyon. On this historical working sheep ranch, which has been going since 1919, the ecosystem includes aspen, oak brush, and evergreen slopes on one of the last major private properties between Vail and Glenwood Springs. By preserving the landscape and wildlife habitat, the easement enables the Bair family to continue sheep ranching.

Other conservation easements on sheep ranches include Gold Run Ranch, which was an original homestead in Grand County near Winter Park. Those acres are now held by the Colorado Headwaters Land Trust. Funds from Great Outdoors Colorado (GOCO) purchased easements on 20 Mile Sheep Ranch in Routt County and on Cross Mountain Ranch in Moffat County, which has the most sage grouse habitat in the state. Near Vail the Jouflas family may put 470 acres into a conservation easement, and near the Utah state line, Jouflas ranch property that was homesteaded on the public domain is now public land again as part of the McInnis Canyons National Conservation Area (NCA). Jouflas Campground on the NCA is a favorite place to camp for mountain bikers on their way to visit Moab, Utah.

Some sheepmen and their families have put their land in conservation easements to give back to Colorado citizens and visitors, while others, like William and Genevieve Clough, have given millions of dollars to provide college scholarships for Garfield County high school students, giving young people a chance to succeed after graduating from high school.

Sheep ranchers also actively participate in Ranching for Wildlife programs with Colorado Parks and Wildlife, which has opened more than a million acres of private wildlife habitat to the public. Cooperating ranchers receive elk hunting licenses that they can sell to out-of-state hunters, with or without guide services, while a percentage of the tags are open to public hunting from in-state hunters for animals of both sexes. Big game hunting for elk, antelope, and mule deer is a huge business; Craig, Colorado, proclaims itself the "elk hunting capital of the world" because of the 55,000 elk within a 50-mile radius. Hunters come from all over the United States, and many access public lands through private ranches where habitat improvements have benefited big game populations.

Aldo Leopold, the father of game management and a devoted wildlife hunter, would approve of these partnerships among private ranches, a state agency, and avid hunters. One of the state's prime sheep ranches, put together by a hardworking Basque sheepman, is now an exclusive hunting preserve bordering public land near Black Canyon of the Gunnison National Park. Because of sheep grazing and also because of elk numbers essential to attracting hunters, the one conflict still simmering but destined to erupt is a movement to reintroduce wolves into Colorado. Of all the ecological areas of concern, nothing will create more controversy than the fight over the future of wolves and their role in public land ecosystems.

Leopold's thinking and writing in *A Sand County Almanac* and his experiences in the Southwest are at the center of this debate. His opinions evolved over time, and he came to see the role of large predators with "wolves as a partner in the evolutionary drama" and their ability "to increase the capacity of the land for self-renewal" by balancing ecosystems.[30]

Sheepmen have always shot predators, and herders can legally do so today. In the 1920s the Bureau of Biological Survey diligently worked to rid Colorado of its last wolves, which had become so famous they had nicknames. Killing wolves represented the true end of the frontier because they were on the wrong side of progress. In one of the most famous essays ever written about animals in the Southwest, Leopold wrote about wolves. Published posthumously in *A Sand County Almanac*, the essay philosophized about our need to "think like a mountain" and not just consider wildlife and habitat from a human-centered perspective.

Having worked as a forester in the backcountry of Arizona and New Mexico at the turn of the twentieth century, Leopold wrote about having shot a wolf and how he later came to regret that decision. He wrote, "I was young and full of trigger-itch," but what he did was entirely commensurate with federal policy at the time. Eventually, he would help to change that policy and become the father of wildlife management. He wrote:

> A deep chesty bawl echoes from rimrock to rimrock, rolls down the mountain, and fades into the far blackness of the night. It is an outburst of wild defiant sorrow, and of contempt for all the adversities of the world. Every living thing (and perhaps many a dead one as well) pays heed to that call. To the deer it is a reminder of the way of all flesh, to the pine a forecast of midnight scuffles and blood upon the snow, to the coyote a promise of gleanings to come, to the cowman a threat of red ink at the bank, to the hunter a challenge of fang against bullet. Yet behind these obvious and immediate hopes and fears there lies a deeper meaning, known only to the mountain itself. Only the mountain has lived long enough to listen objectively to the howl of a wolf.

He explained about wolves and men and how he shot a wolf:

> We reached the old wolf in time to watch a fierce green fire dying in her eyes. I realized then, and have known ever since, that there was something new to me in those eyes—something known only to her and to the mountain. I was young then, and full of trigger-itch; I thought that because fewer wolves meant more deer, that no wolves would be a hunter's paradise. But after seeing the green fire die, I sensed that neither the wolf nor the mountain agreed with such a view.[31]

Though Leopold had had a change of heart, it would be decades before federal policy evolved about killing predators and "varmints."[32]

Wolves are coming. Colorado Parks and Wildlife (CPW) already has a plan. It's over a decade old, but *Findings and Recommendations for Managing Wolves That Migrate into Colorado* by the Colorado Wolf Management Working Group offers interesting scenarios.[33] Strategies involve adaptive management and damage payments for livestock killed. One key idea is that "migrating wolves should be allowed to live with no boundaries where they find habitat," and another is that "wolf distribution in Colorado will

Sheepmen across the Rockies today must contend with protected endangered species. Officially there are no wolves living in Colorado yet, but they are coming south from Yellowstone National Park and they might take up residence in the Flat Tops or Weminuche Wilderness, areas that have long been the summer domain of sheep and sheepherders. *Enchantress of the Forest*. Drawing © Becky Hoyle Lukow. Author's collection.

ultimately be defined by the interplay between ecological needs and social tolerance."

Once wolves are here, CPW staff "will implement programs to make sure that wolves are included as a part of wildlife heritage." *Canis lupus* will be an eco–wild card. With an estimated 250,000 to 280,000 elk in Colorado, we can afford to lose a few to a top predator. The Wolf Management Plan is based on the premise that wolves may reenter the state and recolonize it, but wolf biologists say that's not enough. They believe wolves need to be introduced into the state's wilderness areas on Colorado's Western Slope—wilderness areas now grazed by domestic sheep on summer range allotments. Wolves need to be introduced because not enough single wolves will arrive on their own for genetic variability. Surveys indicate that over 60 percent of Colorado citizens want wolves back in the state.

Of all the environmental controversies over bighorn sheep, sage grouse, and wild or feral horses, bringing wolves back polarizes rural and urban populations. City people want wolves to return, but rural communities will have to live with the consequences, because when deep snows hit the high country and prey populations like elk drift down into lower ranges where ranches lie, wolves will follow.

"Wolves have become a flashpoint in the tension over deep cultural change—one of the last battlefronts in the closing of the American Frontier, the transition from a culture of domination and extermination to one seeking ways to coexist with nature. Whether humans can live with wolves will help determine who we are and what our legacy is to those who come after us," writes the Center for Biological Diversity in the book *A Wild Love*.[34]

The elk population in Colorado currently exceeds the carrying capacity of the range. Wolves will cull elk; an adult wolf kills about 20 elk per year. Wolves have sharp teeth and are not cuddly animals. "People appreciate large carnivores for the cultural, aesthetic, economic, and other values they represent. Other people disdain large carnivores based on fears for human, livestock or pet safety; the negative impact they sometimes cause; and issues of private property rights and government actions," state Richard P. Reading and other editors of *Awakening Spirits: Wolves in the Southern Rockies*. They add, "We know how to protect carnivores, but not how to live with them . . . biologically there is no problem reintroducing wolves successfully; the problem lies in addressing human opposition."[35]

From a Basque family background, Ernie Etchart from Montrose, Colorado, runs sheep on the San Juan National Forest above Silverton, Colorado. The mountain grasses and cool days produce high-quality Colorado lambs. Author photo.

Because of vigorous complaints from hikers, mountain bikers, and San Juan County commissioners, Ernie Etchart socialized his sheep guardian dogs. "We make them people-friendly so they don't view humans as a threat to the sheep," he explains. With the potential for wolves in the high country, his dogs may be too docile. "We don't have wolves yet. They're to the south and to the north of us, so it's only a matter of time. Then I don't know what we'll do, because the guard dogs we have now are so mellow that they don't stand a chance against a wolf and consequently, I don't know that we'll stand a chance."[36]

Sheep and wolves live together in the mountains of Idaho, Wyoming, and Montana, where "constant vigilance replaces bullets as a way of deterring predators."[37] In the Absaroka-Beartooth Wilderness a herder from France has spent summers guarding flocks. "I know from experience and from talking to others that a flock of sheep can co-habit with wolves without a problem. I know that the key to this potential co-habitation depends on the introduction of quality guard dogs," states Pascal Wick. "The latter as their name implies are there to protect the flock from all predators, whether wild, such as wolves, foxes, bears, lynx, wild boar, hooded crow, or domestic such as dogs, which are responsible for ninety per cent of all losses in France."[38]

But herding to ward off predators takes time, patience, and being near the sheep. "Without doubt you need to have endured days outside in the rain, on the mountain, sleeping in a tent pitched on a hollow ledge of the mountain slope, like a quagmire, in muddy shoes and wet clothes, getting into a wet sleeping bag, putting on the same clothes next morning, no drier, and colder, to understand what it means to choose to sleep beside the flock," Wick writes.[39]

Pascal Wick crafted a beautiful shepherd's memoir in *Beartooth: Diary of a Nomadic Herder*, but even a remote Montana wilderness, alive with both gray wolves and grizzly bears, was not immune to federal biologists. "They set down new rules, most of which made the herder's work more difficult, and increased the cost of summer pasturing for the flock owning ranchers. A deeply conflicting situation has emerged."[40]

Becky Weed, a Montana sheep rancher who sells organic lamb and "predator-friendly" wool products made on their farm in a fiber mill, has her own sharp opinions about learning to live with predators:

> We can pick our poison. Castle-building landowners who are busily resurrecting a feudal society while chopping up habitat. Ranchers and politicians who are too quick to put wildlife in the crosshairs as a scapegoat for deeper ills in our agricultural economic system. Energy companies' boom and bust frenzies. The press of all the rest of humanity. It's hard to condemn any one sector without acknowledging the warts and complicity of any other, but collectively we're degrading the magic that makes this region unique. Can we slow down, scale back, and proceed with less of an air of entitlement? The carnivores that seem the most threatening these days are the two-legged kind.[41]

If wolf advocates seek ecological change and habitat rebalance, across the West we've already damaged our forests by fighting too many fires. Now the goal is to create a "natural forest" to replicate the effects of lightning on habitat and ecosystems and to open up a forest canopy for more mosaics, or patchworks of multiaged trees. By thinning in certain ways, foresters are "making meadows," cutting out diseased trees, and creating openings where new trees can get their start.

So what about alpine tundra in isolated areas in high mountain ranges? Tundra has a short growing season. Harsh weather and shallow soils increase its fragility. Scarred tundra may take a century to heal, but sheep regularly graze across it, sometimes with no damage, sometimes with devastating results if they stay too long in the same spot. If sheep arrive too high too early, they can nibble plants that have not yet set seed for reproduction and are not available for pollinators.

Most alpine plants are perennial, but intensive sheep grazing at the wrong time for a lengthy duration can do lasting damage by killing the root system of plants. Scientific knowledge of the Colorado high country is incomplete. No one truly understands the "ramifications of sheep on alpine ecosystems. Also, the increase from sheep dung as a fertilizer needs to be studied to see if some plants benefit more than other plants and if it leads to changes in plant species composition."[42] Mountain meadows must absorb and filter water. Their value as watersheds in a warming West will only increase. Do sheep help or hinder that process?

Public land grazing is shrinking in the Rockies. In the Sangre de Cristo Mountains allotments are understocked, vacant, or closed. "Sheep populations in Colorado exploded between 1880 and 1900, reaching into the millions. During this period in the San Luis Valley alone, ranchers shipped out 250,000 sheep annually, maintaining 500,000 in the Valley," writes environmental historian Tom Wolf.[43] The landscape still suffers from those excesses, and now it rests and recovers with few sheep on the Rio Grande National Forest. Hispanic families that once grazed vast acreages on public lands have much smaller farm flocks.

The West continues to grow and change, with recreational users following the same pattern as many old-time sheep ranchers—summers in the high country and winters in the desert. In the 1930s farming and mining accounted for a third of Colorado employment. By 1962 that was down to 9 percent for ranching and mining. In 2006 it stood at 1.1 percent, and less than 5 percent of the livestock eaten in the United States grazed on public lands.[44] Meanwhile, tourism has increased. The number of registered all-terrain vehicles, or ATVs, in Colorado tripled in the 1990s, and snowmobile numbers have shot up by 60 percent since then.

New residents build second homes, play at "hobby ranching," and bring different values. The number of second homes in the southern Rockies is twice the national average, and "as communities continue to shift from extraction-based economies to service economies, which often rely on marketing local natural amenities, they increasingly recognize the economic benefits of restored and healthy ecosystems."⁴⁵

The sheep and cattle wars of the nineteenth century may become the wolf wars of the twenty-first century. The battleground will be the alpine tundra and mountain meadows of Colorado's national forests and wilderness areas, where old sheep bridges once positioned across swollen creeks will not be replaced in wilderness areas. Sheep helped settle the West. They provided a food source from the very beginning of western history. Sheep ranchers and ranching families worked hard to make a living across diverse landscapes of sagebrush, mountain parks, and desert canyons, but what was once rural and remote is no longer.

It's now contested terrain as new forces—social, economic, and cultural —shape and reshape the Mountain West. Some sheepmen cling to the old ways with bare knuckles and bleeding hands. Others have diversified, sent their children to law school, veterinary school, or Ivy League universities. For that generation, lambing sheds are a distant memory. Cottonwood corrals in deep canyons forgotten. The sweat and labor of shearing unknown.

"City and county land-use planners and conservationists . . . have their hands full. They are wrestling with the musculature of Western cultural and historical geography. While money is certainly a central motivation of developers, it's as if the quiet of the land bothers them, and they turn to the buzz and clatter of platted civilization to blot out the silence," writes John B. Wright in *Rocky Mountain Divide*. "To others, the powerful beauty of the landscape is a catalyst which stimulates intense life experiences and the urge to save geographic rarities. Both options still lie before us. For in the West, you can stand on a rimrock and see a hundred years in either direction, or you can choose not to see at all."⁴⁶

Few historical ranch families still run sheep on public land. The US Department of Labor has forced a change in working conditions and pay scales for herders, many of whom come from Peru on H-2A work visas or permits. They have solar-powered battery chargers for their cell phones, and in this digital age hikers and backpackers can monitor sheep movements on BLM websites to try to avoid confrontations with guardian dogs.⁴⁷ The conduit for herders from northern New Mexican villages ended in the late 1960s.

Like cowboys, sheepherders wanted condensed milk with their coffee. Unlike cowboys, herders reused the condensed milk cans by punching additional holes in the bottom and then stringing the cans through with heavy wire to make a Christmas-wreath sized tambourine that they could rattle and bang to help motivate sheep flocks to move in a specific direction. Hence, the nickname—tin dog. Author photo.

Hispanic groups are suing over better living and working conditions for current herders. No one seems to remember how hard it was a century ago to get started in the sheep business, yet for some immigrant families the isolation, long hours, and lonely working conditions became a time for contemplation, reflection, and development of a financial strategy of grazing, land ownership, and mineral rights that still survives four generations later.

Passage of the Taylor Grazing Act in 1934 permanently quieted cattle and sheep conflicts by creating grazing districts and assigning allotments with the requirement that ranchers have "commensurability" or private land near their public range. Today's foreign herders do not have opportunities to lease or buy sheep or to acquire base properties to start ranches of their own. The living landscape of the working West has become the leisure landscape of skiers, hikers, climbers, and bicyclists. Across most of Colorado, sheepherding in the high country is a fading memory.

But near Craig, Colorado, in 2013 the Visintainer Sheep Company received the prestigious Leopold Conservation Award, sponsored by the Sand County Foundation, the Colorado Cattlemen's Association, and the Colorado Cattlemen's Agricultural Land Trust. Named after Aldo Leopold, the award is presented annually to recognize private landowner achievements in voluntary conservation. For the Visintainers that means moving toward "forage-based" management to improve range health so that their ranch has become a refuge for wildlife species like deer, pronghorn, elk, greater sage grouse, and Columbian sharp-tailed grouse.

"The Visintainers are clearly committed to innovation and testing of practices that further improve stewardship of natural resources under their care," explained Brent Haglund of the Sand County Foundation. "This family exemplifies what it means to be leaders in conservation." T. Wright Dickinson, president of the Colorado Cattlemen's Association, added, "The Visintainer family coexists with nature in one of the most challenging environments in Colorado to produce food and fiber for families across the state and nation. This miracle of agriculture and conservation doesn't happen on its own; but requires tending of the herds, soil, and water through the lens of sustainability."[48] But the future of the ranch is uncertain. The Visintainers have no children, no direct descendants to carry on the family's herding and land stewardship legacy.

In the towns of Meeker and Craig, sheepherding traditions are celebrated. At the Wyman Living History Ranch and Museum near Craig, a sheep wagon rests inside the large facility. Beside it is a framed photo of Lou Wyman's brother from more than half a century ago, standing near a sheep wagon. Each September the Meeker Sheepdog Trials, started by the Halandras family, keep herding traditions alive.

Recently, flags flew from 13 different countries as a dog handler stood near the wooden pole, shepherd's crook in hand, whistling for his dog to bring sheep through a fixed obstacle course. When his border collie drove a small flock through the final gate, the audience, mainly tourists, applauded.

Afternoon storm clouds drift across the Flat Tops, the Elks, and the San Juans. Herders move their sheep for the last round of the day, collies nipping at heels, ewes turning to find lambs, guardian dogs alert on the fringe of flocks. First a few raindrops hit on bare ground and then in tall grass. Aspen leaves tremble, showing their undersides. Spruce limbs begin to rise and fall with the wind. A storm is coming. Change is in the air, but it is not just rain.

Historical Hispanic Herding Terms

borregas	sheep
borregero	sheepherder
calvario	A large cross erected on a scree field or in a high-altitude meadow so that sheepherders who were northern New Mexican Penitentes could offer prayers and devotions. Named after Calvary hill where Jesus Christ was crucified.
caporal	sheep range foreman, sometimes camp tender
carnero entregado, peso contado	a dollar counted out; price paid for each animal sold, because some sellers did not know how to count beyond the fingers of their hands
carneros mesos	rams
chicheros	small, quickly constructed brush pens
corta	stray bunch
descansos	handmade wooden crosses that usually marked where a sheepherder died
el Año de la Nevada	The year in which thousands of sheep died, smothered under wet snow, probably in the winter of 1932. This is vividly remembered in New Mexico and Colorado.
ganado mayor	small hoofed livestock or sheep
ganado preñado	pregnant ewes
goldas	fat ones; bread made by Hispano herders
hediondilla	creosote bush, a remedy for kidney ailments
hijadero	lambing season

Hispano	Term for male sheepherders, primarily from northern New Mexico, who came north to herd sheep. An older term used until the 1950s was "Spanish-American." Today the term "Hispano" also applies to Latin American herders coming into the West on H-2A work visas.
hondas	egg-shaped slings to throw stones, keep stragglers in a flock
la Estrella del Pastor	the morning star, often seen by herders as their flocks begin to graze
los Pastores	Christmas plays about the life of shepherds and sheep camps, ancient pageants brought from Spain
luminarias	small fires lit in bags of sand on Christmas Eve, or Noche Buena, to commemorate the shepherd campfires near Bethlehem and the birth of Christ
majaba	bed-ground
marcadoras	marker sheep, one black sheep per 100
mohoneras	sheepherder stone cairns, also known as monuments
oveja	sheep
pan de pastor	shepherd's bread, round loaves baked in a Dutch oven
partidario	a herder with sheep leased from a rich sheepman; a sheep sharecropper
partido	System in which wealthy sheepmen leased sheep on shares, often forcing Hispano herders deeper into debt at the mercantile stores the sheepman owned. The rigid partido system forced many New Mexican Hispanos to come north into Colorado as sheepherders to be paid in cash and not suffer losses from blizzards, bears, etc.
pastor	shepherd
patrón	boss, owner of sheep
pencos	orphan lambs; herders tied the skin or pelt of a dead lamb on an orphan to fool the mother, or *vieja*, into adopting it

Penitentes	Members of the Brotherhood of Light, a medieval religious group that reconstituted itself in northern New Mexico in the 1700s to help with baptisms, marriages, and funeral rites in remote areas far from churches and priests. Many Penitentes became herders, and by the 1930s they were traveling north into Colorado and Wyoming for work.
pinque	name for the Colorado rubber plant, which is poisonous and causes salivation, nausea, and weakness
reatas	hand-braided leather ropes
rebano	flock
remuda	exchange or replacement from a horse herd
rescoldo	big bed of coals for cooking herder delicacies
rico	a man who owned many sheep and much land
Santa Inés or Saint Agnes	patron saint of sheepherders and those who live outdoors, prayed to over strayed or lost animals
teguas	handmade moccasins worn by herders
vaya con Dios	go with God, a blessing for travelers
yerbas del campo	wild herbs collected by herders both for ailments and cures and for bringing back to their villages in winter

Notes

Introduction

1. Charles Wayland Towne and Edward Norris Wentworth, *Shepherd's Empire* (Norman: University of Oklahoma Press, 1945), 272.
2. Mary Austin, *Land of Little Rain* (1903; repr., New York: Penguin, 1997), 72. Citations refer to the 1997 edition.
3. Aldo Leopold, *A Sand County Almanac* (New York: Ballantine Books, 1970), 197.
4. Nina Leopold Bradley, quote from *Green Fire: Aldo Leopold and a Land Ethic for Our Time* (produced by the Aldo Leopold Foundation, US Forest Service, Humans and Nature, 2011), DVD, 73 minutes.
5. Curt Meine, quote from *Green Fire*, 2011.
6. Sarah Deutsch, *No Separate Refuge: Culture, Class and Gender on an Anglo-Hispanic Frontier in the American Southwest, 1880–1940* (New York: Oxford University Press, 1987). Also see Ruth Lambert, ed., *The Wooden Canvas: Hispanic Arborglyphs along the Pine-Piedra Stock Driveway* (Durango: San Juan Mountains Association with History Colorado, 2014).
7. Carl Abbott, Stephen J. Leonard, and Thomas J. Noel, *Colorado: A History of the Centennial State*, 5th ed. (Boulder: University Press of Colorado, 2013), 40.
8. Stephen J. Leonard, *Trials and Triumphs: A Colorado Portrait of the Great Depression, with FSA Photographs* (Boulder: University Press of Colorado, 1993), 89.
9. Leonard, *Trials and Triumphs*, 89.
10. William Bright, *Colorado Place Names*, 3rd ed. (Boulder, CO: Johnson Books, 2004), 162.
11. Jane Koerner, interview by author, Fairplay, CO, January 24, 2015.
12. John Muir, *My First Summer in the Sierra* (Boston: Houghton Mifflin, 1911).
13. John Muir, journal, August 1875, cited in Edward Norris Wentworth, *America's Sheep Trails* (Ames: Iowa State College Press, 1948), 491.

FIRST SHEEPSCAPE

1. Angie Krall, interview by author, Supervisor's Office, Carson National Forest, Taos, NM, July 26, 2016.
2. Ibid.

Chapter 1

1. Charles Wayland Towne and Edward Norris Wentworth, *Shepherd's Empire* (Norman: University of Oklahoma Press, 1945), 89.
2. Ibid., 22.
3. The best book on Navajo herding and the matriarchal nature of Navajo flock ownership is Marsha Weisiger, *Dreaming of Sheep in Navajo Country* (Seattle: University of Washington Press, 2009). To learn from a Navajo herder's perspective, see Walter Dyk, *Son of Old Man Hat: A Navajo Autobiography* (1938; repr., Lincoln: University of Nebraska Press, 1967); and Louisa Wade Wetherill and Harvey Leake, comps., *Wolfkiller: Lessons from a Nineteenth-Century Navajo Shepherd* (Layton, UT: Gibbs Smith, 2007).
4. William W. Dunmire, *New Mexico's Spanish Livestock Heritage* (Albuquerque: University of New Mexico Press, 2013), 18.
5. Towne and Wentworth, *Shepherd's Empire*, 152.
6. Ibid., 54.
7. Charles F. Lummis, *The Land of Poco Tiempo* (New York: Charles Scribner's Sons, 1893), 20.
8. Lummis, *Land of Poco Tiempo*, 18; Towne and Wentworth, *Shepherd's Empire*, 63.
9. The first caravans of Hispanic traders moved west as soon as Mexico, including New Mexico, became independent of Spain in 1821. They took New Mexican handcrafted woolen goods and were astounded to trade two blankets for one horse. In just one season alone the traders returned to New Mexico on the Old Spanish Trail with 4,000 horses. The legs of those animals contained sagebrush seeds, which flourished on soils eroded and depleted by sheep. Today, greater sagebrush dominates the landscape for miles between Taos and Tres Piedras.
10. Towne and Wentworth, *Shepherd's Empire*, 314.
11. Ibid., 64.
12. Antonio Jose Luna established an empire of wool, business, and politics. His sons Solomon and Tranquilino would come to run 150,000 head of sheep south of the Zuni reservation and across the Rio Puerco watershed, doing immense ecological damage. "By 1900 it was said to be the largest sheep outfit in the United States." Solomon would play a crucial role in writing the bilingual New Mexico State Constitution prior to statehood in 1912. Though married to Adelaida Otero, "thus uniting two of the most influential families in New Mexico," Solomon unfortunately had no children. While inspecting his holdings one night he fell into a sheep vat, probably filled with water, lye, and tobacco to rid sheep of parasites, hit his head, and died. *Tercentennial Exhibit Commemorating the San Clemente Land Grant*, Los Lunas Museum of Heritage and Arts, Los Lunas, NM, July 9–September 17, 2016; Curt Meine, *Aldo Leopold: His Life and Work* (Madison: University of Wisconsin Press, 1988), 121.
13. Edward Norris Wentworth, *America's Sheep Trails* (Ames: Iowa State College Press, 1948), 332.
14. C. E. Gibson Jr. "Stories from Costilla County," manuscript on file with History Colorado, Denver.

15. Sarah Deutsch, *No Separate Refuge: Culture, Class and Gender on an Anglo-Hispanic Frontier in the American Southwest, 1880–1940* (New York: Oxford University Press, 1987), 10.

16. Each sheepman or cattleman moving vast herds across the West dealt with Indian tolls differently. Some paid up after a period of bartering; others bluffed with a show of force and soldiered on. All too often, however, if tolls to adjacent tribes were not paid, stockmen would lose even more stock from Indian raids at night.

17. Towne and Wentworth, *Shepherd's Empire*, 65.

18. Carl Abbott, Stephen J. Leonard, and Thomas J. Noel, *Colorado: A History of the Centennial State*, 5th ed. (Boulder: University Press of Colorado, 2013), 35.

19. Wentworth, *America's Sheep Trails*, 264.

20. Towne and Wentworth, *Shepherd's Empire*, 168.

21. Deutsch, *No Separate Refuge*, 29. A comprehensive look at sheep in New Mexico can be found in Dunmire, *New Mexico's Spanish Livestock*.

22. Towne and Wentworth, *Shepherd's Empire*, 172.

23. Andrew Gulliford, "Eye of the Miracle: Los Ojos, New Mexico," *Durango (CO) Herald*, April 10, 2011.

24. Towne and Wentworth, *Shepherd's Empire*, 330. The bulk of the huge Maxwell Land Grant is now Vermejo Park Ranch, the largest in the United States, owned by Ted Turner, who raises bison where sheep once grazed. Another way that Hispano *ricos* acquired sheep was to buy them from the Utes, who were given livestock by the US government. The Utes turned over to Hispanos, at 50 to 75 cents per head, sheep that the government had purchased for annuities at $2.70 per head. Such shrewd bargaining allowed Bidal Candelaria to own 11,000 sheep by 1883. Frances Leon Quintana, *Pobladores: Hispanic Americans of the Ute Frontier*, 2nd ed. (Notre Dame, IN: University of Notre Dame Press, 1991), 116.

25. Towne and Wentworth, *Shepherd's Empire*, 331. For another perspective on the Bond brothers' sheep empire and New Mexicans kept in *partido* relationships, see Suzanne Forrest, *The Preservation of the Village: New Mexico's Hispanics and the New Deal* (Albuquerque: University of New Mexico Press, 1998), 24.

26. Dunmire, *New Mexico's Spanish Livestock*, 87.

27. Ibid., 102.

28. Frederick Jackson Turner, "The Significance of the Frontier in American History," *Frontier and Section: Selected Essays of Frederick Jackson Turner* (Englewood Cliffs, NJ: Prentice-Hall, 1961), 37–62.

29. *Tercentennial Exhibit*.

30. Deutsch, *No Separate Refuge*, 22–23.

SECOND SHEEPSCAPE

1. Andrew Gulliford, "Art in the Aspens: 40 Years of Searching for Sheepherder Carvings," *Durango (CO) Herald*, August 12, 2015.

2. Antonio Manzanares, interview by author, Tierra Wools, Los Ojos, NM, August 2, 2016.

3. In his interview, Antonio Manzanares stated that the Bond Mercantile in Española, New Mexico, had numerous partidarios and that he had once seen the list, which was two pages long, single spaced.

4. Manzanares, interview. He stated that after centuries of sheepherding in northern New Mexico, there were now only two Hispanic families, his included, that grazed sheep on public lands north of Albuquerque. By October 2017, there was only one. Manzanares had sold his flocks and relinquished his permit.

Chapter 2

1. C. E. Gibson Jr., "The Original Settler at Medano Springs," manuscript on file with History Colorado, Denver.

2. "War on Sheep Men," *Saguache (CO) Crescent*, January 30, 1902.

3. *Monte Vista (CO) Journal*, February 1, 1902.

4. *Center Dispatch* (Saguache, CO), February 7, 1902.

5. Ibid.

6. Gibson, "Original Settler." Also see R. Laurie Simmons and Marilyn A. Martorano, "Guns, Fire, and Sheep: History and Archaeology of the Trujillo Homesteads in the San Luis Valley, Colorado," *Southwestern Lore* 73, no. 3 (Fall 2007). The son's cabin still stands and is now part of the Teofilo and Pedro Trujillo National Historic Landmark in Alamosa County. See Gregory Brill, "The Teofilo and Pedro Trujillo National Historic Landmark: A New Monument for a New Era of American Heritage," graduate paper, Historic Preservation and Public History Program, University of Colorado–Denver, manuscript in possession of the author.

7. To learn more about the architecture of the Trujillo log cabin and its preservation, see Ekaterini Vlahos, "Colorado Ranch Preservation: The Twenty-First Century and the Changing American West," in Andrew Gulliford, ed., *Preserving Western History* (Albuquerque: University of New Mexico Press, 2005), 287–97.

8. For the best books on the Meeker incident and Ute Indian removal from northwestern Colorado, see Robert Emmitt, *The Last War Trail: The Utes and the Settlement of Colorado* (Boulder: University Press of Colorado, 2000); Robert Silbernagel, *Troubled Trails: The Meeker Affair and the Expulsion of Utes from Colorado* (Salt Lake City: University of Utah Press, 2011); Peter R. Decker, *"The Utes Must Go!" American Expansion and the Removal of a People* (Golden, CO: Fulcrum Publishing, 2004); Marshall Sprague, *Massacre: The Tragedy at White River* (Lincoln: University of Nebraska Press, 1980); and Mark E. Miller, *Hollow Victory: The White River Expedition of 1879 and the Battle of Milk Creek* (Boulder: University Press of Colorado, 1997).

9. Ivo E. Lindauer, *Up the Creek: Parachute Creek's Pioneer Families and Energy Development, 1875–2015* (Parachute, CO: Double F Press, 2016), 13–14.

10. Diane Abraham, "Bloody Grass: Western Colorado Range Wars, 1881–1934," *Journal of the Western Slope* 6, no. 2 (Spring 1991).

11. Duane Vandenbusche and Duane A. Smith, *A Land Alone: Colorado's Western Slope* (Boulder, CO: Pruett Publishing, 1981), 156. In northwestern Colorado on Piceance and Yellow Creek, William Wilson of Denver placed 7,000 head; Senator

Chatfield of Aspen located a ranch and put 1,500 head on it; S. S. Green of Douglas County and Mr. Gephat from Elbert brought in 1,500 head and 2,500 head, respectively. See Gracie Petrakian, *Land of Tall Grass* (Flanders, NJ: self-pub., 2010), 111.

12. John Rolfe Burroughs, *Where the Old West Stayed Young* (New York: Bonanza Books, 1962), 68.

13. Edward Norris Wentworth, *America's Sheep Trails* (Ames: Iowa State College Press, 1948), 313.

14. Ibid., 9.

15. Wentworth, *America's Sheep Trails*, 318.

16. Vandenbusche and Smith, *Land Alone*, 157.

17. David Lavender, *One Man's West* (1943; repr., Lincoln: University of Nebraska Press, 1977), 261. Citations refer to the 1977 edition.

18. Wentworth, *America's Sheep Trails*, vii.

19. One of the worst examples of arroyo making and deep, eroded gullies from overgrazing can be found on Highway 139 north of Douglas Pass, south of Rangely, Colorado. Both cattle and sheep denuded the area.

20. Clara M. Love, "History of the Cattle Industry in the Southwest, II," *Southwestern Historical Quarterly* 20, no. 1 (July 1916): 14.

21. Mary Austin, *The Flock* (1906; repr., Santa Fe, NM: William Gannon, 1973), 171. Citations refer to the 1973 edition.

22. The financial panic of 1893 dropped range cattle prices from nine to seven dollars a head, and still there were no buyers. See Eugene Manlove Rhodes, *Beyond the Desert* (1934; repr., Lincoln: University of Nebraska Press, 1967), 4. Citations refer to the 1967 edition. Also see Vandenbusche and Smith, *Land Alone*, 158.

23. See Paul Henley Roberts and L. F. Kneipp, *Hoof Prints on Forest Ranges: The Early Years of National Forest Range Administration* (San Antonio: Naylor, 1963).

24. For the Cattle Growers Protective Association in the Gunnison Valley, see Wilson Rockwell, *New Frontier: Saga of the North Fork* (1938; repr., Lake City, CO: Western Reflections, 2011), 77–79. Citations refer to the 2011 edition. Mary Austin acknowledges that in California, herders, like cattlemen, put poisoned salt on the range for other herders. *The Flock*, 167.

25. Clara M. Love had a different perspective: "The cowboy became more aggressive because of his occupation. He wore a gun as part of his attire. The shepherd was a calmer, quieter man, who carried a gun only when expecting trouble. Frequently, even then, his gun was rusty and useless." "History of the Cattle Industry," 13.

26. Burroughs, *Where the Old West*, 353. Profits from sheep were detailed in the *San Juan Prospector* (Del Norte, CO) on April 2, 1887. The editor wrote, "A pretty sheep story: Judge Davenport, of Montana bought 2,000 ewes for $3,000. He put them in charge of a man who was to care for them and to receive one-half the wool and one-half the increase of the flock. At the end of four years the settlement was to be made, the judge was to have the best 1,000 ewes in the flock, the judge's share in the meantime was $6,500 for wool and $8,000 for the increase. At the end of the four years his profits were $14,500 or 131 3/5 per cent a year."

27. Patti Brady, forest history binder notebook, vol. 1, 1905–1971. Public Lands Center, San Juan National Forest, Durango, CO.

28. Tom Wolf, *Colorado's Sangre de Cristo Mountains* (Boulder: University Press of Colorado, 1995), 78.
29. Wentworth, *America's Sheep Trails*, 522.
30. Ibid., 523.
31. Stewart Udall, *The Quiet Crisis* (New York: Avon, 1963). See chapter 5, "The Raid on Resources."
32. Forest Reserve Act of 1891, cited in Gerald W. Williams, *The USDA Forest Service: The First Century*, FS-650 (Washington, DC: USDA Forest Service, 2000), 8.
33. The 1897 Forest Management Act provided for "proper guidelines for mining, logging, grazing and hydroelectric facilities under the Department of the Interior," but there was no local or state administration.
34. John W. Lowell Jr., acting supervisor, letter to district forester, Denver, April 11, 1910, in response to a circular letter asking for historical information on sheep and cattle conflicts. Denver: National Archives, Rocky Mountain Region, no. 95, records of the Forest Service, Rocky Mountain Regional Office, Historical Files, 1905–1931 (1650), box 12, folder 62.
35. Ibid.
36. Ibid. Also see Len Shoemaker and William R. Kreutzer, "Range Troubles," in *Saga of a Forest Ranger: A Biography of William R. Kreutzer, Forest Ranger No. 1* (Boulder: University of Colorado Press, 1958).
37. "Shot Four Times," *Pagosa Springs (CO) News*, September 1, 1892.
38. *Pagosa Springs (CO) News*, September 8, 1892.
39. *Pagosa Springs (CO) News*, June 23, 1893.
40. *Pagosa Springs (CO) News*, January 12, 1894.
41. Rhodes, *Beyond the Desert*, 4.
42. Vandenbusche and Smith, *Land Alone*, 156.
43. Erlene Durrant Murray, *Lest We Forget* (Grand Junction, CO: Quahada Publishing, 1973), 126.
44. Lindauer, *Up the Creek*, 12. The *Craig (CO) Courier* reported on September 14, 1894, "The owners [of the sheep] are residents of Parachute with rights to adjacent range and the posse made a futile race to apprehend the raiders. John Miller owned 1,700 sheep and Charles Brown, uncle of the wounded man, 2,100." Lindauer notes, "From various reports, John Hurlburt owned many of the sheep killed in this conflict. He attempted to obtain retribution for the loss of a major part of his herd. However no settlement was ever reached in his efforts with the state and he decided he could not fight the whole country, so he sold his remaining sheep."
45. Rifle Reading Club, *Rifle Shots: The Story of Rifle, Colorado* (Rifle, CO: Rifle Reading Club, 1973), 202.
46. Ibid., 203.
47. Ibid.
48. David W. Cayton and Caroline E. Metzler, *James G. Cayton: Pioneer Forest Ranger* (self-pub., 2009), 72.
49. Rifle Reading Club, *Rifle Shots*, 203.
50. Abraham, "Bloody Grass," 10.
51. *Grand Junction (CO) Daily Sentinel*, May 8, 1894.

52. "The Plateau Sheep War," *Grand Junction (CO) News*, January 5, 1895.
53. *Grand Junction (CO) Daily Sentinel*, May 7, 1894.
54. David S. Carpenter, *Jens Nielson: Bishop of Bluff* (Provo, UT: Brigham Young University, 2011), 136.
55. Helen Hawxhurst Young, ed. *The Skin and Bones of Plateau Valley History* (Grand Junction, CO: Wilson and Young Printers, 1976), 24.
56. Ibid.
57. Ibid.
58. *Grand Junction (CO) Daily Sentinel*, May 24, 1894; *Grand Junction (CO) News*, May 26, 1894; June 2, 1894.
59. Burroughs, *Where the Old West*, 141.
60. Ibid. In the same year, on November 17, 1896, the *Grand Junction (CO) Daily Sentinel* reported that 100 cattlemen had rallied to prevent 10,000 Utah sheep from crossing over on Piñon Mesa in Mesa County. "The cattlemen were ready for the sheep and had 100 cowboys armed to the teeth." The sheep stayed in Utah.
61. Burroughs, *Where the Old West*, 138.
62. Ibid., 139.
63. *Craig (CO) Courier*, February 6, 1897, cited in Burroughs, *Where the Old West*, 145.
64. Lindauer, *Up the Creek*, 40.
65. Carpenter, *Jens Nielson*, 135.
66. Ibid., 198. Ohio representative William McKinley's 1890 McKinley Tariff helped some agricultural producers but damaged others. For instance, it eliminated the duty-free status of Hawaiian sugar, causing wholesale prices to plummet 40 percent and resulting in a coup against Queen Liliuokalani. Sugar producers established an independent republic in Hawaii, which requested immediate US annexation.
67. Wilma Crisp Bankston, *Where Eagles Winter: History and Legend of the Disappointment Country* (Cortez, CO: Mesa Verde Press, 1987), 57.
68. Larry D. Ball, *Tom Horn in Life and Legend* (Norman: University of Oklahoma Press, 2014), 271.
69. Ibid., 272.
70. Ibid., 432.
71. *Saguache (CO) Crescent*, January 30, 1902.
72. *Monte Vista (CO) Journal*, February 15 and May 10, 1902.
73. Will C. Barnes, *The Story of the Range* (Washington, DC: US Department of Agriculture, 1926), 37.
74. Coert DuBois, *Report on the Proposed San Juan Forest Reserve, Colorado* (Durango, CO: San Juan National Forest, 1903), 9. Theodore Roosevelt set aside the San Juan National Forest in 1905.
75. Ibid., 11.
76. Ibid., 10.
77. Ibid.
78. Ibid., 12.
79. Austin, *The Flock*, 207.
80. Barnes, *Story of the Range*, 9.

81. Republican boss Mark Hanna quoted in Michael L. Collins, *That Damned Cowboy: Theodore Roosevelt and the American West, 1883–1898* (New York: Peter Lang, 1989), 153.

THIRD SHEEPSCAPE

1. Basque cooking is legendary. One of the 26 books in the Basque Series, published by the University of Nevada Press, is Jose Maria Busca Isusi, *Traditional Basque Cooking: History and Preparation* (Reno: University of Nevada Press, 1987).

2. Joe Mattern, interview by author, Steamboat Springs, CO, September 15, 2015.

3. Beth Sagstetter, excerpts from a detailed personal communication to author, spring 2016. Also see Elizabeth M. and William E. Sagstetter, "Respite from Loneliness," *Denver Post Empire Magazine*, February 7, 1982.

Chapter 3

1. C. B. Mack, letter to Gifford Pinchot, July 15, 1940, in reference to a book Pinchot planned to write about the early Forest Service. San Juan National Forest files, Durango, CO.

2. James G. Lewis, *The Forest Service and the Greatest Good: A Centennial History* (Durham, NC: Forest History Society, 2005), 50. For other references to the early US Forest Service, see Robert D. Baker, Robert S. Maxwell, Victor H. Treat, and Henry C. Dethloff, *Timeless Heritage: A History of the Forest Service in the Southwest*, FS-409 (Washington, DC: USDA Forest Service, August 1988); and Gerald W. Williams, *The USDA Forest Service: The First Century*, FS-650 (Washington, DC : USDA Forest Service, July 2000).

3. Pinchot cited in James G. Lewis, *The Forest Service and the Greatest Good: A Centennial History* (Durham, NC: Forest History Society, 2005), xiii.

4. Len Shoemaker and William R. Kreutzer, *Saga of a Forest Ranger: A Biography of William R. Kreutzer, Forest Ranger No. 1* (Boulder, CO: University Press of Colorado, 1958).

5. Ibid., 99.

6. Lewis, *Forest Service*, 57. Theodore Roosevelt may not have liked sheep, but he admired sheepherders. While he was touring Colorado in 1905, the *Rocky Mountain News* (Denver, CO) reported on April 15 that the president "was also much interested in cowboys and sheepherders that were ranged along the track, and he recognized them, every one. 'That is a very, very lonely life,' remarked Mr. Roosevelt to Governor McDonald referring to the sheepherders. 'The loneliest in the world,' replied the governor. 'And yet they are happy,' said the president, half sadly, as though partly envying the sheepherder in the mountains with his flocks and with no great cares upon his brain. The president envious of a Mexican sheepherder!" See "President Roosevelt Is in Colorado, and Is Glad of It, Will Penetrate the Wilds at Once," *Rocky Mountain News* (Denver, CO), April 15, 1905.

7. Paul Henley Roberts and L. F. Kneipp, *Hoof Prints on Forest Ranges: The Early Years of National Forest Range Administration* (San Antonio: Naylor, 1963), 31.

8. Timothy Egan argues that because of conflicts related to grazing, politicians in the West were ready to dismantle the US Forest Service after Theodore Roosevelt and Gifford Pinchot left office. He believes the mammoth fires of 1910 in Idaho and Montana, and the heroic firefighting of forest crews, forever established the value of the US Forest Service for the public and in essence saved the government bureaucracy. *The Big Burn* (Boston: Houghton Mifflin, 2009).

9. Cited in G. Michael McCarthy, *Hour of Trial: The Conservation Conflict in Colorado and the West, 1891–1907* (Norman: University of Oklahoma Press, 1977), 156.

10. Ibid.

11. Ibid., 160.

12. Ibid., 176.

13. The best book on early opposition to federal forest reserves, with detailed descriptions of Colorado's stockmen's associations and their resolutions, is McCarthy's *Hour of Trial*, which sets the stage for angry cattlemen and the Fred M. Light lawsuit.

14. Lewis, *Forest Service*, 60.

15. Ibid., 59.

16. Roberts and Kneipp, *Hoof Prints*, 83.

17. Gifford Pinchot, *Instructions to Foresters in Public Service*, courtesy San Juan National Forest. Available at the Archuleta County Historical Society, Pagosa Springs, CO. By 1907, only two years after the establishment of the US Forest Service, the *Use Book* had grown to 240 pages.

18. "Roosevelt on Leasing," *Routt County Courier* (Craig, CO), February 21, 1907.

19. McCarthy, *Hour of Trial*, 239. Also see Theodore Roosevelt's May 13, 1908, opening address to the White House Conservation Conference titled "Conservation as a National Duty," in *Proceedings of a Conference of Governors in the White House, May 13–15, 1908* (Washington, DC: Government Printing Office, 1909).

20. Shoemaker and Kreutzer, *Saga of a Forest Ranger*, 93.

21. Ibid. For information on Night Riders, see Wilson Rockwell, "Cow-Land Aristocrats," in *New Frontier* (1938; repr., Lake City, CO: Western Reflections, 2011), 75–81. Citations refer to the 2011 edition.

22. Rockwell, *New Frontier*, 75.

23. *Grand Junction (CO) Daily Sentinel*, April 25, 1907. For locating this source and identifying others related to the Peter Swanson murder, the author is indebted to historian and journalist Bob Silbernagel of the *Grand Junction (CO) Daily Sentinel*, who summarized this Mesa County conflict in his excellent article on October 13, 2014: "In 1908, an 'Army' of 21 Thousand Sheep and Their Guards Crossed Mesa County."

24. *Grand Junction (CO) Daily Sentinel*, May 7, 1907.

25. *Grand Junction (CO) Daily Sentinel*, January 14 and January 21, 1908.

26. *Grand Junction (CO) Daily Sentinel*, March 4, 1908.

27. *Denver News*, January 15, 1908.

28. Arthur Chapman, "Trailing 20,000 Sheep through a Hostile Cattle Country," *San Francisco Chronicle*, February 23, 1908; *Daily Capital Journal* (Salem, OR), March 21, 1908. Also see Silbernagel, "In 1908."

29. "Murder Case Is Dropped; Sole Witness Is Missing," *Grand Junction (CO) Daily Sentinel*, January 11, 1915.

30. Homesteader success with the original 1862 Homestead Act is still being debated. National Park Service staff at Homestead National Monument in Beatrice, Nebraska, are working with researchers at the Center for Great Plains Studies at the University of Nebraska–Lincoln to try to determine a definitive percentage of successful homesteaders. Historical research figures vary from a success rate of 40 percent to 57 percent; hence my estimate that 60 percent of homesteads went to patent.

31. Henry David Thoreau, "Walking," in *The Atlantic*, June 1862.

32. Because of the lack of agricultural land at forest elevations, these June 11, 1906, forest homesteads were of irregular shapes and were often less than 160 acres. Settlers could acquire "a streamwide strip up to one and ½ miles in length, which enabled one settler to control access to a valley," often where there was valuable timber. See Lewis, *Forest Service*, 263.

33. William Voigt Jr., *Public Grazing Lands: Use and Misuse by Industry and Government* (New Brunswick, NJ: Rutgers University Press, 1976), 329.

34. San Juan National Forest, *Forest History*, vol. 1, *1905–1971, San Juan and Montezuma National Forests, Colorado* (Durango, CO: San Juan National Forest), 59.

35. Ernest Shaw, *Annual Grazing Report* (San Juan National Forest, 1908), 15–19.

36. Shaw, *Annual Grazing Report*, 91. By 1915, 82,000 sheep and goats grazed just on the Pagosa Springs District. Cited in San Juan National Forest, letter to the district forester, Riley Smith, from the San Juan forest supervisor, Ernest Shaw, July 30, 1915, historical records, San Juan National Forest, Durango, CO.

37. Shaw, *Annual Grazing Report*, 34–36.

38. Ibid., 82.

39. Andrew Gulliford, ed., *Letters from a Weminuche Homestead, 1902* (Durango, CO: Durango Herald Small Press, 2002). These letters are from Shaw's wife, Edith Taylor Shaw, and describe the hardships of a high-country homestead and a husband who was frequently away working for the US Forest Service.

40. Curt Meine, *Aldo Leopold: His Life and Work* (Madison: University of Wisconsin Press, 1988), 107.

41. Marybeth Lorbiecki, *Aldo Leopold: A Fierce Green Fire* (Guilford, CT: Globe Pequot Press, 2005), 47.

42. Ibid.

43. Governor Bryant B. Brooks to J. D. Linn, May 8, 1907. Gov. Bryant B. Brooks Sheep Raids File, 1907–1910, RG 0001.17, Wyoming State Archives.

44. Governor Bryant B. Brooks to Big Horn County sheriff, May 31, 1907. Gov. Bryant B. Brooks Sheep Raids File, 1907–1910, RG 0001.17, Wyoming State Archives.

45. George S. Walkey to Governor Bryant B. Brooks, April 7, 1909. Gov. Bryant B. Brooks Sheep Raids File, 1907–1910, RG 0001.17, Wyoming State Archives.

46. Judge C. H. Parmelee to Governor Bryant B. Brooks, April 7, 1909. Gov. Bryant B. Brooks Sheep Raids File, 1907–1910, RG 0001.17, Wyoming State Archives.

47. P. W. Metz, Big Horn County attorney, to Governor Bryant B. Brooks, April 9, 1909. Gov. Bryant B. Brooks Sheep Raids File, 1907–1910, RG 0001.17, Wyoming State Archives. Also see the file from the adjutant general, Wyoming National Guard, "Tensleep Murders Incident, 1909–1910," RG 0007, Wyoming State Archives.

48. "Taylor Tells the Story of Attack on His Sheep," *Grand Junction (CO) Daily Sentinel*, May 24, 1909.

49. Ibid.

50. "The Guilty Men Must Be Caught," *Denver Republican* editorial reprinted in the *Grand Junction (CO) Daily Sentinel*, May 26, 1909.

51. "The Sheep Massacre," *Pueblo (CO) Chieftain* editorial reprinted in the *Grand Junction (CO) Daily Sentinel*, May 27, 1909.

52. "Not Guilty of Killing the Sheep of Taylor," *Fruita (CO) Telegram* editorial reprinted in the *Grand Junction (CO) Daily Sentinel*, May 31, 1909.

53. The list of homesteaders' names and the location of their sheep ranges was taken from an exhibit at the Rangely, Colorado, Outdoor Museum, June 2015.

54. "Cunninghams Sell Book Mt. Property," *Grand Valley Times* (Moab, UT), September 4, 1914.

55. "Taylors Incorporate Big Stock Company," *Grand Valley Times* (Moab, UT), November 13, 1914.

56. "$310,000 Paid for Book Mountain Livestock Outfit," *Grand Valley Times* (Moab, UT), March 23, 1917.

57. "S. A. Taylor Loses Sheep," *Grand Valley Times* (Moab, UT), May 28, 1909.

58. "Want to Put In Sheep," *Routt County Courier* (Craig, CO), January 31, 1907.

59. "About the Sheep Question: A Few Letters of Interest from Ranchmen That Show How the Wind Blows," *Routt County Courier*, (Craig, CO), February 14, 1907.

60. Ibid.

61. Ibid.

62. "Are Sheep to Bleat in Routt County?" *Routt County Courier* (Craig, CO), November 14, 1907.

63. William A. Douglass and Jon Bilbao, *Amerikanuak: Basques in the New World* (Reno: University of Nevada Press, 2005), 243.

64. "Northwestern Colorado Ranchmen Take Firm Stand against Sheep on Public Range," *Moffat County Courier* (Craig, CO), April 6, 1911.

65. "Sheep Slaughtered," *Moffat County Courier* (Craig, CO), December 7, 1911.

66. Ibid.

67. "Routt County Sheep Men Can Solve Range Problem," *Steamboat Pilot* (Steamboat Springs, CO), March 20, 1915.

68. Marguerite Lathrop, *Don't Fence Me In* (Boulder, CO: Johnson Publishing, 1972), 125.

69. Muriel Marshall, *Red Hole in Time* (College Station: Texas A&M University Press, 1988), 264.

70. Ibid.

71. Ibid., 265.

72. Ibid., 266.

73. Ibid., 268.

74. Lathrop, *Don't Fence Me In*, 126.
75. Ibid.
76. Ibid., 127.
77. Marshall, *Red Hole in Time*, 286.
78. See "Night Raiders, Bandits and Lions" in Lathrop, *Don't Fence Me In*, 125–33; and "The Shoot-Out" in Marshall, *Red Hole in Time*, 281–90.
79. Shoemaker and Kreutzer, *Saga of a Forest Ranger*, 162.
80. Ibid., 164.
81. Ibid., 172.
82. Ibid., 177.
83. Ibid., 183.
84. Ibid., 190.
85. David W. Cayton and Caroline E. Metzler, *James G. Cayton: Pioneer Forest Ranger* (self-pub., 2009), 72–73.
86. As the law evolved, homesteaders could file grazing claims at higher elevations with no pretense of farming or irrigation. These acres were perfect for sheepmen, who used the land seasonally, but they forfeited any mineral rights, which resulted in the headache called "split estates" that now plagues the West. Contemporary landowners may own their homes, their trees, and their grass, but the BLM controls mineral rights and oil and gas wells.
87. Margaret Duncan Brown, *Shepherdess of Elk River Valley* (Denver: Golden Bell Press, 1967), 34.
88. Ibid., 36.
89. Ibid., 46.
90. Ibid., 53. She continued to write in her journal, and in September 1958 the *Reader's Digest* published her essay "A Little Bunch of Sheep," which received a $2,500 First Person Award.
91. San Juan National Forest, US Forest Service Ranger Daybooks, 1921–1925, archives, Center of Southwest Studies, Fort Lewis College, Durango, CO.
92. This section on wolves and wolfers, or wolf trappers, is excerpted in part from Andrew Gulliford, "The Past and Future of Wolves in Colorado," in Arthur H. Carhart, *The Last Stand of the Pack: Critical Edition*, with Stanley P. Young, ed. Andrew Gulliford and Tom Wolf (Boulder: University Press of Colorado, 2017), 207–11.
93. Annual reports of the Bureau of Biological Survey and books like Michael J. Robinson's *Predatory Bureaucracy: The Extermination of Wolves and the Transformation of the West* (Boulder: University Press of Colorado, 2005) reveal the massive onslaught of poisons and steel traps that permeated the West.
94. Jeremy Johnston, "Preserving the Beasts of Waste and Desolation: Theodore Roosevelt and Predator Control in Yellowstone," *Yellowstone Science*, Spring 2002. For wolves' impact on deer, see Richard Nelson, *Heart and Blood: Living with Deer in America* (New York: Alfred Knopf, 1997).
95. Howard E. Greager, *In the Company of Cowboys* (self-pub., 1990), 135.
96. Ibid., 137.
97. David Lavender, *One Man's West* (Lincoln: University of Nebraska Press, 1977), 250.

98. Ibid., 251.

99. E. W. Nelson, *Report of Chief of Bureau of Biological Survey* (Washington, DC: USDA, August 29, 1918).

100. Tom Wolf, "World Champion Wolfer," *Inside/Outside Southwest*, March 2009.

101. Michael Selle (BLM archaeologist, White River Field Office, Meeker, Colorado), email message to author on split estate, October 29, 2015. Also see the *Grand Junction (CO) Daily Sentinel*, "New Homestead Act," December 30, 1916, and "60,000 New Settlers in Colorado Real Soon," January 2, 1917.

FOURTH SHEEPSCAPE

1. Catherine Moore, manuscript in the archives of the Museum of Western Colorado, Grand Junction.

2. Ibid.

3. "Use Guns to Force Sheepmen off Range," *Grand Valley Times* (Moab, UT), June 19, 1914.

4. Marie Tipping, interview by author, Piñon Mesa, CO, September 22, 2015.

Chapter 4

1. *The Handling of Sheep on the National Forests: La manipulación de las ovejas en los bosques nacionales* (Washington, DC: Government Printing Office, 1920).

2. William A. Douglass and Jon Bilbao, *Amerikanuak: Basques in the New World* (Reno: University of Nevada Press, 2004), 244.

3. David W. Cayton and Caroline E. Metzler, *James G. Cayton: Pioneer Forest Ranger* (self-pub., 2009), 123.

4. Ibid.

5. Ibid., 125.

6. Farrington Carpenter, *Confessions of a Maverick: An Autobiography* (Denver: Colorado Historical Society, 1984), 129.

7. White River Museum, ed., *This Is What I Remember*, vol. 2 (Meeker, CO: Rio Blanco County Historical Society, 1978).

8. Carpenter, *Confessions of a Maverick*, 131.

9. John Rolfe Burroughs, *Where the Old West Stayed Young* (New York: Bonanza Books, 1962), 347.

10. Carpenter, *Confessions of a Maverick*, 131.

11. Olga Curtis, "Farrington R. Carpenter: The Success Story of a 'Failure,'" *Denver Post Empire Magazine*, April 11, 1965.

12. The story of Ferry Carpenter and local teachers is well told in Dorothy Wickenden, *Nothing Daunted: The Unexpected Education of Two Society Girls in the West* (New York: Scribner, 2011).

13. Olga Curtis, "'Yarnin' Champ of Yampa Valley," *Denver Post Empire Magazine*, April 11, 1965. The *Saturday Evening Post* accolade came in 1952. The bull and doorknob story was recorded by this author at the Carpenter Ranch in 1977. The oral history is in "The Years Ahead" collection at the Denver Public Library.

14. Edward N. Wentworth, "Sheep Wars of the Nineties in Northwest Colorado," in Virgil V. Peterson, ed., *The Westerners Brand Book*, vol. 2, *1946–1947* (Denver: The Westerners, 1947), 141.

15. Carpenter, *Confessions of a Maverick*, 132. The rumor that Colorado governor Shoup sent the militia is found in Wentworth, "Sheep Wars," and in a Rio Blanco County Historical Society interview with Regas Halandras, but Ferry Carpenter, who was there, said that what arrived was only a handful of state troopers.

16. Carpenter, *Confessions of a Maverick*, 132.

17. Ibid., 133. Also see "Sheep War Over, Animals to Go by Railroad," *Craig (CO) Empire*, July 13, 1921.

18. Wentworth, "Sheep Wars," 141.

19. Duane Vandenbusche and Duane A. Smith, *A Land Alone: Colorado's Western Slope* (Boulder, CO: Pruett Publishing, 1981), 156.

20. Olga Curtis, "The Best-Known Sheepman in Rio Blanco County," *Denver Post Empire Magazine*, September 25, 1977.

21. Kathy Jordan, "Charlie Glass Was a Dandy Cowpuncher." Archival collection, Museum of Western Colorado, Grand Junction.

22. "Black Cowboy Charley Glass: Man of Mystery," *Real West*, December 1974. Also see J. R. Kirkpatrick, "Who Was Charley Glass?," manuscript at the Museum of Western Colorado, Grand Junction.

23. "Negro Cowboy Slays French Sheep Herder," *Grand Junction (CO) Daily Sentinel*, February 25, 1921.

24. Articles on the shooting are from the *Moab (UT) Times-Independent*, March 24, 1921; August, 11, 1921; November 17, 1921; and "Charles Glass Is Cleared of Murder Charge," December 1, 1921.

25. "Charles Glass Is Cleared."

26. Not one to turn down a poker game, Glass died of a broken neck the night of February 23, 1937, after being invited by two itinerant Basque sheepherders, Joe Savorna of Montrose and Andre Sartan of Grand Junction, to ride in a truck between Thompson and Cisco, Utah. The men had been drinking, and the truck rolled three times. The herders, however, received only minor injuries. Rancher Boots Corn, a local cowman, and Bill Cunningham, the son of one of Charlie's employers, insisted the death was no accident. It was close to Cisco, where Charlie had killed the Basque herder Felix Jesui. Steven F. Mehls also believed it was a revenge killing. *The Valley of Opportunity* (Denver: Colorado State Office, Bureau of Land Management, 1982), 116.

27. "East Utah Range War Is Brewing," *Moab (UT) Times Independent*, January 15, 1921; "French Sheepherders Found Guilty of Attempt to Murder G. A. Harris," January 26, 1922; and "Decision in Burusco Assault Case Reversed," April 12, 1923.

28. Curtis, "Best-Known Sheepman."

29. Virginia Paul, *This Was Sheep Ranching: Yesterday and Today* (Seattle: Superior Publishing, 1976), 59.

30. Diana Allen Kouris, *The Romantic and Notorious History of Brown's Park* (Greybull, WY: Wolverine Gallery, 1988), 259.

31. Paul, *This Was Sheep Ranching*, 80.
32. Robert Laxalt, *Sweet Promised Land* (New York: Harper and Brothers, 1957), 108–9.
33. Shirley Kelly, "Salute to the Sheep-Men," *Fence Post* (Greeley, CO), May 2, 2011.
34. Jeffrey L. Izienicki, "A Study of the Retolaza Boarding House and Its Role in the Life of the Basque Itinerant Sheepherder," *Journal of the Western Slope* 7, no. 1 (Winter 1992): 5.
35. Ibid., 7.
36. Ibid., 7–8. For a fictional, probably autobiographical, account of a young Basque boy growing up in a hotel and boardinghouse and coming of age in sheep camps, see Robert Laxalt, *The Basque Hotel* (Reno: University of Nevada Press, 1989).
37. Iziencicki, "Study of the Retolaza," 12.
38. Donald A. Brown, "Emmett Elizondo: Sheepman Extraordinary," *Fruita (CO) Times*, August 21, 1992, reprinted from the *Wichita Farm Credit Letter*, Spring/Summer 1982.
39. "Colorado Sheepmen Seek Cream of Grand County Winter Ranges," *Moab (UT) Times-Independent*, March 20, 1930; "Resident Stockmen and Settlers of Book Cliff Region Organize to Resist Driveway Withdrawal," March 27, 1930. Also see Lee Bennett, "A History of Selected Ranches on a Twenty-Mile Stretch of the Colorado River in Grand County, Utah" (Monticello, UT: Bennett Management Services, March 2009). Sheepman Henry Revoir was listed as one of 31 members of the Western Slope Wool Growers Association. Document courtesy of the Ouray County Historical Society, RG 15.
40. Herbert P. White, "The Bolten Story: The Last of Colorado's Sheep and Cattle Wars," *Denver Westerners Roundup*, January–February 1971; Sylvia Beeler, "County Profile: Isadore Bolten: The West's Outstanding Stockman," *Hayden Valley*, February 21, 1974; Bill May, "Puncher's Pen," *Saturday Northwest*, January 26, 1991. Also see Dorothy Wickenden, *Nothing Daunted: The Unexpected Education of Two Society Girls in the West* (New York: Scribner, 2011).
41. Lou Wyman, interview by author, Wyman Living History Ranch and Museum, Craig, CO, September 15, 2015.
42. "Six Cattlemen Are Indicted by Federal Grand Jury," *Moab (UT) Times-Independent*, May 3, 1923. For a similar indictment and a reversal in court in Colorado, see "Cattlemen Freed," *Craig (CO) Empire*, May 20, 1925. For the larger context of cattle and sheep conflicts, see Bill O'Neal, *Cattlemen vs. Sheepherders: Five Decades of Violence in the West* (Fort Worth, TX: Eakin Press, 2005).
43. Ottoson story in White River Museum, "The Sheep and Cattle Wars," in *This Is What I Remember* (Meeker, CO: Rio Blanco County Historical Society, 1978).
44. Aldo Leopold, "Erosion as a Menace to the Social and Economic Future of the Southwest," *Journal of Forestry* 44 (September 1946): 627.
45. Ibid., 629.
46. Ibid., 632.

47. Susan L. Flader, *Thinking Like a Mountain: Aldo Leopold and the Evolution of an Ecological Attitude toward Deer, Wolves, and Forests* (Madison: University of Wisconsin Press, 1994), 79.

48. Wesley Calef, *Private Grazing and Public Lands: Studies of the Local Management of the Taylor Grazing Act* (Chicago: University of Chicago Press, 1960), 61.

49. US Tariff Commission, *The Wool-Growing Industry* (Washington, DC: Government Printing Office, 1921), 154.

50. William A. Douglass, "Basque Americans," in *American Folklore: An Encyclopedia*, ed. Jan Harold Brunvand (New York: Garland Publishing, 1996), 74.

51. Ray Stannard Baker, "The Great Southwest: IV. The Tragedy of the Range," *Century Magazine* 4, no. 4 (August 1902).

52. Ibid., 537.

53. Ibid., 538.

54. Will C. Barnes, *The Story of the Range* (Washington, DC: US Department of Agriculture, 1926), 7.

55. Ibid.

56. William Voigt, *Public Grazing Lands* (New Brunswick, NJ: Rutgers University Press, 1976), 249.

57. Grace Petrakian, *Land of Tall Grass* (Flanders, NJ: self-pub., 2010), 112.

58. William Voigt writes, "Dozens of bills to accomplish this purpose were introduced in the Congress in the first quarter of this century. According to one source, eighteen went into the Senate hopper between 1899 and 1925, while twenty-five were introduced in the House between 1900 and 1921. All failed for one reason or another." *Public Grazing Lands*, 246.

59. Voigt, *Public Grazing Lands*, 249.

60. Edward Taylor quote, cited in Douglass and Bilbao, *Amerikanuak*, 293. The chapter "Beyond California" has some of the best explanations and references on itinerant Basque sheepmen as one of the catalysts for passage of the Taylor Grazing Act (1934).

61. Voigt, *Public Grazing Lands*, 251.

62. Farrington Carpenter, "Range Stockmen Meet the Government," *Denver Westerners Monthly Roundup*, October 1967, 6.

63. Ibid., 8.

64. Ibid, 10.

65. Voigt, *Public Grazing Lands*, 255.

66. Ibid., 248.

FIFTH SHEEPSCAPE

1. Joyce and Roger Lawrence, interview by author, Lone Mesa State Park, CO, September 1 and September 28, 2015. List of sheepherder carvings by location courtesy of Joyce Lawrence.

2. Paul R. Wieck, "Opportunity Loans Help the 'Forgotten,'" *Albuquerque Journal*, February 25, 1966.

3. Tony Conrad Gallegos, interview by Joyce Lawrence, June 21, 2005, interview transcript courtesy of Lone Mesa State Park.

4. Mollie Vallejos, interview by Larry Quintana, 1976, for an English assignment for Dolores High School from *Our Past—The Portals to the Future: The Oral History of Dolores and the Surrounding Areas*, 1982, courtesy of Lone Mesa State Park.

5. Scott Elder, interview by author, Lone Mesa State Park, CO, September 28, 2015.

6. Marta Weigle, *Brothers of Light, Brothers of Blood: The Penitentes of the Southwest* (Santa Fe, NM: Ancient City Press, 1976), 191. Also see Alberto Lopez Pulido, *The Sacred World of the Penitentes* (Washington, DC: Smithsonian Institution Press, 2000).

7. Weigle, *Brothers of Light*, 190.

8. Fray Angelico Chavez, *My Penitente Land: Reflections on Spanish New Mexico* (Santa Fe: Museum of New Mexico Press, 1993), 68. Also see Ruben E. Archuleta, *Penitente Renaissance: Manifesting Hope* (Pueblo West, CO: El Jefe, 2007).

9. Peggy Montano, Pete Montano, Shirley Rocha, and Sylvia Montano Trujillo, emails and personal communication to author, March and April 2017.

Chapter 5

1. Marguerite Lathrop, *Don't Fence Me In* (Boulder, CO: Johnson Publishing, 1972), 138.

2. Sarah Deutsch, *No Separate Refuge: Culture, Class, and Gender on an Anglo-Hispanic Frontier in the American Southwest, 1880–1940* (New York: Oxford University Press, 1987), 166.

3. Suzanne Forrest, *The Preservation of the Village: New Mexico's Hispanics and the New Deal*, (Albuquerque: University of New Mexico Press, 1989), 100.

4. Deutsch, *No Separate Refuge*, 38.

5. Ibid., 3.

6. Ibid., 9.

7. Forrest, *Preservation of the Village*, 25.

8. Ibid., 29. To further understand the *partido* system and sheep on shares, see William deBuys, "Manitos," in *Enchantment and Exploitation: The Life and Hard Times of a New Mexico Mountain Range* (Albuquerque: University of New Mexico Press, 1985), 193–214.

9. Frank Clifford, *The Backbone of the World* (New York: Broadway Books), 214.

10. Deutsch, *No Separate Refuge*, 164.

11. Lorin W. Brown, *Hispano Folklore of New Mexico* (Albuquerque: University of New Mexico Press, 1978), 159.

12. "Tin dogs" are in collections at the White River Museum of the Rio Blanco Historical Society in Meeker and the Wyman Living History Ranch and Museum in Craig. Lou Wyman said his sheepherding family preferred Columbine condensed milk cans because they had coupons that could be redeemed.

13. Lathrop, *Don't Fence Me In*, 157.

14. Ibid. Sheepherders could be good cooks, but what they ate was often monotonous. To liven up sheepherders' food at Christmas, Wyoming homesteader Elinore Pruitt Stewart worked with her neighbor to provide a Christmas dinner for 12 sheep camps of 24 men. The ladies cooked six geese, three hams, three

hens, meat loaf, sausage, rye bread, doughnuts, coffee cakes, and fruitcakes. See Elinore Pruitt Stewart, *Letters of a Woman Homesteader* (Boston: Houghton Mifflin, 1914), 68–74.

15. C. B. Mack to Gifford Pinchot, July 15, 1940, files of the San Juan National Forest, Durango, CO.

16. Honore DeBusk Smith, "Mexican Plazas along the River of Souls," in *Southwestern Lore*, ed. J. Frank Dobie (Texas Folklore Society, no. 9, 1931; repr., Hatboro, PA: Folklore Association, 1965), 69. Citations refer to the 1969 edition.

17. San Juan National Forest, US Forest Service Ranger Daybooks, Pagosa Springs Ranger District, June 25, 1924.

18. "Mexican Herder Slays Countryman in Book Mountains," *Moab (UT) Times-Independent*, October 5, 1922.

19. Brown, *Hispano Folklore*, 170.

20. Mike McCole and Scott Davidson, "Oh Hell, I Rode That Bear," oral history with Leo Coca, Montrose High School, *Ptarmigan Quarterly* 3, no. 1 (Spring 1979): 51.

21. See Marsha Weisiger, *Dreaming of Sheep in Navajo Country* (Seattle: University of Washington Press, 2009).

22. See "Voices from the Past," in *Remembrances*, vol. 9 (Pagosa Springs, CO: San Juan Historical Society, n.d.), 5.

23. Deutsch, *No Separate Refuge*, 204.

24. Leonard J. Arrington, *Charlie Redd: Utah's Audacious Stockman* (Provo: Utah State University Press, 1995), 52–53.

25. David S. Carpenter, *Jens Nielson: Bishop of Bluff* (Provo, UT: Brigham Young University, 2011), 276.

26. Arrington, *Charlie Redd*, 45.

27. Ibid., 119.

28. Ibid., 154.

29. Ibid., 144.

30. Ibid., 149.

31. David Lavender, *One Man's West* (Lincoln: University of Nebraska Press, 1977), 160.

32. Arrington, *Charlie Redd*, 172.

33. Ibid.

34. Ibid., 119.

35. "County Stockmen Meet With Board," *Moab (UT) Times-Independent*, April 15, 1937.

36. Throughout her book *Don't Fence Me In*, sheep rancher's wife Marguerite Lathrop does an excellent job of describing the plants growing near various sheep-grazing areas.

37. Charles F. Moore, Everett L. Brown, and Henry E. Snyder, "Early History of Taylor Grazing Act in Colorado," BLM Information Memorandum no. 81–299, change 1 (July 23, 1981).

38. For a solid reference on the CCC in the Southwest, see Wayne K. Hinton, *With Picks, Shovels and Hope: The CCC and Its Legacy on the Colorado Plateau*, with Elizabeth A. Green (Missoula: Mountain Press Publishing, 2008).

39. Ibid.

40. *The Bulletin* (Denver Regional Office, US Forest Service) 18, no. 12 (December 1935): 1–2.

41. *Rocky Mountain Region Bulletin* (San Juan National Forest) 19, no. 11 (November 1936): 10.

42. Paul C. Redington, *Report of the Chief of the Bureau of Biological Survey* (Washington, DC: US Department of Agriculture, 1930), 1.

43. Ibid., 26.

44. Mark Twain, *Roughing It* (New York: Ballantine Books, 1962), 48.

45. Frank C. Clarke, "Facts about, and Experiences with, Coyotes," *National Wool Grower* 30, no. 5 (May 1940): 19.

46. Lathrop, *Don't Fence Me In*, 185.

47. Ibid.

48. Ibid., 186.

49. Ibid., 144.

50. Lavender, *One Man's West*, note to the 3rd ed.

51. Doug Wellman, interview by author, Craig, CO, September 15, 2015.

52. William deBuys, foreword to Forrest, *Preservation of the Village*, ix.

SIXTH SHEEPSCAPE

1. See Polly E. Hammer, Dana Isham, Rand Greubel, and Phil Born, *Cultural Resource Inventory of the Lone Cone Aspen Treatment*, I-84–05–46 (Norwood Ranger District, Uncompahgre National Forest, San Miguel County, CO, December 1988). For an earlier synopsis, see Polly E. Hammer, "Aspen Carvings in the San Juan Mountains" (presentation, annual meeting of the Colorado Council of Professional Archaeologists, Glenwood Springs, CO, March 8 and 9, 1985).

2. Hammer, "Aspen Carvings," 65.

3. Leigh Ann Hunt worked with me for years to understand sheepherder movements and aspen tree carvings. I am grateful for her advice and consultation and for her review of this sheepscape on November 12, 2015. I hope I made all the corrections she suggested.

4. All quotes from Polly Hammer are from the excellent report *Cultural Resource Inventory*.

5. Leigh Ann Hunt, interview by author, Lone Cone Ranger Station, south of Norwood, CO, October 8, 2015, and field notes from our two days walking together in the woods.

6. Leigh Ann Hunt, interview. This author also learned a great deal about aspen carving from Hunt during an interview at the Grand Mesa, Uncompahgre, and Gunnison National Forests (GMUG) office in Delta, CO, on August 3, 2006.

7. Hammer, "Aspen Carvings," 66. Also see Maria Teresa Garcia, "Hispanic Herders Carved Their Cultural Niche," *La herencia del norte* 5 (Spring 1995).

8. Hammer, "Aspen Carvings," 66. Also see Phil Weigand and Celia Garcia de Weigand, "Trails among the Trees," *Canon Journal: Land and Peoples of the Colorado Plateau* 1 no. 1 (Spring 1995): 42–47; and Karen Thurman, "The Wooden Canvas:

Documenting Historic Aspen Art Carvings in Southwest Colorado," *Heritage Matters* (National Park Service), November 2001, 5.

9. Hammer, "Aspen Carvings," 66. Polly Hammer also created a slide show in August 1994 of her aspen carving slides, and the captions for those images, including arborglyph fakes, tell a story. This author interviewed her August 5, 2006, in Hotchkiss, Colorado.

Chapter 6

1. Marguerite Lathrop, *Don't Fence Me In* (Boulder, CO: Johnson Publishing, 1972), 178.

2. William Voigt Jr., *Public Grazing Lands: Use and Misuse by Industry and Government* (New Brunswick, NJ: Rutgers University Press, 1976), 243.

3. Roderick K. Blacker, "History Report—San Juan National Forest," Pagosa Springs Ranger District, CO, February 3, 1948.

4. William deBuys, *The Walk* (San Antonio: Trinity University Press, 2007), 38.

5. Though his facts might be a little off, Pascal Wick, a French herder, writes, "During the Second World War, on the liberty ships carrying the GIs to fight, they only ate lamb [probably mutton]. So the cattle breeders thought the sheep herders had hit the jackpot. But it showed little understanding of human nature. In fact this single menu put off a whole generation of Americans from eating lamb. Once home, they swore never to have to smell it again. This episode had dire consequences for American sheep breeding, the national livestock figure dropping from 40 million to 10 million, from which it hasn't recovered. When the parents don't eat lamb, the children don't either, and once they are adults, the probability of them eating it is practically nil." *Beartooth: Diary of a Nomadic Herder* (Buckingham, UK: Aaranya, 2014), 86.

6. In addition to Aldo Leopold's comments on the dangers of soil erosion, also see the work of another former forester, Ward Shepard, *Food or Famine: The Challenge of Erosion* (New York: Macmillan, 1945).

7. Wesley Calef, *Private Grazing and Public Lands: Studies of the Local Management of the Taylor Grazing Act* (Chicago: University of Chicago Press, 1960), book dedication.

8. Ibid., viii.

9. Voigt, *Public Grazing Lands*, 93.

10. Ibid., 95.

11. Ibid., 96.

12. Charles F. Moore, Everett L. Brown, and Henry E. Snyder, "Early History of Taylor Grazing Act in Colorado," BLM Information Memorandum No. 81–229, change 1 (July 23, 1981).

13. Voigt, *Public Grazing Lands*, 266.

14. Lester Velie, "They Kicked Us off Our Land, *Collier's Magazine*, July 26 and August 9, 1947; Arthur Carhart, "In Defense of Our Public Domain," *The Land*, Summer 1947; Bernard DeVoto, "The West against Itself," *Harper's Magazine*, January 1947; DeVoto, "The Easy Chair," *Harper's Magazine*, June 1947; DeVoto, "Sacred Cows and Public Lands," *Harper's Magazine*, July 1948; DeVoto, "Statesman on the Lam," *Harper's Magazine*, July 1948; DeVoto, "Two Gun Desmond Is Back," *Harper's*

Magazine, March 1951. To understand the larger legacy of Arthur Carhart, see Tom Wolf, *Arthur Carhart: Wilderness Prophet* (Boulder: University Press of Colorado, 2008).

15. Alice Boulton, *Silt, Colorado Homesteads, 1880–1940* (Silt, CO: Silt Historical Park, 2006), 69.

16. Aldo Leopold, *Transactions of the Twelfth North American Wildlife Conference*, San Antonio, TX (Washington, DC: Wildlife Management Institute, 1947).

17. In Leopold's time, the public land grab focused on what became BLM lands. By 1952 cattle and sheep ranchers had refocused their target on the US Forest Service, seeking changes to 24,000 permits and 80 million acres of forestland. Under so-called Uniform Grazing bills, they wanted perpetual lease rights. President Dwight Eisenhower, a Colorado fisherman, failed to support the bills. See Mark Harvey, *Wilderness Forever: Howard Zahniser and the Path to the Wilderness Act* (Seattle: University of Washington Press), 156.

18. Marybeth Lorbiecki, *Aldo Leopold: A Fierce Green Fire* (Guilford, CT: Globe Pequot Press, 2004), 178.

19. William R. Jordan III, *The Sunflower Forest: Ecological Restoration and the New Communion with Nature* (Berkeley: University of California Press, 2003), 30, 31.

20. Aldo Leopold, *A Sand County Almanac* (New York: Ballantine Books, 1970), 134.

21. Ibid., 135.

22. Mike Hudak, *Western Turf Wars: The Politics of Public Lands Ranching* (Binghamton, NY: Biome Books, 2007), 240.

23. Peter Edson, "McCarran Act Backfires on Its Sheepish Author," *Times-News* (Twin Falls, ID), March 13, 1951.

24. Vince J. Juaristi, "Intertwined: The Good Shepherds," *Elko (NV) Daily News*, April 9, 2016.

25. Ibid. In Wyoming the famous Warren Livestock Company in Cheyenne, which once ran cattle and up to 60,000 sheep in several counties and two states, finally came under ownership of the Basque Paul Etchepare. Now the ranch also grazes bison.

26. J. Baird Callicott and Eric T. Freyfogle, eds., *Aldo Leopold: For the Health of the Land* (Washington, DC: Island Press, 1999), 223.

27. Andrew Gulliford, "Echo Park: When Progress Is No Progress," in *Outdoors in the Southwest: An Adventure Anthology*, ed. Andrew Gulliford (Norman: University of Oklahoma Press, 2014), 245–50.

28. Harvey, *Wilderness Forever*, 119. To understand the larger wilderness context, also see Doug Scott, *The Enduring Wilderness: Protecting Our Natural Heritage through the Wilderness Act* (Golden: CO: Fulcrum Publishing, 2004).

29. Harvey, *Wilderness Forever*, 114. To understand the Weminuche Wilderness, the largest in Colorado, see B. J. Boucher, *Walking in Wildness: A Guide to the Weminuche Wilderness* (Durango, CO: Durango Herald and San Juan Mountains Association, 1998).

30. W. R. Harvey, "Winder Wonderland," *Denver Post*, July 15, 1952.

31. Pasquale Marranzino, "Tenders of the Sheep," *Rocky Mountain News* (Denver, CO), August 19, 1960.

32. David Petersen, *Ghost Grizzlies* (Boulder, CO: Johnson Books, 1998), 41.

33. Ibid., 45.

34. La Osa had been one of the oldest sheep allotments and had preceded establishment of the national forest. From 1,800 head, the allotment was reduced to 800 head in 1951. The last permit was issued to Pacheco and Sons in 1973, and the entire Pine River allotment went back to the government in 1984 after three years of nonuse. But nothing will bring the grizzly bear back.

35. A. Starker Leopold, S. A. Cain, C. M. Cottam, I. N. Gabrielson, and T. L. Kimball, "The Goal of Park Management in the United States, 1963," in *Wildlife Management in the National Parks: The Leopold Report* (National Park Service, March 4, 1963). Also see National Park System Advisory Board Science Committee, *Revisiting Leopold: Resource Stewardship in the National Parks* (August 25, 2012), https://www.nps.gov/calltoaction/pdf/leopoldreport_2012.pdf. To understand the *Leopold Report*, wildlife, national parks, and climate change, see Michelle Nijhuis, "The Parks of Tomorrow," *National Geographic*, December 2016.

36. Stanley Temple, interview by author, Aldo Leopold's Mia Casita bungalow, Tres Piedras, Carson National Forest, NM, August 1, 2016. Also see Estella Leopold, *Stories from the Leopold Shack* (New York: Oxford University Press, 2016), 251.

37. Stewart Udall quote in David Duncan and Ken Burns, *The National Parks* (New York: Knopf, 2009), 337. By the end of Udall's tenure visitation to national parks had reached 150 million people annually.

38. Jen Jackson Quintano, *Blow Sand in His Soul: Bates Wilson, the Heart of Canyonlands* (Moab, UT: Friends of Arches and Canyonlands Parks, 2014), 5.

39. Ibid., 6.

40. Ibid., 9.

41. Ibid., 15.

42. Lathrop, in *Don't Fence Me In*, has many excellent descriptions of sheep camps, grazing vegetation, and life as the wife of a sheepman, including traveling to sheep camps with her husband.

43. Lathrop, *Don't Fence Me In*, 172.

44. Ibid., 174.

45. Ibid.

46. Quintano, *Blow Sand in His Soul*, 65.

47. Leisl Carr Childers, "The Angry West: Understanding the Sagebrush Rebellion in Nevada," in *Bridging the Distance: Common Issues of the Rural West*, ed. David B. Danbom (Salt Lake City: University of Utah Press, 2015), 225.

SEVENTH SHEEPSCAPE

1. Thanks to Linda Balough, Jerry Davis, Andy Spencer, Julie Koomler, Jane Goetz, Ruth Martin, and Brian Woodyard for helping with South Park and Park County research and historical site visits. A special thanks to Frank Wolthuis of the Badger Basin Ranch, formerly the Colton Ranch, for letting us visit his property, photograph sheepherder art, and meet his friendly bison herd.

2. Lucinda A. Rogers (91 years old, widow of Joseph Rogers), interview by R. G.

Colwell, September 21, 1944. Pike National Forest History Microfilm, document no. 136.

3. The exception in South Park was Obe Fife, who killed a sheepman named Scribner. See Virginia McConnell Simmons, *Bayou Salado: The Story of South Park* (Boulder: University Press of Colorado, 2002), 242. For additional historical information see R. Laurie Simmons and Thomas H. Simmons, "The History of Ranching in South Park, Colorado," National Register of Historic Places Multiple Properties Documentation Form, December 10, 1999.

4. Midge Harbour, *The Tarryall Mountains and the Puma Hills: A History* (Century One Press, 1982), 82.

5. Jerry Davis, email message to author, December 12, 2016.

6. Simmons, *Bayou Salado*, 215.

7. Will Irwin, "Timber-Line Clover," *Saturday Evening Post*, November 25, 1922, 17.

8. Ibid.

9. Ibid., 70. Census data confirm this. The 1900 census lists the Herrera, Sanchez, Martinez, Trujillo, and Vigil families. The 1910 census includes Herreras, Pachecos, Torreses, and Cordovas. Vigils appear in the 1920 census, and the 1930 census enumerates Garcias, Pachecos, Mondragons, Martinezes, and Guiterrezes. Census data are courtesy of researcher Jerry Davis.

10. Irwin, "Timber-Line Clover." Also see Marie Chisholm, "Sheepherding History in South Park," in *Proceedings of the Sixth South Park Symposium*, Fairplay, CO, June 25–26, 2010, Park County Archives.

11. Alfredo Romero signed the dates "Mayo 22th 1930, 1931, 1934, 1935," and Jose E. Romero also wrote his name on the inside of the shearing shed.

Chapter 7

1. David Lavender, *One Man's West*, 1943 (Lincoln: University of Nebraska Press, 1977), 271.

2. Leisl Carr Childers, "The Angry West: Understanding the Sagebrush Rebellion in Nevada," in *Bridging the Distance: Common Issues of the Rural West*, ed. David B. Danbom (Salt Lake City: University of Utah Press, 2015), 226.

3. Aldo Leopold, *A Sand County Almanac* (New York: Ballantine Books, 1970), 268.

4. Mike Hudak, *Western Turf Wars: The Politics of Public Lands Ranching* (Binghamton, NY: Biome Books, 2007), 372.

5. Steve McMillan, "Area Sheep Ranchers Applaud 1080 Decision," *Grand Junction (CO) Daily Sentinel*, November 2, 1983.

6. Range Management, 2220, "Bear S&G Allotment Management Plan," Norwood District, Uncompahgre National Forest, 1961.

7. Deborah D. Paulson and William L. Baker, *The Nature of Southwestern Colorado: Recognizing Human Legacies and Restoring Natural Places* (Boulder: University Press of Colorado, 2006), 58.

8. Ibid., 279.

9. Ibid.
10. Ibid., 286.
11. David Petersen, *Ghost Grizzlies* (Boulder, CO: Johnson Books, 1998), 145.
12. Ibid., 146.
13. Jason Blevins, "Fourteeners Give Colorado Significant Economic Boost," *Denver Post*, August 8, 2016.
14. Susan Loth, "Sheep Guardians Prove Worth," *Delta County (CO) Independent*, May 4, 1981; Steve McMillan, "Coyote Killers Protect Craig Rancher's Sheep," *Grand Junction (CO) Daily Sentinel*, December 27, 1982.
15. Frank Clifford, *The Backbone of the World: A Portrait of the Vanishing West along the Continental Divide* (New York: Broadway Books, 2002), 77.
16. Ibid., 91.
17. American Sheep Industry Association, "Fast Facts about Sheep Production," 2015, sheepindustrynews.org.
18. Clifford, *Backbone of the World*, 83.
19. A flurry of inquiries and concerns over lost or abandoned sheepdogs ending up in the Rangely, Colorado, animal shelter has been a problem, as have guardian dog attacks. See Colleen O'Neill, "Are Sheep Dogs Lost on the Range?," *Glenwood Springs (CO) Post Independent*, November 22, 2015.
20. Mary Beaber, compiler, "Overview of Attached Letters Which Cover Incidents of Sheep Dog Encounters with Hikers and Bicyclists on Public Lands in San Juan County," September 9, 2011, collection of the author.
21. Nicolle Bellman, letter to whom it may concern, Silverton Property Management, n.d., Beaber compilation.
22. Ibid. Clinton Jacobsen sent the author this email on March 15, 2016, with the title "The Battle of Roncevaux Pass":

> On the Colorado trail, sometime in the summer of 2014—July or August (I can't remember the date exactly—that summer I had started a weekly/biweekly habit of hitchhiking a shuttle to ride the Molas pass to Engineer Mountain segment of the Colorado trail, leaving my car at the top of Coal Bank pass, hitchhiking up to and riding alone back from the top of Molas pass/Little Molas Lake area all along on the CT trail) . . . anyway, the rides blend together after a while, but about 2/3rds of the way into this ride, walking my mountain bike out of the Engine Creek drainage (part of the trail that I couldn't yet ride up, & still can't—there's a pretty steep section of trail coming out of the drainage and onto the "flat"/saddle between Jura Nob and Engineer mountain) I found myself next to a good sized herd of sheep. I was just to the west of the herd and a little downhill—all north of Engineer & close to the foot of Jura Nob. Soon after I noticed the sheep, the barking started. First just the one dog galloped up to me, then another. These were huge, white, Great Pyrenees-looking dogs. The two put themselves between me and the sheep and continued to aggressively bark—at times holding off to look at each other and consult on the issue before returning to barking—you know how groups of dogs do. After the two I then noticed a third was making his way toward us from the middle of the herd, they started advancing toward me again. Still off my bike, I had it between me and the dogs, I picked up my

walking pace to a near run (cycling shoes with cleats—not great for running) further down the trail & south toward Engineer mountain. I was yelling a colorful assortment of obscenities and threats back at the dogs as I was doing this, you can imagine. As soon as I could throw a leg back over the bike and start peddling again I immediately did and sprinted until the dogs blended back to just white specks on the green & red hillside like the sheep. That's about what I remember. I did not see sheep herders with the group, but I imagine they weren't that far away—It was a pretty big herd. Ha! Maybe they watched the whole thing! I was probably pretty entertaining if they did.

23. Will Sands, "From the Editor: Black Sheep," *Durango (CO) Telegraph*, August 25, 2011.

24. Resolution adopted by the San Juan County Board of Commissioners, September 24, 2014.

25. Michael J. Crumb, "Vail-Area Sheepdog Attack Creates Worries across West," *Vail (CO) Daily*, July 8, 2010.

26. Ibid.

27. Tom McGhee, "Vail: Woman Attacked by Rancher's Dogs Receives $1 Million Settlement," *Denver Post*, February 14, 2016.

28. Hudak, *Western Turf Wars*, 350.

29. Edward Abbey, "Even the Bad Guys Wear White Hats: Cowboys, Ranchers, and the Ruin of the West," *Harper's Magazine* 272, no. 1628 (January): 51–55. In contrast to Abbey, a Nevada rancher assumed that his allotment was private property, which has no legal basis. See E. Wayne Hage, *Storm over Range Lands: Private Rights in Federal Lands* (Bellevue, WA: Free Enterprise Press, 1989).

30. Hudak, *Western Turf Wars*, 360.

31. Debra L. Donahue, *The Western Range Revisited: Removing Livestock from Public Lands to Conserve Native Biodiversity* (Norman: University of Oklahoma Press, 1999), 3.

32. Ibid., 4.

33. Ibid., 5, 7.

34. Lynn Jacobs, *Waste of the West: Public Lands Ranching* (Tucson, AZ: self-pub., 1991); George Wuerthner and Mollie Matteson, eds., *Welfare Ranching: The Subsidized Destruction of the American West* (Washington, DC: Island Press, 2002).

35. Andrew Gulliford, "Privatizing Public Lands? Start with Grazing Fees," opinion/editorial column, *Grand Junction (CO) Daily Sentinel*, March 13, 2016.

36. Ben Goldfarb, "The Forever War," *High Country News*, January 25, 2016, 12.

37. Wayne Yonemoto (grazing staff), interview by author, Tres Piedras District, Carson National Forest, July 19, 2016. Also see Andrew Gulliford, "Bureau of Biological Survey: A Century Poisoning the West," opinion/editorial column, *Grand Junction (CO) Daily Sentinel*, August 23, 2015.

38. James Surowiecki, "The Financial Page—Bundynomics," *New Yorker*, January 25, 2016.

39. Ernie Etchart, interview by author, California Gulch, north of Silverton, CO, August 24, 2015.

40. Colleen Schreiber, "Martin Etchart Started Out as Herder and Ended Up a Rancher," *Livestock Weekly*, September 21, 2006.

41. Ibid.

42. Etchart, interview.

43. Garth Nelson (Dolores, CO, field office of the BLM), interview by author, Ernie Etchart's sheep camp, Placer Gulch, August 24, 2015.

44. Colleen Schreiber, "Running Sheep on Federal Land Is Not for the Faint-Hearted," *Livestock Weekly*, September 18, 2014.

45. Kathy McCraine, "Nomadic Sheep Rancher," *Range Magazine*, Winter 2015/2016, 84.

46. Schreiber, "Running Sheep on Federal Land."

47. The lynx section of this chapter is taken in edited form from Andrew Gulliford, "The Missing Lynx: A Ten-Year Eco-Update on the Lynx Re-introduction to Colorado," *Inside/Outside Southwest*, August/September 2007.

48. Dale Rodebaugh, "Biologists Launch Lynx Study," *Durango (CO) Herald*, January 22, 2015.

49. See Doug Scott, *The Enduring Wilderness* (Golden, CO: Fulcrum Publishing, 2004). To learn specifically about the Weminuche Wilderness, the largest in Colorado, see B. J. Boucher, *Walking in Wildness: A Guide to the Weminuche Wilderness* (Durango, CO: Durango Herald and San Juan Mountains Association, 1998).

50. Theodore Roosevelt, *Wilderness Writings* (Salt Lake City: Gibbs Smith, 1986), 57.

51. Ibid., 59.

52. Jack Ballard, *Bighorn Sheep* (Guilford, CT: Falcon Guides, 2014), 17; Colorado Parks and Wildlife bighorn sheep brochure, n.d.

53. Ballard estimates 4,500 bighorns, but the number is higher (*Bighorn Sheep*, 21). See Jonathan Romeo, "Managing the Bighorns," *Durango (CO) Herald*, November 30, 2016. A highly controversial protocol has Colorado Parks and Wildlife killing bighorns that come in contact with domestic sheep. See Romeo, "Managing the Bighorns," and John Mumma, "Agency's Politics Override Responsibility," *Durango (CO) Herald*, December 11, 2016.

54. Bob Broscheid, director, Colorado Parks and Wildlife, speech, 89th Annual Colorado Wool Growers Convention, Montrose, CO, July 14, 2016.

55. John Muir quote, 1894, Sierra Nevada Bighorn Sheep Foundation website, http://sierrabighorn.org/.

56. Ellen Meloy, *Eating Stone* (New York: Pantheon Books, 2005), 134, 205.

57. San Juan National Forest, *Historical Notes: Bighorn Sheep and Domestic Sheep Grazing*, September 6, 2012.

58. Ballard, *Bighorn Sheep*, 68.

59. Ibid., 75.

60. Nike Stevens, pers. comm., April 25, 2017. Also see John D. Wehausen, Scott T. Kelley, and Rob R. Ramey II, "Domestic Sheep, Bighorn Sheep, and Respiratory Disease: A Review of the Experimental Evidence," *California Fish and Game* 97, no. 1 (2011): 7–24; and N. J. Goodson, "Effects of Domestic Sheep Grazing on Bighorn Sheep Populations: A Review," *Biennial Symposium of the Northern Wild Sheep and Goat Council* 3 (1982): 288–313. In a letter to the editor of the *Durango (CO) Herald*

on April 29–30, 2017, David Lien writes, "As detailed in a joint issue statement of the Wildlife Society and the American Association of Wildlife Veterinarians, 'Effective separation of domestic sheep from wild sheep is the only currently available management solution for preventing or minimizing disease transmission.'"

61. Stevens, pers. comm.

62. San Juan National Forest, *Historical Notes*. Also see San Juan National Forest, *Summary of Rocky Mountain Bighorn Sheep and Domestic Sheep Information for the San Juan National Forest—Bighorn Sheep Management on the San Juan National Forest (SJNF)*, Pagosa Ranger District, July 12, 2016.

63. San Juan National Forest, *Historical Notes*; San Juan National Forest, *Summary of Rocky Mountain Bighorn Sheep*.

64. Mary Shinn, "Rep. Tipton Pushes for Clarity on Grazing on National Land," *Durango (CO) Herald*, May 5, 2015; and "Long Recovery of Bighorns," *Durango (CO) Herald*, July 7, 2015.

65. Similar issues are occurring across western national forests. On the Beaverhead-Deerlodge National Forest there are 8,000 sheep and only 35 bighorn. See "News in Brief," *High Country News*, October 26, 2015, hcn.org.

66. Wild Sheep Working Group, *Recommendations for Domestic Sheep and Goat Management in Wild Sheep Habitat* (Western Association of Fish and Wildlife Agencies, 2012), 3.

67. Ibid., 4.

68. Ibid., 6.

69. In 2014 a Colorado bighorn sheep tag auctioned by Colorado Parks and Wildlife sold for $130,000. The accompanying raffle brought in an additional $78,200. See Dale Rodebaugh, "Sheep-Grazing Study Suspended for New Examination," *Durango (CO) Herald*, August 2, 2014. That study in the San Juans resulted in a complete environmental impact statement, or EIS—San Juan National Forest, *Draft Environmental Impact Statement: Weminuche Landscape Grazing Analysis* (USDA Forest Service, February 2016). The EIS discussed domestic sheep and bighorns on 13 forest allotments.

70. Rio Grande National Forest, *Annual Operating Instructions*, East Vega–Treasure S&G Allotment, Conejos Peak Ranger District, 2016.

71. Luciano Sandoval, interview by author, Conejos Peak Ranger District, La Jara, CO, July 21, 2016.

72. Kelly Garcia (acting district ranger), interview by author, Leadville Ranger District Office, Pike and San Isabel National Forests, CO, April 15, 2016.

EIGHTH SHEEPSCAPE

1. Note that sheepherder stone cairns or monuments are not to be confused with Native American cairns, which are often of the same type and in the same landscapes. See Andrew Gulliford, *Sacred Objects and Sacred Places: Preserving Tribal Traditions* (Boulder: University Press of Colorado, 2000).

2. Norman Hallendy, *Inuksuit: Silent Messengers of the Arctic* (Seattle: University of Washington Press, 2000), 21.

3. David B. Williams, *Cairns: Messengers in Stone* (Seattle: Mountaineers Books, 2012), 96.

4. This text is adapted from Andrew Gulliford, "Stone Messengers in Wild Country," *Durango (CO) Herald*, January 11, 2015.

5. Bill Harris, "Stinking Desert Cairns Project," *Southwestern Lore: Journal of Colorado Archaeology* 79, no. 4 (Winter 2013): 19.

6. Ibid., 23. He adds that the Stinking Desert Cairns Project became a fieldwork exercise for the Chipeta Chapter of the Colorado Archaeological Society from Montrose and that more research is needed in terms of sheep rancher and sheepherder interviews.

7. For a northern plains reference, see Pat Hansen, "Stone Johnnies: Vanishing Landmarks of Lonely Hills," *Montana Standard* (Butte), April 4, 2008.

8. To read about hikers hit by lightning, see Dean Cox, "Electrified: Struck by Lightning . . . a Survivor's Story—Weminuche Wilderness," in *Outdoors in the Southwest: An Adventure Anthology*, ed. Andrew Gulliford (Norman: University of Oklahoma Press, 2014), 149–53.

Chapter 8

1. M. K. Thompson, "Colorado's Aspen Trees Uniquely Beautiful," *Durango (CO) Herald*, November 7, 2010. Also see Chris Madson, "Trees Born of Fire and Ice," *National Wildlife* 34, no. 6 (October/November 1996).

2. See David Petersen, *Among the Aspens* (Flagstaff, AZ: Northland Publishing, 1991).

3. Deborah D. Paulson and William L. Baker, *The Nature of Southwestern Colorado: Recognizing Human Legacies and Restoring Natural Places* (Boulder: University Press of Colorado, 2006), 214.

4. For a sample of newspaper articles on SAD, or sudden aspen decline, see Chase Squires, "Aspens Dying across the West, Scientists Say," *Arizona Republic* (Phoenix), September 15, 2006; Kristen Plank, "Forest Officials Measure Sudden Aspen Decline," *Cortez (CO) Journal*, August 21, 2008; Kristen Plank, "Experts Cite Climate Change in Forest Decline," *Durango (CO) Herald*, February 20, 2011; and Dale Rodebaugh, "Thirst Felling West's Aspen: Cortez Native's Stanford Research Pinpoints Cause of Sudden Decline," *Durango (CO) Herald*, December 29, 2011.

5. Hal Borland, *When the Legends Die* (New York: Bantam, 1963), 259.

6. The best book on climate change and its impact on ecosystems in the Southwest is William deBuys, *A Great Aridness* (New York: Oxford University Press, 2011).

7. Paulson and Baker, *Nature of Southwestern Colorado*, 216.

8. Gary Visintainer, interview by author, 89th Annual Colorado Wool Growers Convention, Montrose, CO, July 14, 2016.

9. Aldo Leopold, *A Sand County Almanac* (New York: Ballantine Books, 1970), 6.

10. Shannon Joyce Neal, "Alone on the Range," *Grand Junction (CO) Daily Sentinel*, February 18, 2001. Also see Matt King, "Acker Connects Dots between Human Trafficking and Food Supply," *Western Colorado Clarion*, Autumn 2015, 4; Linda Surbaugh, ed., *Overworked and Underpaid: H-2A Herders in Colorado* (report, Mi-

grant Farm Worker Division of Colorado Legal Services, 2010); Bonnie Brown, "Colorado Wool Growers Association's Response to 'Overworked and Underpaid: H-2A Herders in Colorado'" (handout from Colorado Wool Growers Association, March 12, 2010).

11. Dan Frosch, "Sheepherders Are Set to Get a Raise," *Wall Street Journal*, October 15, 2015.

12. Ibid.

13. Ibid.

14. Anna Boiko-Weyrauch, "Earning Low Wages in Colorado's High Places," *Durango (CO) Herald*, August 1, 2015. Also see Stephen Elliott, "Montrose Group Files Lawsuit over Sheepherder Wages," *The Watch*, October 7, 2015; Julie Stepanek Shiflett, *The Real Wage Benefits Provided to H-2A Sheep Herders and the Economic Cost to Colorado Ranchers* (report prepared for the Colorado Wool Growers Association, March 5, 2010).

15. Julie Stepanek Shiflett, "Non-Traditional Lamb Marketing" (presentation, 89th Annual Colorado Wool Growers Convention, Montrose, CO, July 14, 2016). Also see Julie Stepanek Shiflett, Gary W. Williams, and Paul Rogers, *The Nontraditional Lamb Market: Characteristics and Marketing Strategies*, AFCERC Commodity Market Research Report No. CM-02–10 (March 2010).

16. Shiflett, "Non-Traditional Lamb Marketing."

17. Marija B. Vader, "Shear Agony," *Grand Junction (CO) Daily Sentinel*, May 4, 2000.

18. Ibid.

19. Chris Mooney, "'Massive' Tree Die-Off a Threat in Southwest," *Durango (CO) Herald*, December 24, 2015.

20. Courtney White, *Grass, Soil, Hope: A Journey through Carbon Country* (White River Junction, VT: Chelsea Green Publishing, 2014).

21. Ibid., x. To understand how ranching and ranchers can benefit soils, rangeland, and wildlife, see Marcy Houle, *The Prairie Keepers: Secrets of the Zumwalt* (Corvallis: Oregon State University Press, 2014). She writes, "Needing appreciation and support are conscientious private ranchers who manage their lands with thoughtful stewardship and in ways beneficial to wildlife. To eliminate them from the land could very well eliminate those things we hope to save" (266).

22. Mary Austin, *The Flock* (1906, repr., Santa Fe, NM: William Gannon, 1973), 10.

23. Michael Meuret and Fred Provenza, *The Art and Science of Shepherding: Tapping the Wisdom of French Herders* (Austin, TX: Acres USA, 2014), 11.

24. See Jerry L. Holechek, Hilton Gomes, Francisco Molinar, Dee Galt, and Raul Valdez, "Short Duration Grazing: The Facts in 1999," *Rangelands* 22 (February 2000): 18–22; David D. Briske, Andrew J. Ash, Justin D. Derner, and Lynn Huntsinger, "Commentary: A Critical Assessment of the Policy Endorsement for Holistic Management," *Agricultural Systems* 125 (2014): 50–53; and John Carter, Allison Jones, Mary O'Brien, Jonathan Ratner, and George Wuerthner, "Holistic Management: Misinformation on the Science of Grazed Ecosystems," *International Journal of Biodiversity* 2014, article ID 163431.

25. Davin Montoya, interview by author, Montoya Ranch, Hesperus, CO, December 26, 2015.

26. Ibid.

27. Ibid.

NINTH SHEEPSCAPE

1. Joe Sperry, remarks at the 89th Annual Colorado Wool Growers Convention, Montrose, CO, July 13, 2016.

2. Wayne Brown, remarks at the 89th Annual Colorado Wool Growers Convention, Montrose, CO, July 13, 2016.

3. S. J. Cranshaw, "Concerning the Sheep Industry in Central Wyoming," *Douglas (WY) Budget*, anniversary ed., 1907, Converse County WPA Files, Wyoming State Archives.

4. Tomás Antillon, "Sheep Herder Monuments," interview ca. 1939, WPA Collections, subject file 1396 for Converse County, Wyoming State Archives.

5. Ibid.

6. Ibid.

7. Hal Borland, *When the Legends Die* (New York: Bantam, 1963), 249.

8. Ibid., 250.

9. Pascal Wick, *Beartooth: Diary of a Nomadic Herder* (Buckingham, UK: Aaranya, 2014).

10. Ibid.

11. Rebecca H. Schwendler, Kellam Throgmorton, and Kevin Thompson, *Results of the Solar Potential Areas Class III Cultural Survey, Mesa County, Colorado*, BLM-GJFO CRIR 16712–01, SHPO Report No. ME.LM.R810, for PaleoWest Archaeology (August 2, 2013).

12. Aaron A. Abeyta, "Wilderness in Four Parts, or Why We Cannot Mention My Great-Grandfather's Name," *High Country News*, November 14, 2016, 16–20.

13. Alison Hostad and Michael Kyte, *Canjilon Lakes Sanitation Salvage Project: A Cultural Resources Inventory and National Register of Historic Places Evaluation of Sites for the Canjilon Lakes Recreation Area, Carson National Forest, Rio Arriba County, New Mexico* (Tres Piedras, NM: Tres Piedras Ranger District, August 20, 2015). Also see James B. De Korne, *Aspen Art in the New Mexico Highlands* (Santa Fe: Museum of New Mexico Press, 1970).

14. Elmer O. Bair, *Elmer Bair's Story, 1899 to 1987* (Glenwood Springs, CO: Gran Farnum Printing, 1987), 147. Bair's autobiographical story is one of the most authoritative and well told of all sheepmen's accounts. His descriptions of seeing wildlife, of enduring blizzards on the Flat Tops, of making a sheep ranch work despite skeptical cattlemen, of his Mormon faith, and of moving sheep from Colorado high country to Utah deserts make for an important historical book.

15. Ibid. A good analysis of sheepmen-cattlemen conflicts in that area and along the Colorado River on the Utah-Colorado state line is Mike Milligan, "Cattle versus Sheep," chap. 4 in *Westwater Lost and Found* (Logan: Utah State University Press, 2004).

16. Ruth Lambert, ed., *The Wooden Canvas: Hispanic Arborglyphs along the Pine-Piedra Stock Driveway* (Durango: San Juan Mountains Association with History Colorado, 2014).

17. See Esther Greenfield, *Reading the Trees: A Curious Hiker's Field Journal of Hidden Woodland Messages* (North Charleston, SC: CreateSpace Independent Publishing, 2015).

18. See Andrew Gulliford, "Reading the Trees: Colorado's Endangered Arborglyphs and Aspen Art," *Colorado Heritage*, Autumn 2007.

19. Bridget Roth, interview by author, Routt National Forest, Steamboat Springs, CO, September 16, 2015.

20. Ibid.

21. Scott Ortman, "What Difference Does Archaeology Make?" *El Palacio* 121, no. 2 (Summer 2016): 22.

22. Polly E. Hammer, Dana Isham, Rand Greubel, and Phil Born, *Cultural Resource Inventory of the Lone Cone Aspen Treatment*, I-84–05–46 (Norwood Ranger District, Uncompahgre National Forest, San Miguel County, CO, December 1988).

Chapter 9

1. There are many sources on Butch Cassidy and the West—too many to be listed here—but for purposes of this book it is interesting to note that when Butch, the quintessential western outlaw, left the United States after 1900 for safer territory in Argentina and Patagonia, he and the Sundance Kid went into the ranching business. Yes, they ran cattle, but the former desperados also had a flock of 1,300 sheep.

2. Tom Kourlis, interview by author, 89th Annual Colorado Wool Growers Convention, Montrose, CO, July 13, 2016. One of the Kourlis men married the daughter of Colorado governor John Love. As proof of upward mobility among dedicated Greek sheepmen and their children, Rebecca Love Kourlis became a Colorado Supreme Court judge.

3. Scott Armentrout, interview by author, 89th Annual Colorado Wool Growers Convention, Montrose, CO, July 13, 2016.

4. William Philpott, *Vacationland: Tourism and Environment in the Colorado High Country* (Seattle: University of Washington Press, 2013), 22.

5. Ibid., 8.

6. Ibid., 21.

7. Shirley Welch, "Once Upon a Time: From Ellis Island to Wolcott, Colorado," *Vail Valley Magazine*, Summer 2015, 146.

8. Connie Jouflas, interview by author, Grand Junction, CO, September 21, 2015.

9. Ibid.

10. Welch, "Once Upon a Time," 145. This anecdote about lost lambs in the back seat of Cadillacs appears to be classic sheepman folklore. Another, almost identical version of the story, only this time with the sheepman Howard Lathrop, is told by his wife, Marguerite Lathrop, in *Don't Fence Me In* (Boulder, CO: Johnson Publishing, 1972), 337.

11. Pam Aldasoro Bennett and Cristine Aldasoro Mitchell, interview by author, Telluride, CO, March 5, 2016.

12. Ibid. To understand Basque ranching families in New Mexico, see John M. White, "Ranchers in the Basque Tradition," *New Mexico Magazine*, April 1963, which describes Basque sheepmen and a ranch of 66 sections of 640 acres each in Guadalupe County, New Mexico—a sheep range of 42,240 acres.

13. Philpott, *Vacationland*, 305.

14. Ibid., 299.

15. Andrew Gullliford, "Who Will Speak on Behalf of the Beleaguered Sage Grouse"?, opinion/editorial column, *Grand Junction (CO) Daily Sentinel*, November 17, 2013.

16. Ibid.

17. E. O. Wilson, *The Future of Life*, quoted in Gulliford, "Who Will Speak."

18. Mathew Brown, "Environmentalists Seek to Protect Sage Grouse," *Durango (CO) Herald*, February 27, 2016.

19. Gulliford, "Who Will Speak."

20. Andrew Gulliford, "Too Much of a Good Thing: Wild Horses on Public Lands," opinion/editorial column, *Grand Junction (CO) Daily Sentinel*, February 10, 2013. For a different perspective, see Paula Morin, *Honest Horses: Wild Horses in the Great Basin* (Reno: University of Nevada Press, 2006); and Deanne Stillman, *Mustang: The Saga of the Wild Horse in the American West* (Boston: Houghton Mifflin, 2009).

21. Gary Visintainer, interview by author, 89th Annual Colorado Wool Growers Convention, Montrose, CO, July 13, 2016.

22. Leisl Carr Childers, "The Angry West: Understanding the Sagebrush Rebellion in Nevada," in *Bridging the Distance: Common Issues of the Rural West*, ed. David B. Danbom (Salt Lake City: University of Utah Press, 2015), 231.

23. "Federal-Lands Ranching: A Half-Century of Decline," *High Country News*, June 13, 2016, 6.

24. Ibid.

25. Wayne Yonemoto (grazing staff), interview by author, Tres Piedras Ranger District, Carson National Forest, July 19, 2016.

26. In addition to summer recreation, winter recreation booms in the high country. The Vail Pass Winter Recreation Area encompasses an area the size of 10 Vail Mountain ski areas and attracts 36,000 people a season. But there are parking spaces for only 50 snowmobile trailers and 80 other vehicles. Parking fills to capacity early on winter mornings.

27. Missy Votel, "The Trail Ahead," *Durango (CO) Telegraph*, September 3, 2015, 8.

28. Mark Wilson, interview by author, Meeker Sheepdog Trials, Meeker, CO, September 12, 2015.

29. Ibid.

30. Curt Meine, quotes from *Green Fire: Aldo Leopold and a Land Ethic for Our Time* (produced by the Aldo Leopold Foundation, US Forest Service, Humans and Nature, 2011), DVD, 73 minutes.

31. Aldo Leopold, "Thinking like a Mountain," in *A Sand County Almanac* (New York: Ballantine Books, 1970), 137–41. For other outstanding sources on Leopold,

see Susan L. Flader, *Thinking like a Mountain: Aldo Leopold and the Evolution of an Ecological Attitude toward Deer, Wolves and Forests* (Madison: University of Wisconsin Press, 1994); David E. Brown and Neil B. Carmony, *Aldo Leopold's Wilderness* (Harrison, PA: Stackpole Books, 1990); and Curt Meine, *Aldo Leopold: His Life and Work* (Madison: University of Wisconsin Press, 1988).

32. Michael J. Robinson, *Predatory Bureaucracy: The Extermination of Wolves and the Transformation of the West* (Boulder: University Press of Colorado, 2005).

33. Colorado Wolf Management Working Group, *Findings and Recommendations for Managing Wolves That Migrate into Colorado* (Colorado Parks and Wildlife, December 28, 2004). Also see Andrew Gulliford, "Wolves, Wilderness and Elk: Canis Lupus in Colorado," opinion/editorial column, *Grand Junction (CO) Daily Sentinel*, December 20, 2015.

34. Center for Biological Diversity, *A Wild Love* (self-pub., 2015).

35. Richard P. Reading, Brian Miller, Amy L. Masching, Rob Edward, and Michael K. Phillips, eds. *Awakening Spirits: Wolves in the Southern Rockies* (Golden, CO: Fulcrum Publishing, 2010), 57, 72.

36. Colleen Schreiber, "Running Sheep on Federal Land Is Not for the Faint-Hearted," *Livestock Weekly*, September 18, 2014.

37. "Yellowstone: The Battle for the American West," *National Geographic* 229, no. 5 (May 2016): 166.

38. Pascal Wick, *Beartooth: Diary of a Nomadic Herder* (Buckingham, UK: Aaranya, 2014), 26.

39. Ibid.

40. Ibid., 70

41. "Yellowstone," *National Geographic*, 164.

42. Dr. Julie Korb (Fort Lewis College biology professor), email message to author, April 11, 2016.

43. Tom Wolf, *Colorado's Sangre de Cristo Mountains* (Boulder: University Press of Colorado, 1995), 242. For an overview of sheep raising in the San Luis Valley, see Virginia McConnell Simmons, *The San Luis Valley: Land of the Six-Armed Cross* (Boulder: University Press of Colorado, 1999). For sheep herded near La Garita, see F. Amadeo White, *La Garita: Growing Up in and about the San Luis Valley* (Denver, CO: self-pub., 2007). For the environmental consequences of sheep grazing in the San Luis Valley and subsequent "widespread erosion across the valley floor," see Michael M. Geary, *Sea of Sand* (Norman: University of Oklahoma Press, 2016).

44. Reading et. al, *Awakening Spirits*, 90.

45. Ibid., 87.

46. John B. Wright, *Rocky Mountain Divide: Selling and Saving the West* (Austin: University of Texas Press, 1993), 40.

47. Dale Rodebaugh, "See Guard Dogs on New Web Map," *Durango (CO) Herald*, September 4, 2014.

48. Quotes from the Sand County Foundation website from the story by Kevin Kiley, "Visintainer Family Received Leopold Conservation Award," April 23, 2013, accessed August 13, 2016, https://sandcountyfoundation.org/news/2013/visintainer-family-receives-leopold-conservation-award-in-colorado.

Glossary

allotments. Public land designated for specific cattle and sheep herds; size depends on grazing capacity.

arborglyphs. Herders' carvings on aspen trees, including portraits of themselves, women, horses, religious icons, houses, animals, and other symbols, but almost always with the herders' names, dates, and hometowns. Cowboys usually carved only the brands of the ranches they worked for.

AUM. Animal unit month; federal fees paid by stockmen.

band of sheep. Approximately 1,000 ewes with lambs.

bedding out system. Spending only one night in the same place.

bed-ground. A place where bands of sheep spend one or two nights.

Bureau of Land Management. Agency that manages public lands that were once available for homesteading and then reverted from the General Land Office to the Office of Grazing after the 1934 Taylor Grazing Act. Those lands were consolidated into the BLM in 1946. The organization received its Organic Act or congressional authorization in 1976 under the Federal Land Policy and Management Act.

campfire. Known as a "poor man's blanket."

camp tender. Someone who brings weekly food and other supplies to herders in their remote location.

carrying or grazing capacity. Number of livestock or wildlife that can inhabit an area or ecosystem without damaging the plants and riparian resources.

chahakoa. Basque goatskin wine pouch. Basques drank red wine with sourdough bread and always scratched the sign of the cross on the back of the loaf with a knife before cutting the first slice.

chain migration. Migration that occurred when a Basque, Greek, or Hispano herder found a successful job and encouraged other male family members to work for the same outfit. Often these work relationships lasted generations.

common sage. Along with shadscale, bud brush, wheatgrass, and winter fat, a staple plant eaten by sheep on low-elevation winter range.

"coyote it." To tear out chunks of meat from a piece of lamb or mutton in the same way that coyotes attack sheep.

crutching. Occasional trimming of sheep around the teats, anus, and groin performed by herders in winter or early spring.

cuts. Strayed sheep.

deadlines. Boundaries established during the cattle and sheep wars to keep cattle herds and sheep flocks separate. If herders crossed the arbitrarily imposed deadlines, their sheep could be killed, their wagons burned, and their lives threatened.

drop herd. A segregated herd of ewes. Once ewes were sheared in the spring, pregnant or heavy ewes would be segregated into a drop herd and put into a lambing ground to be watched daily and even hourly.

grazing trespass. Shepherds taking sheep onto a cattle allotment or onto another sheepman's leased grazing land.

gummers and shells. Old ewes unable to forage well because of declining agility and weak or absent teeth.

gunnysackers. Term used especially in Wyoming to describe cowboys wearing gunnysacks as masks to raid sheep camps and shoot sheep, burn wagons, and sometimes kill herders.

harri mutilak. "Stone boys" in Basque. Term for the large stone monuments or cairns stacked by Basque sheepherders across the West.

hobby ranches. In scenic, mountainous areas of the West, working ranches once owned by locals that are now owned by wealthy out-of-state residents, often as a tax write-off or as a real estate investment.

Homestead Act (1862). The first of many laws providing for a person to attain 160 acres of private property on the public domain after living on it for five years and building a house measuring 12 by 14 feet.

hoofed locusts. John Muir's derogatory term for sheep. He was a sheepherder in the high meadows of what became Yosemite National Park.

lamb lickers. Pejorative term for men who worked in lambing sheds.

makila. Basque walking stick.

osha root. The root of a high-altitude plant that is highly regarded by native New Mexicans and Native Americans as a cure-all.

patch cuts. Aspen clear-cuts of approximately 10 acres.

GLOSSARY

permits. Authorization required for grazing on public land allotments. Initially granted to stockmen in the high country and forested areas based on prior use; usually granted in 10-year increments.

public entry. Historical ability of the public to file for private property rights on public land prior to 1934; this limited options for stockmen who once grazed thousands of acres unimpeded by farmers or "nesters."

regulated grazing. Grazing on public land under the rules of the US Forest Service and later the BLM.

relict stands. Small, isolated parcels of original, ungrazed vegetation and timber.

rim-rocked. Sheep driven off a cliff and killed by cowboys.

Rocky Mountain oysters. Nickname for the delicacy of roasted sheep testicles, often first separated from a male lamb by a sheepman's teeth.

shearing. The process of removing wool from sheep after lambing.

sheep on shares. An agreement whereby herders took their wages in sheep, lived frugally with their food and tent or camp wagon provided by their employer, and could start their own flock in five or six years. Earning sheep on shares worked well for Mormon, Basque, and Greek sheepmen, but an untimely spring blizzard could wipe out everyone's profits and years of labor.

sheep outfits. Everything necessary to raise and sustain sheep, including horses, corrals, wagons, herders, burros, and even a ranch itself.

sheepscapes. Archaeological features created by or for sheepherders that remain in high-mountain or canyon landscapes, such as carved aspens, stacked rocks or cairns, paintings inside sheep shearing sheds, troughs for salt, corrals, bridges built in national forests for sheep to cross swollen creeks, and so forth.

sheep wagons. Portable homes for shepherds, including a bed, stove, and supplies. Possibly invented in Rawlins, Wyoming, in 1884 by a blacksmith. Still in production today but much modernized, complete with well-insulated walls and solar panels.

"Stone Johnnies." Nickname for sheepherder monuments or large stacked stone cairns; these indicated allotment boundaries and sometimes served as valuable markers if herders were caught in blizzards.

submit to the count. Annual count of sheep before they enter the forest.

sustained yield. The goal of forests managed for vegetation and tree growth.

Taylor Grazing Act (1934). Legislation that established stockmen-administered grazing districts on public lands that would come under the authority of the Bureau of Land Management.

timber famine. Loss of trees and watershed damage as a result of timber poaching.

tin dogs. Condensed milk cans on a wire loop that could be shaken like a tambourine by a herder moving his sheep.

tramp outfits/sheepmen. Large sheep bands/sheepmen that came onto public land without ownership of local adjacent land; owners paid no local, county, or state taxes; sheep were managed primarily by Basques called range nomads, who herded "alien sheep." Also known as tramp herding.

US Forest Service (1905). Established by President Theodore Roosevelt, with Gifford Pinchot as chief forester. Required permits and range allotments on higher-elevation timbered land by 1906.

watershed. Forest, pasture, and canyons containing creeks and rivers that represent major collecting points for snowmelt and rain prior to flowing into other western rivers.

wet bands. Ewes with lambs.

wethers. Neutered male sheep.

Wilderness Act (1964). Legislation that established congressionally designated wilderness areas on public lands, places "where man is a visitor who does not remain" and where access is only on foot, on horseback, or by paddle. Historic grazing in wilderness areas was continued or "grandfathered in." Ironically, on landscapes dedicated to natural processes and ecosystems, wilderness areas are the only public lands with grazing established by federal statute.

winter range. Lower-elevation land with feed for sheep in the deserts of Utah and Wyoming and for cattle in Colorado; now BLM land. Most of the conflicts between cattlemen and sheepmen revolved around sheep foraging on winter range for cattle. Includes common sage, bud brush, shadscale, winter fat, and wheatgrass.

Selected Bibliography

State and Federal Government Documents and Publications

Baker, Robert D., Robert S. Maxwell, Victor H. Treat, and Henry C. Dethloff. *Timeless Heritage: A History of the Forest Service in the Southwest.* FS-409. Washington, DC: USDA Forest Service, August 1988.

Barnes, Will C. *The Story of the Range.* Washington, DC: US Department of Agriculture, 1926.

Blacker, Roderick K. "History Report—San Juan National Forest." Pagosa Springs Ranger District, CO, February 3, 1948.

The Bulletin (Denver Regional Office, US Forest Service) 18, no. 12 (December 1935).

Cassity, Michael. *Wyoming Will Be Your New Home . . . Ranching Farming, and Homesteading in Wyoming, 1860–1960.* Cheyenne: Wyoming State Historic Preservation Office Planning and Historic Context Development Program, Wyoming State Parks and Cultural Resources, 2011.

Colorado Wolf Management Working Group. *Findings and Recommendations for Managing Wolves That Migrate into Colorado.* Colorado Parks and Wildlife, December 28, 2004.

Cookson, David A. "The Basques in Wyoming." In *Peopling the High Plains: Wyoming's European Heritage*, edited by Gordon Olaf Hendrickson, 95–120. Cheyenne: Wyoming State Archives and Historical Department, 1977.

DuBois, Coert. *Report on the Proposed San Juan Forest Reserve, Colorado.* Durango, CO: San Juan National Forest, 1903.

Hammer, Polly E., Dana Isham, Rand Greubel, and Phil Born. *Cultural Resource Inventory of the Lone Cone Aspen Treatment.* I-84-05-46. Norwood Ranger District, Uncompahgre National Forest, San Miguel County, CO, December 1988.

The Handling of Sheep on the National Forests: La manipulación de las ovejas en los bosques nacionales. Washington, DC: Government Printing Office, 1920.

Hostad, Alison, and Michael Kyte. *Canjilon Lakes Sanitation Salvage Project: A Cultural Resources Inventory and National Register of Historic Places Evaluation of Sites for the Canjilon Lakes Recreation Area, Carson National Forest, Rio Arriba County, New Mexico.* Tres Piedras, NM: Tres Piedras Ranger District, August 20, 2015.

Lambert, Ruth, ed. *The Wooden Canvas: Hispanic Arborglyphs along the Pine-Piedra Stock Driveway.* Durango: San Juan Mountains Association with History Colorado, 2014.

Leopold, A. Starker, S. A. Cain, C. M. Cottam, I. N. Gabrielson, and T. L. Kimball. "The Goal of Park Management in the United States, 1963," in *Wildlife Management in the National Parks: The Leopold Report.* National Park Service, March 4, 1963.

Lowell, John W., Jr. Letter to district forester, April 11, 1910. Denver: National Archives, Rocky Mountain Region, no. 95. Records of the Forest Service, Rocky Mountain Regional Office, Historical Files, 1905–1931 (1650), box 12, folder 62.

Mack, C. B. Letter to Gifford Pinchot, July 15, 1940. San Juan National Forest files, Durango, CO.

Mallea-Olaetxe, Jose. *Recording Arborglyphs in Copper Basin, Elko County, Nevada.* USFS Report No. HM-97-0784. Humboldt National Forest P.I.T. Project, July 20–26, 1997.

Mehls, Steven F. *The Valley of Opportunity.* Denver: Colorado State Office, Bureau of Land Management, 1982.

Moore, Charles F., Everett L. Brown, and Henry E. Snyder. "Early History of Taylor Grazing Act in Colorado." BLM Information Memorandum no. 81–299, change 1. July 23, 1981.

National Park System Advisory Board Science Committee. *Revisiting Leopold: Resource Stewardship in the National Parks.* August 25, 2012. https://www.nps.gov/calltoaction/pdf/leopoldreport_2012.pdf.

Nelson, E. W. *Report of Chief of Bureau of Biological Survey.* Washington, DC: USDA, August 29, 1918.

Pinchot, Gifford. *Instructions to Foresters in Public Service.* Courtesy San Juan National Forest. Available at the Archuleta County Historical Society, Pagosa Springs, CO.

Range Management, 2220. "Bear S&G Allotment Management Plan." Norwood District, Uncompahgre National Forest, 1961.

Redington, Paul C. *Report of the Chief of the Bureau of Biological Survey.* Washington, DC: US Department of Agriculture, 1930.

Rio Grande National Forest. *Annual Operating Instructions.* East Vega–Treasure S&G Allotment, Conejos Peak Ranger District, 2016.

Rocky Mountain Region Bulletin (San Juan National Forest) 19, no. 11 (November 1936).

Roosevelt, Theodore. "Conservation as a National Duty." Speech to the White House Conservation Conference. In *Proceedings of a Conference of Governors in the White House, May 13–15, 1908.* Washington, DC: Government Printing Office, 1909.

Salmon, D. E. *Special Report on the History and Present Condition of the Sheep Industry of the United States.* Washington, DC: US Department of Agriculture, Government Printing Office, 1892.

San Juan County, Colorado, Board of County Commissioners. Resolution adopted September 24, 2014.

San Juan National Forest. *Draft Environmental Impact Statement: Weminuche Landscape Grazing Analysis.* USDA Forest Service, February 2016.

———. *Forest History.* Vol. 1, *1905–1971. San Juan and Montezuma National Forests, Colorado.* Durango, CO: San Juan National Forest.

———. *Historical Notes: Bighorn Sheep and Domestic Sheep Grazing.* September 6, 2012.

———. Letter from Ernest Shaw, supervisor, to Riley Smith, district forester, July 30, 1915.

———. *Summary of Rocky Mountain Bighorn Sheep and Domestic Sheep Information for the San Juan National Forest—Bighorn Sheep Management on the San Juan National Forest (SJNF).* Pagosa Ranger District, July 12, 2016.

———. US Forest Service Ranger Daybooks, 1921–1925. Archives, Center of Southwest Studies, Fort Lewis College, Durango, CO.

Shaw, Ernest. *Annual Grazing Report.* San Juan National Forest, 1908.

Simmons, R. Laurie, and Thomas H. Simmons. "The History of Ranching in South Park, Colorado." National Register of Historic Places Multiple Properties Documentation Form, December 10, 1999.

Smith, Nicole M. "Identification and Documentation of Herding Routes." Project #2003-M1-019, Site #5AA2515 and Site #5AA2516. Durango, CO: San Juan Mountains Association, December 2004.

US Census for Park County, Colorado—1900, 1910, 1920, 1930.

USDA Forest Service. "Allotment Retired." *R-2 Rendezvous,* June 15, 1989.

———. *The Use Book: A Manual for Users of the National Forests.* Washington, DC: Government Printing Office, 1913.

US Tariff Commission. *The Wool-Growing Industry.* Washington, DC: Government Printing Office, 1921.

Wild Sheep Working Group. *Recommendations for Domestic Sheep and Goat Management in Wild Sheep Habitat.* Western Association of Fish and Wildlife Agencies, 2012.

Williams, Gerald W. *The USDA Forest Service: The First Century.* FS-650. Washington, DC: USDA Forest Service, 2000.

Manuscripts and papers

Adjutant General, Wyoming National Guard. "Tensleep Murders Incident, 1909–1910." RG 0007. Wyoming State Archives.

Antillon, Tomás. "Sheep Herder Monuments." Interview ca. 1939. WPA Collections, subject file 1396 for Converse County, Wyoming State Archives.

Beaber, Mary, compiler. "Overview of Attached Letters Which Cover Incidents of Sheep Dog Encounters with Hikers and Bicyclists on Public Lands in San Juan County." September 9, 2011. Collection of the author.

Bennett, Lee. "A History of Selected Ranches on a Twenty-Mile Stretch of the Colorado River in Grand County, Utah." Monticello, UT: Bennett Management Services, March 2009.

Brady, Patti. Forest history binder notebook. Vol. 1, 1905–1971. Public Lands Center, San Juan National Forest, Durango, CO.
Brill, Gregory. "The Teofilo and Pedro Trujillo National Historic Landmark: A New Monument for a New Era of American Heritage." Graduate paper, University of Colorado–Denver. Manuscript in possession of the author.
Brooks, Bryant B. [governor 1907–1910]. Sheep raids, specifically Ten Sleep or Spring Creek Raid in Big Horn County, Wyoming. RG 0001.17, Wyoming State Archives.
Gibson, C. E., Jr. "The Original Settler at Medano Springs." Manuscript on file with History Colorado, Denver.
———. "Stories from Costilla County." Manuscript on file with History Colorado, Denver.
Jordan, Kathy. "Charlie Glass Was a Dandy Cowpuncher." Archival collection, Museum of Western Colorado, Grand Junction.
Kirkpatrick, J. R. "Who Was Charley Glass?" Archival collection, Museum of Western Colorado, Grand Junction.
Lathrop, Howard and Marguerite Collection. Accession #5084. American Heritage Center, University of Wyoming.
Macy, Robert W. "Some Factors in the Development and Destruction of the Open Range." Addendum study in "Several Phases of the Present Sheep Grazing Situation in Northern Wyoming, 1935." MSS 1043. Wyoming State Archives.
Moore, Catherine. Memoir/manuscript. Archival collection, Museum of Western Colorado, Grand Junction.
"Petition to the State Legislature of Wyoming, 1897." Governor William A. Richards, legislative affairs file, Wyoming State Archives.
Smith, Moroni A. "Herding and Handling Sheep on the Open Range in USA." Salt Lake City, UT, 1918.
Surbaugh, Linda, ed. *Overworked and Underpaid: H-2A Herders in Colorado*. Report. Migrant Farm Worker Division of Colorado Legal Services, 2010.
Wentworth, Edward N. Papers, 1805–1959. Accession #73. American Heritage Center, University of Wyoming.
Wyoming Wool Growers Collection. Accession #1350. American Heritage Center, University of Wyoming.

Interviews and Oral Histories

Armentrout, Scott (supervisor, Grand Mesa, Uncompahgre, and Gunnison National Forests). Interview by author. 89th Annual Colorado Wool Growers Convention, Montrose, CO, July 13, 2016.
Bennett, Pam Aldasoro, and Cristine Aldasoro Mitchell. Interview by author. Telluride, CO, March 5, 2016.
Carpenter, Farrington. Interview by author. Carpenter Ranch, July 1977. Oral history in the Western History Collections, Denver Public Library.
Chacon, Pacomio. Oral history interview by Philip L. Born. Grand Mesa, Uncompahgre, and Gunnison National Forests, Delta, CO, May 6, 1987.

Crowther, Leon. Interview by author. Tres Piedras Ranger District, Tres Piedras, NM, July 7, 2016.
Elder, Scott. Interview by author. Lone Mesa State Park, CO, September 28, 2015.
Etchart, Ernie. Interview by author. High country near Silverton, CO, August 24, 2015.
Gallegos, Tony Conrad. Interview by Joyce Lawrence, June 21, 2005. Interview transcript from Lone Mesa State Park, CO.
Garcia, Kelley (acting district ranger). Interview by author. Leadville Ranger District Office, Pike and San Isabel National Forests, CO, April 15, 2016.
Hammer, Polly (retired, Grand Mesa, Uncompahgre, and Gunnison National Forests). Interview by author. Hotchkiss, CO, August 5, 2006.
Hicks, Mona. Interview by E. Steve Cassells. Radio station KQIX, Grand Junction, CO, June 6, 1985.
Hunt, Leigh Ann (archaeologist, Grand Mesa, Uncompahgre, and Gunnison National Forests). Interview by author. Delta, CO, August 3, 2006; Lone Cone Ranger Station, Grand Mesa, Uncompahgre, and Gunnison National Forests, October 8, 2015.
Jack, Beatrice. Transcribed oral history on the sheep industry in Sweetwater, County, Wyoming. OH 255. Wyoming State Archives.
Jouflas, Connie. Interview by author. Grand Junction, CO, September 21, 2015.
Koerner, Jane. Interview by author. Fairplay, CO, January 24, 2015.
Krall, Angie. Interview by author. Supervisor's Office, Carson National Forest, Taos, NM, July 26, 2016.
Lawrence, Joyce and Roger. Interview by author. Lone Mesa State Park, CO, September 1 and 25, 2015.
Mattern, Joe. Interview by author. Steamboat Springs, CO, September 15, 2015.
Montoya, Davin. Interview by author. La Plata County, CO, December 26, 2015.
Nelson, Garth (Dolores, CO, field office of the Bureau of Land Management). Interview by author. Ernie Etchart's sheep camp, Placer Gulch, August 24, 2015.
Rogers, Lucinda A. Interview by R. G. Colwell. September 21, 1944. Pike National Forest History Microfilm, document no. 136.
Roth, Bridget (Routt National Forest). Interview by author. Steamboat Springs, CO, September 16, 2015.
Sandoval, Luciano (range conservationist). Interview by author. Conejos Peak Ranger District, Rio Grande National Forest, La Jara, CO, July 21, 2016.
Snyder, Raymond "Mex." Interview by author. Norwood, CO, October 5, 2015.
Temple, Stanley. Interview by author. Aldo Leopold's Mia Casita bungalow, Tres Piedras, Carson National Forest, NM, August 1, 2016.
Tipping, Marie. Interview by author. Piñon Mesa, CO, September 22, 2015.
Vallejos, Mollie. Interview by Larry Quintana, 1976. In *Our Past—The Portals to the Future: The Oral History of Dolores and the Surrounding Areas*, 1982. Courtesy of Lone Mesa State Park, CO.
Visintainer, Gary. Interview by author. 89th Annual Colorado Wool Growers Convention, Montrose, CO, July 14, 2016.
Wellman, Doug. Interview by author. Craig, CO, September 15, 2015.

Wilson, Mark. Interview by author. Meeker Sheepdog Trials, Meeker, CO, September 12, 2015.
Wyman, Lou. Interview by author. Wyman Living History Museum, Craig, CO, September 15, 2015.
Yonemoto, Wayne (grazing staff). Interview by author. Tres Piedras District, Carson National Forest, NM, July 19, 2016.

Conference Presentations and Personal Communications

American Sheep Industry Association. "Fast Facts about Sheep Production." 2015. sheepindustrynews.org.
Baughman O'Leary, Shirley. "Stone Johnnies: Vanishing Landmarks of the Lonely Buttes." West River History Conference, Keystone, SD, 1995.
Bombaci, Sara P., and Julie E. Korb. "The Effects of Sudden Aspen Decline on Avian Biodiversity in Southwest Colorado." In *The Colorado Plateau V: Research, Environmental Planning, and Management for Collaborative Conservation*, edited by C. van Riper, M. L. Villarreal, C. J. van Riper, and M. J. Johnson, 95–112. Tucson: University of Arizona Press, 2012.
Broscheid, Bob (director, Colorado Parks and Wildlife). Speech, 89th Annual Colorado Wool Growers Convention, Montrose, CO, July 14, 2016.
Brown, Bonnie. "Colorado Wool Growers Association's Response to 'Overworked and Underpaid: H-2A Herders in Colorado.'" Colorado Wool Growers Association, March 12, 2010.
Brown, Wayne. Remarks at the 89th Annual Colorado Wool Growers Convention, Montrose, CO, July 13, 2016.
Chisholm, Marie. "Sheepherding History in South Park." In *Proceedings of the Sixth South Park Symposium*, Fairplay, CO, June 25–26, 2010. Park County Archives.
Farnsworth, Linda, "Dendroglyph Survey and Recording Procedures." Elderhostel Program 1996, Peaks Ranger District, Coconino National Forest, AZ.
Goodson, N. J. "Effects of Domestic Sheep Grazing on Bighorn Sheep Populations: A Review." *Biennial Symposium of the Northern Wild Sheep and Goat Council* 3 (1982): 288–313.
Hammer, Polly E. "Aspen Carvings in the San Juan Mountains." Presentation at the annual meeting of the Colorado Council of Professional Archaeologists, Glenwood Springs, CO, March 8 and 9, 1985.
Jacobsen, Clinton. Email message to author on the Battle of Roncevaux Pass, March 15, 2016.
Korb, Julie. Personal communication with author, April 11, 2016.
Leopold, Aldo. *Transactions of the Twelfth North American Wildlife Conference*, San Antonio, TX. Washington, DC: Wildlife Management Institute, 1947.
Montaño family (Peggy Montaño, Pete Montaño, Shirley Rocha, and Sylvia Montaño Trujillo). Emails and personal communication to author, March and April, 2017.
Schwendler, Rebecca H., Kellam Throgmorton, and Kevin Thompson. *Results of the Solar Potential Areas Class III Cultural Survey, Mesa County, Colorado*. BLM-

GJFO CRIR 16712–01. SHPO Report No. ME.LM.R810, for PaleoWest Archaeology. August 2, 2013.

Selle, Michael (BLM archaeologist, White River Field Office, Meeker, CO). Email message to author on split estate, October 29, 2015.

Shiflett, Julie Stepanek. "Non-Traditional Lamb Marketing." Presentation at the 89th Annual Colorado Wool Growers Convention, Montrose, CO, July 14, 2016.

———. *The Real Wage Benefits Provided to H-2A Sheep Herders and the Economic Cost to Colorado Ranchers*. Report prepared for the Colorado Wool Growers Association, March 5, 2010.

Shiflett, Julie Stepanek, Gary W. Williams, and Paul Rogers. *The Nontraditional Lamb Market: Characteristics and Marketing Strategies*. AFCERC Commodity Market Research Report No. CM-02–10. March 2010.

Sperry, Joe. Remarks at the 89th Annual Colorado Wool Growers Convention, Montrose, CO, July 13, 2016.

Stevens, Nike. Personal communication, April 25, 2017.

Weigand, Phil, and Celia Garcia de Weigand. "The Dendroglyphs of the San Francisco Peaks, Arizona." Paper presented at the 1994 meeting of the Arizona Historical Society, Casa Grande, AZ.

Master's Theses and PhD Dissertations

Connolly, Nicholas J. "Environmental Variables Associated with the Location of Arborglyphs in the Eastern Sierra Nevada, Alpine County, California." PhD diss., University of Nevada, Reno, May 2012.

Sypolt, Charles M. "Keepers of the Rocky Mountain Flocks: A History of the Sheep Industry in Colorado, New Mexico, Utah, and Wyoming to 1940." PhD diss., University of Wyoming, 1974.

Wallace, Jon M. "Livestock, Land and Dollars: The Sheep Industry of Territorial New Mexico." Master's thesis, University of New Mexico, 2013.

Newspapers, 1880 to 1930

"60,000 New Settlers in Colorado Real Soon." *Grand Junction (CO) Daily Sentinel*, January 2, 1917.

"$310,000 Paid for Book Mountain Livestock Outfit." *Grand Valley Times* (Moab, UT), March 23, 1917.

"About the Sheep Question: A Few Letters of Interest from Ranchmen That Show How the Wind Blows." *Routt County (CO) Courier*, February 14, 1907.

"Are Sheep to Bleat in Routt County?" *Routt County (CO) Courier*, November 14, 1907.

"Cattlemen Freed." *Craig (CO) Empire*, May 20, 1925.

Center Dispatch (Saguache, CO), February 7, 1902.

Chapman, Arthur. "Trailing 20,000 Sheep through a Hostile Cattle Country." *San Francisco Chronicle*, February 23, 1908; *Daily Capital Journal* (Salem, OR), March 21, 1908.

"Charles Glass Is Cleared of Murder Charge." *Moab (UT) Times-Independent*, December 1, 1921.

"Colorado Sheepmen Seek Cream of Grand County Winter Ranges." *Moab (UT) Times-Independent*, March 20, 1930.

"Concerning the Sheep Industry in Central Wyoming." *Douglas (WY) Budget*. Anniversary ed., 1907.

"Cunninghams Sell Book Mt. Property." *Grand Valley Times* (Moab, UT), September 4, 1914; *Craig (CO) Courier*, September 14, 1894.

Craig (CO) Courier, February 6, 1897.

"Decision in Burusco Assault Case Reversed." *Moab (UT) Times-Independent*, April 12, 1923.

Denver News, January 15, 1908.

"East Utah Range War Is Brewing." *Moab (UT) Times-Independent*, January 15, 1921.

"French Sheepherders Found Guilty of Attempt to Murder G. A. Harris." *Moab (UT) Times-Independent*, January 26, 1922.

Grand Junction (CO) Daily Sentinel, May 7, May 8, May 24, 1894; November 17, 1896; April 25, May 7, 1907; January 14, January 21, March 4, 1908.

Grand Junction (CO) News, May 26, June 2, 1894.

"The Guilty Men Must Be Caught." *Denver Republican* editorial reprinted in the *Grand Junction (CO) Daily Sentinel*, May 26, 1909.

Lawson, J. W., "Sheep Industry of Famous South Park Rivals Strikes in Gold Fields." *Colorado Springs (CO) Gazette and Telegraph*. Tourist ed., April 7, 1929.

"Linn's Camp Raided." *Basin (WY) Republican*, August 26, 1907.

"Mexican Herder Slays Countryman in Book Mountains." *Moab (UT) Times-Independent*, October 5, 1922.

Moab (UT) Times-Independent, March 24, August 11, November 17, 1921.

Monte Vista (CO) Journal, February 1, February 15, May 10, 1902.

"Murder Case Is Dropped; Sole Witness Is Missing." *Grand Junction (CO) Daily Sentinel*, January 11, 1915.

"Negro Cowboy Slays French Sheep Herder." *Grand Junction (CO) Daily Sentinel*, February 25, 1921.

"New Homestead Act." *Grand Junction (CO) Daily Sentinel*, December 30, 1916.

"Northwestern Colorado Ranchmen Take Firm Stand against Sheep on Public Range." *Moffat County (CO) Courier*, April 6, 1911.

"Not Guilty of Killing the Sheep of Taylor." *Fruita (CO) Telegram* editorial reprinted in the *Grand Junction (CO) Daily Sentinel*, May 31, 1909.

Pagosa Springs (CO) News, September 8, 1892; June 23, 1893; January 12, 1894.

"The Plateau Sheep War." *Grand Junction (CO) Daily Sentinel*, January 5, 1895.

"President Roosevelt Is in Colorado, and Is Glad of It, Will Penetrate the Wilds at Once." *Rocky Mountain News* (Denver, CO), April 15, 1905.

"A Pretty Sheep Story." *San Juan Prospector* (Del Norte, CO), April 2, 1887.

"Resident Stockmen and Settlers of Book Cliff Region Organize to Resist Driveway Withdrawal." *Moab (UT) Times-Independent*, March 27, 1930.

"Roosevelt on Leasing." *Routt County (CO) Courier*, February 21, 1907.

"Routt County Sheep Men Can Solve Range Problem." *Steamboat Pilot* (Steamboat Springs, CO), March 20, 1915.
Saguache (CO) Crescent, January 30, 1902.
"S. A. Taylor Loses Sheep." *Grand Valley Times* (Moab, UT), May 28, 1909.
"The Sheep Massacre." *Pueblo (CO) Chieftain* editorial reprinted in the *Grand Junction (CO) Daily Sentinel*, May 27, 1909.
"Sheep Slaughtered." *Moffat (CO) County Courier*, December 7, 1911.
"Sheep War Over, Animals to Go by Railroad." *Craig (CO) Empire*, July 13, 1921.
"Shot Four Times." *Pagosa Springs (CO) News*, September 1, 1892.
"Six Cattlemen Are Indicted by Federal Grand Jury." *Moab (UT) Times-Independent*, May 3, 1923.
"Taylors Incorporate Big Stock Company." *Grand Valley Times* (Moab, UT), November 13, 1914.
"Taylor Tells the Story of Attack on His Sheep." *Grand Junction (CO) Daily Sentinel*, May 24, 1909.
"Use Guns to Force Sheepmen off Range." *Grand Valley Times* (Moab, UT), June 19, 1914.
"Want to Put in Sheep." *Routt County (CO) Courier*, January 31, 1907.

Newspapers, 1931 to 1980

Baker, Fred, "Wool Fights Back." *Denver Post Empire Magazine*, March 24, 1964.
Beeler, Sylvia. "County Profile: Isadore Bolton; The West's Outstanding Stockman." *Hayden (CO) Valley*, February 21, 1974.
"County Stockmen Meet with Board." *Moab (UT) Times-Independent*, April 15, 1937.
Curtis, Olga. "The Best-Known Sheepman in Rio Blanco County." *Denver Post Empire Magazine*, September 25, 1977.
———. "Farrington R. Carpenter: The Success Story of a 'Failure.'" *Denver Post Empire Magazine*, April 11, 1965.
———. "'Yarnin' Champ of Yampa Valley." *Denver Post Empire Magazine*, April 11, 1965.
Edson, Peter. "McCarran Act Backfires on Its Sheepish Author." *Times-News* (Twin Falls, ID), March 13, 1951.
Harvey, W. R. "Winder Wonderland." *Denver Post*, July 15, 1952.
Leonard, Peg Layton. "Sheep Wagons Created in Rawlins." *Star-Tribune* (Casper, WY), March 25, 1979.
Marranzino, Pasquale. "Tenders of the Sheep." *Rocky Mountain News* (Denver, CO), August 19, 1960.
Pepis, Betty. "New Ideas and Inventions." *New York Times Magazine*, April 23, 1950.
Spring, Agnes Wright. "Sheep Wagon Home on Wheels Originated in Wyoming." *Wyoming Stockman-Farmer* 46, no. 12 (December 1940).
Wieck, Paul R. "Opportunity Loans Help the 'Forgotten.'" *Albuquerque Journal*, February 25, 1966.
Wilkinson, Bruce. "Lopez Shears Slim Profit from Sheep." *Denver Post*, March 7, 1976.

Contemporary Newspapers

Alderman, Jesse Harlan. "Arborglyphs Provide a Window into the Life of Immigrant Sheepherders." *Aspen (CO) Daily News*, July 31, 2006.

Baker, Steve. Letter to the editor. *The Watch* (Ouray and Telluride, CO), October 14, 2015.

Baker, Tess Noel. "Canvas of Bark: Local Woman Photographs Vanishing Tree Etchings." *Pagosa Springs (CO) Sun*, June 10, 2004.

Best, Allen. "USFS Tries to Regenerate Aspen Trees." *Durango (CO) Telegraph*, January 24, 2008.

Blevins, Jason. "Aspens Hold Fading Tales of Loneliness." *Denver Post*, March 3, 2008.

———. "Fourteeners Give Colorado Significant Economic Boost." *Denver Post*, August 8, 2016.

Boiko-Weyrauch, Anna. "Earning Low Wages in Colorado's High Places." *Durango (CO) Herald*, August 1, 2015.

Bowman, Chris. "Forests of History." *Sacramento Bee*, May 3, 1994.

Brown, Donald A. "Emmett Elizondo: Sheepman Extraordinary." *Fruita (CO) Times*, August 21, 1992.

Brown, Mathew. "Environmentalists Seek to Protect Sage Grouse." *Durango (CO) Herald*, February 27, 2016.

Buchanan, Dave. "The Silent Legacy of Forgotten Men." *Durango (CO) Herald*, September 6, 1987.

Buford, Katie. "Drought, Age Harm Trees." *Durango (CO) Herald*, September 13, 2007.

Crawshaw, S. J. "The Irish Highway: The Dust of the Big Sheep Flocks in Wyoming's Big Horn Country Has Faded into History." *Denver Post Empire Magazine*, November 2, 1974.

Crumb, Michael, J. "Vail-Area Sheepdog Attack Creates Worries across West." *Vail (CO) Daily*, July 8, 2010.

Draper, Electra. "Carvings on San Juans' Aspen Speak Volumes to Researchers." *Denver Post*, November 4, 2001.

Elliott, Stephen. "Montrose Group Files Lawsuit over Sheepherder Wages." *The Watch* (Ouray and Telluride, CO), October 1, 2015.

Frosch, Dan. "Sheepherders Are Set to Get a Raise." *Wall Street Journal*, October 15, 2015.

Gilman, Sarah. "Wrangling the Rocky Mountain Bighorn." *Aspen (CO) Daily News*, January 13, 2008.

Greenfield, Esther. "Bittersweet Ending: Arborglyph Story on F. J. Moss Leads to Rest of the Tale." *Durango (CO) Herald*, January 28, 2007.

———. "Ghost in the Trees: Search for F. J. Moss Reveals a Life Carved into Aspens." *Durango (CO) Herald*, November 26, 2006.

———. "Moonlick Meadows and the Sheep Men of Blanco Canyon." *Durango (CO) Herald*, August 8, 2011.

Gulliford, Andrew. "Art in the Aspens: 40 Years of Searching for Sheepherder Carvings." *Durango (CO) Herald*, August 12, 2015.

———. "An Artist among the Aspens." *Durango (CO) Herald*, December 8, 2016.
———. "Bureau of Biological Survey: A Century Poisoning the West." Opinion/editorial column. *Grand Junction (CO) Daily Sentinel*, August 23, 2015.
———. "Eye of the Miracle: Los Ojos, New Mexico." *Durango (CO) Herald*, April 10, 2011.
———. "Privatizing Public Lands? Start with Grazing Fees." Opinion/editorial column. *Grand Junction (CO) Daily Sentinel*, March 13, 2016.
———. "Stone Messengers in Wild Country." *Durango (CO) Herald*, January 11, 2015.
———. "Too Much of a Good Thing: Wild Horses on Public Lands." Opinion/editorial column. *Grand Junction (CO) Daily Sentinel*, February 10, 2013.
———. "Who Will Speak on Behalf of the Beleaguered Sage Grouse?" Opinion/editorial column. *Grand Junction (CO) Daily Sentinel*, November 17, 2013.
———. "Wolves, Wilderness and Elk: Canis Lupus in Colorado." Opinion/editorial column, *Grand Junction (CO) Daily Sentinel*, December 20, 2015.
Hanel, Joe. "Aspen, Pine in State Dying at Record Rates." *Durango (CO) Herald*, January 15, 2008.
Hansen, Pat. "Stone Johnnies: Vanishing Landmarks of Lonely Hills." *Montana Standard* (Butte), April 4, 2008.
Harris, Bill. "The Stone Boys of Delta County." *Montrose (CO) Daily Press*, February 18, 2011.
Herman, Becky. "Audubon Meeting Features Arborglyphs Expert." *Pagosa Springs (CO) Sun*, April 10, 2014.
Kelly, Shirley. "Salute to the Sheep-Men." *Fence Post* (Greeley, CO), May 2, 2011.
King, Matt. "Acker Connects Dots between Human Trafficking and Food Supply." *Western Colorado Clarion*, Autumn 2015. [Grand Junction, CO, newsletter of the Western Colorado Congress.]
Johnson, Pamela. "Bighorn Sheep Herd Rebounding after Disease in 1990s." *Durango (CO) Herald*, October 23, 2016.
Juaristi, Vince J. "Intertwined: The Good Shepherds." *Elko (NV) Daily News*, April 9, 2016.
Lambert, Ruth. "Association Studying Hispano Arborglyphs on a Wooden Canvas." *Durango (CO) Herald*, September 28, 2014.
Lofholm, Nancy. "Annual Sheep Drive in NW Colorado Continues Tradition of Generations." *Denver Post*, November 28, 2014.
Loth, Susan. "Sheep Guardians Prove Worth." *Delta County (CO) Independent*, May 4, 1981.
May, Bill. "Puncher's Pen." *Saturday Northwest*, January 26, 1991.
McGhee, Tom. "Vail: Woman Attacked by Rancher's Dogs Receives $1 Million Settlement." *Denver Post*, February 14, 2016.
McMillan, Steve. "Area Sheep Ranchers Applaud 1080 Decision." *Grand Junction (CO) Daily Sentinel*, November 2, 1983.
———. "Coyote Killers Protect Craig Rancher's Sheep." *Grand Junction (CO) Daily Sentinel*, December 27, 1982.
Mooney, Chris. "'Massive' Tree Die-Off a Threat in Southwest." *Durango (CO) Herald*, December 24, 2015.

Mumma, John. "Agency's Politics Override Responsibility." *Durango (CO) Herald*, December 11, 2016.

Neal, Shannon Joyce. "Alone on the Range." *Grand Junction (CO) Daily Sentinel*, February 18, 2001.

O'Neill, Colleen. "Are Sheep Dogs Lost on the Range?" *Glenwood Springs (CO) Post Independent*, November 22, 2015.

Parkinson, Dan. "Big Decision on Bighorns: Closing Grazing Allotments on Weminuche Essential." *Durango (CO) Herald*, February 12, 2017.

Peel, John. "Herders' History Told on Aspen Trees." *Durango (CO) Herald*, August 6, 2001.

Pierce, Shari. "Arborglyph Photo Display Opens June 17." *Pagosa Springs (CO) Sun*, June 15, 2005.

Plank, Kristen. "Experts Cite Climate Change in Forest Decline." *Durango (CO) Herald*, February 20, 2011.

———. "Forest Officials Measure Sudden Aspen Decline." *Cortez (CO) Journal*, August 21, 2008.

Rodebaugh, Dale. "The Aspen Conundrum: Rates of Decline Increasing Experts Say at FLC Workshop." *Durango (CO) Herald*, February 21, 2008.

———. "Aspen Die-Off, Deadly Hantavirus Linked? FLC Researcher Finds Possible Connection." *Durango (CO) Herald*, January 24, 2011.

———. "The Bark Chronicles: Old Carvings in Aspen Attest to Sheep Camps." *Durango (CO) Herald*, September 20, 2013.

———. "Biologists Launch Lynx Study." *Durango (CO) Herald*, January 22, 2015.

———. "Out on a Limb: National Experts Converge on Durango for Tree Disease Conference." *Durango (CO) Herald*, July 16, 2009.

———. "See Guard Dogs on New Web Map." *Durango (CO) Herald*, September 4, 2014.

———. "Sheep-Grazing Study Suspended for New Examination." *Durango (CO) Herald*, August 2, 2014.

———. "Shrubs Winning Race: Fewer Grasses Replacing Dead Aspen, Cortez Researcher Finds." *Durango (CO) Herald*, September 13, 2012.

———. "Sudden Death: Forest Service Hopes to Rejuvenate Aspen Stands Northeast of Mancos." *Durango (CO) Herald*, January 22, 2009.

———. "Thirst Felling West's Aspen: Cortez Native's Stanford Research Pinpoints Cause of Sudden Decline." *Durango (CO) Herald*, December 29, 2011.

Romeo, Jonathan. "Grazing in the Wilderness." *Durango (CO) Herald*, February 18, 2016.

———. "Managing the Bighorns." *Durango (CO) Herald*, November 30, 2016.

Sagstetter, Elizabeth M., and William E. Sagstetter. "Respite from Loneliness." *Denver Post Empire Magazine*, February 7, 1982.

Sands, Will. "From the Editor: Black Sheep." *Durango (CO) Telegraph*, August 25, 2011.

———. "Sudden Aspen Rebound: Regional Aspen Tree Infestation Starts to Stabilize." *Durango (CO) Telegraph*, April 8, 2010.

Shinn, Mary. "Long Recovery of Bighorns." *Durango (CO) Herald*, July 7, 2015.

———. "Rep. Tipton Pushes for Clarity on Grazing on National Land." *Durango (CO) Herald*, May 5, 2015.
Silbernagel, Robert. "In 1908, an 'Army' of 21 Thousand Sheep and Their Guards Crossed Mesa County." *Grand Junction (CO) Daily Sentinel*, October 13, 2014.
Simmons, Marc. "Trail Dust: The Great Sheepherders of New Mexico." *Santa Fe New Mexican*, February 1, 2003.
Smith, Erin. "Forget Me Nots: Sheepherders Used Aspen Trees as Message Boards." *Pueblo (CO) Chieftain*, September 26, 2002.
———. "'Quakie Grafitti': Messages in the Trees." *Pueblo (CO) Chieftain*, reprinted in the *Durango (CO) Herald*, October 3, 2002.
Squires, Chase. "Aspens Dying across the West, Scientists Say." *Arizona Republic* (Phoenix), September 15, 2006.
Thompson, M. K. "Colorado's Aspen Trees Uniquely Beautiful." *Durango (CO) Herald*, November 7, 2010.
———. "West's Aspen Groves Hit Hard This Year." *Telluride (CO) Watch*, August 15, 2006.
Tuttle, Regan. "Living History: Sheepherders Etched Their Lives into Local Aspen Trees, a History That Will One Day Vanish." *Telluride (CO) Watch*, September 30, 2015.
Vader, Marja B. "Shear Agony." *Grand Junction (CO) Daily Sentinel*, May 4, 2000.
Votel, Missy. "The Trail Ahead." *Durango (CO) Telegraph*, September 3, 2015.

Journals/Magazines

Abbey, Edward. "Even the Bad Guys Wear White Hats: Cowboys, Ranchers, and the Ruin of the West." *Harper's Magazine* 272, no. 1628 (January).
Abeyta, Aaron A. "Wilderness in Four Parts, or Why We Cannot Mention My Great-Grandfather's Name." *High Country News*, November 14, 2016.
Abraham, Diane. "Bloody Grass: Western Colorado Range Wars, 1881–1934." *Journal of the Western Slope* 6, no. 2 (Spring 1991).
Anderegg, Leander D. L., William R. L. Anderegg, John Abatzoglou, Alexandra M. Hausladen, and Joseph A. Berry. "Drought Characteristics' Role in Widespread Aspen Forest Mortality across Colorado, USA." *Global Change Biology* 19, no. 5 (2013): 1526–37.
Anderegg, William R. L. "Complex Aspen Forest Carbon and Root Dynamics during Drought: A Letter." *Climatic Change* 111, no. 3–4 (2012): 983–991.
Anderegg, W. R., L. D. Anderegg, C. Sherman, and D. S. Karp. "Effects of Widespread Drought-Induced Aspen Mortality on Understory Plants." *Conservation Biology* 26, no. 6 (2012): 1–9.
Anderegg, William R. L., Joseph A. Berry, and Christopher B. Field. "Linking Definitions, Mechanisms, and Modeling of Drought-Induced Tree Death." *Trends in Plant Science* 17, no. 12 (December 2012): 685–744.
Anderegg, William R. L., Lenka Plavcová, Leander D. L. Anderegg, Uwe G. Hacke, Joseph A. Berry, and Christopher B. Field. "Drought's Legacy: Multiyear Hydraulic Deterioration Underlies Widespread Aspen Forest Die-Off and Portends Increased Future Risk." *Global Change Biology* 19, no. 4 (2013): 1188–96.

Arnold, Peg. "Wyoming's Hispanic Sheepherders." *Annals of Wyoming* 69, no. 1 (Winter 1997).
Baker, Ray Stannard. "The Great Southwest: IV. The Tragedy of the Range." *Century Magazine* 4, no. 4 (August 1902).
"Black Cowboy Charley Glass: Man of Mystery." *Real West*, December 1974.
Briske, David B., Andrew J. Ash, Justin D. Derner, and Lynn Huntsinger. "Commentary: A Critical Assessment of the Policy Endorsement for Holistic Management." *Agricultural Systems* 125 (2014).
Brower, Barbara Anne. "Sheep Grazing in National Forest Wilderness: A New Look at an Old Fight." *Mountain Research and Development* 20 (May 2000).
Carhart, Arthur. "In Defense of Our Public Domain." *The Land*, Summer 1947.
Carpenter, Farrington. "Range Stockmen Meet the Government." *Denver Westerners Monthly Roundup*, October 1967.
Carter, John, Allison Jones, Mary O'Brien, Jonathan Ratner, and George Wuerthner. "Holistic Management: Misinformation on the Science of Grazed Ecosystems." *International Journal of Biodiversity* 2014, article ID 163431.
Clarke, Frank, C. "Facts about, and Experiences with, Coyotes." *National Wool Grower* 30, no. 5 (May 1940).
Coggan, Catherine. "Grafitti in the Wild: Time's Almost Up for Arizona Tree Carvings." *Preservation* 51, no. 3 (May/June 1999): 19.
DeVoto, Bernard. "The Easy Chair." No. 140. *Harper's Magazine*, June 1947.
———. "Sacred Cows and Public Lands." *Harper's Magazine*, July 1948.
———. "Statesman on the Lam." *Harper's Magazine*, July 1948.
———. "Two Gun Desmond Is Back." *Harper's Magazine*, March 1951.
———. "The West against Itself." *Harper's Magazine*, January, 1947.
Ehrlich, Gretel. "A Sheepherder's Life." *High Country News*, April 18, 1980.
"Federal-Lands Ranching: A Half-Century of Decline." *High Country News*, June 13, 2016.
Garcia, Maria Teresa. "Hispanic Herders Carved Their Cultural Niche." *La herencia del norte* 5 (Spring 1995).
Goldfarb, Ben. "The Forever War." *High Country News*, January 25, 2016.
Gulliford, Andrew. "Aldo Leopold, Estella Bergere, Mia Casita and Sheepherding in New Mexico and Colorado." *Natural Resources Journal*, Summer 2017.
———. "The Missing Lynx: A Ten-Year Eco-Update on the Lynx Re-introduction to Colorado." *Inside/Outside Southwest*, August/September 2007.
———. "Reading the Trees: Colorado's Endangered Arborglyphs and Aspen Art." *Colorado Heritage*, Autumn 2007.
———. "Sheepherder Carvings on the White River Plateau." *Waving Hands Review: Literature and Art of Northwest Colorado* 9, no. 9 (2017).
———. "Sheepmen of Northwest Colorado: A Hidden History of the Wooly West." *Waving Hands Review: Literature and Art of Northwest Colorado* 8, no. 8 (2016).
Harris, Bill. "Stinking Desert Cairns Project." *Southwestern Lore: Journal of Colorado Archaeology* 79, no. 4 (Winter 2013).
Hayes, A. A. "The Shepherds of Colorado." *Harper's New Monthly Magazine* 60, no. 356 (January 1880): 193–211.

Hoffman, Daniel. "Sheep v. Sheep." *High Country News*, October 1, 2007.
Holechek, Jerry L., Hilton Gomes, Francisco Molinar, Dee Galt, and Raul Valdez. "Short Duration Grazing: The Facts in 1999." *Rangelands* 22 (February 2000).
Holliday, J. S. "The Lonely Sheepherder." *The American West: Magazine of the Western History Association* 1, no. 2 (Spring 1964).
Huang, Cho-Ying, and William R. L. Anderegg. "Large Drought-Induced Aboveground Live Biomass Losses in Southern Rocky Mountain Aspen Forests." *Global Change Biology* 18, no. 3 (2012): 1016–27.
Irland, Frederic. "In the Big Dry Country." *Scribner's Magazine* 36 (1904).
Irwin, Will. "Timber-Line Clover." *Saturday Evening Post*, November 25, 1922.
Izienicki, Jeffrey, L. "A Study of the Retolaza Boarding House and Its Role in the Life of the Basque Itinerant Sheepherder." *Journal of the Western Slope* 7, no. 1 (Winter 1992).
Johnston, Jeremy. "Preserving the Beasts of Waste and Desolation: Theodore Roosevelt and Predator Control in Yellowstone." *Yellowstone Science*, Spring 2002.
Kildare, Maurice. "Sheepherder's Home." *Relics* 1, no. 4 (Spring 1968).
Leopold, Aldo. "Erosion as a Menace to the Social and Economic Future of the Southwest." *Journal of Forestry* 44 (September 1946): 627–30.
Lopez, M. Leon. "Well-Bred Mutts." *International Harvester World*, July 1963.
Love, Clara M. "History of the Cattle Industry in the Southwest, II." *Southwestern Historical Quarterly* 20, no. 1 (July 1916).
Madson, Chris. "Trees Born of Fire and Ice." *National Wildlife* 34, no. 6 (October/November 1996).
McCole, Mike, and Scott Davidson. "Oh Hell, I Rode That Bear." *Ptarmigan Quarterly* 3, no. 1 (Spring 1979) [oral history with Leo Coca, Montrose High School].
McCraine, Kathy. "Nomadic Sheep Rancher." *Range Magazine*, Winter 2015/2016.
National Geographic Society. "Yellowstone: The Battle for the American West." *National Geographic* 229, no. 5 (May 2016).
"News in Brief." *High Country News*, October 26, 2015. hcn.org.
Nijhuis, Michelle. "The Parks of Tomorrow." *National Geographic*, December 2016.
Ortman, Scott. "What Difference Does Archaeology Make?" *El Palacio* 121, no. 2 (Summer 2016).
Rock, Luanne. "The Life of the Sheepherder . . . Then and Now." *Journal of the Western Slope* 6, no. 2 (Spring 1991).
Schreiber, Colleen. "Martin Etchart Started Out as Herder and Ended Up a Rancher." *Livestock Weekly*, September 21, 2006.
———. "Running Sheep on Federal Land Is Not for the Faint-Hearted." *Livestock Weekly*, September 18, 2014.
Seaman, Cindy. "Sheep Dogs—For Greater Efficiency and Profit." *National Wool Grower*, May 1978.
"The Sheepherder." *Saturday Evening Post*, September 13, 1924.
Simmons, R. Laurie, and Marilyn A. Martorano. "Guns, Fire and Sheep: History and Archaeology of the Trujillo Homesteads in the San Luis Valley, Colorado." *Southwestern Lore* 73, no. 3 (Fall 2007).

Smith, Honore DeBusk. "Mexican Plazas along the River of Souls." In *Southwestern Lore*, edited by J. Frank Dobie. Texas Folklore Society, no. 9, 1931. Reprint, Hatboro, PA: Folklore Association, 1965.

Sterling, Terry Greene. "Write and Wrong." *Arizona Highways*, May 2016.

Surowiecki, James. "The Financial Page—Bundynomics." *New Yorker*, January 25, 2016.

Thurman, Karen. "The Wooden Canvas: Documenting Historic Aspen Art Carvings in Southwest Colorado." *Heritage Matters* (National Park Service), November 2001, 5.

Tory, Sarah. "Sheepherders Get a Pay Raise." *High Country News*, February 22, 2016.

Velie, Lester. "They Kicked Us off Our Land. *Collier's Magazine*, July 26 and August 9, 1947.

"Voices from the Past." In *Remembrances*, vol. 9. Pagosa Springs, CO: San Juan Historical Society, n.d.

Wehausen, John D., Scott T. Kelley, and Rob R. Ramey II. "Domestic Sheep, Bighorn Sheep, and Respiratory Disease: A Review of the Experimental Evidence." *California Fish and Game* 97, no. 1 (2011): 7–24.

Weigand, Phil, and Celia Garcia de Weigand. "Trails among the Trees." *Canon Journal: Land and Peoples of the Colorado Plateau* 1, no. 1 (Spring 1995): 42–47.

Welch, Shirley. "Once Upon a Time: From Ellis Island to Wolcott, Colorado." *Vail Valley Magazine*, Summer 2015.

Wentworth, Edward N. "Sheep Wars of the Nineties in Northwest Colorado." In *The Westerners Brand Book*, vol. 2, *1946–1947*, edited by Virgil V. Peterson. Denver: The Westerners, 1947.

White, Herbert P. "The Bolten Story: The Last of Colorado's Sheep and Cattle Wars." *Denver Westerners Roundup*, January–February 1971.

White, John M. "Ranchers in the Basque Tradition." *New Mexico Magazine*, April 1963.

Wolf, Tom. "World Champion Wolfer." *Inside/Outside Southwest*, March 2009.

Worrall, James J., Suzanne B. Marchetti, L. Egeland, Roy A. Mask, Thomas Eager, and Brian Howell. "Effects and Etiology of Sudden Aspen Decline in Southwestern Colorado, USA." *Forest Ecology and Management* 260, no. 5 (2010): 638–48.

Worrall, James J., Gerald E. Rehfeldt, Andreas Hamann, Edward H. Hogg, Suzanne B. Marchetti, Michael Michaelian, and Laura K. Gray. "Recent Declines of *Populus tremuloides* in North America Linked to Climate." *Forest Ecology and Management* 299, no. 1 (2013): 35–51.

Worrell, Chris, "The Woodland Archives: Interpretive Use of Arborglyphs." *Legacy: The Magazine of the National Association for Interpretation*, July/August 2009.

Books

Abbott, Carl, Stephen J. Leonard, and Thomas J. Noel. *Colorado: A History of the Centennial State*. 5th ed. Boulder: University Press of Colorado, 2013.

Archuleta, Ruben E. *Penitente Renaissance: Manifesting Hope*. Pueblo West, CO: El Jefe, 2007.

Arrington, Leonard J. *Charlie Redd: Utah's Audacious Stockman.* Logan: Utah State University Press, 1995.
Austin, Mary. *The Flock.* 1906. Reprint, Santa Fe, NM: William Gannon, 1973.
———. *The Land of Little Rain* 1903. Reprint, New York: Penguin, 1997.
Bair, Elmer O. *Elmer Bair's Story: 1899 to 1987.* Glenwood Springs, CO: Gran Farnum Printing, 1987.
Baker, Steven G. *My Name Is Pacomio! The Life and Works of Colorado's Sheepherder and Master Artist of Nature's Canvases.* Lake City, CO: Western Reflections Press, 2016.
Ball, Larry D. *Tom Horn in Life and Legend.* Norman: University of Oklahoma Press, 2014.
Ballard, Jack. *Bighorn Sheep.* Guilford, CT: Falcon Guides, 2014.
Bankston, Wilma Crisp. *Where Eagles Winter: History and Legend of the Disappointment Country.* Cortez, CO: Mesa Verde Press, 1987.
Boucher, B. J. *Walking in Wildness: A Guide to the Weminuche Wilderness.* Durango, CO: Durango Herald and San Juan Mountains Association, 1998.
Boulton, Alice. *Silt, Colorado Homesteads, 1880–1940.* Silt, CO: Silt Historical Park, 2006.
Bright, William. *Colorado Place Names.* 3rd ed. Boulder, CO: Johnson Books, 2004.
Brown, David E., and Neil B. Carmony. *Aldo Leopold's Wilderness.* Harrison, PA: Stackpole Books, 1990.
Brown, Lorin W. *Hispano Folklore of New Mexico.* Albuquerque: University of New Mexico Press, 1978.
Brown, Margaret Duncan. *Shepherdess of Elk River Valley.* Denver: Golden Bell Press, 1967.
Brunvand, Jan Harold, ed. *American Folklore: An Encyclopedia.* New York: Garland Publishing, 1996.
Burroughs, John Rolfe. *Where the Old West Stayed Young.* New York: Bonanza Books, 1962.
Calef, Wesley. *Private Grazing and Public Lands: Studies of the Local Management of the Taylor Grazing Act.* Chicago: University of Chicago Press, 1960.
Callicott, J. Baird, and Eric T. Freyfogle, eds. *Aldo Leopold: For the Health of the Land.* Washington, DC: Island Press, 1999.
Carhart, Arthur H. *The Last Stand of the Pack.* With Stanley P. Young. New York: J. H. Sears, 1929.
———. *The Last Stand of the Pack: Critical Edition.* With Stanley P. Young. Edited by Andrew Gulliford and Tom Wolf. Boulder: University Press of Colorado, 2017.
Carpenter, David S. *Jens Nielson: Bishop of Bluff.* Provo, UT: Brigham Young University, 2011.
Carpenter, Farrington R. *Confessions of a Maverick: An Autobiography.* Denver: Colorado Historical Society, 1984.
Cayton, David W., and Caroline E. Metzler. *James G. Cayton: Pioneer Forest Ranger.* Self-published, 2009.
Center for Biological Diversity. *A Wild Love.* Self-published, 2015.
Chavez, Fray Angelico. *My Penitente Land: Reflections on Spanish New Mexico.* Santa Fe: Museum of New Mexico Press, 1993.

Childers, Leisl Carr. "The Angry West: Understanding the Sagebrush Rebellion in Nevada." In *Bridging the Distance: Common Issues of the Rural West*, edited by David B. Danbom. Salt Lake City: University of Utah Press, 2015.

Clifford, Frank. *The Backbone of the World*. New York: Broadway Books, 2002.

Collins, Michael L. *That Damned Cowboy: Theodore Roosevelt and the American West, 1883–1898*. New York: Peter Lang, 1989.

Danbom, David B. ed. *Bridging the Distance: Common Issues of the Rural West*. Salt Lake City: University of Utah Press, 2015.

deBuys, William. *Enchantment and Exploitation: The Life and Hard Times of a New Mexico Mountain Range*. Albuquerque: University of New Mexico Press, 1985.

———. *A Great Aridness*. New York: Oxford University Press, 2011.

———. *The Walk*. San Antonio: Trinity University Press, 2007.

Decker, Peter R. *"The Utes Must Go!" American Expansion and the Removal of a People*. Golden, CO: Fulcrum Publishing, 2004.

De Korne, James B. *Aspen Art in the New Mexico Highlands*. Santa Fe: Museum of New Mexico Press, 1970.

Deutsch, Sarah. *No Separate Refuge: Culture, Class and Gender on an Anglo-Hispanic Frontier in the American Southwest, 1880–1940*. New York: Oxford University Press, 1987.

Dobie, Frank J., ed. *Southwestern Lore*. Texas Folklore Society, no. 9, 1931. Reprint, Hatsboro, PA: Folklore Associates, 1965.

Donahue, Debra L. *The Western Range Revisited: Removing Livestock from Public Lands to Conserve Native Biodiversity*. Norman: University of Oklahoma Press, 1999.

Douglass, William, A., and Jon Bilbao. *Amerikanuak: Basques in the New World*. Reno: University of Nevada Press, 2005.

———. "Basque Americans." In *American Folklore: An Encyclopedia*, edited by Jan Harold Brunvand. New York: Garland Publishing, 1996.

Duncan, David, and Ken Burns. *The National Parks*. New York: Knopf, 2009.

Dunmire, William W. *New Mexico's Spanish Livestock Heritage*. Albuquerque: University of New Mexico Press, 2013.

Dyk, Walter. *Son of Old Man Hat: A Navajo Autobiography*. 1938. Reprint, Lincoln: University of Nebraska Press, 1967.

Egan, Timothy. *The Big Burn*. Boston: Houghton Mifflin, 2009.

Emmitt, Robert. *The Last War Trail: The Utes and the Settlement of Colorado*. Boulder: University Press of Colorado, 2000.

Flader, Susan L. *Thinking like a Mountain: Aldo Leopold and the Evolution of an Ecological Attitude toward Deer, Wolves, and Forests*. Madison: University of Wisconsin Press, 1994.

Forrest, Suzanne. *The Preservation of the Village: New Mexico's Hispanics and the New Deal*. Albuquerque: University of New Mexico Press, 1998.

Geary, Michael M. *Sea of Sand*. Norman: University of Oklahoma Press, 2016.

Gilfillan, Archer B. *Sheep*. Boston: Little, Brown, 1929.

Greager, Howard E. *In the Company of Cowboys*. Self-published, 1990.

Greenfield, Esther. *Reading the Trees: A Curious Hiker's Field Journal of Hidden Woodland Messages*. North Charleston, SC: CreateSpace Independent Publishing, 2015.
Gulliford, Andrew, ed. *Letters from a Weminuche Homestead, 1902*. Durango, CO: Durango Herald Small Press, 2002.
———, ed. *Outdoors in the Southwest: An Adventure Anthology*. Norman: University of Oklahoma Press, 2014.
———, ed. *Preserving Western History*. Albuquerque: University of New Mexico Press, 2005.
———. *Sacred Objects and Sacred Places: Preserving Tribal Traditions*. Boulder: University Press of Colorado, 2000.
Hage, E. Wayne. *Storm over Range Lands: Private Rights in Federal Lands*. Bellevue, WA: Free Enterprise Press, 1989.
Hallendy, Norman. *Inuksuit: Silent Messengers of the Arctic*. Seattle: University of Washington Press, 2000.
Harbour, Midge. *The Tarryall Mountains and the Puma Hills: A History*. Century One Press, 1982.
Harvey, Mark. *Wilderness Forever: Howard Zahniser and the Path to the Wilderness Act*. Seattle: University of Washington Press, 2005.
Hinton, Wayne K. *With Picks, Shovels and Hope: The CCC and Its Legacy on the Colorado Plateau*. With Elizabeth A. Green. Missoula: Mountain Press Publishing, 2008.
Houle, Marcy. *The Prairie Keepers: Secrets of the Zumwalt*. Corvallis: Oregon State University Press, 2014.
Hudak, Mike. *Western Turf Wars: The Politics of Public Lands Ranching*. Binghamton, NY: Biome Books, 2007.
Isusi, Jose Maria Busca. *Traditional Basque Cooking: History and Preparation*. Reno: University of Nevada Press, 1987.
Jackson, John Brinckerhoff. *A Sense of Place, a Sense of Time*. New Haven, CT: Yale University Press, 1994.
Jacobs, Lynn. *Waste of the West: Public Lands Ranching*. Tucson, AZ: Self-published, 1991.
Jocknick, Sidney. *Early Days on the Western Slope*. 1913. Reprint, Ouray, CO: Western Reflections Press, 1998.
Jordan, William R., III. *The Sunflower Forest: Ecological Restoration and the New Communion with Nature*. Berkeley: University of California Press, 2003.
Kouris, Diana Allen. *The Romantic and Notorious History of Brown's Park*. Greybull, WY: Wolverine Gallery, 1988.
Lathrop, Marguerite. *Don't Fence Me In*. Boulder, CO: Johnson Publishing, 1972.
Lavender, David. *One Man's West*. 1943. Reprint, Lincoln: University of Nebraska Press, 1977.
Laxalt, Robert. *The Basque Hotel*. Reno: University of Nevada Press, 1989.
———. *Sweet Promised Land*. New York: Harper and Brothers, 1957.
Leonard, Stephen J. *Trials and Triumphs: A Colorado Portrait of the Great Depression, with FSA Photographs*. Boulder: University Press of Colorado, 1993.

Leopold, Aldo. *A Sand County Almanac*. 1949. Reprint, New York: Ballantine Books, 1970.

Leopold, Estella. *Stories from the Leopold Shack*. New York: Oxford University Press, 2016.

Lewis, James G. *The Forest Service and the Greatest Good: A Centennial History*. Durham, NC: Forest History Society, 2005.

Lindauer, Ivo E. *Up the Creek: Parachute Creek's Pioneer Families and Energy Development, 1875–2015*. Parachute, CO: Double F Press, 2016.

Lorbiecki, Marybeth. *Aldo Leopold: A Fierce Green Fire*. Guilford, CT: Globe Pequot Press, 2005.

Lummis, Charles F. *The Land of Poco Tiempo*. New York: Charles Scribner's Sons, 1893.

Mallea-Olaetxe, Jose. *Shooting from the Lip: Bertsolariak Ipar Amerikan—Improvised Basque-Verse Singing*. Reno, NV: North American Basque Organization, 2003.

———. *Speaking through the Aspens: Basque Tree Carvings in California and Nevada*. Reno: University of Nevada Press, 2000.

Marshall, Muriel. *Red Hole in Time*. College Station: Texas A&M University Press, 1988.

———. *Uncompahgre: A Guide to the Uncompahgre Plateau*. Lake City, CO: Western Reflections Press, 1998.

Mathers, Michael. *Sheepherders: Men Alone*. Boston: Houghton Mifflin, 1975.

McCarthy, Michael. *Hour of Trial: The Conservation Conflict in Colorado and the West, 1891–1907*. Norman: University of Oklahoma Press, 1977.

McPherson, Robert S. *Life in a Corner: Cultural Episodes in Southeastern Utah, 1880–1950*. Norman: University of Oklahoma Press, 2015.

Meine, Curt. *Aldo Leopold: His Life and Work*. Madison: University of Wisconsin Press, 1988.

Meloy, Ellen. *Eating Stone*. New York: Pantheon Books, 2005.

Meuret, Michael, and Fred Provenza. *The Art and Science of Shepherding: Tapping the Wisdom of French Herders*. Austin, TX: Acres USA, 2014.

Miller, Mark E. *Hollow Victory: The White River Expedition of 1879 and the Battle of Milk Creek*. Boulder: University Press of Colorado, 1997.

Milligan, Mike. *Westwater Lost and Found*. Logan: Utah State University Press, 2004.

Morin, Paula. *Honest Horses: Wild Horses in the Great Basin*. Reno: University of Nevada Press, 2006.

Muir, John. *My First Summer in the Sierra*. Boston: Houghton Mifflin, 1911.

Murray, Erlene Durrant. *Lest We Forget*. Grand Junction, CO: Quahada Publishing, 1973.

Nelson, Richard. *Heart and Blood: Living with Deer in America*. New York: Alfred Knopf, 1997.

Niland, John. *A History of Sheep Raising in the Great Divide Basin of Wyoming*. Cheyenne, WY: Lagumo, 1994.

O'Neal, Bill. *Cattlemen vs. Sheepherders: Five Decades of Violence in the West*. Fort Worth, TX: Eakin Press, 2005.

Paul, Virginia. *This Was Sheep Ranching: Yesterday and Today*. Seattle: Superior Publishing, 1976.

Paulson, Deborah D., and William L. Baker. *The Nature of Southwestern Colorado: Recognizing Human Legacies and Restoring Natural Places*. Boulder: University Press of Colorado, 2006.

Petersen, David. *Among the Aspens*. Flagstaff, AZ: Northland Publishing, 1991.

———. *Ghost Grizzlies*. Boulder, CO: Johnson Books, 1998.

Petrakian, Gracie. *Land of Tall Grass*. Flanders, NJ: Self-published, 2010.

Philpott, William. *Vacationland: Tourism and Environment in the Colorado High Country*. Seattle: University of Washington Press, 2013.

Pulido, Alberto Lopez. *The Sacred World of the Penitentes*. Washington, DC: Smithsonian Institution Press, 2000.

Quintana, Frances Leon. *Pobladores: Hispanic Americans of the Ute Frontier*. 2nd ed. Notre Dame, IN: University of Notre Dame Press, 1991.

Quintano, Jen Jackson. *Blow Sand in His Soul: Bates Wilson, the Heart of Canyonlands*. Moab, UT: Friends of Arches and Canyonlands Parks, 2014.

Reading, Richard P., Brian Miller, Amy L. Masching, Rob Edward, and Michael K. Phillips, eds. *Awakening Spirits: Wolves in the Southern Rockies*. Golden, CO: Fulcrum Publishing, 2010.

Rifle Reading Club. *Rifle Shots: The Story of Rifle, Colorado*. Rifle, CO: Rifle Reading Club, 1973.

Roberts, Paul Henley, and L. F. Kneipp. *Hoof Prints on Forest Ranges: The Early Years of National Forest Range Administration*. San Antonio: Naylor, 1963.

Robinson, Michael J. *Predatory Bureaucracy: The Extermination of Wolves and the Transformation of the West*. Boulder: University Press of Colorado, 2005.

Rockwell, Wilson. *New Frontier: Saga of the North Fork*. 1938. Reprint, Lake City, CO: Western Reflections, 2011.

Roosevelt, Theodore. *Wilderness Writings*. Layton, UT: Gibbs Smith, 1986.

Rowley, William. *US Forest Service Grazing and Rangelands*. College Station: Texas A&M University Press, 1985.

Scott, Doug. *The Enduring Wilderness: Protecting Our Natural Heritage through the Wilderness Act*. Golden, CO: Fulcrum Publishing, 2004.

Shepard, Ward. *Food or Famine: The Challenge of Erosion*. New York: Macmillan, 1945.

Shoemaker, Len, and William R. Kreutzer. *Saga of a Forest Ranger: A Biography of William R. Kreutzer, Forest Ranger No. 1*. Boulder: University Press of Colorado, 1958.

Silbernagel, Robert. *Troubled Trails: The Meeker Affair and the Expulsion of Utes from Colorado*. Salt Lake City: University of Utah Press, 2011.

Simmons, Virginia McConnell. *Bayou Salado: The Story of South Park*. Boulder: University Press of Colorado, 2002.

———. *The San Luis Valley: Land of the Six-Armed Cross*. Boulder: University Press of Colorado, 1999.

Sprague, Marshall. *Colorado*. New York: W. W. Norton, 1976.

———. *Massacre: The Tragedy at White River*. Lincoln: University of Nebraska Press, 1980.

Steinel, Alvin T. *History of Colorado Agriculture, 1858–1926*. Fort Collins: Colorado State Board of Agriculture, 1926.

Stewart, Elinore Pruitt. *Letters of a Woman Homesteader*. Boston: Houghton Mifflin, 1914.

Stillman, Deanne. *Mustang: The Saga of the Wild Horse in the American West*. Boston: Houghton Mifflin, 2009.

Towne, Charles Wayland, and Edward Norris Wentworth. *Shepherd's Empire*. Norman: University of Oklahoma Press, 1945.

Twain, Mark. *Roughing It*. New York: Ballantine Books, 1962.

Udall, Stewart. *The Quiet Crisis*. New York: Avon, 1963.

Vandenbusche, Duane, and Duane A. Smith. *A Land Alone: Colorado's Western Slope*. Boulder, CO: Pruett Publishing, 1981.

Voigt, William, Jr. *Public Grazing Lands: Use and Misuse by Industry and Government*. Rutgers, NJ: Rutgers University Press, 1976.

Weidel, Nancy. *Sheepwagon: Home on the Range*. Glendo, WY: High Plains Press, 2001.

Weigle, Marta. *Brothers of Light, Brothers of Blood: The Penitentes of the Southwest*. Santa Fe, NM: Ancient City Press, 1976.

Weisiger, Marsha. *Dreaming of Sheep in Navajo Country*. Seattle: University of Washington Press, 2009.

Wentworth, Edward Norris. *America's Sheep Trails*. Ames: Iowa State College Press, 1948.

Wetherill, Louisa Wade, and Harvey Leake, comps. *Wolfkiller: Lessons from a Nineteenth-Century Navajo Shepherd*. Layton, UT: Gibbs Smith, 2007.

White, Courtney. *Grass, Soil, Hope: A Journey through Carbon Country*. White River Junction, VT: Chelsea Green Publishing, 2014.

White, F. Amadeo. *La Garita: Growing Up in and about the San Luis Valley*. Denver: Self-published, 2007.

White River Museum, ed. *This Is What I Remember*. Vol. 2. Meeker, CO: Rio Blanco County Historical Society, 1978.

Wick, Pascal. *Beartooth: Diary of a Nomadic Herder*. Buckingham, UK: Aaranya, 2014.

Wickenden, Dorothy. *Nothing Daunted: The Unexpected Education of Two Society Girls in the West*. New York: Scribner, 2011.

Williams, David B. *Cairns: Messengers in Stone*. Seattle: Mountaineers Books, 2012.

Wolf, Tom. *Arthur Carhart: Wilderness Prophet*. Boulder: University Press of Colorado, 2008.

———. *Colorado's Sangre de Cristo Mountains*. Boulder: University Press of Colorado, 1995.

Wright, John B. *Rocky Mountain Divide: Selling and Saving the West*. Austin: University of Texas Press, 1993.

Wuerthner, George, and Mollie Matteson, eds. *Welfare Ranching: The Subsidized Destruction of the American West*. Washington, DC: Island Press, 2002.

Young, Helen Hawxhurst, ed. *The Skin and Bones of Plateau Valley History*. Grand Junction, CO: Wilson and Young Printers, 1976.

Books, Fiction

Borland, Hall. *When the Legends Die*. New York: Bantam, 1963.
Doig, Ivan. *English Creek*. New York: Penguin Books, 1984.
Krumgold, Joseph. . . . *And Now Miguel*. New York: HarperCollins, 1953.
Maclean, Norman. *A River Runs through It and Other Stories*. Chicago: University of Chicago Press, 1976.
Rhodes, Eugene Manlove. *Beyond the Desert*. 1934. Reprint, Lincoln: University of Nebraska Press, 1967.

Media

Green Fire: Aldo Leopold and a Land Ethic for Our Time. Produced by the Aldo Leopold Foundation, US Forest Service, Humans and Nature, 2011. DVD, 73 minutes.
Lords of Nature: Life in a Land of Great Predators. Green Fire Productions, 2009. DVD, 60 minutes.
Sweetgrass. Cinema Guild, 2010. DVD, 100 minutes.
Wild by Law: Aldo Leopold, Bob Marshall, Howard Zahniser and the Redefinition of America Progress. Film documentary by Lawrence Hott and Diane Garey, Florentine Films, 1991.

Index

NOTE: Page numbers in *italic* type indicate photographs, or illustrations; those in **bold** type indicate maps.

Abbey, Edward, 245–46
Abeyta, Aaron A., 289
Abraham, Diane, 46
accidents and injuries (non-antagonistic), 18, 154, 172, 198, 203, 283. *See also* herbology
Acker, Tom, 274
Agriculture Appropriations Act, 84
Albuquerque Journal, 153
Aldasoro family, 302–4
alpine ecosystem, overview, 320–21
alpine willow, 32
American Flats, 176
America's Sheep Trails (Wentworth), 48
Animal Damage Control Act (1931), 179–80
animal unit months (AUMs), 246, 247, 309
Antillon, Tomás, 285–86
Aragon, Emiliano, 153
Aragon, Luis, 119
arborglyphs, definition, 18. *See also* carvings (arborglyphs); sheepscapes (site studies)
Arches National Monument, 220
Arrington, Leonard J., 172, 175
"aspen porn," 13, 284, 293
aspen trees, *21*, *201*; choice of for carving, 14; conservation techniques, 186; disease and decline of, 7, 70; physiology and life cycle, 154, 268–70. *See also* carvings (arborglyphs)
Aspinall, Wayne, 214–15
associations: cattlemen's, 50, 57, 58, 60, 84–85; sheepmen's, 100, 104
attacks on sheep/sheepmen, *50*; barring Utah influx into Colorado, 59, 61, 119, 125, 335*n* 60; barring Wyoming influx into Colorado, 60–61, 62, 93–95; Battle of Yellow Jacket Pass, 128–29; Dickey brothers incident, 43–45; Escalante Sheep War, 101–3; and forest reserve laws, 86; Grand Junction incident, 95–96; Hayden, Colorado, 138; Moffat County massacre, 100; murders, 51, 59, 62, 85–86, 94–95, 125, 131–32; "Oh-Be-Joyful Raid," 103–5; overviews, 50–52; Peach Day Massacre, 54–59, *58*; Plateau Valley incident, 54; Spring Creek sheep raid, 93–95
Aubert family, 116, 119, 120, 134, 238, 302
Austin, Mary, 2, 49, 64, 276–77
Awakening Spirits (Reading, ed.), 317
Aztec symbols, 235

Backbone of the World, The (Clifford), 242
Bair family, 290, 313
Baker, Ray Stannard, 143–44
Baker, William L., 238, 239
Ballard, Jack, 254
barbed wire, 89–90

bark beetles, 270–71
Barnes, Will C., 47, 65, 80, 144
Basque sheepherders: Aldasoro family profile, 302–4; cairns of, 18, 260; carvings of, *117*, 120; character profiles, 72–73, 130–31, 134–37; Etchart family profiles, 103, 248–50, 274, 318; hotels run by, 122–23, 135–36, 303; influx of, early 1900s, 78, 106, 113; integration into American life, 129–30, 163; murder of sheepherder, 131–33; post-WWII influx, 120, 212–13; as tramp herders, 143, 145–46
Bassett, Anne, 297–98
Battle of Yellow Jacket Pass, 128–29
bears, 18, 217, 239–40
Beartooth (Wick), 288, 319
Beaver Park, 187
beavers, 153
beef and cattle prices, 47, 56, 85, 125, 129, 333*n* 22
behavior and anatomy of sheep: grazing habits, 25, 47, 48, 51–52, 64, 144, 189, 276–77; water requirements, 28, 96
Bergon, Peggy, 34, *36*, 37, 39
Big Flats area, 183, 220–21
bighorn sheep, 32, 90–91, 253–58
big ranchers *vs.* small stockmen, 83, 90, 98
bison, 229, 231
Black Hand Society, 195
blazes (trail markings), 17. *See also* markers
bobcats, 109, *179*
Bolten, Isadore "Izzie," 137–38
Bond, Ann, 263–64
Bond family operations, 31, *166*
Borland, Hal, 269–70, 287–88
breeding sheep (crossbreeding), 25–26, 47, 61, 228
bridges, sheep, 20, 101–2, 116, 118
Brock, J. Elmer, 208–9
Brooks, Bryant B., 94
Broscheid, Bob, 255
Brothers of Light, Brothers of Blood (Weigle), 156
Brown, Bonnie, 245
Brown, J. Paul, 310
Brown, Margaret Duncan, 106–7

Bruner, Travis, 247
Buckles Lake area, 40–42
Bureau of Biological Survey, 109, 179, 314
Bureau of Land Management: and contemporary grazing fees, 247; ecosystem management issues, 237, 249, 307–8; endangered species efforts, 306–7; formation of, 206; recreational land use, acceptance of, 222
burros, 237, 307–8
Burroughs, John Rolfe, 47, 51, 60

cairns (markers), 18, 19, 170, 260–66, 285–86
Cairns (Williams), 261
Calef, Wesley, 207, 208
California, sheep taken to, 26–29
calvarios (crosses), 20. *See also* Penitentes
Campbell, Randy, 250
campsites, 53, *273*, *287*; characterizations of, 19, 107, 153, 167–68, 173, 175–77, 233, 235–37, 288; modernized conditions, 305, 311, *312*, 321; routines, 287–88; sheep wagons, 6, *49*, *53*, 311–13; tenders, 2, 72, 236, 283; tourist "camps," *312*, 313
Canyonlands National Park, 219–20, 221–22
carbon sequestration, 276
Carhart, Arthur, 78, 142, 210
Carpenter, David S., 61, 172
Carpenter, Farrington "Ferry," 124–25, 126–29, 145–48
carrying capacity of range, 124, 210, 308, 317. *See also* stocking rates
Carson, Kit, 28
Carson National Forest, 91–92, 290
carvings (arborglyphs): arborglyphs, definition, 18; as communication/messages, 14, 188, 199–200; and loss of aspen trees, 7, 13–14, 37, 70, 291; overviews, 2, 4–5, 187–88, 200, 291–96; technique and skill, 73, 190, 279–80, 284, 291. *See also* sheepscapes (site studies); symbols/themes in sheepscapes
Cassidy, Butch, 359*n* 1

Cayton, James G. "Jim," 106, 123
Caywood, "Big Bill," 109, 113
Center Dispatch (Saguache), 44
Century Magazine, 143
Chacon, Pacomio, *279*
"chaining," 211
Chavez, Angelico, 156
Cheyenne Leader, 59–60
Childers, Leslie Carr, 222, 309
churros (Spanish sheep), 25–26, 276
Civilian Conservation Corps (CCC), 177–79, 187
Clarke, Frank C., 180
Clifford, Frank, 242
cliffs, running livestock over. *See* "rim-rocking"
climate change, impact of, 269–70, 276–77
clubbing of sheep. *See* attacks on sheep/sheepmen
Coca, Leo, 169–70
Collier, John "Sheep Killer," 171
Colorado Parks and Wildlife (CPW): bighorn sheep recovery and protection, 255, 257; Lone Mesa State Park, 152–55; lynx restoration program, 250–51; Ranching for Wildlife program, 314; wolf management plan, 315–19
Colorado River Valley, 12, 27, 46–47, 78, 116
Colton, Dan, 146
commensurability of land, 145, 175, 209. *See also* land control strategies
Compound 1080, 238, 247
condensed milk, 19, 167, *322*
Confessions of a Maverick (Carpenter), 124–25
conservation easements, 313–14
conservation movement, 32, 52, 70, 78–79, 237. *See also* ecological balance; environmentalism; Leopold, Aldo; restoration programs
contemporary challenges and impacts, 5, 7
Coronado, Juan Francisco de, 23–24
cougars. *See* mountain lions
counting corrals, 18, 40–42, 90
"coyote-getter," 247

coyotes, 111, 179–80, 238, 247, 285
Craig, Colorado, 83, 98–100, 215–16, 314, 323
Craig Courier, 61, 125
Cranshaw, S. J., 285
crossbreeding sheep, 25–26, 47, 61, 228
crosses. *See under* symbols/themes in sheepscapes
"crutching," 288
Cultural Resource Inventory of the Lone Cone Aspen Treatment (Hammer), 200
Curtis, Olga, 133

dams, 141, 213
Darnell, John, 125
Davis, Jerry, 226
"deadlines," 84, 87
debt servitude, 25, 32, 41, 165
deBuys, William, 182–83, 204–5
Delta Independent, 102
dendroglyphs. *See* carvings (arborglyphs)
Denver and Rio Grande Railroad, 37, 57, 92, *171*, 182, *208*, *218*, 227, 301
Denver News, 87
Denver Post, 133, 209
Denver Republican, 96, 118
Department of Agriculture, US, 65, 144, 247
desert bighorn sheep, 254. *See also* bighorn sheep
Desert Land Act (1877), 89
Deutsch, Sarah, 163–64, 164–65, 166, 172
Dickey brothers, 44
Dickinson, T. Wright, 323
diet in herder/ranger camps, 19, 110, 167–68, 177, 236
Dinosaur National Monument, 213
DiSalvo, Nina, 274
diseases/afflictions: plant, 7, 70, 270–71, 296; sheep, 253, 254–58. *See also* illness and medicine
Division of Wildlife, Colorado (DOW), 250, 251. *See also* Colorado Parks and Wildlife (CPW)
dogs, herders,' 1, 72–73, *241*. *See also* guardian dogs, aggression incidents
Donahue, Debra L., 246
Don't Fence Me In (Lathrop, M.), 102, 181, 220–21, **222**

Douglas Budget (Wyoming), 285
Douglass, William A., 123, 143
driveways, stock: definition, 17; maintenance and management of, 71, 123–24; objectives of, 105; profiles of, 12–13, 68–75, 119, 127–29, 136–38, 189, 291, 294; signage for, 17, 71, 123, 294
drought, 145, 170–71, 172, 205, 269
DuBois, Coert, 63–64
Dunmire, William W., 31
Durango, Colorado, 39, 51, 55–56, 263, 310
Durango Telegraph, 244
Dust Bowl, 145
dynamite in range wars, 52, 59

eagles, 109–10, 238
Eating Stone (Meloy), 255
ecological balance: concept of, 141–43, 204, 210–11, 267–68, 307, 314; holistic range management, 276–77; national park efforts, 217–19. *See also* environmentalism; restoration programs
ecological impacts: erosion and overgrazing, 49, 141–42, 144; extinctions, 32; gullies, 141–42, 178, 205–6; invasive plants, 25, 32, 51, 112–13, 178, 211; predator extermination, 79–80, 109–10, 207, 237–38; sheep, destructive power of, 6, 25, 48, 239
economic issues: beef and cattle prices, 47, 56, 85, 125, 129, 333*n* 22; Great Depression, impact of, 161–63, 166, 176–77, 177–79; profitability of sheep vs. cattle, 51, *53*, 61, 97–101, 182, 189, 277–79; recreation, profit potential, 220–22; sheep industry and local economies, 216, 226–27, 228; wages of sheepherders, 25, 129, 130, 173, 198, 271, 273–74, 289, 321. *See also* grazing fees; winter storms and herd losses
Edson, Peter, 212
educational programs, 313–14
Edwards, Jack, 60
Egan, Timothy, 337*n* 8
ejidos (common lands), 3, 165
Ekker, Art, 219

Elder, Scott, 152, 154
Elizondo, Emmett, 136
elk, 79, 90, 112, 314, 317
Elkhorn Stock Driveway, 68–75
Enchantress of the Forest (Lukow, painting), *316*
endangered species, advocacy of, 219, 238–40, 253, 305–7
English sheepmen/herders, 299
environmentalism, 141, 213, 305–7. *See also* conservation movement
Environmental Protection Agency (EPA), 237
erosion and overgrazing, 49, 141–42, 144. *See also* gullies
erotica in carvings, 13, 21, 284, 293. *See also* nude (women) carvings/art
Escalante Sheep War, 101–3
Etchart, Ernie, 249, 274, 277, 318
Etchart, Martin, 103, 248–50

farmers, 30. *See also* Homestead Act (1862)
fences: for conservations efforts, 178; on range, 29, 32, 89–90, 116, 128
firearms/guns, 50–51
fires: Forest Service efforts against, 337*n* 8; intentional by herders, 64; intentional in range wars, 44–45, 95; and loss of arborglyphs, 37; mismanagement of, 270, 271, 319
fish, 20, 70, 72
Fish and Wildlife Service, US, 179
Flat Tops Wilderness, 12, 263
Flock, The (Austin), 276–77
food, herders.' *See* diet in herder/ranger camps
Forest, Melvin, 153
Forest Homestead Act (1906), 89
Forest Reserve Act (1891), 52–54, 83–84
Forest Service, US, overviews, 65, 77–79, 113. *See also* Bureau of Biological Survey; grazing fees; grazing rights; national forest program; rangers, forest
Forest Service and the Greatest Good, The (Lewis), 82
Forrest, Suzanne, 165
Fraternidad Piadosa de Nuestro Padre

Jesus Nazareno (The Pious Fraternity of Our Father Jesus the Nazarene), 155–60
Fruita Telegram, 96
Fulton Amendment, Forest Reserve Act, 83–84

Gallegos, Tony, 153–54
Garcia, Kelly, 228
Gardner, Jack, *170, 179*
Ghost Grizzlies (Petersen), 217, 239
Gila, National Forest, 142
Gilbert, Carl, 102
Glade Park, 116–20
Glass, Charlie, 131–33, 138–39
global warming, 270, 276
"Goat Creek Incident," 188
gold rushes, 6, 26, 28
Gomez family, 171
Goodnight, Veryl, 241
Goslin, Walt T., 118
Grand Junction area: agriculture in, 30; attacks on sheepmen in, 57–59, 95–97, 131–32; Basque presence in, 120, 123, 134–37; Museum of Western Colorado, 116; sheepmen's solidarity in, 78, 80, 86; stockmens's meeting in, 147
Grand Junction Daily Sentinel, 58, 59, 86, 87, 96
Grand Junction News, 59
Grand Mesa Uncompahgre Gunnison (GMUG) National Forests, 299
Grand Valley Times, 97, 118
Grass, Soil, Hope (White), 276
grasses. *See* overgrazing; plants; sustainable grazing practices
grazing fees, 78, 81–82, 246–47. *See also* stocking rates
Grazing Office (Taylor Grazing Act), 147–48, 206
grazing rights: environmental restrictions on, 249, 254, 258; grazing districts, 145, 146–48, 178; under partido system, 31–32; perpetual lease rights, 349*n* 17; sheep permits, Forest Service, 99, 104, 207; Taylor Grazing Act (1934), 46, 124, 145–48. *See also* grazing fees; public lands
Greager, Howard E., 111

"Great Barbecue, The," 52
Great Depression, impact of, 161–63, 166, 176–77, 177–79
Great Outdoors Colorado, 152, 313
Great Pyrenees dogs, 72–73
Greek sheepmen/herders, 4, 6; influx of, 106; integration into American life, 163; profiles, 130, 133–34, 298; and Vail, development of, 300–301
Greenfield, Esther, 39
grizzly bears, 217, 239–40
Groundhog Stock Driveway, 291, 294
guardian dogs, aggression incidents, 241–45, 318, 352–53*n* 22
gullies, 141–42, 178, 205–6. *See also* erosion and overgrazing
Gulliford, David Oliver, 205
Gunnison Forest Reserve, 103–4
Gunnison National Forest, 105
Gunnison National Park, 314
Gunnison River Valley, 27, 101–3, 262–63
Gunnison sage grouse, 305–7

H-2A visas, 272, 274, 321
Haglund, Brent, 323
Halandras family, 14, *15*, 130, 131, 133–34, 171, 291
Haley, Ora, 47, 297–98
Hallendy, Norman, 260
Hammer, Polly, 186, 187, 188–89, 194, 199–200
Hansmire, Julie, 250
Harper's Magazine, 245–46
harri mutilak "stone boys," 18, 170, 260
Harris, Bill, *262*, 263
Harris, G. A., 133
Hatch, Julian, 211–12
Hawaii, 335*n* 66
herbology, 169, 268. *See also* illness and medicine
Hickenlooper, John, 306
high altitude grazing, 78
High Country News, 247
hiking, 241–42, 243–45. *See also* recreation and tourism
Hispanic herders: and Depression era racism, 161–63; loyalty and dedication of, 172–74, 175; migrant lifestyle and home ties, 163–66; overviews,

3, 25–27, 28–32; Penitentes faith, 155–60; profiles of, 166–69
Hitchcock, Ethan, 61
Homestead Act (1862), 87–89
homesteaders: forested acreage, 338*n* 32; and Forest Reserve Act, 53; "proving up" claims, 88, 89, 119, 130; Stock-Raising Homestead Act (1916), 78, 106, 113, 122, 129–30; success rate of, 338*n* 30
Hoover administration, 113, 144–45
Horn, Tom, 62–63
horses: carvings/art of, 74, *230, 272*; and sagebrush migration, 25; and sheepherders, 198; wild, 237, 307–8
Horsethief Trail, 264–65, *266*
hospitality and goodwill, 72, 131, 173–74, 219–20
hotels, Basque-run, 122–23, 135–36, 303
Hour of Trial (McCarthy), 81
Howe, William, 55–56
humorous carvings, 14
Hunt, Leigh Ann, 186, 188, 189–90, 194, 197, 199
hunting, 79, 154, 206, 254, 257, 314. See also under predators

Ickes, Harold, 145
Iliff, John W., 29
illness and medicine, 93, 169, *292*. See also accidents and injuries; herbology
immigrant sheepherders, highlights, 106, 120, 129–30, 212–13. See also Basque sheepherders; Greek sheepmen/herders; Peruvian sheepherders
Indians, American: aspen as medicine, 268; cairns by, 261–62, 263, 265, 355*n* 1; forced removal of, 46; symbols in arborglyphs, 190, *191, 234, 235*; tolls charged by, 23, 28. See also Navajo Indians; Ute Indians
interstate highway system, 206, 300
Inuksuit (Hallendy), 260
inuksuk (Inuit cairn), 260, 265
Irish sheepmen, 31, 285
Irvine, Van, 237–38
Irwin, Will, 227–28
itinerant sheepmen. See "tramp" sheepmen

Izienicki, Jeffrey, 135

Jacobs, Lynn, 246–47
Jacques family, 278
Jacquez, Harry, 9
James Mark Jones State Wildlife Area, 231
Jefferson, Thomas, 87
Jesui, Felix, 131–32
Jewish sheepmen, 137–38, 284
Jolly brothers, 105–6
Jordan, William R. III, 211
Jouflas family, *4*, 300–301, 313
Journal of the Western Slope (Izienicki), 135
Juaristi, Vince J., 212–13
junipers, 276

Khung, Kevin, 34
Kilroy symbols, 193–94
Koerner, Jane, 5
Kourlis, Tom, 298
Krall, Angie, 20–21
Kreutzer, William "Bill," 80, 84, 103–5

Lambert, Ruth, 39
lambing pens, 18
lambing process, 167
lamb/mutton: early west demand for, 6, 23–24, 28, 99; markets for, post-WWII, 205–6, 274–75, 301; profit margin and recreation incursion, 242
land awareness, 271–72, 283–84, 287–88, 305
land control strategies: and commensurability of land, 145, 175, 209; early homesteading tactic, 278, 303–4; failed mortgages, purchase of, 51, 118, 173; forested acreage in homesteading, 338*n* 32; homesteading fraud, 89, 119; mining claims, 176–77; railroad land, 27, 48, 60–61; Stock-Raising Homestead Act (1916), 78, 106, 113, 122, 129–30
language barriers, *71*, 166, 168, 284
La Plata Mountains, *234*
larkspur, 40, 169, 189, 238
Lathrop, Howard, 101–3, 180–82, 203, 220, 248

Lathrop, Marguerite, 102, 181, 220–21, **222**
Lavender, David, 50, 111, 174–75, 182, 236
Lawrence, Roger and Joyce, 152
Laxalt, Robert, 134
LeFors, Joe, 62, 95
legal actions in range conflicts, 55–56, 58, 82, 95, 125, 132–33, 138–39
Legro, Renee, 244–45
Leonard, Stephen J., 5
Leopold, Aldo: on arborglyphs, 211; background and career profile, 3, 91–93, 140–44, 204, 207; dams, fight against, 213; on ecological balance, 210–11, 267, 307, 314; on land awareness, 271–72; on predator control, 237, 315
Leopold, A. Starker, 217–19
Lewis, James G., 82
Light, Fred M., 81–82
lightning, 265, *266*, 283, 288
Lizard Head Wilderness, 187
Lone Cone Ranger Station, 186
loneliness and isolation of herders, 2, 107, 168, 282–83
Lone Mesa State Park, 152–55
Lougheed, Robert, *85*
Love, Clara M., 333*n* 25
Lowe, Ben, 80, 103
Lowell, John, 54
Lukow, Becky Hoyle, *316*
Lummis, Charles, 25
Luna family, 27
Luna-Ortega family, 3, 91
lynx, reintroduction of, 250–52

Mack, C. B., 168
Maestas, Joe, *287*
La Mano Negra (Black Hand Society), 195
Manzanares, Antonio, 40–42, 276, 289
markers: cairns, 18, 19, 170, 260–66, 285–86; directional carvings, 73; stock driveway signage, 17, 71, 123, 294
Marshall, Muriel, 101
Martinez, Joe R., 291–95
Mattern, Joe and family, 68–70, 72–73, 74
Matteson, Mollie, 247

Maxwell Land Grant, 31
McCarran, Pat, 209, 212
McCarthy, Michael, 81
McCarty, Sylvester, 59
McKinley Tariff (1890), 61
Medicine Bow National Forest, 68–75
Meeker, Nathan, 46
Meine, Curt, 3
Meloy, Ellen, 255
memorials/monuments, 18–19, 283, 285–86. *See also* cairns (markers)
Mexicans. *See* Hispanic herders
mineral rights, 340*n* 86
mining industry, 122, 130, 176–77, 303–4
Moab, Utah, 219
Moab Times-Independent, 132, 136–37, 139
modernization: and Hispanic migrant herders, 163–64; homeowners association rules, 310–11; and land awareness, 271–72, 283–84; post WWII consumerism, 205–6, 305; Progressive Era, 79; and sheep camps, 305, 311, *312*, 321
Moffat County Courier, 100
Montaño family, 155–60
Monte Vista Journal, 44
Montoya, Davin and family, 277–79
Montoya, Juan and family, 54–56, 290
Montrose, Colorado, 46, 86, 102–3, 123, *147*
monuments/memorials, 18–19, 283, 285–86. *See also* cairns (markers)
Moore, Catherine, 116, 118
Mormon sheepmen/herders, 52, 61, 124, 139, 172–77, 216, 290, 313
Moss, Frank, 220
mountain lions, 63, 109, 111, 254, 285
Muir, John, 6, 214, 255
Multiple Use Sustained Yield Act, 214
Mumma, John, 251–2525
murders of sheepmen, 51, 59, 62, 85–86, 94–95, 125, 131–32. *See also* attacks on sheep/sheepmen
museum, New Castle, 108–9
Museum of Western Colorado, 116
Muslims, 274, 275
mutton. *See* lamb/mutton
My Penitente Land (Chavez), 156

National Environmental Policy Act (NEPA), 237
national forest program, 63, 77, 83–84
National Wool Grower, 180
Native Americans. *See* Indians, American
Nature of Southwestern Colorado, The (Paulson and Baker, W.), 238, 239
Navajo Indians: carvings and symbology, 9, 190, *191*; drought, 170–71; herders, 289; sheep, importance of, 24; stones and memory, 262; sweat lodges, 19
Nelson, E. W., 111
Nelson, Garth, 249
Nepalese sheepherders, 279
New Mexico's Spanish Livestock Heritage (Dunmire), 31
New Yorker, 248
New York Sun, 87
Nez Perce Indians, 261
Northwest Ordinance (1787), 87
No Separate Refuge (Deutsch), 163–64
nude (women) carvings/art, 187, 192, *196*, *236*, 284, *296*. *See also* erotica in carvings
numbers of sheep: contemporary decline, 242; modern decline of, 277, 284–85, 320

Old West, legacy and romance of, 245–50
Oñate, Juan de, 24
One Man's West (Lavender), 174–75, 236
Open Range Encounter (Lougheed, painting), *85*
Ortman, Scott, 294
Orwick, Peter, 245
Otero family, 27
Ottoson, Hans, 139
overgrazing, 31, 32, 112–13. *See also* behavior and anatomy of sheep; erosion and overgrazing

Pacific Railroad Grant, 87
Pagosa Springs, Colorado, 34, 37, 54–56, 204, 277
Pagosa Springs News, 55
paint, sheep-marking, 229–32
Parks and Wildlife. *See* Colorado Parks and Wildlife (CPW)
partido system, 25, 31, 32, 41, 165

pastores (herders), 3, 25
Paulson, Deborah D., 238, 239
Peach Day Massacre, 54–59, *58*
Penitentes, 20, 155–60
perpetual lease rights, 349n 17
Peruvian sheepherders, 71, 249, 250, 271–72
Petersen, David, 217, 239, 240
Philpott, William, 300, 305
Pinchot, Gifford and family: appointed Forest Service chief, 65, 77; on economic importance of sheep, 80; on grazing fees, 81; and greatest good philosophy, 79; *Use Book*, 80, 83; Yale School of Forestry endowment, 140
pine peels, 20
pine trees, threats to, 270–71, 276
Piñon Mesa, 116–20
plants: herbology, 169; invasive, 25, 32, 51, 112–13, 178, 211; poisonous, 28, 40, 104, 169, 189, 238; recovery and regrowth, 240; re-seeding programs, 178, 204. *See also* overgrazing
Plateau Valley, 54, 58–59
pneumonia in sheep, 254–58
poetry/philosophy in carvings, 74–75
poisoning: of predators, 79, 108, 109–10, 111, 237–38, 247; of sheep, 52, 139
poisonous plants, 28, 40, 104, 169, 189, 238
Pollan, Michael, 276
Potter, Alfred, 81
Power, Thomas, 248
Predator and Rodent Control (US Fish and Wildlife), 179–80
predators: of cattle *vs.* sheep, 278; contemporary conditions, 284–85; and ecological balance, 207, 237–38; extermination by government, 79–80, 108–13, 179–80, 217, 247–48; and guard dogs, 241–42, 245, 318–19; reintroduction programs, 250–52, 314–19
Preservation of the Village (Forrest), 165
Price, James E., 125
Private Grazing and Public Lands (Calef), 207
privatization arguments (public lands), 207–10

Progressive Era developments, 78–79
"proving up" claims, 88, 89, 119, 130
Public Grazing Land (Voigt), 149, 204
Public Land Commission, 63
public land ranching tradition and heritage, 245–50, 320, 321
public lands: early conflicts, 30–31; land control strategies, 48; privatization arguments, 207–10; regulation of grazing on, 57, 61; reservation of, 52–54, 63, 90–91; state control arguments, 113, 144–45, 208–9. *See also* Forest Service, US; homesteaders
Pueblo Chieftain, 96
Pueblo culture. *See* Navajo Indians

Quick, Bill, 193
Quintana, Larry, 154
Quintano, Jen Jackson, 219

rabbits and lynx reintroduction, 251
racism, 49–50, 52, 161–63, 197
Raftopoulos, Steve, 298
railroads: and consumerism, 31; and land control strategies, 48, 60–61; land grants from, 87; proximity to, 209; rights-of-way, 27; and sheep transport, 37, 102, 126, 227. *See also* Denver and Rio Grande Railroad
rangeland management, contemporary theory, 276–77, 320–21, 323
rangers, forest, 77–78, 80, 82–83, 108, 123–24
Reading, Richard P., 317
Reading the Trees (Greenfield), 39
real estate development, contemporary, 300–301, 304–5
recreation and tourism: growth and impact of, 5, 7, 320; heritage tourism, 243, 310, 324; post-WWII boom, 206, 300; sheepdog aggression incidents, 241–45; *vs.* sheepmen and fight for public lands, 210, 219–23, 248–49; tourist "sheep camps," *312*, 313; under US Forest Service, 78–79; and wilderness preservation programs, 215
Redd family, 61, 152, 153–54, 155, 172–77
Red Hole in Time (Marshall), 101

Redington, Paul G., 179
Rees, Claude Harp and son, 145
refuges, wildlife, 90–91
religion: and bigotry, 52; Hispanic herders' practices, 155–60, 167, 168; symbology in sheepscapes, 14, 20, 34, *35*, 155–60, 284
restoration programs: bighorn sheep recovery and protection, 255, 257; Civilian Conservation Corps (CCC), 177–79; cutthroat trout, 70; Leopold's concept, 204; lynx restoration program, 250–51; re-seeding and regrowth programs, 178, 204, 240; and stock limits, 238–39; wild animal populations, 219; wolf management plan, 315–19
Retolaza, Antonio, 135
ricos (rich sheep owners), 3, 25, 162
Rifle Shots, 58
"rim-rocking," 46, 50, 105, 188, 297
Rincón de la Osa, 217, 239
Ringland, Arthur "Ring," 91
Rio Grande Valley, New Mexico, 24, 27, 91
Robertson, E. V., 208
Robinson, Sam, 242, 245
Rocha, Shirley, 159
Rockwell, Wilson, 85
Rocky Mountain bighorn sheep, 5, 254, 257. *See also* bighorn sheep
Rocky Mountain Divide (Wright), 321
Rocky Mountain News, 216, 336n 6
rodent control programs, 179–80
Romero, Alfredo, 230, *232*
Roosevelt, Theodore: on bighorn sheep, 253, 254; as cattleman, 47; and conservation movement, 79, 84; dislike of sheep, 80; on durability of environmental policy, 308–9; experience and vision of, 63, 65; sheepherders, admiration for, 336n 6
Roth, Bridget, 293
Routt County Courier, 83, 98, 99
Routt National Forest, 20, 68–75

Saga of a Forest Ranger (Shoemaker), 80
sagebrush, invasion by, 25
sage grouse, 305–7

Sagstetter, Bill and Beth, 68, 73–75
Saguache Crescent, 44, 62
Salazar, Jose Emilio, 195–97
San Angelo, Texas, 275
Sand County Almanac, A (Leopold, Aldo), 210–11, 314
Sandoval, Luciano, 258
Sands, Will, 244
Sangre de Cristo Mountains, 27, 44, 264
San Juan Mountains: aspens, beauty of, 269–70; impact of sheep on, 63–64, 178, 242–44; lynx reintroduction program, 251, 252; Penitentes in, 155–57; predator control in, 217; recovery highlights, 299
San Juan National Forest, 34–42, 90–91, 242, 255, 256, 292. *See also* Weminuche Wilderness
San Luis Valley, 27, 29, 44, 264
Santa Fe Railroad, 27
Saturday Evening Post, 127, 227–28
Scottish sheepmen/herders, 299
see also public lands
set-guns, 247
sexual carving themes. *See* erotica in carvings
Shaw, Ernest W., 90–91
shearing, 176, 275
"The Sheep Army," 78, 86–87
"Sheepherder Bills" (post-WWII), 212–13
sheepherders, overviews: historical profile of Southwest, 23–32, 213–314, 227–28; hospitality and goodwill of, 72, 131, 174, 219–20; legacy of, 1–7, 324; profiles, contemporary operations, 271–74, 321, 323; profiles, typical operations, 226–29, 234, 235–37; sheepherder characterization, 1–2
sheep permits, Forest Service, 99, 104, 207
sheepscapes (site studies): cairns, 260–66; definition and characterization of, 17–21; Glade Park and Piñon Mesa, 116–20; Lone Mesa State Park, 152–55; Medicine Bow–Routt National Forests, 68–75; San Juan National Forest, 34–42; South Park and sheepshed art, 226–32; Uncompahgre National Forest, 186–201; White River National Forest, 12–17
sheepshed art, 229–32
sheep wagons, 6, *49*, *53*, 311–13
Shepherdess of Elk River Valley (Brown), 106–7
Shiflett, Julie Stepanek, 274–75
Shoemaker, Len, 80
signs, stock driveways, 17, 71, 123, 294
Silverton, Colorado, 242–44
Simos family, 6, 300
ski resorts/developments, 300–301
Smith, Duane, 56, 129
Smith, Honora DeBusk, 168
Society for the Mutual Protection of United Workers, Sociedad Protección Mutua de Trabajadores Unidos (SPMDTU), *159*
South Park, Park County, Colorado, 226–32
South Park National Heritage Area, 227
Southwestern Lore, *262*, 263
Spanish colonial era, 23–24
Spanish influenza, 118
Sperry, Joe, 285
"split estates," 340*n* 86
Spring Creek sheep raid, 93–95
spruce trees, threats to, 270–71, 276
stealing of sheep, 119
Steamboat Pilot, 100
Steamboat Springs, Colorado, 20, *69*, 74, 97, 100
Stinking Desert, 262–63
stocking rates, 81, 90, 210, 246, 254, 299. *See also* carrying capacity of range
Stock-Raising Homestead Act (1916), 78, 106, 113, 122, 129–30
"stone boys," 170, 260, 263. *See also* cairns (markers)
stone markers. *See* cairns (markers)
stone structures, 18, 19, 265, *266*
stories and lore, 110, 169–70, 283–84, 286–91, 302
Story of the Range, The (Barnes), 47, 144
Stransky, Kip, 250–52
sudden aspen decline (SAD), 7, 70, 269

Sundance Kid, 359*n* 1
Sunflower Forest (Jordan), 211
Surowiecki, James, 248
sustainable grazing practices, 154, 239, 299, 309
Swanson, Peter, 85–86
sweat lodges, 19
Sweet Promised Land (Laxalt), 134
symbols/themes in sheepscapes: animals, 9, 42, 74, *230*, *231*, *272*; hands, 195; houses, *16*, 284; humorous, 14; Indian symbols, 190, *191*, *235*; Kilroy figures, 193–94; overviews, 2, 4–5, 39, 187–88, 200, 291–96; penmanship, 37, *38*, 39; portraits, *36*, 37, 68, *69*, 194, *229*; religious, 14, 20, 34, *35*, 155–60, 284. *See also* women, carvings/art of

Taylor, S. A., 95–96, 97
Taylor Edward T. "Ed," 145, 146–48
Taylor Grazing Act (1934), 46, 124, 145–48, 323
Ten Sleep sheep raid, 93–95
Theos family, 133–34, 245, 277
Thoreau, Henry David, 88, 214
Tierra Wool Cooperative, 40, 276
Timber and Stone Act (1878), 89
Timber Culture Act (1873), 89
Times-News (Twin Falls, Idaho), 212
"tin dogs," 167, *322*
Tipping, Marie, 116, 118, 119, 120
tolls charged by Indians, 23, 28
tourism. *See* recreation and tourism
Towne, Charles, 2, 24–25, 25–26
trail markers. *See* cairns (markers); signs, stock driveways
"tramp" sheepmen, 49, 52, 98–99, 136, 143, 145
trapping: bear, 18, 217, 239–40; predators, 18, 108, 110–12, 247; for relocation, 252
trees, replanting programs, 178
Trek to the High Country (Goodnight, painting), 241
trenches and troughs, 19
Trujillo, Solomon, *36*, 37
Trujillo, Teofilo and family, 28, 43–45, 290

Turner, Frederick Jackson, 32
Turner, Oscar, 131–33, 138–39
Turner, Ted, 331*n* 24
Twain, Mark, 180
Two-Bar Ranch, 297–98

Udall, Stewart, 52, 214–19
Uncompahgre National Forest, 116, 158, 186–201, **222,** 238–39
Uncompahgre Plateau/Valley, *30*, 46, 101–3, 249
unemployment issues, 161–63
Uniform Grazing bills, 349*n* 17
urban/suburbanization, 249, 310–11, 320
Urruty, Jean, 134–35
Use Book, The (Pinchot), 80, 83
Utah Desert, 220
Ute Indians, 12, 23, 46, 263, 265, 331*n* 24
Ute Trail, 12

Vacationland (Philpott), 300
Vail Valley, development of, 300–301
Valastegui, Serapio, 272–73
Valdez family, 27
Valencia, George "Junior," 197–99
Vallejos, Joe, 154
Vandenbusche, Duane, 56, 129
Vermejo Park Ranch, 331*n* 24
Vigil, Ben, 68, *69*
Villa, Francisco "Pancho," 101
visas, 272, 274, 321
Visintainer family, 271, 309, 323
Voigt, William, 148, 149, 204, 209, 344*n* 58
V Rock landmark, 40, *41*

wages of sheepherders, 25, 129, 130, 173, 198, 271, 273–74, 289, 321
wagons. *See* sheep wagons
Wait, Scott, 252
Walkey, George S., 95
Wall Street Journal, 273
Wangelin, Sharon, 186, 189–90, 194
Warren, Francis, 83
wars, range conflicts: compromise and amity, 131; early conflicts, 30–31; legal actions, 55–56, 58, 82, 95, 125, 132–33, 138–39; overviews, 2, 50–52; protests

against permit policies, 99–100. *See also* attacks on sheep/sheepmen
Waste of the West (Jacobs), 246–47
water: rights, 231; sheep requirements for, 28, 96; tables, 142
weaving, Navajo, 24
Weed, Becky, 319
Weigle, Marta, 156
Welfare Ranching (Wuerthner and Matteson), 247
Weminuche Wilderness, 27, 37, 217, 239–40, 263. *See also* San Juan National Forest
Wendell, John, 109
Wentworth, Edward, 24–25, 25–26
Wentworth, Edward Norris, 2, 48
Western Range Revisited, The (Donahue), 246
Western Slope profiles, 46–48, **140**, *164*
wether, definition, 29
When the Legends Die (Borland), 269–70, 287–88
Where the Old West Stayed Young (Burroughs), 47
White, Courtney, 276
White River National Forest, 12–17, *21*, 125, 138, 242
White River Plateau Timber Reserve, 53
Wick, Pascal, 288, 318–19, 348*n* 5
Wilderness Act (1964), 215, 223
wilderness preservation programs, 142–43, 213–15
Wilderness Society, 213, 214
Wild Free-Roaming Horses and Burros Act (1971), 237, 307–8
Wildlife Services (of USDA), 247–48

Wild Love, A (Center for Biological Diversity), 317
Williams, David B., 261
Wilson, Bates, 219–20
Wilson Camps, 311
Winder, G. Norman, 208, 215–16
winter storms and herd losses, 18, 30, 41, 47, 53, 170–71
Wolf, Thomas, 51
wolves, 108–13, 314–19
women, carvings/art of, 74, 194, 195–97, 231, *232*, *236*, *279*, 280, 294–95. *See also* nude (women) carvings/art
Woodyard, Brian, 226, 227, 231
Wool Growers Association, 81, 86, 93
wool industry, *130*; military uniforms, 28, 100–101, 205, 228; production and market data, 32, 37, 61, 206, 228, 242, 275–76; and synthetics, competition from, 37, 205
Wootton, "Uncle Dick," 23, 27
work permits. *See* visas
World War I, 100–101, 106, 122, 135
World War II, 205–6
Wright, John B., 321
Wuerthner, George, 247
Wyman, J. N. "Jap" (family), 128, 138

Yakama Indians, 261
Yampa Leader, 81
Yampa River Valley, 59, 100, 128, 138, 297
Yellowstone National Park, 53, 108
Yosemite National Park, 6

Zahniser, Howard, 214–15

Other Books in the Elma Dill Russell Spencer Series in the West and Southwest

Aspects of the American West Three Essays
Joe B. Frantz and W. E. Hollon

Trader on the American Frontier: Myth's Victim
Howard R. Lamar and Kristin E. Parsons

America's Frontier Culture: Three Essays
Ray A. Billington and W. T. Jackson

How Did Davy Die?
Dan Kilgore

Grave of John W. Hardin: Three Essays on Grassroots History
C. L. Sonnichsen

Juan Davis Bradburn: A Reappraisal of the Mexican Commander of Anahuac
Margaret S. Henson

Civil War Recollections of James Lemuel Clark
L. D. Clark

Texas Longhorn: Relic of the Past, Asset for the Future
Donald E. Worcester

Red Hole in Time
Muriel Marshall

Travels in Mexico and California
A. B. Clarke

Mexican War Journal and Letters of Ralph K. Kirkham
Robert R. Miller

Regional Studies: The Interplay of Land and People
Glen E. Lich

Immigrant Soldier in the Mexican War
Frederick Zeh and William J. Orr

Where Rivers Meet: Lore from the Colorado Frontier
Muriel Marshall

Massacre on the Lordsburg Road: A Tragedy of the Apache Wars
Marc Simmons

Geronimo's Kids: A Teacher's Lessons on the Apache Reservation
Robert S. Ove and H. Henrietta Stockel

Defiant Peacemaker: Nicholas Trist in the Mexican War
Wallace L. Ohrt

Life among the Texas Indians: The WPA Narratives
David La Vere

Plains Indians
Paul H. Carlson

Conquest of the Karankawas and the Tonkawas, 1821-1859
Kelly F. Himmel

Chiricahua Apache Women and Children: Safekeepers of the Heritage
H. H. Stockel

Hispanics in the Mormon Zion, 1912-1999
Jorge Iber

Comanche Society: Before the Reservation
Gerald Betty

True Women and Westward Expansion
Adrienne Caughfield

Robertsons, the Sutherlands, and the Making of Texas
Anne H. Sutherland

Life Along the Border: A Landmark Tejana Thesis
Jovita González and Maria E. Cotera

Lone Star Pasts: Memory and History in Texas
Gregg Cantrell and Elizabeth H. Turner

Secret War for Texas
Stuart Reid

Colonial Natchitoches: A Creole Community on the Louisiana-Texas Frontier
H. S. Burton and F. Todd Smith

Yeomen, Sharecroppers, and Socialists: Plain Folk Protest in Texas, 1870-1914
Kyle G. Wilkison

More Zeal Than Discretion: The Westward Adventures of Walter P. Lane
Jimmy L. Bryan

On the Move: A Black Family's Western Saga
S. R. Martin

Texas That Might Have Been: Sam Houston's Foes Write to Albert Sidney Johnston
Margaret S. Henson

Tejano Leadership in Mexican and Revolutionary Texas
Jesús F. De la Teja

Texas Left: The Radical Roots of Lone Star Liberalism
David O. Cullen

How Did Davy Die? And Why Do We Care So Much?
James E. Crisp and Dan Kilgore

*Drumbeats from Mescalero: Conversations with
Apache Elders, Warriors, and Horseholders*
H. H. Stockel

Turmoil on the Rio Grande: History of the Mesilla Valley, 1846-1865
William S. Kiser

Texas Right: The Radical Roots of Lone Star Conservatism
David O' Donald Cullen and Kyle G. Wilkison

*We Never Retreat: Filibustering Expeditions into
Spanish Texas, 1812–1822*
Ed Bradley

General Alonso de León's Expeditions into Texas, 1686–1690
Lola Orellana Norris

*Comanches and Germans on the Texas Frontier:
The Ethnology of Heinrich Berghaus*
Daniel J. Gelo and Christopher J. Wickham,
with contributions by Heide Castañeda

*Murder and Intrigue on the Mexican Border: Governor
Colquitt, President Wilson, and the Vergara Affair*
John A. Adams